EDUCATION IN THE RURAL AMERICAN COMMUNITY

EDUCATION IN THE RURAL AMERICAN COMMUNITY

A *Lifelong Process*

Edited by
Michael W. Galbraith

KRIEGER PUBLISHING COMPANY
MALABAR, FLORIDA
1992

Original Edition 1992

Printed and Published by
KRIEGER PUBLISHING COMPANY
KRIEGER DRIVE
MALABAR, FLORIDA 32950

FROM A DECLARATION OF PRINCIPLES JOINTLY ADOPTED BY A COMMITTEE
OF THE AMERICAN BAR ASSOCIATION AND A COMMITTEE OF PUBLISHERS:

> This publication is designed to provide accurate and authoritative information in
> regard to the subject matter covered. It is sold with the understanding that the
> publisher is not engaged in rendering legal, accounting, or other professional
> service. If legal advice or other expert assistance is required, the services of a
> competent professional person should be sought.

Library of Congress Cataloging-In-Publication Data
Education in the rural American community : a lifelong process /
    edited by Michael W. Galbraith. — Original ed.
        p. cm.
    Includes bibliographical references and index.
    ISBN 0-89464-383-5 (alk. paper)
        1. Education, Rural—United States. 2. Education, Rural—Canada.
I. Galbraith, Michael W.
    LC5140.E38   1992
    370.19'346'0973—dc20   91-31536
                                                                        CIP

10   9   8   7   6   5   4   3   2

This book is dedicated to PAUL A. SUNDET,
the community educator's educator

Contents

PART THREE
RESOURCES AND FUTURE PROSPECTS FOR RURAL
LIFELONG EDUCATION

Preface

Learning is a lifelong process and the educational opportunities to engage in formal, nonformal, and informal learning are available within each community, although many times unrecognized. This is especially true for rural communities in the United States and Canada because of their diversity in population, institutions, governments, resources, economics, cultures, and lifestyles. Community members draw on their own powers of creativity and sensitivity to make their learning rewarding. In essence, the rural community becomes a natural setting for the lifelong educational process.

Although an acceptable definition of *rural* is difficult to determine, the recognition that rural America is different from urban America is not, and as a result unique responses to its educational needs are warranted. Because the rapidly changing nature of rurality is affected by economic, social, political, and technological factors, all institutions, including the educational process, must change and adapt. Understanding and participating in lifelong education is one way of addressing such change. It encourages unique responses to unique concerns confronting rural Americans. It suggests that education over the life span can be dispensed and acquired through a multiplicity of formal, nonformal, and informal means, and existing institutions of all types in the rural community can be used to enhance educational purposes.

Until now, no books on rural education have addressed lifelong education and the rural community. The central purpose of *Education in the Rural American Community: A Lifelong Process* is to provide a conceptual and practical framework for understanding lifelong education and how the various facets of the total rural community enhance this process. Basic premises are:

● Learning opportunities should exist for all people of all ages.

- Formal and nonformal community organizations should take part in providing educational opportunities.

- The rural community should be the locus for planning and conducting such learning.

From this discussion, it is hoped that educational programs involving new combinations of services and new organizational arrangements will be constructed and ·that individuals will become resourceful, autonomous, and continuous learners within the various contexts of their community.

The intended audiences for this book are rural school administrators and teachers, school board members, college and university faculties, educational researchers, adult and continuing educators, educational policy makers, community based educators, members of funding agencies, and all lifelong educators. The book can be used as a primary or supplemental textbook for undergraduate and graduate courses concerned with rural education or in professional seminars focusing on topics in social work, community development, extension education, community psychology, sociology, and so forth. It is also a general reference book for those who need to investigate lifelong education in the American rural community and its associated issues.

Education in the Rural American Community: A Lifelong Process has three parts. Part One is concerned with the conceptualization of lifelong education, community, and rurality. In Chapter 1, I examine the concepts of lifelong education and community and in a practical manner attempt to connect the two. This chapter also suggests that lifelong education within the community can be accomplished through formal, nonformal, and informal processes and that learners, community organizations, and educators are confronted with important choices. Daryl Hobbs, in Chapter 2, discusses the concept of rurality. He examines the rural context for education and suggests that present day images of rural America need to be adjusted to fit reality.

Part Two consists of twelve chapters that examine various educational programs and providers in the rural community. Ivan D. Muse and Gloria Jean Thomas, in Chapter 3, discuss rural elementary education. They explore the responsibilities of rural elementary schools and the external and internal challenges that confront them, the characteristics of the students, teachers, and administrators, and the preparation and recruitment of teachers and principals. Curricular issues are also discussed with a look to the future and the societal and educational changes promised by the twenty-first century. Paul Nachtigal examines rural secondary education in Chapter 4. He suggests we take a careful look at the reality of rural secondary schools and points out their strengths and weaknesses as a result of adopting the urban industrial model of schooling. In the latter part of his chapter he purports that opportunity exists to capitalize on the strengths of rural schools and rural communities as the country moves from an industrial to an information/service society. The authors of Chapter 5, David Little and Robert Priebe, explore the existing structures of vocational education in rural and urban sectors of society in relation to formal, nonformal, and informal settings for learning. These descriptions provide a basis for reconceptualizing and restructuring learning opportunities based on a distinction between the occupational and social dimensions of vocational education. Doris Helge, in Chapter 6, examines special education in the rural context. She describes factors that distinguish rural individuals with disabilities from those in nonrural settings and then examines the unique needs of rural families having members with special needs. Resources needed for appropriate services, service delivery considerations, and model development strategies are also discussed. Douglas Treadway discusses higher education in the rural environment in Chapter 7. He looks at the accelerating forces of societal change and suggests how higher education institutions in rural America can provide support and assistance in coping with such dynamic trends. In Chapter 8 John Pelham focuses on the role of university extension in the lifelong educational process. He discusses the unique contributions university extension has made to education for rural citizens, the elements of extension programs, and how these have changed to reflect changed needs and opportunities. In addition, he provides a modest look into the future of extension programs for rural Americans and the kinds of changes that may be needed in organizational affiliations, programs and services offered, and funding sources.

Chapter 9 is concerned with rural community adult education. David Price and I examine the concepts of community, rurality, and community adult education and discuss various organizational frameworks within adult education and the types of programs and providers associated with each. A brief discussion concerning the future of rural community adult education concludes the chapter. William Griffith in Chapter 10 details some of the social, fraternal, and economic organizations found in nonmetropolitan areas and their special relationship to the rural population. He explores the kind of adjustments that seem essential in the social, fraternal, and economic organizations of rural America and Canada if they are to be effective contributors to the lifelong educational process. The rural public library is the topic of Chapter 11. Bernard Vavrek describes the layers of educational and informational services provided by the typical American rural public library and how these contribute to the opportunities for lifelong learning. Paulette Beatty and Barbara Robbins in Chapter 12 address the rural church and religious education. They explore the question of the continued vitality of the rural church and examine its current educational mission by addressing specific areas such as goals and functions, the programs and content, the delivery processes employed, the participants, and the leadership. In addition, they identify some of the ongoing concerns experienced in the delivery of rural church education and describe some of the adaptive strategies and emerging practices. Their chapter concludes with a discussion on how the rural church can advance the concept of lifelong learning.

Vicki Luther and Marian Todd in Chapter 13 describe the changing educational needs of rural women. They explore the changes in the lives of rural women and families and analyze the variety of responses by educational service providers. In conclusion, they offer a framework for the development of programs targeted at rural women. The final chapter of Part Two is concerned with rural education and minorities. In Chapter 14 Ray Barnhardt discusses how the educational equation is changed when "minority" is factored in. He explores the particular and unique ways in which diversity is manifested in rural communities as well as the consequences of such diversity for educational planning, policy making, and program development. He suggests ways in which educational institutions can be more accommodating to this cultural diversity.

Part Three of the book provides a look at some of the resources for rural lifelong education and a discussion concerning the future. In Chapter 15 Jacqueline Spears, Gwen Bailey, and Sue Maes present a brief overview of the various resources within three broad categories: rural schools, higher education, and nonformal education. In each of the categories they provide information on clearinghouses/centers, programs, organizations/associations, and publications. The appendix, which they also authored, supplements this with a complete list of the various resources. In the last chapter of Part Three, Chapter 16, I look at the future of rural lifelong education, examining the influence of certain trends and factors. The chapter also summarizes aims and priorities and how they relate to new directions and attitudes concerning dispositional change, school and lifelong education curriculum, and the role of educators in rural America. Finally, the benefits of lifelong education are discussed in the context of the rural American community.

Education in the Rural American Community: A Lifelong Process gives the reader a new perspective about learning and education. It suggests that the rural American community holds the potential to contribute to the lifelong educational opportunities of all its individuals, both youth and adult. The challenge confronting each rural community is whether or not it will respond to the "calling" that warrants a unique personal and organizational response. Rural America does not need to look to urban America for its answers. What is required is a collective effort in critical reflective thought, imagination, and action.

Acknowledgments

To the many colleagues who have given their ideas and time to write chapters for this book goes my sincere gratitude. I believe this book is something unique in its approach to rural education and it is through your efforts that this uniqueness is realized. One colleague has been particularly influential. Over the years we have worked to develop new ideas and concepts relating to education in the rural American community. The results of our many discussions fill the following pages. It is with a sense of friendship and scholarship that I dedicate this book to my lifelong friend and valued colleague, Paul A. Sundet.

To T.J., my wife and best friend, goes a loving thank you for supporting me through the best and worst of times. Sincere gratitude goes to Robert Krieger, Mary Roberts, Marie Bowles, and all the people at Krieger Publishing Company for the continuous support of my ideas and for making them into a readable reality. Finally, to all the people of rural America, a special thank you for allowing me to pop in and out of your unique world throughout my life.

The Editor

Michael W. Galbraith is associate professor of adult education and coordinator of graduate studies in adult education at Temple University. He received his B.Ed. degree (1973) in social studies education and an M.Ed. degree (1981) in social foundations and gerontology from the University of Toledo, and his Ed.D. (1984) in adult education from Oklahoma State University.

Galbraith's main research activities have been in the areas of adult learning, community adult education, rural education, professional certification, and educational gerontology. He is an active member in the Commission of Professors of Adult Education, American Association for Adult and Continuing Education, American Educational Research Association as well as in various state and regional adult education associations. He has held numerous voluntary leadership roles with adult education professional associations and presently serves on the editorial boards of *Adult Education Quarterly: A Journal of Research and Theory* and *Educational Gerontology: An International Bimonthly Journal*. For his contributions to the field of adult education, he has been the recipient of numerous state, regional, and national awards. He has written numerous journal articles, book chapters, monographs, and several books including *Elder Abuse: Perspectives on an Emerging Crisis* (1986), *Professional Certification: Implications for Adult Education and HRD* (1986, with Jerry W. Gilley), *Adult Learning Methods: A Guide for Effective Instruction* (1990), *Education Through Community Organizations* (1990), and *Facilitating Adult Learning: A Transactional Process* (1991). In addition, he serves as editor-in-chief of Krieger Publishing Company's *Professional Practices in Adult Education and Human Resource Development* book series.

Before coming to Temple University, Galbraith served on the faculties of the University of Missouri-Columbia and Oklahoma State University. Prior to his appointments in institutions of higher education, he worked for several community-based organizations in rural settings.

The Contributors

Gwen Bailey is the project coordinator for the Rural Clearinghouse for Lifelong Education and Development at Kansas State University. She has directed a number of regional projects supported by the Rural Clearinghouse and currently edits its newsletter, *Rural Adult Education Forum*. Prior to joining the Clearinghouse, she taught in both secondary and alternative school settings.

Ray Barnhardt is a professor of cross-cultural education and rural development at the University of Alaska-Fairbanks, where he has been involved in teaching and research related to rural and minority education issues since 1970. He has served as the director of the Cross-Cultural Education Development Program, the Small High Schools Project, the Center for Cross-Cultural Studies, and the Center for Cross-Regional Education Programs. His research interests include minority teacher education, distance education, institutional adaptations to rural and cross-cultural settings, and alternative approaches to management and organization.

Paulette T. Beatty is an associate professor of adult education and program leader for the graduate program in adult and extension education at Texas A&M University. She has worked for over eighteen years in the area of adult religious education and for over eight years served as director of a retreat and renewal center in upstate New York. She has served as editor for *Lifelong Education: An Omnibus of Practice and Research,* a publication of the American Association for Adult and Continuing Education. Special areas of research include adult religious education, collaborative educational programs for and with older adults, staff development, and program development and evaluation in nonformal settings.

Michael W. Galbraith is an associate professor of adult education and coordinator of graduate studies in adult education at Temple University. He is the author of numerous publications including several books in the areas of adult learning, community-based education, professional certification, and gerontology. He is a frequent speaker at state, regional, and national adult education conferences and has received various awards for his contributions to the field. In addition, he serves on several editorial boards for national and international professional journals.

William S. Griffith is a professor of adult education at the University of British Columbia in Vancouver, Canada. He has been a member of the Executive of the Canadian Society of Extension and a member of the editorial board of the *Journal of Extension*. He was co-editor for the 1980 handbook series in adult education which was sponsored by the Adult Education Association of the U.S.A. In 1990/91, he served as president of the American Association for Adult and Continuing Education.

Doris Helge is the executive director of the National Rural Development Institute and the American Council on Rural Special Education (ACRES), both located at Western Washington University in Bellingham, Washington. She is the author of numerous articles concerning special education, rural special education, and at-risk students.

Daryl Hobbs is the director of the University of Missouri's Office of Social and Economic Data Analysis and is a professor of rural sociology. His academic specialities include social change and rural development. He has written extensively on rural education with an emphasis on education reform, policy, and linkages between education and rural development. He is a past president of the Rural Sociological Society.

David Little is an associate professor of vocational and technical education at the University of Regina in Saskatchewan, Canada. He has worked in the field of adult vocational/technical education in Canada and the United States for over thirty years. His research interests are in educational action research applying critical psychology, activity theory, and critical sociology, in particular, Habermas' theory of communicative action to adult vocational and technical education.

Vicki Luther is the co-director for the Heartland Center of Leadership Development in Lincoln, Nebraska. She has developed training programs for community leaders and conducted research projects on economic development, citizen participation, and skills of decision makers in the public and private sector. She has worked with small rural towns throughout the Midwest in the area of strategic planning to rural issues.

Sue C. Maes is the co-director of the Rural Clearinghouse for Lifelong Education and Development and the associate director of the Division of

Continuing Education at Kansas State University. She has served as executive director of the University of Man, a community education program, for sixteen years and was responsible for a number of projects related to the adaptation of the free university model to rural community settings. She has been a founding member in the efforts to explore and understand rural adult education.

Ivan D. Muse is a professor and the current chair of the Department of Educational Leadership at Brigham Young University. He has written extensively in the area of rural education and is the co-author of the book *One Teacher Schools in America.* Other research interests include preparation practices for rural school principals and health appraisal of rural school administrators.

Paul M. Nachtigal is the director of the rural institute, Midcontinent Regional Educational Laboratory (McREL) located in Aurora, Colorado. Prior to joining McREL, he was with the Education Commission of the States where he directed a national study of efforts to improve rural education, *Rural Education: In Search of a Better Way.* He has been with the Ford Foundation monitoring and evaluating school improvement programs and a rural school superintendent. Recently, he has served as a consultant to the Lilly Endowment, the Public Education Fund, the National Governor's Association, and the National Conference of State Legislators.

John T. Pelham is the program director of Family Strengths and Youth Development for University Extension for the University of Missouri system, Columbia, Missouri. His efforts have been directed toward farm and rural crisis recovery and the establishment and training for rural human services coalitions and rural health care delivery. He maintains professional memberships in the Rural Sociological Society, the National Rural Health Association, and the National Collaboration of Social Work and Human Services in Rural Areas.

David W. Price is currently completing his Ph.D. in higher and adult education at the University of Missouri-Columbia. He has served in the U.S. Peace Corps in Micronesia as a community dvelopment worker and as a training officer of Peace Corps–Micronesia. He has been a community development specialist with the Cooperative Extension Service in Missouri and a program development and evaluation specialist with the National Geographic Society's Missouri Geography Education Program. His research interests include community development and community adult education.

Robert Priebe is the director and associate professor of vocational and technical education at the University of Regina in Saskatchewan, Canada. For the past twenty-five years he has worked with school boards, technical institutes, community colleges, governmental agencies, as well as a range of private and public sector agencies in the development of programs and related services in vocational education. His research interests are focused on the role of vocational education in affecting the meaning of work and work reform.

Barbara P. Robbins is a research associate at the Texas Center for Adult Literacy and Learning at Texas A&M University. She has served as an editorial assistant for *Lifelong Education: An Omnibus of Practice and Research* and is presently involved in activities such as GED preparation, work place literacy, parenting education, and Christian education. Her volunteer interests include literacy teaching, tutor training, Sunday School staff development, telephone crisis counseling, and public speaking.

Jacqueline D. Spears is the co-director of the Rural Clearinghouse for Lifelong Education and Development at Kansas State University. She has worked in the field of rural adult education since 1984 and has written extensively on the impact of state policy on rural adults' access to postsecondary education.

Gloria Jean Thomas is an assistant professor in the Department of Educational Administration, Center for Teaching and Learning, at the University of North Dakota. She teaches education law, microcomputers, and higher education administration at the university. One of her research interests is in the area of rural elementary education.

Marian Todd is a senior associate with the Strategic Leadership Group, a consulting firm based in Lincoln, Nebraska. She has experience as a community development specialist with the Community Energy Planning Project and the Nebraska Energy Office and with a rural Nebraska community action agency. Her areas of research include educational needs of rural women, and eco-feminism as a force in planning and development.

Douglas M. Treadway is president of Southwest State University in Marshall, Minnesota, a rural institution with a curriculum and organization specifically oriented to the issues of rural development. He has been an administrator, professor, and counselor in rural settings for twenty years. He is the author of numerous journal publications including the book *Higher Education in Rural America: Serving the Adult Learner*. He is currently the chair of the Agriculture and Rural Development Committee for the American Association of State Colleges and Universities and serves as well on the Joint Council on Food and Agricultural Sciences for the U.S. Department of Agriculture.

Bernard Vavrek is a professor of library science in the College of Library Science at Clarion University of Pennsylvania and coordinator of the Center for the Study of Rural Librarianship. In addition, he is the coordinator of the Small Library Development Center and has served as Interim Dean for the College of Library Science for 1988–1990. His main research activities include the rural public library and its development and contribution to lifelong learning. He has written over fifty articles for the library literature and has served on the National Commission on Libraries and Information Science's Advisory Board for Rural Information Needs.

PART ONE

LIFELONG EDUCATION, COMMUNITY, AND RURALITY

CHAPTER 1

Lifelong Education and Community
MICHAEL W. GALBRAITH

When the words *lifelong education* and *community* are voiced, a plethora of images is generated. Some will consist of a singular dimension while others will be multifaceted in perspective. The purpose of this introductory chapter is to provide a framework for examining these concepts and to detail in a practical manner the connection between lifelong education and community. It is suggested that lifelong education within the community can be accomplished through formal, nonformal, and informal educational processes and that learners, community organizations, and educators are confronted with important choices.

LIFELONG EDUCATION

Lifelong education and lifelong learning have become popular slogans within the lexicon of American language. The two phrases have been used interchangeably within the literature as well as synonymously to mean and promote adult and continuing education. The very nature of the words suggests that lifelong learning and lifelong education do not take place only in adulthood but throughout life from birth to death. To conceptualize and understand lifelong education, definitional distinctions between lifelong learning and lifelong education must be made. In addition, words such as *life, lifelong, learning,* and *education* must be examined.

The word *life* conjures up definitions that range from political, religious, sociological, historical, anthropological, and psychological perspectives. Understanding life involves determining how society measures it and views it in relationship to these various perspectives. Life is composed of the growth and development of the human being that takes place from birth to death. *Lifelong* denotes this timespan. Differentiating

3

between *learning* and *education* also creates operational and definitional dilemmas as is evidenced by the frequency with which writers use the terms interchangeably. Apps (1985) suggests that "Learning is defined as those internal changes that occur in our consciousness" (p. 4). When one accepts the tenets of *lifelong*, the definition of *learning* can be broadened to mean a process of transforming experience into knowledge, skills, and attitudes through a variety of processes (Kolb, 1984). This definition recognizes the experiential nature of learning, namely that individuals arrive at meaningful learning through different processes. *Education* therefore can be defined as those processes, events, activities, and conditions that assist and encourage learning. Peterson (1979) states that education can be described as deliberate (planned) or unintentional (random). Deliberate education is that which is provided by schools such as elementary and secondary, college and university, proprietary schools, university extension, and community education. It is also provided by nonschool organizations such as private industry, professional associations, trade unions, military services, community organizations, and churches. The third source of deliberate education is by oneself through various forms of individual and self-directed study. Unintentional education, as suggested by Peterson (1979), is provided from everyday work experiences; from friends and contact with family and home experiences; from the mass media, such as television, movies, and radio; and from everyday contact with the environment through, for example, recreation and entertainment, travel, and community activities.

Considering these terms, *lifelong learning* means those changes in consciousness that take place throughout the life span which result in an active and progressive process to comprehend the intellectual, societal, and personal changes that confront each individual human being. Lifelong learning therefore, is not synonymous with adult learning nor is it accepted that lifelong learning begins with the completion of preparatory education such as elementary, secondary, or postsecondary schooling. The words themselves suggest life span learning and the transformation process that takes place from birth to death.

How then should *lifelong education* be defined? Is it just an abstract goal or ideal that cannot be realized; or is it a concrete term that can be considered a defined reality? The rational answer is that it probably is a little of both. However, drawing from the definition of terms above, lifelong education will be defined as a process of deliberate and unintentional opportunities that influence learning throughout the life span. Dave (1976) best describes lifelong education when he states that it "seeks to view education in its totality. It covers formal, nonformal, and informal patterns of education, and attempts to integrate and articulate all structures and stages of education . . ." (p. 35) . . . "it is a process of accomplishing personal, social, and professional development throughout the life span of individuals in order to enhance the quality of life of both individuals and their collectives" (p. 34). From this definition, lifelong education is incorporated into every aspect of society through the multitude of institutions and individuals within that society. According to Ireland (1978), "it links up the whole of the community's educational activities resources, aiming alike at the full development of the individual's potentialities and at the advancement of a society undergoing transformation . . ." (p. 18).

Dimensions of Lifelong Education

Numerous writers have attempted to clarify the complexity and multidimensional aspects of lifelong education (Cropley, 1977; Dave, 1973, 1976; Jarvis, 1986, 1987; Lengrand, 1975; Long, Apps, & Hiemstra, 1985). The concept of lifelong education includes three aspects:

1. Formal education, which relates to education within any formal bureaucratic organization such as the school or university

2. Nonformal education, which relates to education outside the framework of the formal system that provides selected types of learning through YWCAs, libraries, museums, and so forth

3. Informal education, which relates to the education obtained through the interaction of people by means of the workplace, friends, family, and so on

If one accepts this conceptualization, then education must be viewed in its totality: at the center of society is a very visible lifelong educational structure. Cropley and Dave (1978) suggest that lifelong learning has two dimensions: vertical integration and horizontal integration. A third category, learning to learn, must be considered as well.

Vertical Integration

This dimension of lifelong education stresses the notion that schooling and education are not synonymous processes and that learning itself is a continuous process throughout life. Schooling is only "one educative influence in life, and that schooling is incapable, by itself, of providing all the education needed for life" (Cropley, 1977, p. 34). This dimension does not reject the concept of formal schooling, but it does affirm that the most "rapid and enduring changes during the process of personal development take place prior to the commencement of formal schooling [and that] the longest period of life by far is the one that commences after schooling ends" (p. 34). Therefore, education is a major component of life and the strongest educational influences come from outside the formal school setting through the media, relationships with peers and family, the community, workplaces, and so on. In addition, any learning is a result of prior learning and such learning influences the nature and extent of future learning, whether it be through formal, nonformal, or informal processes. Education is for all age levels and the ability to learn and grow is cumulative over a lifetime through the integration of various processes.

Horizontal Integration

This dimension stresses the notion that education and life are linked. Horizontal integration views education as life-wide whereby school learning is coordinated with other components in the society in which learning occurs. Cropley (1977) states that a "very wide range of the members of society should be involved in education, and that knowledge itself should be seen as a broad integrated network, rather than a series of more or less unrelated, narrow and discrete disciplines" (pp. 33–34). Educational processes should not be divided into school and non-school in which knowledge in school is unrelated to knowledge acquired outside of school. Education must be viewed as continuous throughout the life span and on a continuum that accepts the integration of school and life and the various educational components that influence life.

Learning to Learn

A prerequisite to any educated community or society is that its people acquire the skill to learn how to learn. This dimension suggests that the educated person learns how to adapt and change, either out of self-motivation to be more efficient or out of sheer necessity from societal and personal influences and changes. Smith (1982) writes that learning how to learn "involves possessing, or acquiring, the knowledge and skill to learn effectively in whatever learning situation one encounters" (p. 19). The process includes not only "how" to learn but what, why, when, and where to learn. Knowles (1980) and a host of others have encouraged self-directed learning whereby learners acquire the ability to identify their own learning needs, formulate learning objectives, locate and identify appropriate resources and strategies to accomplish objectives, carry out the planned learning, and evaluate learning outcomes. These abilities are paramount for all learners and an essential component of lifelong education. In the development of self-direction and independence, whether in formal, nonformal, or informal processes, learning to learn draws on the aspects of individuality and human potential. Learning to learn suggests that all learners begin to question the habitual givens about their thoughts, values, attitudes, and knowledge and become critically reflective thinkers. Through this dimension lifelong education truly becomes vertically and horizontally integrated. Consequently, the concept of lifelong education then becomes a reality and not an abstract ideal for the community and the society.

Psychosocial Aspects of Lifelong Education

Lifelong education does not take place in a vacuum. It involves human beings and the society in which they live. If lifelong education is to be a reality, profound implications of a psychological as well as a social nature must be considered. Lifelong education is education for a changing world. Psychologically, individuals of all ages must extend their cognitive, affective, and motivation domains to cope with the changing intellectual demands of a society (Cropley, 1977). The ability to understand the social and technological aspects of their culture as well as the ability to understand themselves is vital. Lifelong education should facilitate healthy personal and emotional growth as well as a sense of independence. Learning to learn relates to this psychological aspect in that it begins to equip learners with the ability and skill of how, what, why, when, and where to learn. Lifelong education premises its process on the ability to understand and adapt to the psychological needs of individuals who are at different stages of their development.

Individuals grow and mature within the context of social living, thus becoming to some degree a reflection of the social situation (Jarvis, 1987). Within the social context, individuals endeavor to understand the personal, social, and intellectual aspects of their world. They begin to change as a result of their experiences. However, the social milieu is also continuously changing and this change is the norm rather than the exception. Consequently, educational structures are the recipients of the pressures for change as well as the initiators. Within this scheme, individuals also exert their will and become an agent for change. In doing this they become an active and progressive component in the learning process.

The psychosocial aspects mesh within the vertical and horizontal dimensions of lifelong education. It is recognized that lifelong education must be flexible enough to accommodate individual options and social differences. It should promote personal development and unity as well as a greater understanding of fellow human beings and the social environment in which they live. By incorporating all the dimensions and aspects of lifelong education into a conceptual framework, education and learning can begin to be viewed in its totality and take its place within the community of formal, nonformal, and informal processes.

COMMUNITY

Individuals in any social milieu are all members of some kind of community and they all, whether deliberately or unintentionally, participate in some aspect of education and learning. The primary focus of this section is to explore the concept of community and the difficulty of defining it in simple and definitive terms. Several approaches to studying community are also examined.

The Concept of Community

Community is multidimensional in scope and perspective (Bellah et al., 1985; Effrat, 1974; Fellin, 1987; Galbraith, 1990a, 1990b; Galbraith & Price, 1991; Luloff & Swanson, 1990; Warren & Lyon, 1988). The term generates a host of definitions, missions, aims, and images. Community is a value laden term that evokes a variety of descriptions by a plethora of individuals.

Galbraith (1990b) suggests that in reality we live in a mega-community that is international, national, and local in scope. A mega-community is a large scale systematic community that is connected by cultural, social, psychological, economic, political, environmental, and technological elements. It is a community that is depicted by its vertical pattern in which each identified community and its social systems' relationships are oriented to the international and national society and culture (Warren, 1978).

A community may also be depicted by its horizontal pattern which is concerned with the relationship of local units to each other. It is through the community's horizontal pattern that the social system performs locality and relevant functions; provides education, employment, and income; and establishes a link between various social units and individuals in the community. The horizontal pattern of community assists us in understanding geographic communities as well as how people relate to each other.

Tonnies (1957) used the German terms *gemeinschaft* and *gesellschaft* to describe two ways of how people relate to each. A *gemeinschaft* community is characteristic of families, neighborhoods, and friendship groups that relate to each other in a sense of mutuality, stability, common identity and concerns, and a common subscription to social norms, bonds, and obligations. A geographic community calls forth an awareness of mutual assistance and development in the interrelationship and cohesiveness of its membership that will ensure a harmonious existence. A *gesellschaft* community is one in which people relate to each other in a means-ends relationship. It is characterized by various forms of exchange with other people for the primary purpose of serving individual interests. There is little sentiment involved and the rationality within the *gesellschaft* community is high in that shared identity, mutuality, and a common concern is absent.

Defining Community

Warren (1978, p. 1) suggests that the idea of community is deceptively simple, "so long as one does not ask for a rigid definition." He found through a meta-analysis of some ninety-four definitions of community that sixty-nine such definitions included social interaction, common ties, and locational criteria as definitive of the concept. The emphasis on human interaction and relationships within places, and commonalities in interests, values, and mores are frequently cited attributes of community. Warren (1978) ultimately considered a community to be "that combination of social units and systems which perform the major social functions having locality relevance" (p. 9). This definition suggests that people within the community have local access to a diversity of activities which are necessary in day-to-day living.

While the above is considered a geographic and locational definition of community, others suggest that the emphasis should focus on the commonalities of interests, concerns, and functions of people (Bellah et al., 1985; DeLargy, 1989; Fellin, 1987; Galbraith, 1990a; Hamilton & Cunningham, 1989, Hiemstra, 1972; Roberts, 1979; Wright, 1980). Brookfield (1983) declares that, aside from the familiar locational expression of community, there are "communities of interest" and "communities of function" which may supersede geographic boundaries. Communities of interest are those groups of individuals bound by some single common interest or set of common interests such as leisure interests, civic and special political interests, or spiritual and religious beliefs and affiliations. Wright (1980, p. 101) echoes this by stating that "a community is a collectivity of people differentiated from the total population by a common interest." Communities of function are those groups identified by the function of major life roles such as teacher, attorney, doctor, farmer, student, homemaker, parent, and so forth. As is readily apparent, geographic communities, communities of interest, and communities of function intersect and overlap into the broad conceptualization of community. Another typology of the concept of community is derived from the field of educational marketing in which demographic and psychographic communities exist. Demographic communities are those groups bound by common demographic characteristics such as race, age, and sex. For example, to speak of "the black community" or "the elderly community" is to address a demographic community. Psychographic communities are those formed by commonality of value systems, social class, and life style such as "the yuppy community" or "the gay community."

Thus there are numerous frameworks for understanding and defining the word *community*. A community that is characterized by *gemeinschaft* seems most appropriate as it subscribes to a democratic and harmonious existence. From that perspective, Galbraith (1990b) suggests that a community may be defined as "the combination and interrelationship of geographic, locational, and non-locational units, systems, and characteristics that provide relevance and growth to individuals, groups, and organizations" (p. 5).

The Good Community

Warren (1970) coined the phrase "the good community" and pointed to a number of issues embodying it. The issues that follow coincide with what has been described as a *gemeinschaft* community as well as the definition of community just provided. The good community is concerned with primary group relationships, autonomy, viability, power distribution, participation, degree of commitment, degree of heterogeneity, the extent of neighborhood control, and the extent of conflict. Warren suggests that the good community is people-oriented, controlled, and democratic in nature. It is concerned with the capacity of local people to confront their problems through concerted actions, directing themselves to the distribution of power, arranging for participation and commitment in community affairs, understanding how differences among people can be tolerated, and debating the extent of neighborhood control and conflict. Warren suggests that these important issues demand critical reflection, debate, and difficult choices if such a community is to exist.

Fellin (1987) echoes similar characteristics of a good community by describing a community as a group in which membership is valued as an end in itself. The community's members share a commitment to stability, subscribe to a set of common social norms, and maintain a sense of shared identity. In addition, the people have enduring and extensive personal contact with each other. Lastly, a community concerns itself with many significant aspects of the members' lives, tolerates competing factions, and has procedures for handling conflict. Kanter (1972) contends that the search for the good community is a quest for direction and purpose in the collective anchoring of the individual life.

While the authors have addressed the good community and its characteristics from a local or neighborhood community perspective, they say much to us about the hope and challenge of developing the good megacommunity that affects the national and international dimensions of our lives.

Studying the Community

The diverse approaches to studying the community, as well as their contributions, emphasize the complexity of the concept of community. One approach is to study the community as space and spatial relationships (Warren, 1978). In this approach we investigate people and institutions and their distribution throughout geographical space, for example, studying rural or urban communities. Another approach is to study the community as people, that is, the individual character of the community created by the kinds of people who live there. Here a careful analysis is made of the kinds of people who reside in the community, based on age, race, nationality, sex, mobility factors, and the rates of change by the inhabitants over a period of time.

In addition, the community can be investigated according to the notion of shared institutions and values. This approach suggests that certain institutions and shared values are held in common by the local population. Warren (1978) suggests that "the shared institutional services are thought to constitute a shared way of life. . . . and that the function of making accessible locally the various institutional facilities for daily living needs is, from the ecological standpoint, the chief reason for existence of the community" (p. 34). He continues by declaring that shared values "are thought of not only as a basic component of what is meant by the community, but also as an important item on which communities often differ greatly from each other" (p. 34). A fourth approach to studying the community is through the interaction of local people and their association with one another, and through their behavior with regard to one another and such major institutional areas as the family, the church, government, and education. Points of departure arise through social processes such as conflict, competition, disorganization, dissociation, and the degree and dimensions of community action.

The final two approaches involve studying the community as a distribution of power and as a social system (Rothman & Tropman, 1987; Suttles, 1972; Warren, 1978). Power is concerned with how and by whom social behavior is influenced, whether this be through individuals or by formal or informal organizations that exist in the community. This approach focuses on power structures and the consequences of policy decisions on the lives of individuals, groups, and organizations within the community (Zander, 1990). The social system concept, by contrast, is based on the idea of "structured interaction between two or more units" (Warren, 1978, p. 46). It is concerned with how the various structures of the interaction endure through time. Warren contends that to study the community one must recognize that it is a system of systems, that it is not structurally and functionally centralized in the same sense as a formal organization, and that as a social system it is implicit in nature as compared with the explicitness of a formal organization.

The concept of community is multidimensional in scope, both in practice and in theory. The concept of lifelong education is also multidimensional in that it utilizes formal, nonformal, and informal educational mechanisms to effect individual, group, and community change. The connection between community and lifelong education seems to be a natural process. Conceptualizing community and lifelong education assists us in understanding the connection they both have to society at large.

CONNECTING LIFELONG EDUCATION AND COMMUNITY

Merging of the concepts of lifelong education and community can be identified in works by Cropley (1977), Dave (1973, 1976), Galbraith (1990a), Lengrand (1975), Long, Apps, and Hiemstra (1985), and Peterson and Associates (1979). Each author operates from some framework of community, whether from a locational or nonlocational perspective (i.e., communities of interest, communities of function) and ties it to a lifelong education perspective. It is through the nonlocational features that formal, nonformal, and informal lifelong education is facilitated. It can be considered an intervening process that affects change in individuals, groups, and the locational and nonlocational communities which comprise a larger community context. Within this scope of inquiry, lifelong education has the potential to impact individuals, groups, and communities in the way they live, inform, and educate themselves. Lifelong education can serve as a mechanism for self-fulfillment as well as for social, political, and psychological empowerment. When lifelong education and community are connected both conceptually and in practice, a unique relationship is developed that gives individuals and communities a sense of hope and dignity, a sense of responsibility for their own communities and lives, and a sense of voice within the social and political arenas. The connection suggests an inclusionary and liberating significance for individuals, groups, and communities.

There are many ways of discussing the connection between lifelong education and community. One is by viewing the community as a context for formal, nonformal, and informal education for individuals across the life span. From this perspective, the agencies, organizations, and activities that exist within the community are connected with the process of lifelong education. It suggests how lifelong education can serve as an intervention in bringing about change and growth for learners, groups, and communities.

Figure 1.1 depicts a framework for connecting lifelong education and community. It begins with the assumption that lifelong education exists and that it is available across the life span from youth through adulthood, from birth to death. Lifelong educational opportunities exist in each community in three distinct educational forms: formal, nonformal, and informal. Each process is a valid means of assisting lifelong learners in acquiring and meeting their educational needs. This framework suggests that lifelong learners can make choices in fulfilling their educational concerns and desires in a multitude of ways (Galbraith, 1990c).

Formal Education

This category consists of for-profit and nonprofit bureaucratic organizations within the community who have as their primary function the delivery of formal education in which youth and adult learners may participate. The goal of the organization is to provide some type of credential such as a diploma, certificate, or degree. Examples of such providers include high schools, state and regional universities and colleges, community colleges, proprietary schools, vocational and technical institutes, external degree agencies, and public adult education schools. Because of the nature of the settings, instructors or teachers are professional educators who hold expertise in the area of specialization. Learners in such settings have little control over what is taught and how it is taught. Educators make value and prescriptive judgments of what is appropriate for learners to acquire within their formal educational pursuits.

Nonformal Education

Communities contain a number of organizations and agencies that use education as a secondary or allied part of their mission. The YMCA or YWCA, cooperative extension, religious institutions, health institutions, service clubs, voluntary organizations, business and industry human resource development programs, correctional institutions, libraries, museums, senior citizen organizations, and a plethora of other community-based agencies are examples of such nonformal education providers. In these settings learners are more likely to participate voluntarily and are not seeking any type of credentials or degrees but may receive in some cases a certificate of completion. They can also retain some control over what they want to learn as well as when, how, and where this learning takes place. The educational settings range from nonstructured to structured. The instructors may or may not be professionally trained but overall seem to be quite successful in helping learners reach their learning needs.

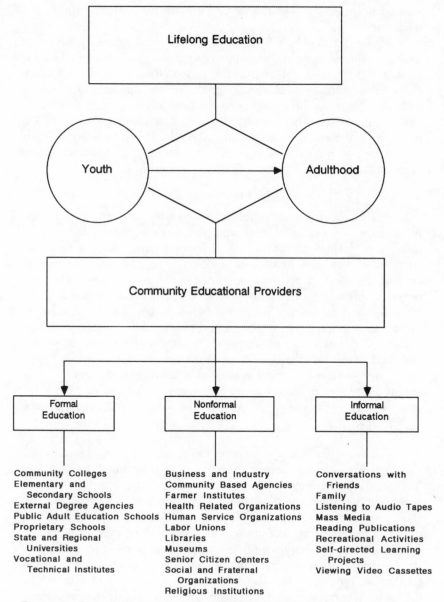

Figure 1.1 Framework for connecting lifelong education and community.

Informal Education

This category encompasses the vast majority of education that takes place within community structures. It is independent of institutional and organizational providership. The community itself is the instrument of education and learners are guided by their own desires and learning processes. Learning within this context may be deliberate or fortuitous, but is always personally meaningful to the learner. Informal education is characterized by interaction between human and material resources. Examples include informal debates and conversations in the work, family, or community setting; television and other mass media viewing; travel, recreational and leisure-time activities; and listening to audio cassettes, reading publications, or viewing video tapes. The learner is in complete control over how, what, and where the learning will occur. Although the learner may consult with others concerning a project, in most cases a professionally trained educator is absent. The community serves as the educator as well as the learning resource and laboratory.

CONCLUSION

Both lifelong education and the community are multidimensional in scope and perspective. Connecting lifelong education with the community stimulates and contributes to the lifelong learning process. The ultimate goal of any community should be to develop a democratic and educated citizenry. As Lindeman (1926) stated "The whole of life is learning, therefore education can have no endings" (p. 6). The concept of lifelong education suggests that it occurs throughout the entire life span (the vertical dimension) and that education and life are linked (horizontal dimension). Through the three modes of education—formal, nonformal, and informal—a lifelong education community develops consisting of individuals, groups, and communities of interest and function. This is the foundation on which learners recognize their identity, human potential, and inclusionary significance. It is a way of creating the good community which is one that demonstrates the elements of a harmonious existence.

At the heart of a lifelong education community is the notion that "building a community of learners requires choices" (Galbraith, 1990c, p. 89). These choices are made by learners, community organizations, and educators. As suggested above, learners may be members of several communities, each contributing to a different dimension that fulfills some specific, culturally constructed, and contextual need in their lives, whether personal, professional, social, spiritual, or recreational. Learners then make choices when it comes to what, why, where, and how learning will occur. Will these choices maintain what Peshkin (1982) calls community integrity—that is, will they allow for a sense of unity and wholeness shared by members of that community? When choices are made, how do they affect individualism, self-reliance, and moral, social, and political discourse? How do these choices affect with the work, school, religious, and family communities? Learners choose their mode of education. Will learning be voluntary or involuntary? While most learning is voluntary, sometimes learners have little choice in deciding what will be learned, i.e., human resource development activities sponsored by employers. Overall, learners must make choices, both philosophical and practical, concerning learning needs and the purpose of learning something new. How will the learning contribute to fulfilling the identified need? Can an organization within the community be located to fulfill the identified need? Is that organization private or public? Can a learner participate as a member of the community at large? Participation or nonparticipation, according to Galbraith (1990c) "will be determined by learners' decisions in relation to the community organization in which they seek educational opportunities" (p. 90).

Organizations within the community must also make numerous choices about how they utilize education to meet their varied missions. As Galbraith (1990c) states "they too must begin with philosophical choices concerning their provision of education. The foremost question that must be addressed relates to the issue of why provide education?" (p. 90). Community organizations must wrestle with the question of whether or not education is a component of their mission or is the rationale based on a market-driven mentality. If the determination is that education is a vital component, then decisions of who should they serve, to what population should it be directed, and how often should educational programs be offered must be addressed. Other questions also must be raised. Who in the organization should decide what programs will be offered? How will the programs be supported? Should they be cost-effective? Should learners be charged a fee and if so on what basis should fees be established? Should programs be organized on the premise that learners are independent and self-directed? The specific community organization must make choices grounded in ethical behavior and sound decision making when it comes to the provision of educational opportunity.

Educators must also conduct an ethics check and in doing so must engage in choices that relate to programmatic issues and the teaching and learning process. The primary determination is: Are their instructional approaches, activities, and programs grounded in solid learning procedures and principles? Is there, for example, an understanding of how learners learn and how their shifting needs influence the teaching and learning encounter? What educational philosophy does the educator practice? How do philosophy and teaching style influence instructional methods? Should learners be helped to become more reflective and critical?

Lifelong education and community are the foundation of a free and democratic society. Galbraith (1990c) states that "Building communities of independent, thoughtful, and autonomous learners is one way to sustain the democratic process" (p. 92). Lifelong education through formal and nonformal community organizations contributes to the good community that is anchored in individualism and opportunity for free choice. By understanding and then engaging in a lifelong educational process, individuals of all ages find satisfaction through context-specific, value-laden, and socially constructed learning experiences. Through formal and nonformal community organizations, individuals contribute to the community at large by gaining a better understanding of themselves; by finding meaning in school, work, family, religion, and community; by contributing something to the public welfare; and by providing a different voice in a common tradition.

REFERENCES

Apps, J. (1985). Lifelong learning examined. In H. Long, J. Apps, & R. Hiemstra, *Philosophical and other views on lifelong learning* (pp. 1–38). Athens: The University of Georgia.

Bellah, R., Madsen, R., Sullivan, W., Swidler, A., & Tipton, S. (1985). *Habits of the heart: Individualism and commitment in American life.* New York: Harper and Row.

Brookfield, S. (1983). *Adult learners, adult education and the community.* New York: Teachers College Press.

Cropley, A. (1977). *Lifelong education: A psychological analysis.* New York: Pergamon.

Cropley, A., & Dave, R. (1978). *Lifelong education and the training of teachers: Developing a curriculum for teacher education on the basis of the principles of lifelong education.* Oxford: Pergamon.

Dave, R. (1973). *Lifelong education and the school curriculum.* Hamburg: UNESCO Institute for Education.

Dave, R. (Ed.). (1976). *Foundations of lifelong education.* Oxford: Pergamon.

DeLargy, P. (1989). *Public schools and community education.* In S. Merriam & P. Cunningham (Eds.), *Handbook of adult and continuing education* (pp. 287–302). San Francisco: Jossey–Bass.

Effrat, M. (Ed.). (1974). *The community: Approaches and applications.* New York: The Free Press.

Fellin, P. (1987). *The community and the social worker.* Itasca: Peacock.

Galbraith, M. W. (Ed.). (1990a). *Education through community organizations.* New Directions for Adult and Continuing Education, no. 47. San Francisco: Jossey–Bass.

Galbraith, M. W. (1990b). The nature of community and adult education. In M. W. Galbraith (Ed.), *Education through community organizations* (pp. 3–11). San Francisco: Jossey–Bass.

Galbraith, M. W. (1990c). Building communities of learners. In M. W. Galbraith (Ed.), *Education through community organizations* (pp. 89–92). San Francisco: Jossey–Bass.

Galbraith, M. W., & Price, D. W. (1991). Community adult education in America: An overview. *New Horizons in Adult Education, 5*(1), 3–18.

Hamilton, E., & Cunningham, P. (1989). Community-based adult education. In S. Merriam & P. Cunningham (Eds.), *Handbook of adult and continuing education* (pp. 439–450). San Francisco: Jossey–Bass.

Hiemstra, R. (1972). *The educative community.* Lincoln: Professional Educators Publications.

Ireland, T. (1978). *Gelphi's view of lifelong education.* Manchester: The University of Manchester.

Jarvis, P. (1986). *Social perspectives of lifelong education and lifelong learning.* Athens: The University of Georgia.

Jarvis, P. (1987). *Adult learning in the social context.* London: Croom Helm.

Kanter, R. (1972). *Commitment and community: Communes and utopias in sociological perspective.* Cambridge: Harvard University Press.

Knowles, M. (1980). *The modern practice of adult education* (revised and updated). New York: Cambridge.

Kolb, D. (1984). *Experiential learning.* Englewood Cliffs: Prentice–Hall.

Lengrand, P. (1975). *An introduction to lifelong education.* London: Croom Helm.

Lindeman, E. (1926). *The meaning of adult education.* New York: New Republic.

Long, H., Apps, J., & Hiemstra, R. (1985). *Philosophical and other views on lifelong learning.* Athens: The University of Georgia.

Luloff, A., & Swanson, L. (Eds.). (1990). *American rural communities.* Boulder: Westview.

Peshkin, A. (1982). *The imperfect union.* Chicago: University of Chicago Press.

Peterson, R. (1979). Present sources of education and learning. In R.

Peterson & Associates, *Lifelong learning in America* (pp. 13–74). San Francisco: Jossey–Bass.

Roberts, H. (1979). *Community development: Learning and action.* Toronto: University of Toronto Press.

Rothman, J., & Tropman, J. (1987). Models of community organization and macro practice perspectives: Their mixing and phasing. In F. Cox, J. Erlich, J. Rothman, & J. Tropman (Eds.), *Strategies of community organization* (pp. 3–26). Itasca: Peacock.

Smith, R. (1982). *Learning how to learn.* New York: Cambridge.

Suttles, G. (1972). *The social construction of communities.* Chicago: University of Chicago Press.

Tonnies, F. (1957). *Community and society.* East Lansing: Michigan State University Press.

Warren, R. (1970). The good community—What would it be? *Journal of the Community Development Society,* 1(1),14–23.

Warren, R. (1978). *The community in America* (3rd. ed.). Chicago: Rand McNally.

Warren, R., & Lyon, L. (Eds.). (1988). *New perspectives on the American community* (5th ed.). Chicago: Dorsey.

Wright, J. (1980). Community learning: A frontier for adult education. In R. Boyd, J. Apps & Associates, *Redefining the discipline of adult education* (pp. 99–125). San Francisco: Jossey–Bass.

Zander, A. (1990). *Effective social action for community groups.* San Francisco: Jossey–Bass.

CHAPTER 2

The Rural Context for Education: Adjusting the Images

DARYL HOBBS

Consideration of today's rural communities is hampered by an absence of any clear definition of either *rural* or *community*, or a consensus about what they mean. Both terms tend to be somewhat like beauty; their existence and meaning is in the eye of the beholder. But whether precisely defined or not, both terms are widely used in everyday discussion and both share a capacity to evoke images and emotions. Indeed these widely held images are being combined by advertisers to form an image of country as an ethic, idea, and lifestyle, distinguished from city and suburb. The images of country, as exemplified in the marketing of products from blue jeans to music to suburban housing developments, tend to cast country as escape from the constraints, pressures, and fast-paced life of the cities.

But the commercialized images of country tend to be at substantial variance with current facts concerning rural America and its communities. Images persist which portray rural America as the bastion of hard work and tradition, of simple lifestyles, and communities where people know and care about each other. Rural people are seldom portrayed as wealthy, but nevertheless are thought to be enjoying the good life. These images, reinforced by commercialism, are still prevalent—public opinion polls over the past several years continue to reveal that most Americans, rural and urban, if offered a choice, report they would prefer to live in a rural area or small town. Current facts portray a different picture. In 1987 median family income for metropolitan areas (urban) was $33,131 compared with $24,397 in nonmetropolitan areas (rural); urban income is 36 percent greater than rural and growing more rapidly. The poverty rate in nonmetro areas is 35 percent higher than metro. Unemployment is 25 percent higher in rural areas, but underemployment is a more serious

21

problem. About 10 percent of rural counties are classified as "persistent poverty" counties, having been in the lowest 20 percent in income over the past forty years. Further, "rural" U.S. counties with the most rapid population and income growth are generally those which are closest to major metropolitan areas and have become more urban than rural in lifestyle and occupation.

Times have blurred what were once clear distinctions between rural and urban America. The extremes (e.g., midtown Manhattan compared with a small ranching town in the Nebraska Sand Hills) are still easy to find and classify as either urban or rural, but most Americans now live somewhere between those extremes. Over the past several decades American society has been transformed into a mass society dominated by urban lifestyles, economic activity, and institutions which have extended into and engulfed the country. Rural people, however they are defined, now watch the same TV programs, consume most of the same products, and work at many of the same jobs as their urban counterparts.

Thus much of what has affected rural Americans originated in and around cities. Indeed those changes have forced some redefinition of rural and urban. First a bit of history about the cities to give us a better foundation for understanding today's version of rural.

Because agricultural mechanization reduced the need for labor on the nation's farms and because economic and job growth have occurred disproportionately in the cities, rural Americans have, throughout this century, moved in a steady stream to urban areas for employment. American cities were literally built on immigration. The rural to urban immigrants did not, however, leave rural values completely behind when they moved. One manifestation was the dramatic growth of suburbs around the larger cities especially following World War II. To a great extent the suburbs reflected a kind of rural-urban compromise: compromising an economic necessity to live near where the better paying jobs were, with many people's preference for more open space and other features of rural life style. Suburbs were quite literally an invention to accommodate economic necessity with some rural based values.

CONVERSION OF CITIES TO METROPOLITAN AREAS

Beginning with the close-in suburbs, urban areas have continued to sprawl and grow outward, making the boundaries of cities less and less distinct. Cities have become the focal point for metropolitan regions which extend far out into the countryside. The continuing sprawl has been energized both by urban people retaining their city job and moving to smaller outlying "rural" communities and by small town and rural people regularly commuting to metropolitan area jobs. As improved transportation shriveled distances, a concomitant blending of countryside into town, town into suburb, and suburb into city gave rise to the concept of a rural-urban continuum to replace the rural-urban dichotomy. The automobile and the vast infrastructure that supports it emancipated rural people from the land and released urban people from the city. It became possible for more people to live in a rural area or small town and enjoy access to urban jobs and other amenities. Correspondingly cities grew out, more than up.

The U.S. Bureau of the Census has recognized this urban sprawl and developed the concept of the *metropolitan area* along with the technical definitions to classify it. Although the definition of a metropolitan area is detailed and complex, simply defined, metropolitan counties are those that include a city of 50,000 or more and/or are counties that are near large cities and have a highly urbanized population. Counties are the basis for classification. Of the 3,067 U.S. counties, 626 (20 percent) are currently classified as metropolitan and 2,441 as nonmetropolitan. Together the metropolitan counties included 77 percent of the U.S. population in 1986: nonmetropolitan counties included 23 percent. All fifty states include at least one metropolitan area, but in California 96 percent of the population lives in a metro area; in Idaho only 20 percent.

Accordingly metropolitan areas such as Atlanta, St. Louis, Minneapolis-St. Paul, continue to expand horizontally and have become labor and service market regions as large as 100 miles or more in diameter. The St. Louis (Missouri, Illinois) metropolitan area is illustrative. The officially designated St. Louis standard metropolitan statistical area (SMSA) includes ten counties - five in Missouri and five in Illinois with a total 1988 population of 2.4 million. Movement out from the central city is reflected by St. Louis City's population having declined from 850,000 in 1950 to only about 400,000 in 1988. Only one sixth of the metro area population resides in the place that gives the region its name. The ten St. Louis SMSA counties include more than 200 incorporated places, many of which were once smaller rural trade centers but which have been engulfed and have become "bedroom" towns, that is, places where people live, although their livelihood is in the city.

The urban sprawl is important also because many of the more rapidly growing and higher income nonmetropolitan counties are within the reaches of this sprawl. Indeed as the sprawl continues, more nonmetropolitan counties at the periphery are becoming reclassified as metropolitan. It is probable for example that because of continued population growth on the periphery, at least three additional counties will be added to the St. Louis SMSA following the 1990 census, increasing the number of counties in the SMSA from ten to thirteen. Thus a part of metro growth and nonmetro decline is attributable to statistical reclassification. The number of U.S. metropolitan counties increases at the expense of the number of nonmetropolitan counties.

FROM URBAN-RURAL TO METROPOLITAN-NONMETROPOLITAN

The distinction *metropolitan-nonmetropolitan* has largely taken the place of *urban-rural* in public policy analysis, legislation, research, and so forth because that has become the most frequently used basis for reporting demographic and economic data. Indeed the term *metropolitan area* has generally replaced *urban* or *city* as a description for large population concentrations. The classification is more than a statistical artifact. For example, in recent years federal legislation has provided for a lower level of reimbursement for Medicare services performed by nonmetro physicians and hospitals than for the same services performed by metro area physicians and hospitals.

Although the definition of metropolitan is relatively precise, the definition of nonmetropolitan (rural) isn't. Nonmetropolitan is a residual, that is, it is what is left over after the metropolitan areas have been defined and taken out. Indeed the very label *nonmetropolitan* indicates clearly that it is whatever isn't metropolitan. The only consistent basis for differentiation is population density—the basis on which a county is officially defined as metropolitan. The concept of rurality once had significant economic, social, and political associations, but the nonmetropolitan concept that has replaced it is primarily, though perhaps not totally, geographic: one of the still distinctive features of rural areas is the distances that separate the homes of rural people (Gilford, Glenn & Ingram, 1981). So rural (nonmetropolitan) is that 23 percent of the population which is less tightly squeezed together than the 77 percent that is defined as metropolitan. Because of the broad definition, nonmetro includes cities of just under 50,000 as well as open country residents and inhabitants of the smallest villages. The economic span is even greater, ranging from very high income resort communities such as Aspen, Colorado, down to some of the poorest communities and neighborhoods in the nation.

Traditionally the idea of community in rural areas has been linked with a town. Indeed town and community are often used interchangeably in rural localities. Certainly there are far more towns and places to inspire a sense of community in nonmetropolitan America. Altogether there are 19,205 incorporated places - villages, towns, cities in the United States. Only 12 percent of those places have a population of more than 10,000; 88 percent (16,872) have a population of less than 10,000; and 60 percent (11,428) have a population of less than 2,500 (Johansen & Fuguitt, 1984).

INCORPORATION OF RURAL AMERICA INTO THE MASS SOCIETY

Important to understanding contemporary rural America and rural communities is to understand how much rural distinctiveness has been lost in recent decades and why. Until rather recently, the concept of rurality represented a whole bundle of closely interrelated economic, social, and political traits. Rural referred to more than a geographic category; there was a identifiable rural way of life, a rural culture. Rural life could be more easily understood because there were so many factors that reinforced each other. Today the bundle has come apart, and the various characteristics that once were closely associated under the broad rubric of rurality are now almost completely unrelated (Gilford, Glenn, & Ingram, 1981). It is that uncoupling which complicates easy generalizations about rural.

Reinforced by great improvements in transportation and communication technology, rural America has been transformed and incorporated first into the mass society and more recently into a global economy. National markets replaced local markets for rural goods and products, and mass merchandising and franchises began to replace local merchants as the distributors of goods. Transportation and communication technologies played a prominent role. Improvements in transportation made it possible to get to more centralized services and shopping centers and improvements in communication exposed rural people to the same information and same advertisements as urban people. Not only do rural people watch the same TV programs, read the same newspapers, and rent the same movies but they also purchase the same goods, usually from franchise stores bearing the same names as found in urban shopping malls. Indeed, because of regionalization of services they often make those purchases in urban shopping malls. What rural people have in common across the country is not so much a distinctive rural lifestyle, but rather consumption of the same goods and exposure to the same media. That causes rural residents to have as much or more in common with urban residents as with each other. Rural America has simply been incorporated into the consumption-oriented mass society.

This transformation was not due alone to market forces and technology. It was greatly reinforced by public policies. In recent decades the goals of rural improvement and development programs and policies have been largely oriented toward making rural America more like urban America. Public policies encouraged school consolidation to make rural schools larger and more like urban schools. Infrastructure investments and training facilitated the movement of lower skill industries from urban to rural areas which also expedited the concentration of health, retail, and other services in larger rural trade centers, and so on.

Incorporation into a mass society has affected rural people beyond their role as consumers of goods and services. Other national trends have affected rural areas as well, with similar effects on lifestyles. For example, nationwide, rural women have entered the work force outside the home in nearly as great numbers as urban women. In the process a demand has been generated for child care, more meals are eaten away from home, and more stress has been placed on families. That is especially important considering that rural workers, especially women, generally work for lower wages than their urban counterparts. For many farm and small town residents the necessity to travel to larger places for work, shopping, and so forth takes added time, further reducing the amount of time available for community activities and family life. In view of these changes, along with the greater rural incidence of poverty, low income and marginal employment, it is not surprising that rural social service workers, mental health workers, and other helping professionals report increased incidence of stress related problems in rural areas. The commercialized image of country doesn't include those problems but they are there.

ECONOMIC CHANGES

It seems somewhat contradictory to emphasize that while rural America has been incorporated into the mass society it has at the same time become increasingly diverse. While rural people have become more alike in what they consume, they have become more different from each other in what they produce and how.

As late as the 1950s most rural counties could count agriculture as the principal basis for their economy and if not agriculture, then it was mining, timbering, fishing, or some other natural resource based industry. However that has changed greatly. In recent years manufacturing employment and retirement income have grown to account for much more rural income than farming. A recent U.S. Department of Agriculture study classified nonmetropolitan counties according to the principal source of their economic base (Henry, Drabenstott, & Gibson, 1987). About 25 percent (618) of the nonmetro counties were classified as manufacturing. They are mostly concentrated in the southeast and include about 36 percent of the total nonmetro population and 36 percent of total nonmetro income. Those rural counties were converted to a manufacturing economy in the 1950s, 60s, and 70s as mature product industries (generally low skill) moved from cities in the northeast to rural areas, principally drawn by cheaper and unorganized rural labor and reinforced by public investments in highways, industrial parks, vocational training centers, and so forth. Another 25 percent (602 counties) is classified as farming, but those counties account for only 11 percent of the nonmetro population and 12 percent of total nonmetro income. Most of the counties classified as farming are located in the upper midwest and the plains states. Other classifications include: mining and energy extraction (7 percent of counties); retirement, mostly in the mid-South (9 percent); government, those having a military base, major university, etc. (10 percent); and trade, counties with a larger town serving as a regional trade and service center (15 percent).

This classification is particularly cogent for understanding rural America today because most rural localities are reliant on one major source for their economic base. Metropolitan areas generally have a diversified economy; rural localities don't. The rural locality therefore is much more economically vulnerable. A corporation can decide to move a branch factory to a rural locality and create a local economic boom. It can just as easily several years later leave the community holding the bag if it decides to relocate somewhere else. Communities principally dependent on farming tend to experience economic peaks and valleys as farm prices fluctuate in response to national and international market forces. Most rural localities have become heavily dependent for their well-being on economic decisions and forces over which they have relatively little control (Padfield, 1980).

It is this economic transformation of rural America from mostly production agriculture and other natural resource based industries to regions of different and more specialized economic activity that has contributed most to the diversification of rural America. These changes have greatly affected communities throughout rural America but in very different ways. A key to understanding rural communities begins with a determination of a community's economic base and how that is affecting the community's current and long term prospects. There are now rural factory towns, ski resort towns, cattle ranching towns, coal mining towns, oil drilling towns, retirement communities, and so on. These are more than just labels; the lifestyle, social organization, social class structure, demographic composition, leadership, wealth, and so on of a community are greatly affected by its economic base. As one example, most farming communities have been losing population for years; most rural retirement, government, trade, and commuting communities have been growing.

ECONOMIC VULNERABILITY OF RURAL RESIDENTS

It was emphasized earlier that per capita income in nonmetropolitan America is well below metropolitan areas and is falling further behind. A principal reason is to be found among the major sources of rural income. Nationwide, real income (constant dollars) for professional, managerial, technical, and complex manufacturing workers has been increasing. The number employed in those occupations is increasing as well. However most of the higher skill, professional, and managerial employment is located in metropolitan areas and is increasing more rapidly there. On the other hand both income and employment have declined among natural resource based occupations and routine (low skill) manufacturing. Those occupations are far more prevalent in nonmetropolitan areas. So very simply, higher paying occupations are disproportionately located and growing in metropolitan areas and lower paying occupations are disproportionately located in rural areas (Falk & Lyson, 1988). Thus the income gap is widening and is continuing to serve as an inducement for more highly educated rural people to relocate to metropolitan areas, leaving behind a higher proportion of working age rural residents struggling to make ends meet.

Low paying occupations are a contributing factor to the greater amount of rural poverty. Data from the 1987 Census of Poverty reveals that 70 percent of rural families living below the poverty line have at least one employed family member; 40 percent have two or more (Greenstein, 1988). The profile of rural poverty that emerges is that of a "working poor." The rural poor tend also not to have equal access to various kinds of benefits targeted toward low income people because the criteria do not apply as well to rural people (Tweeten, 1980). For example recent studies reveal that the actual rate of rural unemployment is much higher than official estimates largely because of the higher percentage of rural workers are self-employed and "informally" employed. Self-employed people are not counted as unemployed, although they may be seriously underemployed. A person is considered underemployed if operating a business or service that attracts insufficient business to keep the operator fully employed. A declining population usually means a loss of business for local establishments.

The greater economic vulnerability of many rural residents lies not only in lower paying jobs, underemployment, and lack of employment stability but also in the absence of benefits usually associated with employment. Because more rural people are self-employed, irregularly employed (seasonal work, for example), and employed part-time they do not have the same coverage and protection of unemployment compensation, manpower training programs, etc. Recent studies also reveal that low wage workers and employees of small businesses are far less likely to have health insurance coverage as a employee benefit (The State of Small Business, 1987). This economic marginality of so many rural residents creates a great potential demand for adult education and skill training, but such training needs to be accessible and linked with realistic prospects for improved income of the participants if it is to be effective (Lichter & Costanzo, 1987).

Interdependence or Dependence?

Economic changes have diversified the rural economy but the effects have been very uneven. Some rural localities have reaped great dividends in income and employment while others have had persistent poverty reinforced. Most have experienced the widening gap between metro and nonmetro income. The reality is that whether economic winners or losers, rural localities have become more dependent on economic forces beyond their control. Not only the economy has been affected. Incorporation into the mass society and increasing centralization of institutions and services such as education and health care have also reduced local control. Not only is the rural community economy directly connected with national and international markets, but so also have rural schools, health care, and other services become a part of national systems. A consequence is greater rural community dependency, less rural community autonomy.

That traditional foundation of the rural economy, agriculture, exemplifies the growing interdependence. Most rural communities came into existence a century or more ago to meet the production and consumption needs of the surrounding farmers. Most of what farmers needed was obtained in the closest small town, but that has changed greatly. Today's commercial farmers have become accustomed to operating in an environment of national and international markets and streams of technology, inputs, and finance. Farming has become less local and more national and international; it has become less dependent on local community services and markets and more dependent on regionalized services and terminal markets. Farming has been extended to become a component of an elaborate agribusiness sector. Consequently although most farmers claim a rural community as their residence, their farm business may not be very dependent on the services of the local community. Much the same could be said about rural factories, mining and energy corporations, and other businesses.

Many rural communities have also become dependent on other towns for retail and other necessary services. As the concepts of the mass society—specialization, centralization, and standardization—affected rural areas, many businesses and services closed in smaller towns and were replaced by businesses concentrated in larger rural trade and service centers. Although the size of such centers varies from one part of the country to another, they are typically towns with a population of 10,000 or more in which there are substantial concentrations of retail stores, physicians and other health services, media and so forth. A significant concomitant of this regionalization has been the extension of franchise businesses, such as discount stores, fast food restaurants, and hardware chains into these trade centers. Significantly, which communities become the location of these businesses is determined more by market analysts in corporate headquarters than by local independent entrepreneurs. Indeed many rural communities compete for the location of such franchise businesses just as they compete for factories to relocate in their town.

Centrifugal Effects on Rural Communities

A consequence of this expanded economic dependency has been to diminish the economic and service role of the thousands of small rural communities across the country. Whereas those communities were once places where people went to church, worked, shopped, went to the doctor, and went to school, many have become places where people live, while depending on other larger communities for necessary services. Often the community has come to mean less to people who live there because it doesn't satisfy as many needs. Figure 2.1 shows some of the centrifugal influences affecting smaller rural communities. It is increasingly difficult to maintain a sense of community in many rural localities when so many things residents depend on are located somewhere else. The effects are comprehensive. With modern mass media people frequently obtain more and better information about what is going on in the world outside the community than close to home. An increasing number of rural residents obtain their retirement income from Social Security and other transfer payments. If people don't depend on the locality for their livelihood, that tends to diminish interest in the locality. As a growing proportion of the funding for schools and other government services comes from state and federal sources it also causes local school, hospital and government boards, and commissions to pay as much or more atten-

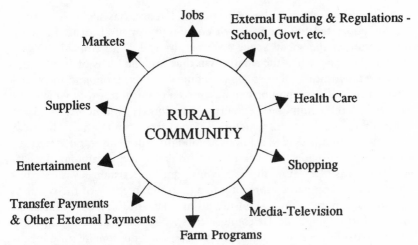

Figure 2.1 External effects on rural communities.

tion to the sources of those funds than to the locality. All these influences compete for time and attention with the community and make the task of retaining a strong sense of community that much more difficult, even if people know each other well and have a traditional attachment to a place.

COMMUNITY AND CHANGES IN BOUNDARIES

Community can be thought of as a social space occupied by members who perceive common traditions and ways of doing things as well as problems that affect the vitality and viability of their community. Communities become effective when they organize themselves to address and resolve their commonly perceived problems. It is that quality that Peshkin (1982) refers to as community integrity - a sense of unity and wholeness shared by members. A part of integrity involves boundaries: what are the boundaries of the community? who is a member and who isn't?

We refer to community as social space in order to emphasize a quality of community beyond geographic or physical space. Everyday experience makes it clear that people living close to each other, such as in an urban apartment building or neighborhood, do not necessarily share a sense of community. They may not even know each other and make no attempt to become acquainted. Social space refers to a sense of belonging whether physically close or not.

Proximity, sharing the same physical space, has historically been closely associated with the idea of community in rural areas. In many rural localities the social space and the physical space coincided, especially in the days when the small town that was the focus of community was also the location where people met most of their economic and social service needs. The community represented a physical territory which was essential to the community's identity. Accordingly community residents generally resisted changes which threatened those boundaries. The great controversy that attended school consolidation in many rural American communities provides an example. To residents of a community threatened with loss of a school through consolidation, resistance was based as much or more on perceptions of damage to the integrity of the community than on more technical considerations of curriculum, cost, efficiency, and so forth (Smith & DeYoung, 1988). Not only did consolidation threaten loss of a valued community possession, but in many rural localities the school was also the centerpiece of community activity and therefore crucial to maintaining community identity. School and community reinforce each other greatly in many rural localities.

Not only school consolidation, but the whole array of external influences described above are contributing to restructuring the social and physical boundaries of today's rural community. New community boundaries are being formed, while the grip of the older boundaries is being loosened. Because of the centrality of the school, many rural informants emphasize that today the boundaries of the school district, usually including several towns, has become a more meaningful community social space than the trade area of the closest town. To a great extent the boundaries of community and the network of relationships that give it meaning are expanding horizontally in rural areas. As this occurs, however, there is a diminished sense of community and a reduced integrity of the communities that were once clearly defined and gave a distinctive identity to their residents. Consequently the idea of social space is beginning to replace physical space as a delineation of community in rural areas.

Developing and Preserving a Sense of Community

The emergence of new rural trade and service areas and the replacement of proximity by social space compound the task of community development for many smaller rural localities. There is a quality about community that can transcend economic influences and demographic classifications; it is a "sense of community." As suggested by Peshkin (1982):

Census data permit the creation of a useful picture of a place, one that allows ready comparisons and contrasts. What such data do not reveal is the sense that the residents of such a place have about themselves and about their relationship with other places, a sense that is derived from a compound of historical and contemporary fact and fiction. (p. 12)

If a place is both small and rural, it improves the probability of residents feeling and working to retain a sense of community, but it doesn't guarantee it. Social and economic changes make a sense of community more problematic, more difficult to sustain. In rural communities experiencing population decline and loss of businesses, residents can develop a sense of fatalism and resign themselves to continued decline. On the other hand, rural localities experiencing substantial population growth involving retirees or metropolitan workers face a task of integrating such people into the history and fiction of the old community if it is to be retained, or of creating new history and fiction if a new sense of community is to be created. Indeed for many residents of such communities, the presence of newcomers can be threatening because community is more than space, it is involved with individual identity. As observed by Jonassen (1968):

A community may be bound up with one's identity such that it has become an extension of an inhabitant's ego so that any action which seems to diminish the status of the community and its security becomes, in effect, a threat to the self and security . . . of the individual involved. (p. 32)

Changes originating outside the community can also produce intense conflicts. All these changes make it more difficult for a community consensus to survive today. That is important because rural communities have traditionally strived for consensus and avoidance of conflict (Padfield, 1980). Indeed the absence of conflict has been one of the persistent images of rural community life; it is also at variance with the facts.

New Bases for Conflict

"The mixing of rural with urban values, lifestyles, and vocations is generating vitality, change, and growing conflict over the current state and future path of rural communities" (Gilford, 1981, p. 4). As new social and physical boundaries of rural communities are established, this brings into potential conflict different interests and values that were often sublimated within smaller communities of the past.

As emphasized, there are substantial differences in income, employment, and other measures of economic well-being between rural and urban America. Reducing or eliminating those differences has been a prominent rationale for rural development initiatives from the federal level on down to the local level. That has translated into a need for rural community (regional) economic growth. Thus rural development has largely been defined in terms of growth in income, population, and employment, and the addition of services that growth would facilitate. A broad spectrum of rural leaders has bought into that idea. Even very small rural communities are likely to have organized a community industrial development committee to attract industries and expand the economic base.

Because growth requires change, an emphasis on growth very often conflicts with preserving the integrity of the community as it has existed. Accordingly community advocates of growth and change often find themselves at odds with residents whose identity and preference are linked with preservation. Such conflict can be intractable. Indeed Padfield (1980) suggests that of all the contradictions inherent in American society, the contradiction between "growth fundamentalism" and "rural fundamentalism" is one of the more persistent and profound. If growth is achieved, it appears to come at the price of some loss of community integrity. Although not always the case, evidence has accumulated that community growth results in greater incorporation into the mass society and a corresponding increase in community dependency.

The attitudes and beliefs associated with "growth fundamentalism" and "rural fundamentalism" can be at the heart of numerous specific community conflicts, including education.

THE CENTRALITY OF THE SCHOOL AND LIFELONG EDUCATION

Because schools are the most inclusive of all community institutions, requiring nothing more for affiliation than that one be a resident, the school is potentially everyone's. In many rural localities this sense of ownership (and the sense of community that often accompanies it) is reinforced by the school being the largest employer, the largest claim on the local public treasury, and the location of most events that are community wide and open to the public. In the words of one rural community resident:

> This community school, it's the only thing that's a hub or a center, a common thing for everybody in the community. Church isn't 'cause we go to different churches. You'll eventually meet in the school, you'll finally end up at the school, 'cause that's the hub. (Peshkin, 1982, p. 114)

Schools and education often become the battleground for conflicts between growth and tradition in many rural localities largely because schools are at the same time intimately linked with community identity and yet the most visible manifestation of the mass society in the community. Correspondingly, conflicts emerge concerning what the school does and who controls it. Conflicts regarding what the school does are often confined to within the community. Illustrative is the research of Cummings, Briggs, and Mercy (1977) and their analysis of a community conflict concerning textbooks. They stress that the school symbolizes some of the conflict between the local and the mass society and that some community traditionalists conceptualized the school, ". . . as an alien social institution, staffed and controlled by individuals subscribing to cosmopolitan value orientations and beliefs" (p. 16).

Conflicts can also occur between "communities" regarding "ownership and control" of the school. Peshkin's (1982) analysis of school consolidation describes a twenty year long process of intercommunity conflict regarding school location. It was location, far more than the program, that was the basis for the conflict, because of the implications of school location for persistence and survival of community.

Conflict regarding schools and education can also be framed in terms of a community consensus in favor of greater local control opposed to the mass society emphasis on greater standardization, regulation, and accountability (DeYoung, 1987). The trend of modern society has been toward diminishing prerogatives for individuals and small towns. A school symbolizes community autonomy because it is what remains of local control in most states. Indeed education as a function of the state versus a function of the community (locality) is a central issue in school restructuring proposals originating in the early 1990s.

EDUCATION AND RURAL DEVELOPMENT

Education, broadly defined, is coming to be regarded by advocates of change and growth as a necessary foundation for rural localities to arrest the widening rural-urban income gap. The question is what kind of education and for which people. That question is pertinent because expanded investments in traditional education, by themselves, appear unlikely to contribute much more to rural economic development (Reid, 1990).

Rural communities lag behind in the proportion of college graduates and in occupations requiring higher levels of education and training. That is both cause and effect for the continuing migration of some of the most highly educated youth from rural communities. They leave because of an absence of jobs offering a good return on their education, but their departure reinforces a rural deficit in educational attainment. As those youth leave the community for careers elsewhere, they also take with them the value of the community's investment in their education. That has made it difficult for rural communities to capture a return on their educational investment (Deaton & McNamara, 1984). Because of this long-term transfer of educational investment from rural to urban areas, some economists (Tweeten, 1980) have argued for greater public subsidy of rural education on equity grounds. While such subsidies would address funding inequities for traditional education, they would not necessarily improve prospects for rural community economic development. Other approaches are needed.

Additional industrial relocation to rural areas is a diminishing prospect (Reid, 1990) and even where it occurs, it contributes little to narrowing the rural-urban income gap because low-skill manufacturing wage rates are low (Falk & Lyson, 1988). Consequently rural development specialists are directing more attention to rural community self-development strategies, including greater emphasis on knowledge-based rural development (Hobbs, 1986). Those strategies emphasize a need for greater attention to, and investment in, adult and continuing education.

Numerous kinds of adult education are needed to support more knowledge-based rural development efforts. There is a need for skill training of residents whose income and productivity is limited by a lack of skills. As Lichter and Costanzo (1987) emphasize, such training should be coordinated with local economic development efforts so that persons with improved skills can find local employment. Skill training without more productive employment is not likely to be of much benefit either to the recipient or the community. There is a need for retraining for some rural residents who are displaced from an occupation or career. In recent years many farmers have been forced from farming, factory workers have lost jobs when a factory has relocated, workers have been displaced in mining and energy occupations, and so on. Such persons are confronted with a transition to other, different sources of employment. There is a need for additional education and training to support entrepreneurship. A higher proportion of rural workers are self-employed and small businesses are creating most of the new jobs in rural areas as well as across the nation. Education is needed to provide prospective entrepreneurs with necessary skills and with the techniques to identify "niches," such as viable business and service opportunities.

Just as importantly there is a need for informal and continuing education to support new forms of community self-development. Specifically there is a need for continuing education regarding the impact of regional and national changes on the rural community. Such education is needed to enable leaders and citizens to more effectively identify realistic options for community change and development. Education can help community members more effectively utilize information and analyze the needs and development possibilities of the locality. Traditional education has been much more focused on the world outside the locality, than on the locality itself (Nachtigal & Hobbs, 1988). Now some rural localities are beginning to experiment with modifications of the role and procedures of the traditional school and school program in order to encompass a broader concept of community education. If adult and continuing education is going to be effective in supporting rural community development efforts, it must improve understanding of the community and how outside influences are affecting it.

COMMUNITY DEVELOPMENT

While a community may be defined as the social space in which people perceive common problems, an added feature, a contributing factor to the strength of the community, is the extent to which members organize themselves to effectively confront those problems. The degree of organization and the process by which decisions are made are fundamental to many analysts reference to development of the community, in contrast to developments that occur in the community but with little local participation (Wilkinson, 1986).

Recent research confirms that there are differences between communities in their ability to achieve self-development. Flora and Flora (1988) directed their research toward identifying characteristics of those rural towns and communities which have continued community improvements and which have diversified their local economy despite being hard hit by market forces outside the community. They describe the communities which were effective in adapting to macroeconomic changes and achieving some degree of self-determination as entrepreneurial:

> Entrepreneurial communities must set priorities and develop appropriate strategies and tactics. Such communities support local government, have a realistic perspective on the future and are able to overcome capacity limits, weigh alternatives, share new technologies, explore institutional innovation and mobilize new partners. (p. 2).

They found the following attributes associated with entrepreneurial communities:

- Acceptance of controversy

- A long-term emphasis on education

- Adequate resources to facilitate collective risk taking

- Willingness to invest in local private initiatives

- Willingness to tax themselves to invest in community improvements

- Ability to define community broadly, to envision larger boundaries for smaller communities

- Ability to network vertically and horizontally to obtain resources, particularly information

- A flexible, dispersed community leadership

Knowing these characteristics provides a starting point for public institutions who are suppliers of adult and continuing education. Their task is to design programs to help more rural communities become entrepreneurial. Doing so will require not only new methods and approaches but also the ability to separate the images about rural communities from the facts.

CONCLUSION AND IMPLICATIONS

Education, broadly defined, will likely have as much or more to contribute to the future well-being of rural residents and the quality of life and economic sustainability of their communities as the location and natural resources of their locality. Natural resource based industries, the traditional backbone of the rural economy, have been a sector of declining employment—a trend which is likely to continue. New forms of economic activity are needed and new creative approaches to providing community services will be necessary. There is a need for knowledge-based economic and community development across rural America. The capabilities of rural workers and citizens, and the knowledge and creativity of rural community leaders, will be pivotal factors in determining which rural communities thrive during the 1990s. A variety of educational and training services will be needed to support those efforts.

While education will be essential, there are some caveats. First, education will need to be tailored to meet very different local needs and circumstances. That is contrary to much of the past conventional wisdom pertaining to education which has tended to stress standardization more than adaptation to local circumstances. As we have emphasized throughout the chapter, rural America has become remarkably diverse over the past couple of decades, and different communities and regions face very different constraints and opportunities. Providers of educational services must be prepared to work collaboratively with rural communities in identifying needs and how they can best be met. Indeed, doing such needs assessments, if they effectively involve community residents, can be a pertinent form of education for participants. Some rural communities are finding that involving secondary school students in such a process is an effective form of learning and influences the students' attitudes and perceptions about their community. In effect secondary students can become an important community resource while they are learning. Community leaders and educational providers should take advantage of all available resources to assist with such assessments including the local office of land-grant university extension services, community colleges, regional development agencies, and so forth.

Second, education to support knowledge-based rural development will need to be nontraditional as well as traditional, continuing, and oriented to the different needs, ages, and circumstances of residents. For many rural communities it is the adults who have a greater stake in the future of the community because of the long-term pattern of out-migration of many youth and high-school graduates. Technology and the economy have been changing so rapidly that most workers require frequent retraining to retain their skills. Economic changes in a substantial number of rural communities, e.g., a factory closing, being forced out of farming, and so forth, have forced many rural residents into midlife occupational changes. Education and training are needed to facilitate a productive transition. In addition community and organization leaders need ongoing informational and educational services to improve their ability to make decisions and devise new strategies for delivery of services and for community development. One noted rural development specialist contends that the most important rural need is for a more informed local leadership.

Third, in order to be most effective, education and training programs and services need to be collaborative, not only among various providers of education and training, but also with a broader spectrum of community groups, agencies, and organizations. Education and training should be an integral component of achieving individual and community goals rather than representing a separate set of goals. An obvious connection involves closer collaboration between education and training and economic development efforts. Providing skill training for which there are no jobs, or no prospects for jobs, is of little benefit to anyone, least of all those who receive the training. This need for collaboration extends to all facets of community life. Educational agencies, largely by neglect, have failed to make it easy for students, especially adults, to make a transition from one level of educational attainment to the next. Clearer communication is needed. As noted, in many rural communities the school is the most prominent community institution and the one that contributes most to community identity. Where that is the case, it is logical to consider the school as the location for a broader range of community education activities, especially after normal school hours. It could be a logical place for community seminars, adult counseling, manpower training services, and off-campus courses from community colleges, universities, and vocational school.

Education in rural localities has reflected the mass society trends toward institutional specialization and separatism. It has become more incorporated into a national system and correspondingly less attune to local needs and circumstances. From our review of the status of rural localities today, we conclude that there is a need for a broadened role for education and training, and for those services to become a more integral part of community activity. That will require some institutional innovation and more conscious attention to the types and purposes of education and training, if the needs of rural residents and communities are to be met.

REFERENCES

Cummings, S., Briggs, R., & Mercy, J. (1977). Preachers vs. teachers: Local cosmopolitan conflict over textbook censorship in an Appalachian community. *Rural Sociology,* 42 (1), 7–21.

Deaton, B., & McNamara, K. (1984). *Education in a changing environment.* Mississippi State, MS: The Southern Rural Development Center.

DeYoung, A. J. (1987). The status of American rural education research: An integrated review and commentary. *Review of Educational Research,* 57 (2), 123–148.

Falk, W. W., & Lyson, T. (1988). *High tech, low tech, not tech: Recent industrial and occupational change in the South.* Albany, NY: State University of New York Press.

Flora, C., & Flora, J. (1988). Characteristics of entrepreneurial communities in a time of crisis. *Rural Developoment News,* 12 (2), 1–4.

Gilford, D. M., Nelson, G. L., & Ingram, L. (Eds.). (1981). *Rural America in passage: Statistics in policy.* Washington, DC: National Academy Press.

Greenstein, R. (1988, August). *Barriers to rural development.* Paper presented at the Annual National Rural Electric Cooperative Manager's Conference, Baltimore, MD.

Henry, M., Drabenstott, M., & Gibson, L. (1987). Rural growth slows down. *Rural Development Perspectives, 3* (3), 25–30.

Hobbs, D. (1986, September). *Knowledge based rural development: Adult education and the future rural economy.* Paper presented at the National Invitational Conference of Rural Adult Postsecondary Education, Arlie House, VA.

Johansen, H. E., & Fuguitt, G. (1984). *The changing rural village in America.* Cambridge: Ballinger.

Jonassen, C. T. (1968) *Community conflict in school district reorganization.* Oslo: Universitetsforlaget.

Lichter, D. T., & Costanzo, J. A. (1987). Nonmetropolitan underemployment and labor force composition. *Rural Sociology, 52* (3), 329–344.

Nachtigal, P., & Hobbs, D. (1988). *Rural development: The role of the public schools.* Washington, DC: National Governor's Association.

Padfield H. (1980). The expendable rural community and the denial of powerlessness. In A. Gallaher, Jr. & H. Padfield (Eds.), *The dying community* (pp. 159–185). Albuquerque, NM: University of New Mexico Press.

Peshkin, A. (1982). *The imperfect union.* Chicago: The University of Chicago Press.

Reid, J. N. (1990, April). *Education and rural development: A review of recent evidence.* Paper presented at the American Educational Research Association Annual Conference, Boston, MA.

Smith, D. T., & DeYoung, A. J. (1988). Big school vs. small school: Conceptual, empirical and political perspective on the re-emerging debate. *Journal of Rural and Small Schools, 2* (2), 2–11.

The State of Small Business: A Report of the President. (1987). Washington, DC: U.S. Government Printing Office.

Tweeten, L. (1980). Education has a role in rural development. *Rural Development Perspectives, 1,* 9–13.

Vidich, A., & Bensman, J. (1958). *Small towns in mass society.* New York: Anchor Books.

Wilkinson, K. P. (1986). Communities left behind - again. In U.S. Congress, Joint Economic Committee, *New dimensions in rural policy: Building upon our heritage* (pp. 341–346). Washington, DC: U.S. Government Printing Office.

PART TWO

EDUCATIONAL PROGRAMS AND PROVIDERS

CHAPTER 3

Elementary Education

IVAN D. MUSE
GLORIA JEAN THOMAS

The elementary school of a hundred years ago conjures up warm thoughts of the little red schoolhouse topped by a bell tower, heated by a pot-bellied stove, and furnished with hard desks, a map of the United States, and a picture of George Washington. Vigilant schoolmasters and schoolmarms are remembered fondly as capable of quelling the largest farm lads with just a look (or a rap on the knuckles with a wooden ruler) as pupils came to learn the rudiments of reading, writing, and 'rithmetic. Fascinating reading are the tales in the *Hoosier Schoolmaster* and *The Legend of Sleepy Hollow*. Whittier captured the essence of schooling in this earlier year with his poem "In School-Days" (1869):

> Still sits the school-house by the road,
> A ragged beggar sunning;
> Around it still the sumacs grow
> And blackberry vines are running.
>
> Within, the master's desk is seen,
> Deep scarred by rays official,
> The warping floor, the battered seats,
> The jack-knife's carved initial.

The American elementary school, or common school as it was called in the 1800s, suggested a belief that education would provide opportunity to individuals from every walk of life. That all Americans should be able to read and write was an idea embraced by its advocates with fervor and dedication. The theme of this time, "Common Schools— The Hope of Our Country," served as a focal point for many communities and small villages (Gross, 1962).

The elementary school in the rural area often became the center of the community, used as the gathering place for a multitude of functions.

After the school day, the schoolhouse was quickly transformed into a meeting area for quilting guilds, spelling bees, box socials, church services, Grange discussions, political gatherings, and even funerals. Imperfect as they may have been in the nineteenth century and into the early part of this century, elementary schools served as a major instrument in shaping the lives of countless millions who used schooling as a means of improving opportunity and the quality of life.

The inevitable growth of America into a major industrialized nation impacted the small rural elementary school. In 1820 only thirteen cities in the country had over 8,000 people, and the educational programs for youth were primarily rural. From the mid-nineteenth century onward, the power of industrialization was pervasive. Mechanized factories in rapidly growing cities required workers, and the needed manpower was on the farms. As cities grew, rural areas decreased in population and in ability to keep up with urban centers in providing adequate support services (Muse, 1977).

Within the expanding cities, a more formal and well-defined notion of schooling evolved. The necessity of schooling at a secondary level (high school) was accepted, and teacher training colleges were created to provide schooling for future teachers. Standards of excellence were established by the larger school districts, and the idea that bigger was better took root in urban soil. Rural schools came to be considered inferior simply because they were small and out of the mainstream of progress.

Reformers attempted to improve rural schools by making them more like their urban counterparts. Decision makers in cities and state offices began to feel that the lay people in rural areas did not know what was best for their children and that professionals skilled in modern urbanized theories of education could serve better the needs of rural youth. Armed with their rational arguments for school structure, efficiency, and effectiveness, professional educators used principles of consolidation to eliminate small schools and to build bigger ones. Their success was phenomenal. Within a hundred years, thousands of rural schools were closed, children bused to other communities to attend school, and the life of countless communities disrupted (Nachtigal, 1982).

Although the theme of "one best system of education" manifest in larger schools maintains a persuasive influence in public policy in the states today, the positive aspects of smallness are being increasingly recognized and appreciated. Conformity to some distant educational model does not always work well in the rural community. Rural schools must be far more diverse than urban ones to meet the diversity of the communities they serve. Demographic, economic, cultural, and social differences make comparisons of rural schools almost impossible (Jess, 1989).

Much evidence supports the contention that the quality of school life in many rural elementary schools equals and often exceeds that found in urban schools (Sher & Tompkins, 1976; Nachtigal, 1982; Barker & Muse, 1983; Hovey, 1987). Small pupil-teacher ratios, individualized attention to student needs, community support for schools, low dropout rates, familiarity with families and community citizens, and safe and orderly educational opportunities create an environment in rural elementary schools that benefits their students. Yet, like all schools, rural elementary schools face tremendous responsibilities and challenges as they look toward the next century.

In this chapter, the responsibilities of rural elementary schools and the external and internal challenges they face will be explored. Characteristics of the students, teachers, and administrators of rural schools will be discussed. The preparation and recruitment of teachers and principals and the challenges and rewards of teaching in rural schools will be analyzed. Curricular issues will be discussed with a look to the future and the societal and educational changes promised by the twenty-first century.

RESPONSIBILITIES AND CHALLENGES

Just as rural elementary schools have changed in appearance, their purpose has changed and expanded with the needs of rural children and larger society. Rural America is no longer isolated from urban America, which has lessened many of the differences between rural and urban schools. No longer are rural children as likely to remain on the farm or in the small town as they once were. No longer are rural children naive about urban life because paved highways, television, satellite disks, and computers provide indelible links between farm and town. Rural elementary schools are not immune to society's problems as latch-key children, single parent homes, and drug and alcohol abuse affect home and school. Although the primary purpose of rural elementary schools is still to provide a foundation to enable a child to advance in the educational system, a system which now includes college for many of the students, schools must also prepare children to become citizens in an increasingly complex society.

As for all schools in America today, rural elementary schools are beseiged by critics and by pressures from within and without. Nostalgic longings for the simple good life may persuade some to believe that media-reported attacks on schools are directed only at large urban schools. Yet, rural elementary schools must shoulder responsibilities very similar to those of urban schools.

Responsibilities

Rural elementary schools are responsible for guiding a child's first tentative forays into the world of education and establishing a foundation upon which the child will build all future experiences. The attitudes developed by a child in the early grades will largely determine attitudes toward schools for a lifetime. If a love of learning is to be instilled, it must be done when a child is in elementary school.

Because rural elementary schools typically have smaller teacher-pupil ratios, the education available in this setting often may be more child centered than teacher or school centered. The needs of indiviudal children can be identified and attention paid to meeting those needs much more easily when the focus is on the child. The ideal of an individualized education for every child may be more feasible in rural elementary schools than in large urban schools.

A major responsibility of elementary schools is the social development of children, whereby youngsters learn about themselves and their relationships with peers. Although rural schools often lack the diversity in student population of urban schools, rural students may more easily be taught principles of self-esteem, cooperation, service, leadership, and teamwork when they have daily opportunities to experience and practice them.

Fostering positive relationships between children and adults, community, and country is yet another responsibility of elementary schools. In small communities, children have opportunities to know more adults as relatives and family friends and to see teachers, police officers, ministers, and farmers not only in their official roles but as neighbors, cousins, or the parents of friends. Pride in community should be encouraged, even when the overall morale of some rural communities is sinking as their economic future seems bleak. The positive aspects of clean air and water, outdoor recreation opportunities, low crime rates, and community spirit need to be impressed upon children. Community commitments to work ethics and democratic values have to be imparted by the rural elementary school. Because those linkages between school and community are stronger and less complex in rural communities, elementary children are better able to understand their current and future roles as citizens.

Although the elementary school curriculum will be addressed in depth later in this chapter, the responsibilities of the rural school for teaching a formal curriculum must be mentioned. Because of widespread availability of modern books, resources, and materials, rural schools have access to the same basic curriculum as urban schools. The days are past when rural schools had to depend on castoffs from city schools. The development and implementation of a well-rounded curriculum to prepare an elementary child to progress successfully into secondary school is the responsibility of the rural elementary school. The information/technological age has affected rural schools as surely as urban schools, and satellite disks are found in rural schoolyards in many areas. Rural elementary schools have the responsibility to stay up to date in their use of technology, curricular advancements, and resource development so that their students receive an education comparable to that available in any school in the nation.

Therefore, rural elementary schools have many of the same responsibilities as their urban counterparts but those responsibilities may go beyond the education of the children to providing a focal point for community pride and activity. The schools' abilities to fulfill those responsibilities are impacted, however, by challenges from within the school environment and from the larger socioeconomic-technical environment surrounding rural schools and communities. Many of these pressures are similar to those felt by urban schools, but some are unique to the rural setting.

Internal Challenges

From the beginning, schools in America have had internal problems and pressures. Students, parents, teachers, administrators, support staff, and school board members create tensions for and among each other, whether the school is in a metropolitan area or in a rural town. However, internal pressures for rural elementary schools differ from those in urban settings.

Multigrade classrooms require teachers to coordinate activities of children at more than one age and ability level simultaneously. Multigrade and multilevel schools often require teachers to hold credentials in not only one school level (K-6) but possibly K-8 or even K-12. Lack of subject matter specialists often means that music, special education, physical education, and art teachers, for example, have responsibilities for entire K-12 programs in their subjects. Subject matter may be broadly defined for these specialists, too. For example, a music teacher in an urban setting may be able to specialize in teaching only elementary band while the same teacher in a rural setting may be solely responsible for all instrumental and vocal music instruction—classroom and performance groups—for all schools and school levels in the rural district.

Turnover of teachers and administrators in some rural areas may be high, and the difficulty of recruiting competent educators means that rural schools may sometimes have less qualified teachers or administrators. In other areas, turnover of teachers and administrators may be very low, but the staff may become static in their approach to teaching, failing to keep up with innovations and new knowledge. Of course, teacher turnover and burnout are not unique to rural elementary schools. Yet, the impact on students can be greater in rural schools than in urban schools where there are many more teachers and one teacher leaving or one teacher's information becoming obsolete does not impact all the students in the school for several years.

Some rural elementary schools may lack the services and opportunities available in urban schools. Curricula may be limited to basic information because of constraints of money, equipment, facilities, and teacher ability. Funding problems for rural schools are legendary, and the local base for raising additional funds may leave schools in rural areas at a disadvantage. The best intentions and efforts of the local parents' organization may not provide the additional resources for computers, playground equipment, and field trips available in some urban schools.

Rural elementary principals sometimes teach part of the day, which means they have administrative duties sandwiched around teaching duties or vice versa. In addition, seldom do rural schools have a complement of support staff as do urban schools, which means the rural principal is also often the attendance taker, phone answerer, disciplinarian, counselor, coach, custodian, bus driver, and substitute teacher. One rural elementary principal in a southern Utah district regularly becomes responsible for snow removal at his school because he owns the only small snow plow in the community. Even when funds are allocated for support staff, qualified people may not be available, and a pool of substitutes or replacements is often not present in rural areas. Administrators and teachers in rural schools must assume support duties for the school to function smoothly.

Although many of the internal pressures on rural elementary schools are different from those felt by urban schools, other internal pressures are similar in nature, if not in scope and magnitude. Societal problems are increasingly impinging on rural elementary schools through students and their families. Latchkey children are not unknown in rural schools as economic problems force both parents to work away from home, sometimes at great distances from home. Yet, most rural areas do not have day care centers, and schools are left with the responsibililty of caring for young children for several hours before and after school. In a survey of seven predominately rural western states, 10 percent of the principals of rural elementary schools indicated that they had initiated programs for latchkey children in the last five years (Muse & Thomas, 1989). Single parent families are increasing, creating even more need for before and after school care as well as the need for schools to deal with the emotional scars some children may bring from broken or battered home lives. Children of drug and alcohol abusers are found in rural schools, some with the congenital effects of addicted parents and others with the behavior and emotional disabilities brought on by living with such parents. Children born with Fetal Alcohol Syndrome and AIDS are arriving at rural schools as well as urban schools. Schools are attempting to deal with these problems by establishing special programs. According to survey results, 36 percent of the principals of rural elementary schools in seven states indicated that programs for at-risk children had been developed, and 82 percent had established drug and alcohol education (Muse & Thomas, 1989). Unfortunately, rural schools are often alone in dealing with troubled students and families while urban schools often have many social and civic agencies to which to turn for additional resources.

External Challenges

Many of the problems facing rural elementary schools continue to result from the distance and relative isolation of the schools and their communities. Political power, once held by agrarian communities, has moved inexorably to the centers of population as reapportionment mandates have confirmed our democratic principle of equal representation. Yet, rural elementary schools may be left with only a very weak voice in the state legislature, state office of education, and even the school district, if the district includes both town and country schools. Concerns of rural elementary schools often are ignored because of lack of political clout when competing with the demands of urban schools.

State certification standards often may be established and/or raised with little thought for the impact on rural schools. When the Utah legislature mandated that a teacher had to have certification for every subject he or she taught, the negative effect on rural school districts was not considered. Teachers in urban areas may teach but one subject at one grade level; teachers in rural areas often teach several subjects at more than one level. Recruiting of teachers may become even more difficult for some rural schools as state certification standards are changed.

Laws at state and national levels are often passed with scant attention paid to their effect on thousands of small rural elementary schools. P.L. 94–142, which mandates the provision of a free, appropriate public education for every child with a handicapping condition, has been difficult and expensive to implement in rural schools. The removal of asbestos has proven to be an impossible burden for many rural schools, which have been forced to close. Although legislative purpose in both of these examples was certainly to provide better, safer education for children, the regulations for implementation were not written with consideration paid to small rural elementary schools.

Economic conditions in rural areas have generally worsened in the last decade, spawning many repercussions for schools. When farmers are threatened with foreclosure, small businesses with bankruptcy, and the local mine or mill with closure due to a takeover of the parent company, the very existence of the community is jeopardized and citizen morale drops into depression. Young families leave, parents turn to alcohol or drugs, and school enrollments plummet. The tax base and discretionary family funds are eroded, and financial support for the school tapers off. Poverty stalks many rural communities, and the schools suffer along with the people.

Of course, loss of enrollment in schools and loss of population in rural areas eventually lead to the question of whether a rural elementary school can or should be maintained. Pressures from within the community to keep a school open may clash with pressures from school districts, state officers, and legislatures to consolidate schools where possible. Issues of how far elementary children should be bused, what type of minimal education program must be offered, and what types of cooperative arrangements among schools and districts are possible are continually debated with states offering both sticks (mandates to consolidate) and carrots (incentive grants to consolidate) to rural schools. The greatest external pressures ever in their history are now on rural elementary schools that must prove their viability or face closure.

According to doomsayers, rural elementary schools will soon have grass and weeds growing between the floorboards; however, optimists point to some young families returning to rural America in order for their children to attend school in a safe, secure environment. Teachers and administrators of rural elementary schools need to promote traditional strengths of the rural elementary school in order to perpetuate those strengths and to prepare students for a changing society.

THE RURAL ELEMENTARY STUDENT

In the United States approximately one student in every three attends school in a nonmetropolitan area. Although most attend schools in small towns or villages, a few students attend the 800 or so remaining one-teacher schools located in every state in the union on islands, mountaintops, valleys, deserts, and prairies. Most rural elementary schools operate as self-contained units, although some schools have both elementary and secondary levels in one building. Students are generally in single grade level classrooms, but in small enrollment schools, students may be in classrooms with two or three grade levels combined.

Rural elementary students are more likely to be in classrooms where the average pupil-teacher ratio is lower than that in metropolitan schools. Their particular abilities and needs can be more easily addressed in schools where teachers work with smaller numbers of students and are more likely to know the family backgrounds of their students. The potential for the positive development of learning abilities, personality traits, and social skills is enhanced in rural elementary schools. In 1964 Barker and Gump found that the proportion of students who participated in out-of-school activities was greater in small schools than in large ones. Muse and Thomas (1989) learned that rural elementary schools offer a variety of activities for schoolchildren, including science fairs, art shows and exhibits, music performing groups, spelling bees, geography contests, and athletic competitions.

Student Achievement

A continuing concern about rural schools relates to student achievement as many opponents of small schools argue that rural schools lack the resources to allow students to perform as well as their large-school counterparts on various indicators of achievement. However, Barker, Muse, and Smith (1984–85) found that superintendents of rural school districts of under 300 students stated that their students performed statistically better than national averages. They reported that fewer than 7 percent of their students fell below the national average on standardized tests. In 1989 Doud reported that unsatisfactory student performance was viewed as a major problem by only 22 percent of principals in rural schools and 19 percent of principals in small town schools but by 30 percent of principals in urban areas.

In their study of seven western states, when Muse and Thomas (1989) asked rural elementary principals to report student performance on tests in mathematics and reading, 60 percent of the principals indicated that their students were above the national average in mathematics and reading. Average scores were reported by 23 percent and 22 percent of the rural principals on mathematics and reading tests, respectively. Only 7 percent reported scores below national figures.

Problems of Rural Elementary Students

Rural elementary students face some unique problems but others are representative of societal problems throughout the nation. The incidence of poverty is greater among rural students than among students in metropolitan areas; about 20 percent of the nation's rural children come from families that meet official definitions of poverty (Parks, 1980). Yet, members of poor nonmetropolitan families are much more likely to be working. More than two-thirds of poor families in rural areas had at least one worker in 1985, and more than one-fourth had at least two workers. In metropolitan areas, only 58 percent of poor families had even one worker (Brown, 1989).

In many of the poorest rural areas in the country, academic performance of students falls below the national average. Altering this situation is difficult because the amount of money available for education is often one determinant of educational program quality. Typically, the poorer the economic base, the lower the teacher salaries and the more limited the services (programs for at-risk students, curriculum specialists, social workers, counselors, etc.) available to support students and families. However, states with regional educational service centers and districts that work cooperatively to provide extra services are able to counteract many of the harmful effects that poverty may have on students.

Rural schools have tended to respond less rapidly to the needs of latchkey children and single parent families than urban schools where these problems are more prevalent. In 1988, 19 percent of rural elementary principals reported that less than 20 percent of their students come from single parent families, compared to 6 percent of urban principals. In the same study, 15 percent rural principals reported that at least 40 percent of their students come from single parent families, compared to 45 percent of urban principals. Similar figures were reported for latchkey children (Doud, 1989).

Therefore, many rural elementary students have the advantages inherent to small school size and a safe, secure school, community, and family environment. Yet, other students struggle as victims of poverty and limited social services, thereby requiring teachers of rural schools to cope with ever-increasing challenges.

THE RURAL ELEMENTARY TEACHER

The rural elementary teacher is the thirty-five-year veteran who was born and raised in a Kansas community, leaving only for college but returning to teach her classmates' children in the same school she attended and where her father's initials are carved into one of the desks. The rural elementary teacher is the first-year novice, nervous about teaching first, second, and third graders all in the same room but who grew up on one of the islands off the coast of Maine and who always wanted to return. She is the beginning teacher who would have preferred staying in the Oregon city where she went to college, but no jobs were available and so she took a job in a small town to get experience to qualify for a different position as soon as possible. She is the teacher in a Georgia hill country school who came for one year, met and married a local mill worker, and will now stay to teach and raise a family. He is an art specialist who travels between four elementary schools in Iowa every week. She is the only teacher for a one-room school in the Colorado mountains. In western North Dakota she is also the principal and does all the administrative tasks for the four-teacher school. He is the former Nevada teacher who quit teaching to work at the mine but who updated his credentials and returned to teaching when the mine closed. Rural elementary teachers, a married couple, fly into their school in northern Alaska. Another rural elementary teacher traded her car for a four-wheel drive Jeep in order to reach her school on a reservation in Arizona.

The rural elementary teacher—like the rural school—cannot be stereotyped. The only definite descriptors are that the number of women greatly outnumber men (over 80 percent to 20 percent), and most have ties to a rural background. However, regardless of where they teach or what their backgrounds are, their major responsibilities are the same: to teach children fundamental educational knowledge and skills to prepare them to advance to secondary school and to begin learning their roles as productive citizens of a democratic society.

Rewards, Challenges, Solutions

One quaint, out-of-date view of the rural elementary teacher is of a tough maiden lady who carries a switch to enforce discipline, who stokes the fire before school and sweeps out the ashes of the stove at the end of the day, and who instills trembling respect in parents, students, and the board. Another view is of the young city woman who comes to the country school and loves her students into loving her and school and who becomes the community's educational leader. The contemporary view of an elementary teacher in rural areas is of one who faces tremendous challenges but also great rewards, particularly if he or she is willing to devise solutions to the problems that accompany the position.

The opportunity to individualize instruction for children is rewarding for most rural teachers. At the same time, individualized learning requires an energetic, organized, creative teacher who can keep a classroom controlled while fostering learning on different levels simultaneously. For the teacher of a multi-grade level school, organizing instruction in several subjects on different levels at the same time is a requirement. Many rural elementary teachers have the opportunity to teach all subjects, including art, music, physical education, foreign language, and so forth, because few rural districts have curriculum specialists. The challenge of being responsible for all instruction can be daunting for a teacher who thought that someone else would take care of music instruction or art. Many teachers thrive on the infinite variety and challenge of such individualized instruction; those who want the same lesson to apply to every child in the room will never succeed in most rural schools.

Although rural teachers may have the advantage of having fewer students in the classroom, they do not always capitalize on this advantage. In one study of rural schools in twenty-one states, the following report was made:

> Kindergartens were full of color and variety; they had multiple learning centers entailing lofts, tents, sandboxes, fish ponds or bowls, animal cages, music and art centers, and other nooks and crannies of fascination. The students were curious, active, bright-eyed, and smiling. The teachers, in all instances women, were relaxed, complimentary, active, smiling, and caring. (Schmuck & Schmuck, 1989, p. 10)

However, the investigators noted that too often the teachers were lecturing to the students and not involving them in learning experiences. Cooperative learning was not noted to be as widely used in the schools visited as was reported by the schools.

The rural elementary teacher with a multilevel assignment has an opportunity to incorporate peer teaching right in the classroom. Older students or those with greater ability in a subject can easily become tutors or peer teachers for other students, thereby learning the subject better themselves. The option of grouping students and directing learning according to ability can be facilitated in small classrooms. For example, at the West Desert School in western Utah (located fifty-five miles from the nearest paved road), peer tutoring is commonly used by the three teachers for the fifty-seven students in grades K-12.

The rural elementary teacher often has more opportunity for participating in the management and administrative decision making of the school than in larger schools with more teachers, administrators, and support staff. Rural schools usually have less of a hierarchy because the principal may also be a teacher or there are few teachers, all of whom must work with the administrator for the benefit of the school. When administrative duties are expected of teachers in addition to regular classroom responsibilities, the rural elementary teacher may have a greater burden than urban colleagues.

The isolation of some rural elementary schools from cities and other schools is one of the greatest challenges faced by rural elementary teachers. The lack of readily available supplies, much less teaching aids and resources, may be a problem. Class planning has to be done far enough ahead that supplies, equipment, and materials can be ordered in time to arrive for the lesson. Rural teachers have to be well organized in their class planning and use of resources; they may have to be more innovative with fewer resources.

The rural elementary teacher often has to be willing to travel great distances to district meetings, in-service workshops, or state teacher conventions as such meetings are generally held in population centers. As one example, at the fall 1989 North Dakota teachers' convention, the sole teacher of a one-room elementary school received the award for traveling the farthest—535 miles.

When only a few teachers are in a school, exchange of ideas with many teachers of varying backgrounds and experiences is not possible. Although small staffs usually have very open communication among themselves, broad interaction is limited. Fewer teachers may mean fewer solutions to problems are suggested whereas in larger schools, several teachers may be experiencing the same problem and can brainstorm among themselves and with the entire staff, including counselors, social workers, and psychologists. Staying current on learning strategies, curricular advances, instructional techniques, and resources may be more difficult for rural teachers with less access to other educators.

Living in a rural area can be both a reward and a challenge for rural elementary teachers. If they are natives of the area, then they have the advantage of already knowing the community, its resources, its benefits, the people, the social problems, and the expectations for teachers and the school. Moving into a new area is often difficult for anyone, but small towns generally welcome new teachers. However, getting acquainted may also mean the beginning of life in a fishbowl as small town citizens often pay closer attention to the conduct of each other—especially persons such as teachers—than in large urban areas where anonymity is practically guaranteed. Seldom do urban school districts provide housing for teachers; in some rural areas, there may be no choice but the "teacher's trailer" for a new teacher. Transportation costs may be greater, but crime and drug use are usually much lower than in cities. There is often a lifestyle associated with rural living, and the successful, satisfied teacher will take advantage of the positive aspects and not concentrate on the disadvantages.

A teacher in a rural elementary school often has a chance to be a greater, longer lasting influence on a child than may be possible in an urban school. The teacher often may know the family, may teach several children in the same family, and so may influence the educational attitudes and habits of an entire community. When a teacher can spend more time with children as individuals, helping each one discover and use individual talents, the rewards are great as the children—and parents—return often to express gratitude for the teacher.

Preparation

In very few states are rural elementary teachers allowed to teach without credentials equal to those required of any teacher in the state. Therefore, the preparation of rural elementary teachers is generally the same as that of urban teachers because they all attend the same colleges and universities and are trained in the same teacher education programs. Future elementary teachers may expect to need more diversified training—if not actual credentials—if they are looking at teaching in multilevel schools or becoming, for example, the physical education teacher for all grades K-12 in a rural district.

Unfortunately, too many college and university teacher preparation programs do not prepare young teachers for rural schools. All coursework is geared to urban districts with examples, case studies, and exercises related only to typical city districts (usually those nearest the university). Even if students know they will be teaching in rural districts, they have few experiences to prepare them for their future positions. Few student teachers are assigned to rural districts because the distance between the school and the university is inconvenient for the student teachers and the university supervisor. For students who have no rural background, this lack of experience means they are faced with all the challenges and few solutions if their first teaching positions are in rural elementary schools. Many universities and colleges need to adjust their teacher education programs to include rural school experiences for all students, not only to prepare prospective rural teachers better but also to encourage more competent young teachers to consider teaching in rural schools.

Recruitment

In many rural districts, recruitment of elementary teachers is becoming increasingly difficult. Rural teachers most often come from rural communities; yet fewer students from small towns are going into education in college. High turnover is a problem when teachers come for only a year or two and schools constantly are recruiting for the same positions. In a study of seven western states, only 25 percent of rural elementary principals said they had had to fill no positions in the last year, 29 percent said they had had to fill one position, and 25 percent said they had had to fill two (Muse & Thomas, 1989). Hiring one or two new teachers in a large urban school may be simple and an expectation; however, if having two vacant positions means that half of the positions in a school turn over in one year, then recruitment of teachers is a major problem for the school. Rural communities and school boards need to take some pro-active steps toward recruiting and keeping good teachers. Simply posting vacancies in state office of education bulletins or college placement office listings is not enough. Knowing that teachers with rural ties are more likely to come to rural communities and stay, rural districts should con-centrate on attracting teachers with rural backgrounds.

Rural districts need to encourage their own youth to consider teach-ing as a career. They should work with teacher training institutions in order to encourage placement of student teachers, internships, and obser-vation opportunities in rural schools. Few students from cities will choose to go to rural districts if they have had no experience at all in such districts, and students who desire rural positions will benefit from experi-ences in districts like those where they may later apply for jobs.

Socialization of first-year teachers is difficult in rural elementary schools and districts with few teachers. Yet, making the new teacher feel a part of the educational team and part of the community is crucial to that teacher's success. Collegial mentoring arrangements—even if by tele-phone when distances are great—can mean the difference between feel-ings of acceptance and isolation for new teachers. Rural districts can do much more to ensure that teachers' first years in their elementary schools are positive experiences that encourage them to stay.

Job opportunities for spouses of teachers may be limited in rural areas. However, recruitment of student couples in education, social work, health-related fields, and agribusiness may prove benficial for the young professionals and the community. Advertising the positive aspects of rural living for young families has already been successful in attracting some people to rural areas.

In-service/Staff Development

Distances from district offices, universities or colleges, or state popu-lation centers often preclude in-service opportunities for rural elementary teachers. Administrators who are inexperienced or only part time may not have the expertise or time to organize in-house staff development programs. Rural elementary schools often lack resources to provide travel funds for teachers, who may not be able to take the time to travel to conferences anyway because no qualified substitutes are available.

Rural districts must support leaves of absence, in-service efforts, and increased travel funds for staff development. The use of technology, including distance learning, may bring conferences and workshops to the school. Regional service centers and state offices of education provide help for many teachers in rural areas.

Rural elementary teachers cannot be stereotyped because rural America differs from area to area. Although they often face challenges with few resources the rewards are generally great. Teaching in a rural community is not a nameless, faceless, thankless job. Everyone in a rural community knows who the teachers are, and the teachers are able to feel they are making a substantial contribution to the lives of students and the education of the community.

THE RURAL ELEMENTARY PRINCIPAL

Originally there were no administrators of any kind for the nation's schools, but as school size grew, one teacher was often appointed or assumed duties as a head, or principal, teacher. As administrative tasks evolved, so did the position of school principal. The rural principal of today is not only the building manager, staffing director, program developer, staff evaluator, and student disciplinarian, but is also expected to serve as the educational leader. Creating a positive school climate characterized by teacher productivity, student achievement, and creative thought and activity has become as much the trademark of the successful rural elementary principal in the 1990s as conducting the school spelling bee was for the principal-teacher of the 1890s.

Characteristics of the Rural Elementary Principal

The growth in size and complexity of schools eventually led to the appointment of full-time school administrators for all but the smallest schools. The first principal-teachers were usually women because they were promoted from the ranks of the teachers by seniority or ability. Later, men took over the administrative roles in the nation's schools until approximately 80 percent of current rural principals, 85 percent of small town principals, and 74 percent of urban principals are men (Doud, 1989). Few principals in rural elementary schools are racial or ethnic minorities. In rural communities only one in fifteen principals is likely to be a minority, compared to one in five in urban population centers. Doud also notes that 2 percent of rural elementary principals are Hispanic, 3 percent are Native American, and 2 percent are black. The majority of rural elementary principals tend to have been reared in rural areas. Muse, Thomas, and Newbold (1989) found that 69 percent of those in rural principalships had taught in rural schools before becoming administrators. In fact, 41 percent of rural principals had taught in their present districts before becoming administrators.

Rural elementary principals tend to be satisfied with their assignments and have served as administrators in their current positions for approximately ten years. However, when asked where they will likely be in five years, the majority see themselves in other positions. Because few of these principals plan to leave the ranks of educational administration, the desire for change may be one of striving for career advancement rather than dissatisfaction with the principalship (Doud, 1989).

Rural principals' salaries are not as high as those of urban school administrators, which is a factor causing a number of administrators to consider moving to urban schools. Although 56 percent of rural elementary principals in a seven-state western region expressed satisfaction with their salary arrangements, 29 percent reported that they were dissatisfied. Another 15 percent were neither satisfied or dissatisfied (Muse & Thomas, 1989). In 1987 the average salary for urban and suburban principals was $43,911, but the average salary for small town and rural principals was $36,128. Doud (1989) found that 47 percent of the principals of schools with enrollments of less than 400 earned less than $35,000.

Rural elementary principals are burdened with sole responsibility for many tasks and duties that assistant principals, administrative assistants, and support staff assume in urban schools. Muse and Thomas (1989) found that rural elementary principals wanted their faculty to be more involved in school governance and decision making (87 percent) and more concerned about the learning of students (52 percent). The quality of instruction was perceived to be good in 92 percent of the rural elementary schools in this study. Although 73 percent of the principals reported that hiring outstanding teachers was not a problem, another 20 percent indicated that the hiring of quality teachers was a problem for them. When asked if they had any teachers who should be released from teaching for any reason, 46 percent of the rural principals said they had one or more teachers who should be released.

Recruitment of Rural Elementary Principals

Studies indicate that few educators in rural elementary schools are currently prepared to become elementary principals should any current principal decide to leave. When rural elementary principals were asked to indicate the number of administrative certificate holders in their schools who were available for administrative positions, 59 percent stated that there were none available. Another 21 percent of the respondents reported that only one candidate was prepared for consideration as a school administrator. Of those teachers holding administrative certificates but not working as administrators, 43 percent were not actively pursuing principalship positions (Muse, Thomas, & Newbold, 1989).

With the number of administrators planning on retirement during the next five years estimated to be about 25 percent (Feistritzer, 1988), and with others considering job movement, rural schools need to consider seriously the pool of replacements. Some thought needs to be given to encouraging promising educators in rural districts to pursue administrative training in preparation for potential vacancies. In Utah a program for administrative preparation gives rural districts ways to select and support the training of outstanding educators for future positions. A relevant feature of this program is the practical training and experiences that take place in the rural setting rather than exclusively in urban districts (Wasden, Ovard, & Muse, 1987).

Professional Preparation of Rural Elementary Principals

Rural school administrators are among the most educated adults in the communities in which they live. Practically all principals have completed at least five years of college. The master's degree is a standard level of academic attainment for today's elementary principals with a sizable number possessing an educational specialist or doctorate degree.

When asked to rate the quality of professional preparation for their positions, elementary principals are generally positive and state that the training was of value. However, Doud (1989) found that 57 percent of elementary principals indicate that their graduate education was only of some value. Information gleaned by Muse and Thomas (1989) about the value of graduate education was somewhat similar in that 54 percent of the respondent principals reported their training to be helpful, 40 percent reported it to be somewhat helpful, and 6 percent reported that it was not helpful. One of the difficulties is the lack of attention given to problems of rural schools by university-based preparation programs. Twenty-three percent of the rural principals reported that what was presented in graduate programs about rural school administration was poor, and 34 percent reported that educational administration for rural areas was not even discussed. Colleges of education in areas that serve rural schools need to be more aware of the needs of small schools and to focus administrative training on rural schools as well as schools in urban areas.

The coming shortage of school administrators is likely to have a detrimental effect or rural schools because so few rural teachers are pursuing administrative credentials. Current principals should become more involved in the identification, recruitment, and encouragement of teacher leaders. Then rural school districts should do all that they can to facilitate the preparation of these leaders by supporting their work on credentials. Qualified educational leaders for the rural elementary schools of tomorrow must be prepared today.

THE RURAL ELEMENTARY SCHOOL CURRICULUM

The original rural elementary school curriculum emphasized the three "R's," the fundamental knowledge a rural child was thought to need to progress on to high school or to leave school after the sixth or eighth grade to become a full-time worker on the family farm or in the mill or mine. However, the typical rural elementary school curriculum of today includes modern subject matter taught with contemporary methods using up-to-date materials and resources. Teachers and students use computers, telecommunications equipment, and videodiscs just as in urban schools. The elementary curriculum in a rural school must prepare young students to continue on to secondary school; the strengthening of compulsory education laws and the need for additional schooling in order to become productive citizens have led nearly all rural students to go on to high school and many to higher education.

Postitive Aspects of Rural Elementary Curricula

A love of learning can be imparted in a rural elementary school where the instruction can be centered on the children and their unique needs and experiences rather than centered on subject matter or school objectives. Of course, when the learning needs of children are met, the school's primary objectives will have been met, and the development of habits and attitudes necessary for lifelong learning is the result. Children can be given the opportunity to develop individual talents in a supportive, nonthreatening atmosphere in rural elementary schools.

> There is an increasing pride in the benefits that good, small, rural schools with lower class sizes can give. Many rocognize that situations in which students receive a great deal of individual attention can foster personal and academic growth. (Kennedy, 1989, p. 50)

Instead of using workbook exercises, a rural elementary teacher can use examples from the environment most familiar to the children to bring the lesson objectives to life. Commonality of experiences—even if those experiences may be somewhat narrower than those of children in urban schools—leads teachers and students to understand the applications of class to real life.

Even though some critics emphasize the scarcity of opportunities for field trips and cultural experiences, rural teachers can creatively employ the resources that are at hand as part of the curriculum. As one example, cooperating with the National Park Service, rural elementary schools in southern Utah have developed the opportunity for their students to explore Canyonlands National Park through a program especially designed for schoolchildren. Rudiments of botany are learned through studying wildflowers, geology through hiking around towering rock formations, and archeology through veiwing ancient cave drawings and fossils. Few museums can compete with this setting for field trips.

The community is more likely to become involved in the elementary school curriculum in rural areas than in urban areas. Local businesses often offer prizes for outstanding student work in art or writing. The winning entires are displayed in places of prominence in the community. Essays and poems are published in the local weekly newspaper along with the young artists' or writers' pictures on the front page. Banks, offices, and stores display school artwork, and students are invited to perform musical numbers, dramatic readings, or poetry at social and service organization meetings. Business people, government employees, and farmers willingly buy ads for the school paper and candy bars and placemats to finance the purchase of computers or playground equipment. Elementary band or chorus performances, boys' or girls' basketball games, and class plays bring together townspeople because everyone knows someone in the presentation and the school activity is the priority event on the community calendar.

This unique community/school relationship benefits the school in ways besides financial support and sponsorship, attendance at activities, and promotion of school spirit. Parents who volunteer to help with reading or arithmetic groups at school know almost every child, not just their own. Parents and others are willing to serve as assistant coaches, to provide transportation to and from school events, and to serve as judges for science fairs, livestock shows, and music competitions. Speakers can be easily selected from the community to come to school for career days or special holiday programs because they have ties to the school and welcome opportunities to participate in school activities.

Multigrade level schools have long incorporated learning strategies and teaching techniques that urban schools claim to be discovering. Peer teaching incorporates the concept that one learns best by teaching. Learning groups can be formed and re-formed in multigrade schools easily to account for ability in subject matter without risking permanent placement and the stigmatizing effects often associated with ability grouping. Young students may benefit from examples set by older students and may more readily listen to some lessons—as on drug abuse—from older students rather than from teachers (Johnson, 1989).

The advantages to be gained from cooperative learning are readily available in rural elementary schools where small class size means that everyone can learn from everyone else and everyone has an opportunity to help others. Leadership can be learned through experience because every child can have the oppportunity to be a leader at something. Teamwork is learned because if students, teachers, and the community do not work as a team, the school may flounder. The old-fashioned verities of work, patriotism, and citizenship are among the concepts that can be learned by firsthand experience in rural elementary schools where children do not have to be afraid for their personal safety and where the environment is conducive to learning.

Problems and Challenges

In spite of the many positive aspects of the curriculum in rural elementary schools, there are a great many challenges. At one time, local needs and resources determined the curriculum, but much of this local discretion in curricular issues has been assumed by the state. Statewide curriculum committees and state office of education curriculum specialists often decide what subjects should be taught at each grade level, and some states have adopted core curricula that define learning objectives and outcomes for all subjects at all levels. Although consistency in curricular offerings, standardization of curricular scope and sequence, and control of educational quality are necessary in today's complex educational system, some rural elementary schools have problems reconciling local resources and needs with state requirements.

Lack of funding is the major reason for the challenges facing the curriculum in rural elementary schools. Materials and equipment for laboratories, learning centers, and libraries are often in short supply in rural schools. Even though audio-visual equipment and computers are generally available, rural schools may lack the resources to keep updating equipment and support materials or to provide for service, maintenance, and training. Finding out what films, tapes, software, books, and other materials may be available can be a difficult task in an isolated rural school where the principal may also be the audio-visual specialist, purchasing agent, teacher trainer, and technician.

Although field trip opportunities may be available, local on-site visits in small towns may give students very different impressions than would visits to similar enterprises in larger cities. For example, visiting the local newspaper printing department with its typesetting equipment would be a different experience from visiting the computerized production facilities of a large city daily newspaper. Yet, transportation costs and distance may preclude taking trips to any but local establishments.

Some program offerings just may not be possible in rural areas. Few rural elementary schools can offer full instrumental music programs, sports teams, or gifted and talented programs, for example. When nearly all children ride the bus, before and after school programs are not feasible even if money were not an issue. Providing basic instruction in required curricular areas may be the best some rural schools can do.

Teachers in rural elementary schools may not be qualified to teach classroom subjects plus additional courses, such as music or foreign languages. Also, in small schools, the small number of staff members naturally limits the number of curricular subjects and activities that can reasonably be offered. The distance that teachers have to commute to school each day may also preclude before and after school or weekend programs. Teachers may have difficulty staying current in subject matter, instructional techniques, and available materials. Lack of in-service opportunities, distance from colleges and universities, lack of financial support for participation in workshops, and limited interaction with other elementary teachers may result in instruction becoming outdated.

The poor economic situation of many rural areas is also impacting the curriculum both directly and indirectly. The direct result of economic problems is a drop in funds for materials, equipment, teacher salaries, and student resources. The indirect result may be more insidious and damaging in its long-term effects. When students have long believed that they will be farming when they grow older and then the family farm is lost in foreclosure or when they have always believed that they will be business owners in their small towns and then watch businesses close one after another, a sense of hopelessness can invade the curriculum. Real life applications no longer mean as much because the child's security about what is "real" is threatened.

Although the value of learning cooperation over competition in elementary schools cannot be overlooked, sometimes the lack of opportunity for interaction and competition does have some detrimental effect on the rural student. When student achievement is devalued because the students come from the farm or a small town, those students learn to doubt their abilities to compete in the larger society. Students in a school of very few students may have a difficult time adjusting if they transfer to a larger elementary school or go to a much larger secondary school. Sometimes growing up in a rural area can lead to a built-in sense of inferiority that the school must attempt to overcome with lessons in community pride and personal self-esteem.

Therefore, the challenges facing the rural elementary school curriculum are great, and proponents of consolidation continually point out the limitations of the curriculum, generally ignoring the positive aspects. However, many rural elementary educators are taking steps to overcome some of these problems in order to guarantee rural children a comparable education to any received at urban schools.

Trends

Technology has been a boon for many rural elementary schools. For example, distance learning has great potential for solving many of the curricular problems in rural elementary schools. Schools with the most to gain from distance learning technologies are those with low student enrollments and/or those faced with teacher shortages (Barker, 1987). Interaction among student of many different schools can be facilitated through interactive video. Courses for gifted and talented students can be offered through computer networks as well as interactive video. Materials and resources, including personnel, can be shared by several districts through the use of technology. In-service workshops for teachers via satellite and other telecommunications hookups can overcome the isolation of rural teachers from up-to-date methods, materials, and knowledge while providing an opportunity for them to interact with other teachers. Coordination of resources can make technology a solution to many of the problems inherent to small, isolated rural elementary schools.

Many states are providing incentives for districts and schools to share resources so that program offerings can be expanded. Subject matter specialists and support personnel, such as counselors, social workers, and speech therapists, provide services for multiple schools, thereby bringing additional course offerings and services for children and relief for overburdened teachers and administrators. Regional service centers in many states are coordinating personnel, services, materials, and equipment for several districts or schools. Some serve as brokers for equipment purchasing and sharing while others have central depositories of resources available to all schools in the area.

Other curricular changes have also been successful in rural areas. According to a survey of principals of rural elementary schools in seven states, computers have brought about the greatest number of innovations in the curriculum in the last five years, as indicated by 88 percent of the respondents (Muse & Thomas, 1989). The survey also indicated that responsibility for initiating these innovations in elementary school curriculum seems to be fairly evenly divided among the state (17 percent), community (17 percent), teachers (17 percent), the principal (20 percent), the district office (14 percent), and other sources (15 percent).

Other specific examples of program innovations include the Native American Curriculum written for the schools of North Dakota as part of its centennial celebration. The primary and elementary programs introduced school children throughout this rural state to the contribution Native Americans have made and continue to make to North Dakota. In the face of economic decline, some rural schools have on their own and sometimes in partnership with local businesses taught lessons in entrepreneurship, introducing elementary students to the possibilities of owning one's own business, of contributing significantly to rural communities, and of capitalizing on creative ideas. Some schools and businesses have jointly established school-based business enterprises. Just the surface of the possibilities for such joint programs has been touched as only 7 percent or rural elementary schools surveyed had established school-business partnerships in the last five years (Muse & Thomas, 1989).

In summary, the curriculum in rural elementary schools must include core subjects taught by master teachers using equipment and material as contemporary as possible. Then rural elementary schools are free to match their curriculum to the needs of the student and local community so that schools remain responsive to the everchanging needs of rural America.

THE FUTURE OF RURAL ELEMENTARY SCHOOLS

As long as there is a rural America, there will be rural elementary schools. The solid educational foundation that has been laid for hundreds of years by earnest students, diligent teachers, concerned parents, and involved community members will not be altered soon by societal changes, reform rhetoric, or consolidation proposals. The role of rural elementary schools in fulfilling the highest ideals for education in America will continue.

This is not to suggest that that role is static or that rural elementary schools will not change in the years ahead just as they have changed in the past. Slates have given way to computers, the three "R's" have expanded to include social studies, multicultural awareness, and drug and alcohol education, and students now talk of college after high school instead of farm, mill, or mine work after the eighth grade. Rural elementary schools have proven to be receptive of change, accepting of innovation, and resilient in the face of adversity. Many challenges are ahead, but rural elementary schools have unprecedented opportunities to welcome challenges, initiate change, and emerge as a stronger force in the nation's educational system.

Living in picturesque, unpolluted rural areas today does not necessarily result in a positive outlook for the future. Stereotypes of "city people" and "country folks" have always existed, but now televisions and VCRs ensure that everyone is aware of the exaggerated differences between rural and urban life. *Newsweek's* estimation of the largely rural states of North and South Dakota, Montana, Wyoming, and Idaho constituting America's "outback" does not dispel images of rustic frontier days remaining a way of life (McCormick & Turque, 1989). The suggestion for turning a majority of the Midwest into a "Buffalo Commons" intimates that so few people live in the area that they and their lifestyle would scarcely be missed (McCormick & Turque, 1989). When an earthquake occurred recently near the Idaho-Utah border, UPI reported it having occurred "in an uninhabited area." The residents of the small town (population 75) and the 100 farm families in the epicenter were not so cavalier toward the quake. Remaining upbeat about the future in rural America is becoming more and more difficult when these reports are broadcast, especially when coupled with the reality of decreasing populations and long-term economic recession.

Changes are inevitable for rural elementary schools, but the attitudes taken by teachers, administrators, parents, taxpayers, and community citizens will determine the direction of those changes. Will they unite to determine what is best for the children of the school or will they argue endlessly among themselves while protecting selfish interests? Will they articulate a clear mission and visionary goals for the school or complacently let the status quo be good enough? Will they actively participate in the political process or let voters in urban areas determine their school's future? Will they present a strategic plan for the budget, staff, and curriculum of the school to state officials or will they let the state office inform them of mandatory guidelines? Will they implement curricular changes to benefit students and the community or will they ignore innovations in favor of "the good old ways"? Will they initiate and direct the changes that affect them or will they allow others to determine their future? How these questions are answered will determine the fate of rural elementary schools.

Rural elementary educators and patrons must learn to capitalize on their strengths: strengths that have always been part of a rural lifestyle and so too easily taken for granted, strengths to which urban areas look with envy. Consciously evaluating the advantages of a rural elementary education will often lead state decision makers to a conviction that such schools should be preserved. A vision for the future of the school and the community needs to be promulgated throughout rural areas so that citizens can realize that the goals of school and community, of their children and their neighbors' children, are inextricably entwined. The role of the school in the education of the community and its contribution to lifelong learning must be emphasized. Taking an optimistic, proactive approach to determining the future of rural elementary schools and the surrounding community must precede any other strategy.

Not all rural elementary schools will survive; some probably should not. The days when every hamlet must have a school because of lack of transportation between towns are long past. Consolidation of some rural elementary schools may be one solution to problems of inadequate facilities, resources, teachers, curriculum, and activities. However, consolidation is not the only solution and may not be the most efficient nor the one that promotes children's welfare the most. Cooperation through the sharing of teachers, materials, equipment, curricula, and activities often allows better education but no loss of community identity with the school. Rural elementary educators must be willing to explore current cooperative arrangements and initiate new ones in order to remain current on subject matter, offer up-to-date materials and equipment, and conserve scarce resources. Distance learning and shared telecommunications networks may be an important but as yet untapped resource for all rural elementary schools. This technology should not seem threatening but a key to continual educational improvement for rural schools.

Funding will remain a major problem for rural elementary schools. Yet, approaching the state for more and more money too often leads to consideration of consolidation in order to decrease state expenditures for rural schools. Evidence of willingness to cooperate with other schools and districts is more likely to encourage increases in funding than stoic demands for funds so that a school can remain independent.

The recruitment of quality teachers and administrators for rural elementary schools is likely to become more difficult as fewer students choose education as a career and even fewer come from rural backgrounds. Enticing people with no rural ties to a rural school is difficult; retaining them for more than a year or two is nearly impossible. Rural elementary schools need to start encouraging young children to consider teaching as a career and emphasize continually the positive aspects of teaching. Schools and communities need to work together to make teaching and administrative positions attractive to local persons and to those who inquire about positions. However, a rural community cannot allow just anyone—only because the person is available and willing—to be responsible for educating their children. The best possible people must be recruited and selected for those positions.

Even though rural schools and communities have always shared interests and responsibilities, the need for community involvement in elementary schools has never been greater. Schools must involve the community in more than parent "back-to-school" nights and sending newsletters and lunch menus home with students. Local money-raising projects have always been a mainstay of rural schools, but even though economic conditions are discouraging, the time has come for more than bake sales. Representatives of the school and the community need to determine the long-term educational goals and financial needs of the school and form a partnership for planning, organizing, and implementing local school funding efforts to meet the goals. Such efforts in the past have largely been uncoordinated and short term. For example, the local parents' organization may have purchased a computer or two a few years ago; now there is a need for new software, a better printer, and training for teachers in how to use computers for instructional and administrative purposes. Examples of the benefits of long-term planning and budgeting for rural elementary schools be educators and community citizens are innumerable. Teachers, administrators, board members, parents, and community leaders need to band together to soften the impact inadequate funding will continue to have a rural elementary schools.

Formal school-business partnerships have the potential to strengthen rural elementary schools in ways that go beyond merely funding equipment or progams. Such a partnership involves more than having the president of the local chamber of commerce speak to the students on career day. A partnership denotes equal roles in making decisions that impact both partners, and certainly decisions about the school or the community affect the other significantly. Based on mutual need, help, and support, a school-business partnership could be instrumental in directing the changes that will affect the future of both.

The future of rural elementary schools can be either a story of continual struggle for recognition and survival or a tale of success in educational achievement for students and community. Rural elementary educators must decide now which direction they want their schools to take, thereby determining which story will be told about their schools in the future.

REFERENCES

Barker, B. O. (1987). *Interactive distance learning technologies for rural and small schools: A resource guide.* New Mexico State University, Las Cruces, NM: ERIC Clearinghouse on Rural Education and Small Schools.

Barker, B. O., & Muse, I. D., (1983). National small schools study. *Rural Education News, 34*(3), 4–5.

Barker, B. O., Muse, I. D., & Smith, R. B. (1984–85). A status report of rural school districts in the United States under 300 students. *The Rural Educator, 6,* (1), 1–4.

Barker, R. G., & Gump, P. V. (1964). *Big schools, small schools: High school size and student behavior.* Stanford: Stanford University Press.

Brown, D. L. (1989). Demographic trends relevant to education in

72   EDUCATION IN THE RURAL AMERICAN COMMUNITY

nonmetropolitan America. In *Rural education: A changing landscape* (pp. 19–30). Washington, DC: Department of Education.

Doud, J. L. (1989). *The K-8 principal in 1988: A ten-year study.* Alexandria: National Association of Elementary School Principals.

Feistrizer, E. D. (1989). *Profile of school administrators in the United States.* Washington, DC: National Center for Educational Information.

Gross, R. E. (1962). *Heritage of American education.* Boston: Allyn & Bacon.

Hovey, S. (1987). Rural educators: Ready to fish. *Journal of Rural and Small Schools, 2*(1), 8–9.

Jess, J. D. (1989). A local school perspective. In *Rural education: A changing landscape* (pp. 43–46). Washington, DC: Department of Education.

Johnson, C. (1989). The role of the community in effective policymaking. In *Rural education: A changing landscape* (pp. 5–8). Washington, DC: Department of Education.

Kennedy, J. L. (1989). An education writer's reflections on rural education. In *Rural education: A changing landscape* (pp. 47–54). Washington, DC: Department of Education.

McCormick, J., & Turque, B. (1989, October 9). America's outback. *Newsweek*, pp. 76–80.

Muse, I. D. (1977). *Pre-service programs for educational personnel going into rural schools.* Austin: National Educational Laboratory Publishers.

Muse, I. D., & Thomas, G. J. (1989). *The rural elementary school principal: A seven-state study.* Unpublished manuscript, Brigham Young University, Department of Educational Leadership, Provo, UT.

Muse, I. D., Thomas, G. J., & Newbold, B. L. (1989, October). *Becoming a rural school principal: A seven-state study.* Paper presented at the National Rural Education Association Annual Conference, Reno, NV.

Nachtigal, P. (1982). *Rural education: In search of a better way.* Boulder: Westview Press.

Parks, G. A. (1980). Rural education in the eighties. *PTA Today, 5*(4), 3–4.

Schmuck, P., & Schmuck, R. (1989). *Democratic participation in small-town schools.* Unpublished manuscript, Lewis and Clark College, Portland, OR.

Sher, J. P., & Tompkins, R. B. (1976). *Economy, efficiency, and equality: The myths of rural school and district consolidation.* Washington, DC: National Institute of Education, United States Department of Health, Education, and Welfare.

Wasden, F. D., Ovard, G. R., & Muse, I. D. (1987). Preparing principals in a school-university partnership. *Principal, 66*(9), 16–18.

Whittier, J. G. (1869). *In school-days.* (a poem).

CHAPTER 4

Secondary Education

PAUL M. NACHTIGAL

The rural high school represents a significant piece of American public education. While the pride of rural communities, as its students graduate and go on to "better things", and its athletic teams provide a focus for community spirit and entertainment, it has also been under siege from the education bureaucracy for what are seen to be serious deficiencies. Because rural high schools are for the most part smaller than urban schools and cannot offer the wide range of courses offered in larger systems, they are seen as second best. To get better they must get bigger, therefore school consolidation is always lurking just around the corner.

This chapter takes a careful look at the reality of rural schools, their strengths and weaknesses, many of which have been dictated by the urban industrial model of schooling which has been adopted by public education. As the country moves from an industrial to an information/service society, the opportunity exists to capitalize on the strengths of rural schools and rural communities. The latter half of this chapter suggests ways in which this might happen.

RURAL AND URBAN DIFFERENCES

The rural secondary school has traditionally been the cornerstone, if not the capstone, of formal educational opportunities available in rural communities. For those not continuing their education, the high school years represent the last chance in an organized setting for young people to learn the skills and acquire the knowledge to make their way in the world. For those going on to higher education, the high school experience frequently represents the last substantive involvement with the local community. This "export" phenomena of schooling is an integral part of the urbanization and industrialization that has characterized society since the

73

turn of the century. Reflecting this society, the public schools adopted a factory model of schooling designed to prepare students for life in the city where they would become part of the growing labor force needed for the large corporate institutions (Tyack, 1974). Preparing high school graduates to succeed in college and achieve success in the larger society is a source of pride for the local school, and considered to be a measure of the quality of education received.

The rural secondary school, even though it has tended to serve the purposes of a society which has become more and more urban over the years, operates within the context of a rural culture and therefore is different in a number of significant ways. Let us look briefly at some of these urban/rural differences. Obvious ones are size and, for most rural communities, isolation. Rural schools tend to be smaller and, depending on the section of the country, sufficiently small so that the existing mass production model of schooling does not work very well. In the upper Midwest, for instance, as high as 83 percent of the secondary schools would fall below the 100 students per grade level that conventional wisdom suggests is necessary to provide a comprehensive educational program.

Size brings with it a number of related characteristics. Students are not redundant; each is important in the ongoing life of the school. Social connections are tightly linked. Rural youth and adults interact with the same people in multiple social settings, e.g., you see the same people at the market, at church, at work, and at school functions. Everyone knows everyone else's business. Because of size, organizations can be less bureaucratic, communications tend to be verbal rather than written, who said it is as important as what's said. Rural people tend to be generalists, rather than specialists. Communities are more homogeneous ethnically as well as economically. Because rural people live close to the land, particularly in agricultural regions of the country, their stance toward life tends to be more reactive than proactive. Strategic planning, a popular strategy designed to shape the future, makes less sense when that future is clearly mediated by the natural environment. Time is still dictated more by the seasons of the year than the timeclock. Out of necessity, rural people tend to be more self-sufficient than their urban counterparts. The values held by the local community are generally more traditional or conservative.

Communities that have grown up around the recreation industry or energy boom towns where a large number of "outsiders" have moved into the community represent exceptions to the norm. It is not unusual for these communities to experience turbulent years as conflicting expectations and values get sorted out, turbulence which frequently includes the school as these differences relate to what content should be included in the curriculum, or what books are appropriate for the library.

In addition to the above cultural differences, a number of other characteristics are unique to the rural secondary school. In many, if not most rural communities, the school is *the* single largest enterprise. Because this is so, what happens in the school is much more central to life in that community than in urban areas. Athletics, musical productions, and plays are very likely the major source of entertainment. Problems experienced around the school take on a greater significance in the life of the community. The lack of anonymity results in the personalizing of issues to a much greater extent than in urban areas.

Schmuck and Schmuck (1989) liken ". . . the small town school to a vortex, drawing everyone into it and serving as a foundation for the community. The school engages virtually everyone, regardless of age, because, like the river's eddy, it irresistibly draws the community's residents into it" (p. 2).

The teachers and administrators of the rural secondary school represent the best educated and one of the largest, if not the largest, collection of human resources in the rural community. They are public figures and must be concerned with propriety and public relations. Accepted standards of propriety can vary widely from one region of the country to the next. Expected behaviors in the ethnic communities of the Midwest with a strong religious orientation are very different than those of ranching communities in the Rocky Mountains. In the former, those wishing to indulge in a beer on Friday night will need to leave the community. In the latter, acceptance in the community may depend on joining the locals in sharing a bottle. While secondary school educators' salaries are generally lower than urban educators, they are among the highest paid people in the community. Where local boards are made up of nonprofessionals, salary levels are frequently a matter of heated debate. Furthermore, as employees of the school (one of the few examples of a bureaucracy in the rural community) teachers and administrators have different life and work orientations than those who are self-employed or running small businesses. Bureaucratic employees have come to expect security, predictability, and consistency in their jobs; the entrepreneurs must take initiative and risks in order to maintain their income (Schmuck & Schmuck, 1989).

LIFE IN THE RURAL SECONDARY SCHOOL

Rural high schools are exceptionally busy places with many extracurricular activities, including sports, music, drama, and special interest clubs. A study by Barker and Gump (1964), *Big School, Small School,* found that the proportion of students who participated in district music festivals and dramatic, journalistic, and student government competitions was highest in high schools with enrollments between 61 and 150, with participation being three to twenty times as great as in schools of 2,000 or more. Academically, small-school students took more courses, with greater variety (many being "nonacademic"), than urban students, who tended toward more specialized programs even though large schools offered a greater range of courses.

Relationships tend to be less formal and students are known by name. Teachers and administrators may well have relationships with students outside, as well as within, the school setting. Many of the characteristics identified by the "effective schools" research around interpersonal relationships, shared expectations, and a safe learning environment are an inherent part of the rural school environment. However, just because these characteristics are present, one cannot assume that this automatically translates into a rich, exciting learning environment.

Rural schools are typically strapped for financial resources. Consistent with the need to "make do" which characterizes rural life, the physical facilities are more often than not phased construction with the original building dating back to the turn of the century with classroom wings, a larger gymnasium, and perhaps a vocational shop added as dictated by educational trends and availability of funds. Instructional resources are frequently in short supply and laboratory facilities antiquated. With multiple class preparations and extracurricular assignments, teachers do not have the planning time needed to move the teaching-learning process much beyond the traditional textbook, lecture, paper and pencil mode of instruction. A walk down the hall of a typical rural school will more than likely confirm what Ned Flanders (1970) once called the two thirds rule, i.e., two thirds of the classroom talk is teacher's talk and two thirds of that is unidirectional lecturing.

In spite of these less than ideal conditions, teachers in rural schools, when asked about general job satisfaction, respond more positively than teachers in urban areas. For those who choose the rural lifestyle, the advantages outweigh the disadvantages.

Rural Secondary Teachers

The typical faculty of a rural school is likely to be bimodal in terms of experience and tenure within the district. A fairly large percentage of teachers will be young, in their first years of teaching. Many are in the rural school because they were unable to get a job in a larger urban or suburban community. While a few will choose to remain in rural schools, the majority will use this experience as a stepping stone, moving to larger and larger communities as opportunities avail themselves. At the other end of the continuum are those teachers who, for whatever reasons, have determined that this is where they wish to stay. They have taught in the community for fifteen or twenty years. They may be part-time farmers or people whose spouses are engaged in local business. Teachers in the midrange of experience and age are represented least often.

By far the majority of rural secondary administrators and teachers come from communities very much like those they are now teaching in. Schmuck and Schmuck (1989) interviewed 84 principals and 119 teachers in 80 rural schools and found that 80 percent of the administrators had grown up close to the district in which they were currently employed and over 90 percent of the teachers had grown up very close to where they were now teaching. There is clearly a selection process in place in which compatibility of values and lifestyle play an important role. Alan Peshkin, in *Growing Up American: Schooling and the Survival of Community* (1978), notes the reassurance resulting when the school board in the rural community being studied hired personnel because they were "country."

As mentioned earlier, one of the inherent characteristics of the rural school as it implements the mass-production/factory model of schooling, is the multiple teacher preparations. Because course content has been defined narrowly and taught in fifty to fifty-five minute classes, and because in small schools teachers are often one of a kind, they must prepare for a variety of classes every day. The following quote from a letter written by a rural science teacher in Colorado provides insight into the frustrations of what might well be a typical situation.

> I am a science teacher at Custer High School which has an enrollment of 87 students. I teach every science class that the high school offers. This year my schedule includes earth science, biology (2 sections), health, eighth grade physical science, and physics. This schedule includes 6 classes per day with 5 different preparations and 5 required classes. Physics in the only elective, and this is rotated every other year with chemistry. I have also taught an advanced placement biology course which could not be worked into my schedule this year. I have two concerns . . . (1) How does a rural science teacher do a better than adequate job with the demands put on him/her? (2) In view of the recent criticism of science education in the United States, how should rural schools restructure their programs to ensure scientific literacy for the students graduating from rural schools?

A related problem to a small teaching staff includes the overexposure of students to individual teachers. If, for instance, there are only one or two English teachers in the high school, a student could have the same teacher for up to six years. Even the best of teachers have only so many instructional strategies and illustrations. This lack of variety in teachers, along with the limited repertoire of teaching strategies mentioned earlier, may well be one of the contributing factors to the typical student response of "boring" when asked about impressions of the school program.

Teachers in rural secondary schools are likely to have received their college education from regional state and/or small local private colleges. Because institutions of higher education are not in close proximity, rural teachers have fewer advanced degrees. Teachers most desired by rural schools are those with a broad preparation which will certify them to teach in more than one content area. Our science teacher quoted above is such a generalist with a degree in biology plus twenty graduate hours; a minor in chemistry (lacking only seventeen hours for a degree in that area); fourteen hours in physics; and twenty-eight hours of general education courses.

With multiple teaching assignments and the fact that as many as half of the teachers must serve as coaches, sponsors, or advisors for afterschool activities, teaching in the rural setting is a full-time commitment. Educators interested in a forty hour work week are not likely to stay in a rural community.

Secondary Principal

The rural secondary principal, like the rural teacher, must be a generalist. Only in the largest of rural schools is there likely to be an assistant to help with all the expected duties. In fact, in many rural schools the position of the secondary principal is not a full-time assignment. The position is either combined with that of the district superintendent or with part-time teaching duties. *The Great Plains Rural Secondary Principal: Aspirations and Reality* (Chance & Lingren, 1989), which surveyed 462 small school principals (high school enrollments of 150 students or less) in the states of South Dakota, North Dakota, Kansas, and Nebraska, sheds some light on those holding the position and the nature of that position.

In the study, 97 percent of the principals were male, and 3 percent were female. The typical principal had been a classroom teacher for 7.95 years before becoming an administrator. Those interviewed had been administrators for an average of 10.8 years. A common pattern is for a teacher in a district to move into the principal's role with the average administrator having been in the current school district in some capacity for approximately 9.2 years. Of those responding, 75 percent indicated that they taught periodically in their teaching area while 48 percent were contractually assigned both teaching and administrative duties.

When asked to identify their primary responsibility 58 percent stated that the first priority was to be an instructional leader. Discipline (20 percent) and management (19 percent) were a distant second and third. However, fulfillment of the instructional leadership role is not evidenced upon further examination of the data. Estimates of the percentage of time spent on a daily basis in four areas resulted in 48.3 percent on general managerial duties, 11.5 percent on working directly with teachers, 22.3 percent on disciplining students and, 6.8 percent on meeting with parents. The study concludes, "It is difficult, if not impossible, to be an instructional leader when a typical day is spent as indicated. It is especially difficult for rural principals to be instructional leaders when 48 percent of them teach and the average teaching load is 35.6 percent of the school day" (p. 9).

In keeping with the smaller size and lack of bureaucratic structure, the relationships between the administration and the teachers are more likely to be informal and open. These relationships tend to change, however, during salary negotiations. The negotiating process required in most states pits "management" against "labor" and in much more suited to the anonymity of large urban school systems. The rural principal, who as we have seen is frequently both administrator and teacher and typically experiences a close relationship with teachers, occupies a very difficult position.

The Curriculum

Because of the bigger/more is better syndrome which permeates the urban society, rural schools as seen by state education agencies and the education profession generally are considered to be "second best." Typically this judgment is made because rural schools cannot offer what is considered to be a comprehensive high school program. Monk and Haller, at the request of the New York State Legislature, conducted an extensive study of school size and class offerings. The study, *Organizational Alternatives for Small Rural High Schools* (1986), examined (1) school size related to the number of classes offered; (2) the number of teacher preparations; and (3) the availability of classes, e.g., whether classes were offered more than one period a day, thus reducing scheduling conflicts. The study confirmed that the number of class offerings did indeed increase as school populations increased from 100 up to 3,000. It concludes:

> . . . the curricular offerings of the very smallest secondary schools in New York State are seriously deficient. These deficiencies begin to appear when enrollment levels in grades 9–12 begin to fall below 400 and become more serious as enrollments fall further. Several of the deficiencies, most notable

the availability of courses, accessibility to the offered courses and the degree to which teachers can specialize, become especially acute when the grade 9–12 enrollment drop below 100. It follows, then that there is very little good that can be said about attempts by the State, or anyone else, to increase enrollment levels in grades 9–12 beyond 400. The only benefit we were able to identify is the fact that variety of course offerings continues to grow beyond the 400 pupil level. But this growth of courses is highly unpredictable and does not lead systematically to the offering of a coherent, widely agreed upon curriculum. (p. 62)

The smaller the school, the more likely it is that the curriculum becomes primarily a college prep curriculum. This has been particularly true with the advent of A Nation At Risk (1983), subsequent calls for reform, and the resulting reform legislation. Rural schools in Canada are experiencing similar pressures, not from a formal reform agenda, but from the growing competitive climate related to the global economy, More advanced math, science, and foreign language classes are being required. With limited teachers, students, and hours in the day, vocational and other courses designed for those not continuing their formal education tend to be pushed aside.

Are rural students at a disadvantage because of this more limited access to course offerings? While the definitive data needed to answer this question is not currently available, the answer is likely to be both yes and no. Clearly if a student wishes to pursue a career in engineering and has no access to the advanced math and science courses at the high school level which are prerequisites needed for an engineering major in college, the student is at a disadvantage as long as it is the course titles that colleges pay attention to. If, however, as more and more scholars are beginning to realize, there are certain basic skills such as problem solving and creative thinking that are equally as important, students in rural schools may not be at such a disadvantage. Rural schools, because of their size, provide or could create learning environments much more conducive to acquiring these and other skills needed for an information age than the mass production model of schooling.

Furthermore, educational critics such as Goodlad (1983) and Boyer (1983) are being joined by others such as the National Council of Teachers of Mathematics (1989) and the American Association for the Advancement of Science (1989) in their questioning the notion that more is better. They point out that the structure of the curriculum which packages knowledge to be learned into discrete disconnected courses, taught in fifty-five minute classes may not be educationally sound if we are to educate students for the twenty-first century. This factory model of schooling was fine for an industrial society, but not for the emerging information age. Their recommendations include teaching fewer, more integrated courses in longer time periods. Rural secondary schools, because they offer fewer courses and because teachers often teach in more than one content area, are of necessity closer to realizing these recommendations than large schools. With permission to depart from the mass production one-best-system and with some outside assistance, rural schools could lead the way in the development of a more effective curriculum, a point that we will come back to later in the chapter.

Rural School Performance

As indicated earlier, in order to serve a rapidly growing urban/industrial society, the public schools adopted a mass production/factory model of schooling. In order to operate effectively and efficiently such a school needed large numbers. Without large numbers it was not economically feasible to have the number of specialized teachers needed to teach a comprehensive array of narrowly defined courses. School *quality* was, and to a large extent continues to be, equated with *quantity*, measured by the number of courses offered, the number of teachers with advanced degrees, and the number of books in the library.

With this defintion of quality, small rural schools could never be as good as larger urban schools. The logical solution to this "rural school problem" was to make schools bigger, more like urban schools. Thus emerged what Jonathan Sher (1977) has called the most successful public policy initiative in education, the consolidation of schools. The 128,000 school districts which existed in America in 1930 have been reduced to approximately 16,000 today.

This bigger-is-better belief continues in spite of the lack of empirical evidence that it is true. James Guthrie (1980) in *Organizational Scale and School Success* concludes:

> Though there certainly exists no definitive study regarding the effects of organizational scale upon schooling outcomes, there is sufficient evidence to suggest that the quality of school life for students is not always made better by attending schools that are bigger. At the least, from available research findings, one would have to counsel school decision makers to examine closely their motives for consolidating or closing small schools, be they situated in rural or urban settings. (p. 129)

This conclusion has since been supported by other studies. Ardy Clark (1989) examined the issue of small schools versus large schools in relation to the adequacy of academic preparation for college. Responding to a proposed consolidation bill in Montana, the study found:

1. Size of high school attended in Montana does not appear to determine students' subsequent success in college. Academically, students from the smallest high schools did just as well as, and in some cases better than, students from the largest high schools.

2. Attending a small high school in Montana is not a handicap. It appears that students in smaller high schools obtain a more personalized education with a strong basic skills background which enables them to succeed academically in college; in fact, it may be that a strong basic skills background is the most powerful determinant of college success.

3. Students from the very smallest high schools remained in college and were as likley to graduate from college as were those from the largest high schools.

On another accepted indicator of school performance, dropout rates, Jonathan Sher (1988) in a study of Nebraska schools found that rural schools far outperformed the two large urban school systems in the state. (Note: The reasons for students leaving school before graduation are complex and may be as related to other options, e.g., job opportunities, as the quality of education.)

With a combined 7–12 membership of 29,399 students, Omaha and Lincoln accounted for 26% of all the 112,690 secondary level students enrolled in public, K-12 school systems across the state. However, these two school systems accounted for 52% of all the dropouts in Nebraska's K-12 districts. In other words, more students in the two; largest school districts dropped out last year than in all the other 279 K-12 districts combined. By contrast, there were 93 small rural K-12 systems which had *no* (zero!) dropouts at all last year. In fact, Nebraska can boast of fifteen entire counties (all rural) in which no secondary students dropped out during 1986–87. The Class II school districts (all of which are small rural K-12 systems) have a record that is nothing short of phenomenal in this regard. Last year, the Class II systems had only 31 dropouts among them—an annual dropout rate *well under 1%.* (p. 22)

Further evidence that the assumptions underlying the school consolidation solution to the rural school problem comes from the state of New Jersey. In a study *Expenditure and Size Efficiencies of Public School Districts,* Walberg and Fowler (1988) concluded "Generally, it appears that the smaller the district, the higher the achievement when the SES and per-student expenditures are taken into account. Why should small districts do well? Superintendent and central staff awareness of citizen and parent preferences, the absence of bureaucratic layers and administrative complexity, teacher involvement in decision making, and close home-school relations—these may account for the apparent efficiency of small districts" (p. 19).

RURAL SECONDARY SCHOOLS: THE NEW STORY

The description provided above represents rural secondary schools as we know them today. While they continue to be a central player in providing formal learning opportunities for residents of rural communities, their capacity for providing quality education continues to be suspect in the eyes of the larger education establishment, in spite of a growing body of evidence that such is not the case. Because the schools were designed to serve an urbanized industrial society, rural communities have not been well served by their schools.

The public school is the single largest enterprize in many rural communities. It has the largest budget, the largest physical facility, and represents the largest, best educated cadre of human resources. The school is important to the continued vitality of the rural community. However, historically it has also been the largest economic drain on the local community. It is supported by local tax dollars, and the community provides the community's most important resource, its children. As stated before, the school is then deemed to be a success when these students are educated to leave for work or to continue their education. Most of them never return. Clearly, if this continues over time and no one from the outside moves in, the rural community withers away and dies. This has already happened in many cases.

The larger societal story is, however, now changing. The industrial economy is giving way to an economy based on information and service. We would be amiss in talking about rural secondary schools and their contribution to lifelong learning if we did not speculate about the implications of these important changes for secondary education.

The driving principles of industrialization were *standardization, specialization,* and *centralization.* The attributes of an information society are very different. Standardization is being replaced by *diversity;* instead of specialists, the new society will need *generalists;* centralization is being replaced with *decentralization.* This is good news for rural America, for these characteristics are very consistent with those found in a rural society. In an information society, what one does for a living is no longer as tightly connected to where one lives. More and more new job opportunities are such that given access to the information infrastructure, enjoying a rural lifestyle becomes an option. A broker who works for the French stock exchange lives in a small town in northeast Kansas. An international gem exchange operates from the shores of Lake Dillon, high in the Colorado Rockies. Computers, fax machines, and voice mail are increasingly providing options to the deteriorating quality of life in the cities. The new jobs, we are told, will be created by small entrepreneurial enterprises, not the large corporations. To live productively in the twenty-first century it will be at least as important, if not more important, to have the skills to create a job as to be trained to find a job. As society makes the transition from an urban/industrialized to an information/service society, we have a window of opportunity to reexamine the future of rural communities generally and more specifically the role of rural secondary schools.

The Rural Secondary School of the Future

In the old story, rural secondary schools were always at risk because they could not measure up to the efficiency and effectiveness criteria established by an urban model of schooling. Often consolidation resulted in rural communities losing their schools. In the new story, the rural school will be a major player in how rural communities adapt to the changes of the information society. In order to serve this function, schools will change in a number of significant ways. First, the school will take on an expanded mission, both in terms of how the curriculum is defined and who constitutes the student body. The curriculum will be redesigned to prepare students for the information age: collecting and processing data; analyzing that data and translating it into useful information for problem solving; and learning entrepreneurial skills. This will allow students to choose their future. They will have the option to stay, leave, or return to their rural communities. The student body will no longer be the kindergarten through grade twelve age range, but will include preschoolers and adults as well. In many of the smaller rural communities, the school is the last viable social service agency in the community. As such, it will become the "general store" for all human services, health and welfare as well as education. This does not mean that the already stretched staff will need to take on a whole range of additional duties. Rather, staff members will be deployed in more effective ways and be members of a team which includes itinerant specialists from outside the community, allowing the school to become a full-service institution.

The Curriculum

With the factory model of schooling in the old story, learning has become more and more abstract and increasingly fragmented. Textbooks and workbooks, while useful, if used exclusively provide only a symbolic medium which is drained of vitality and meaning. In the new story, a school will recapture the relevance of learning by engaging students far more actively with their surrounding—not just in the context of science or social studies, but as fresh subject matter for artistic expression, mathematical analysis, astronomy, and history, as well as reading and writing.

Shifting the focus of study from abstract artifacts to the real world - to the local community - is a shift which rural schools, because of size and logistics, can accomplish much more easily than large schools. It holds the potential for:

- Integrating learning. Real life is not neatly compartmentalized into mathematics, economics, history, and science.

- Bringing the process of learning alive. The content is real, not a distilled replication of real events.

- Eliminating some of the traditional weaknesses of rural schools, such as limited lab facilities, through the use of the community and the environment as a living laboratory.

- Conducting studies that are useful to the planning and decision-making process of the community's future.

- Using the microcosm of the rural community to understand complex concepts such as economics or the operation of social systems.

- Changing attitudes and perceptions of students so they consider the option to stay in rural communities. What one knows and understands, one can learn to love and appreciate.

Engaging students in learning from the real world builds on the rural tradition of learning by doing; it is real learning which comes from doing real work.

Perhaps the best existing example of using the community as the focus of study is the Foxfire program in north Georgia. Elliot Wigginton, frustrated with attempts to get his students interested in becoming better writers, put the textbook aside and with the help of his students agreed that they would learn language skills through the process of interviewing local residents, writing up what they had learned, and turning their interviews into articles for a magazine of local history and customs. The local magazine was a success and led to a contract with a major publisher for the bestselling *Foxfire* series. While not every school can become a successful publisher of books, teachers can use similar projects to involve students in the community and in the process make learning real.

The high school in Belle Fourche, South Dakota, as a part of a larger effort to involve the school in community development, decided that the journalism class should do brief stories on local business establishments. An agreement was reached with the community newspaper that once written and polished up, the stories would be published. The students learned about local entrepreneurs, gained a better understanding of how the local economy works, and discovered that writing for the public created a very different level of expectations around the quality of writing than did writing for a class assignment.

R. W. Colton, in *The Science Program In Small Rural Secondary Schools* (1981), asserts

> If science is learning facts from a book and carrying out more or less complicated "experiments" to demonstrate something that is already well-known to the teachers, and perhaps to the students, if science is always a distillation of reality and never the real thing itself, and if scientific disciplines are specialized, distinct areas of knowledge unallied and unalloyed with the other subject areas, then the rural school is a serious disadvantage. If, on the other hand ... we look upon science as an exploration of our surroundings, as a method of finding out about things, and as something that, through the medium of technology, has a profound effect on all our live, then the rural school is at an advantage. (p. 1)

Rural schools have ready access to a living laboratory for science right outside the school door.

Through the process of studying the local community, whether it be the physical environment, the economy by doing sales leakage surveys, or local history, opportunities are provided for students buy into and invest in their local community. When viewed as full participants in the life of the community, rather than being hidden away in school until they graduate and become "adults," youth are more likely to entertain the notion that life in rural communities is a real option.

Learning Is Both Local and Global

While the basics can be learned in the local community, not all of what we need to know can be found within its immediate confines. Here, the information technologies will link the rural secondary school with neighboring communities whether they are fifteen miles down Route 15 or halfway around the world. Schools will share teachers and other resources through interactive networks. Specialists can be brought into the classroom via satellite. Computers with a modem can access an unending array of data sources anywhere in the world. Isolation and insulation need no longer be a problem for rural communities. Rural schools can have the best of both worlds—access to information and resources while enjoying all the strengths and benefits which accompany small size.

School Organization

The rural secondary school will become less well defined in many ways. High school students may elect to be part-time students, combining learning with work. Earning a high school diploma may take either more or less than twelve years. Adults will be served by a wide variety of job related, life enrichment, or leisure time activities. Recreational learning will reside side by side with training and re-training for changing job opportunities. Adult learners will be integrated into many instructional options currently reserved only for traditional high school students.

The schedule will be more flexible with most courses being taught in blocks of time at least two hours in length. With electronic networking and many students having computers at home, daily attendance at school may no longer be necessary. With a shift from "time-based" to "outcomes-based" measures of student achievement, meeting the traditional time clock based schedule of the school becomes less important.

Districts, while preserving their identity and control through local boards, will form consortia with other districts, institutions of higher education, and private sector agencies to provide the various functions of schooling that cannot effectively and efficiently be provided by a single district. Higher level courses need not be duplicated by high schools if accessible via technology from community colleges or universities. Contract arrangements with higher education or the private sector for vocational education can replace expensive vocational facilities.

PREPARING STAFF FOR RURAL SECONDARY SCHOOLS

Few programs exist for the specific preparation of teachers, counselors, and administrators for rural schools. The assumption underlying education preparation programs is that the one-best-system is a generic system. Education is education, whether rural or urban. Preparation for teaching, administrating, or counseling is also generic, leaving it up to the individual to make the minor adaptations needed for the local context. As long as all schools, rural and urban, ascribed to the mass production model of schooling this assumption had some validity. What was absent from this school of thought was the understanding of the rural context differences. However, this has been addressed through the process of rural districts hiring individuals who grew up in rural areas. This practice provides the necessary mechanisms to adapt the centralized/national curriculum to fit the values and mores of the local community (Nachtigal, 1989).

The proposed reforms in teacher preparation that require graduate study in major research universities will create problems for rural faculties (Haas, 1989). Since the majority of rural teachers are trained by regional state institutions, programs that take place at a distance argue against participation by rural residents, particularly those who prefer postsecondary education close to home, in small scale institutions (Bagenstos & Haas, 1987).

As the future for rural secondary schools unfolds, preparation for rural educators will need to change. Different pedagogical skills will enable them to focus on the community for teaching problem solving, higher order thinking skills, and entrepreneurship. Since schools will be involved in community development, educators will need to have an understanding of rural economics and rural sociology. They will need to understand technology, using its capabilities to manipulate data, access information, and bring in resources from around the world. They will be co-learners and facilitators of learning for secondary school students, both youth and adults.

SUMMARY

The rural secondary school represents a unique learning environment which, because of the demands of an urban/industrialized society and the mass-production school system, has not been able to capitalize on its inherent strengths. As society moves into the information age, the opportunity exists to redesign rural secondary education in such a way as to provide a quality education for rural youth and serve as a resource for community development as well.

REFERENCES

American Association for the Advancement of Science. (1989). *Science for all Americans: A project 2061 report on literacy goals in science, mathematics, and technology.* Washington, DC: Author.

Bagenstos, N., & Haas, T. (1987). *Alternative systems for accreditation: National and McREL state responses to issues of teacher quantity and quality.* Aurora, CO: Mid-Continent Regional Educational Laboratory.

Barker, R. C., & Gump, P. V. (1964). *Big school, small school.* Stanford: Stanford University Press.

Boyer, E. (1983). *High school: A report on secondary education in America.* New York: Harper & Row.

Chance, E., & Lingren, C. (1989). The great plains rural secondary principal: Aspirations and reality. *Research In Rural Education, 6* (1), 7–11.

Clark, A. (1989). The relationship between the size of high school and college success for students graduating from Montana high schools. *The Rural Educator, 10* (3), 24–25.

Colton, R. W. (1981). *The science program in small rural secondary schools.* Las Cruces, NM: ERIC Clearinghouse on Rural Education and Small Schools.

Flanders, N. (1970). *Analyzing teacher behavior.* Reading: Addison–Wesley.

Goodlad, J. (1984). *A place called school.* New York: McGraw Hill.

Guthrie, J. (1980). Organizational scale and school success. In United States Department of Health, Education and Welfare, The National Institute of Education. In *Education finance and organization research perspectives for the future: Program on educational policy and organization* (pp. 119–134). Washington, DC: U.S. Government Printing Office.

Haas, T. (1989). *Why reform doesn't apply to education in rural America.* Aurora, CO: Mid-Continent Regional Educational Laboratory.

Monk, D. H., & Haller, E. J. (1986). *Organizational alternative for small rural schools.* Final report to the New York State Legislature. Ithaca: New York State College of Agriculture and Life Sciences at Cornell University.

Nachtigal, P. (1989). *Rural grassroots organizations: Their agendas for education.* Aurora, CO: Mid-continent Regional Educational Laboratory.

National Commission on Excellence in Education. (1983). *A nation at risk: The imperative for educational reform.* Washington, DC: U.S. Government Printing Office.

National Council of Teachers of Mathematics. (1989). *Curriculum and evaluation standards for school mathematics.* Washington, DC: Author.

Peshkin, A. (1978). *Growing up American: Schooling and the survival of community.* Chicago: The University of Chicago Press.

Schmuck, R. A., & Schmuck, P. A. (1989). *Democratic participation in small-town schools.* Unpublished manuscript. University of Oregon, Eugene, OR & Lewis and Clark College, Portland, OR.

Sher, J. (1988). *Class dismissed: Examining Nebraska's rural education debate.* Lincoln: Nebraska Rural Community Schools Association.

Tyack, D. (1974). *The one best system: A history of American urban education.* Cambridge: Harvard University Press.

Walberg, H., & Fowler, W. (1988). Expenditure and size efficiencies of public school districts. *The Heartland Institute: A Heartland Policy Study, 22,* 1–22.

CHAPTER 5

Vocational Education

DAVID LITTLE
ROBERT PRIEBE

Historically social scientists have been interested in what distinguishes rural from urban life, or in the language of sociologists, the relationship between hinterlands and metropolis. This interest continues to grow as the dissociation of the two sectors escalates and as people living in the two settings become increasingly polarized in their disinterest or misunderstanding of each other. The significance of this dissociation is that it represents a growing discordance or a widening gap between those working in rural regions, the source of material well-being, and those working in urban centers, the place where raw materials are processed and consumed (Mirkovic, 1980).

A contemporary view of vocational education must reflect its function in both rural and urban sectors: that is, in the case of the rural it must teach people who participate in the nurturance or extraction of raw materials, while in the urban situation it must teach those who produce and distribute products derived from raw materials. A contemporary view of vocational education must also address how people relate with each other as they go about their vocational practice in both of these sectors. In addition, it must educate people to understand the reciprocal relationship between these two sectors of society and to be able to make the transition between the two if they so desire. If we believe that the dissociation of the rural and urban sectors tends to prevent them from fulfilling their distinct but not separate purposes, it becomes incumbent on us to restructure vocational education in such a way as to contribute to the amelioration of the growing separation between the two. Therefore, this chapter examines rural vocational education from an alternative perspective that is grounded in a philosophical and sociological framework.

In the opening section of this chapter, distinctive features of rural society are examined in the context of the dissociation between the rural and urban sectors of society. Then, existing structures for vocational education in rural and urban sectors are described and located in relation to formal, nonformal, and informal settings for learning. These descriptions provide a basis for reconceptualizing and restructuring learning opportunities based on a distinction between the occupational and social dimensions of vocational education. Finally, rural vocational education is placed in the context of community-based lifelong education.

RURAL SOCIETY AS A CONTEXT FOR VOCATIONAL EDUCATION

The critical dynamic to be considered in reconceptualizing rural vocational education is the tension between the rural and urban sectors. This historical tension represents an everpresent opportunity for either positive or negative societal change. The challenge is to influence this tension in a manner that is morally acceptable to both rural and urban members of society. We are interested in the role vocational education can play in this mediation process. Our understanding of this role is grounded in views concerning specific dimensions of rual society, namely: occupational pursuits, population demographics, physical distances and space, architectural features, community activities, and the rural worldview associated with these characteristics. Studying these various dimensions can reveal something about the mediation process of these tensions for the purposes of attaining a more equitable and productive relationship between the rural and urban sectors.

Earlier chapters have examined the demographics, economics, and social forces of the rural community to determine their impact on educational processes. Discussion here will highlight some of the more prominent features from which implications for vocational education can be derived.

Traditionally, work in rural society was directly associated with primary resource development, namely, trapping, fishing, mining, and farming. In fact, North America, like most frontiers, was originally opened up to provide raw materials for processing in Europe. So, in the early years of both Canada and the United States, the major occupational pursuits were centered around these basic industries. It was logical that as these fledgling resource development industries matured, an infrastructure of related support industries evolved around them.

From this historical beginning, the essential makeup of rural society was established with resource development as its core surrounded by a configuration of ancillary industries and services. However, that early balance did not persist. With the evolution of technology, urban centers came into being as large-scale manufacturing sites for the processing of raw materials. Over the years rural demographics have changed. Significantly fewer people are directly involved in resource development, and more are engaged in related industries and support services. The number of people who choose to live but not work in rural communities continues to increase. In order for the production and distribution processes to operate effectively, a mutual respect between the rural and urban areas must be maintained.

Great physical distances separate people in rural society. Villages and towns abound while only a few small cities exist in strategic locations for regional support and service. Interspersed among these population centers are the fields, mines, timberlands, lakes, and oceans which are the wellsprings of primary resources. These features of distance, space, and sparsity are the essence of rural existence; they color the way we view and relate to rural people as well as the way in which they view themselves. Yet in spite of the physical distances between them, people in rural society have been able to develop a personal closeness that urban dwellers, packed together in increasingly dense arrangements, have failed to attain. In fact in the urban settings it seems that a paradox has emerged: the closer the physical proximity, the greater the personal distance from one's neighbors. In the rural situation, the patterns in which fields are arranged, buildings configured, and highways and streets connected convey an apparent unity that contributes to the worldview of inhabitants of small communities and thus to personal closeness.

Another distinctive characteristic of rural communities is the architectural dimension or the forms of the commercial, public, and residential structures. At the physical center of rural communities, on Main Street, we find the commercial buildings portraying the character and often the names of their individual owners. They are neither ostentatious nor ornate; they exist to meet the material needs of the community. The social center of a rural community is represented by noncommercial structures such as the churches, courthouses, schools, libraries, service clubs and lodge halls, playgrounds, and parks. Although the architecture may be more formal, it still retains a fundamental unpretentiousness. Around these centers, relatively small and unadorned homes are situated which reflect the lifestyle of their owners. The above mentioned configuration of forms and structures conveys the paradoxical nature of rural society in which, on the one hand, functionality is manifested in the architecture, while on the other hand aesthetics is reflected in the natural surroundings.

Since rural communities are usually separated from each other by substantial distance, social activities organized around church, sports, benevolent, and civic endeavors take on personal dimensions seldom found in their urban counterparts. Through participation in these relatively small, face-to-face community groups, individuals gain a special sense of collective life particularly through an awareness of members' contribution to the formation and maintenance of community. Through their participation in community groups, a rural identity forms which is fostered through personal connectedness with other members. The heightened personal interaction fostered through rural community activity creates a rich source of information about various social roles played by community members.

For rural people, the way to go about life is fairly obvious. In their daily life around their occupational pursuits, church and civic activities, recreational events, and the like, relatively clear-cut patterns of action seem to hold. This patterned aspect of rural living gives people a straightforward view of life. These traditions for doing things and viewing the world that have been historically generated are, in a sense, unquestioned. People in the rural setting are comfortable with these rules of action that appear to operate efficiently and effectively in this particular social milieu. This contentment tends to disintegrate, however, under the onslaught of new technology, particularly in communications, where through the medium of television, a countless array of material goods and social alternatives are preferred. However, the use of this new technology creates the need for a reconstruction of the straightforward understanding of how the world operates. On the one hand, the traditional worldview of rural society tends to produce a sense of contentedness regarding the structure of existing social roles, while on the other, it tends to inhibit the potential contribution of people to change the structure of social roles to reflect a more effective social organization.

FUNCTIONS OF VOCATIONAL EDUCATION

Vocational education is often viewed as focusing solely on the acquisition of capacities and dispositions necessary for success in the occupational world. In this view, vocational education is seen as synonymous with occupational or job training where indiviudals learn to play occupational roles that make possible the production and distribution of goods and services, that is, the *intellectual reproduction of society*. The problem with this orientation is that it overlooks a vital aspect of vocational education which goes beyond the notion of merely producing and distributing goods and services to one which also includes an emphasis on a more equal distribution of the goods and services themselves as well as the social relations (power relations) of those producing them. This latter dimension, the redistribution of materials and services and the reconstruction of social relations required to produce them, is referred to as the *spiritual reproduction of society* (Kosik, 1976). The dispositions and capacities associated with intellectual and spiritual reproduction of society are thought to be acquired in school settings as well as in settings for learning outside the school (Habermas, 1984). The idea here is that in order for individuals to learn or acquire the skills necessary to fulfill societal functions, learning sites must be configured so as to reflect society itself rather than as a special learning site at which skills are acquired before a transition to society takes place. The notion of a *metaschool* is invoked included in which there are learning sites strategically placed in various societal locations.

Vocational education, in its fullest meaning, has a contribution to make to both the intellectual and spiritual reproduction of society. In order for these distinct but not separate functions to be fulfilled, individuals who play the social roles associated with them require technical as well as social tools. Technical tools are used by human beings to influence nature and can be thought of as having to do with external changes in an object (nature). That is the kind of change we might expect to occur within the intellectual reproduction of society where goods and services are produced. Social tools are used by human beings to influence others as well as themselves and can be thought of as having to do with *inter* and *intrapersonal* functioning among and within human subjects. That is the kind of change we might expect to occur within the spiritual reproduction of society where the distribution of material well being is considered as well as the social relations between those producing them. In the case of social tools we mean the use of language and in particular, concepts (Wertsch, 1985).

For purposes of description, rural vocational education in Canada and the United States can be seen as taking place on two levels, the secondary and post secondary. When the structures for instruction as well as the less obvious structures for curriculum development, research, and administration are situated within the school institution they are referred to as *formal* settings for learning, while those located in non-school institutions such as industry, government, and hospital institutions are referred to as *non-formal* settings for learning (LaBelle, 1982). Finally, when learning occurs without the benefit of instruction in such institutions as the family, recreation, business, and others, it is referred to as occuring within the *informal* setting for learning. The two levels of education, secondary and post secondary, and the three settings for learning, formal, non-formal, and informal, form a basis for conceptualizing the educational structures as well as the intended outcomes and processes for achieving them.

Recent developments in social theory regarding the relationships between theory and practice have helped to clarify relationships between the settings for learning. Whereas until recently, theory was thought to drive practice, now a new view in which theory and practice are thought to mutually modify each other, intertwine, and produce a new emergent has come to the fore (Carr & Kemmis, 1986). This idea that theory constantly evolves as people put it to use allows for a conceptualization of the relationships between the settings for learning in which the theory is taught in the formal setting, applied in the nonformal setting, reframed in the informal setting, and finally reconstructed back in the formal setting.

RURAL SECONDARY EDUCATION

Often secondary education is viewed as occurring exclusively in schools, when, in fact, considerable education takes place in familial, community, and work locations. This multisetting view is particularly relevant to vocational education in that the nonformal and informal settings are found in all societal institutions. This provides potential learning sites for not only occupational training experiences but also training experiences related to those skills required for the ongoing development of society itself. The interrelationship between these settings is particularly important because in the formal setting learners are exposed to the theoretical knowledge essential for occupational and civic pursuits, while in the nonformal and informal settings the theory is put to practice in a variety of real life situations. In other words, the establishment of multisettings for learning is essential to ensure that learners engage in occupational theory and practice (*intellectual reproduction*) as well as the theory and practice necessary for the ongoing development of society (*spiritual reproduction*).

Secondary Vocational Education in the Formal Setting

Secondary vocational education in the formal setting is found in at least three forms that vary in their degree of emphasis on occupational versus general education. Typically these forms consist of regional comprehensive high schools, composite high schools, and vocational high schools.

In the rural context a typical and often preferred form is the regional comprehensive high school in which a vocational program encompassing a number of conventional technical or occupationally related curricula is offered alongside a broad academic program. These comprehensive high schools are established in urban centers or in strategic locations within a region to draw the volume of students required to sustain an institution with such an array of offerings. The underlying concept of the comprehensive high school is based on the notion of providing vocational subjects as alternatives or supplements to the standard academic offerings, thereby widening the array of career development paths for all students. The idea is to provide, through diverse subject offerings and extracurricular activities, a well-rounded selection of learning opportunities so students acquire the capacities and dispositions required for work and other societal responsibilities. In this form, occupational capacities are balanced with more broadly conceived social capacities.

In areas with a population density too low to sustain a comprehensive high school, probably the most common form of secondary school is the composite high school. In this case the curriculum is much more limited than in the comprehensive high school. Emphasis is placed on a constricted range of subjects oriented toward success in the acquisition of capacities and dispositions necessary for participation in the ongoing development of society with only nominal attention paid to the immediate demands of the occupational world. The overall goal here is to provide students with a basic intellectual repertoire generally considered necessary for the successful negotiation of continuing educational pursuits, particularly of an academic nature, and with only limited provision for further vocational development. Once again, it is important to note the theoretical form in which knowledge is acquired in this formal setting, regardless of whether it is of an occupational or broader social nature. This theoretical form makes it necessary to establish other learning sites where the theory can be applied and modified.

The third type of secondary school structure, the vocational high school, is almost entirely focused on the provision of learning opportunities for those people deemed for one reason or another to have poor chances at success in subjects oriented to the acquisition of those capacities required for participation in the ongoing development of society. Rather, the emphasis is upon the acquisition of basic occupational skills that allow individuals to function at a rudimentary level in the occupational world. These curricula often include basic life skills along with rudimentary vocational skills. These life skills reflect essential capacities and dispositions necessary for negotiating social aspects of life, but more often than not these essential life skills are taught as superficial behaviors rather than as intentionally directed capacities related to broader social functions.

These vocational high schools have evolved as a "special educa-tion" approach intended to make possible "appropriate" employment opportunities for the academically less fortunate. Often essential skills and dispositions are taught in this formal setting with no concomitant linkages to real life situations. Lacking in this educational process is the understanding of the relationship between theory and practice.

Secondary Vocational Education in the Nonformal Setting

Because instruction is usually associated with schools, its occurrence outside of schools in civic, military, work, aesthetic, and recreational-related sites is often overlooked or downplayed. Organizations such as 4H, scouts, military cadets, junior achievement, band, and athletic clubs pro-vide instructional programs that incorporate generic occupational skills that contribute directly and indirectly to vocational competence as well those social skills that are pertinent to the given institution in which the nonformal setting is embedded. Here in the context of the everyday activi-ties comprising the practice of a given organization, members, through an integrated process of instruction and pursuit of an organization's objec-tives, acquire generic occupational skills such as the use of basic technical tools and social skills required to function in the particular institution. Often in these settings the distinct but not separate generic occupational and social capacities that underpin abilities to participate in the institu-tional worlds are acquired in the course of members' engagement in the everyday activities of the organization.

In this situation the theoretical knowledge acquired in the formal setting is enlarged and applied. With the aid of a competent coach or guide (theoretician), learners (practitioners), rather than just learning the language as they do in the formal setting, learn how to play the actual role through the use of language (Schön, 1987). In the process of recipro-cal reflection and action, theory (the instructor) and practice (the learner) mutually modify each other.

Secondary Vocational Education in the Informal Setting

Formal and nonformal settings do not always accompany each other, but every formal and nonformal setting is accompanied by an informal setting. The informal setting is one in which no instruction occurs. Here intended and unintended outcomes merge and become virtu-ally indistinguishable. Members pursue the organization's interest as well as their own idiosyncratic interests. In the case of the military cadet corp, a cadet, through exposure to navigation experience, might develop an interest in astronomy that awakens an ecological awareness that eventu-ally leads to a view of military operations that is incongruent with that of the organization. An adolescent youth working in a local business situation often learns or acquires habits of punctuality, responsibility, and social skills that serve occupational purposes but also civic purposes as well. Cremin's comments (1976) about the ecology of education help clarify the relationships between settings for learning:

> . . . . a complex process, fraught with irony and contradiction. The teacher and the taught often differ in educational aim and outlook, as do both in many instances from the sponsor. What is taught is not always what is desired, and vice versa. What is taught is not always what is learned, and vice versa. And when what is taught is actually learned, it is frequently learned over lengthy periods of time and at the once, twice, and thrice removed, so that the intended and the incidental end up merging in such a way as to become virtually indistinguishable. Moreover, there are almost always unintended consequences; indeed, they are often more significant than those that are intended. (p. 44)

The efforts of competent teachers have long reflected an awareness of the role that intrinsic motivation plays in learning. When this knowledge and the related skills of motivating learners is contextualized by teachers in terms of the various configurations of settings for learning and the intellecutal and spiritual reproduction of society, the total educational experiences that each setting potentially provides are maximized. Given the integrated nature of rural life, vocational educators functioning at the secondary level are potentially better able than their urban counterparts to recognize the configurations of educational experiences and thus are better able to plan and execute instruction that incorporates both the intellectual and spiritual reproduction functions of society.

The informal setting can be viewed as one in which the learner practices with various possibilities for implementing a theory that need not be located within the constraints of the institution in which the activity is occurring. This is not to suggest that constraints do not always exist but, learners are thought to have untold resilience for reshaping these constraints.

RURAL EDUCATION AT THE POST SECONDARY LEVEL

In vocational education at the post secondary level, many participants have identified a particular occupational orientation and are seeking either preservice education or additional continuing education opportunities. As at the secondary level, individuals learn in the formal school-located setting as well as in the nonformal and informal settings.

Post Secondary Vocational Education in the Formal Setting

Rural vocational education at the post secondary level tends to take the form of technical training offered through a diverse array of institutions such as institutes of technology, technical institutes, community colleges, colleges of applied arts and sciences, and regional or district vocational/technical institutes. Collectively, these institutions exist for the purpose of preparing skilled labor market entrants at certificate, diploma, and other paraprofessional levels. Formal settings for professional development learning for those in instructional and administrative roles in these post secondary vocational institutions are generally located in university departments of vocational and continuing adult education.

Institutes of technology generally offer two or three year curricula. This type of institution is concerned with the preparation of paraprofessionals or technologists who function in the halfway zone between professional and lesser skilled occupations. There is some balance here between training for the occupational world and education for participation in the ongoing development of society. In order to provide educational opportunities in this latter area, institutes of technology often have liberal arts faculties or affiliated status with universities.

Technical institutes are also concerned with the preparation of paraprofessionals and technicians, but unlike the institutes of technology, they place less emphasis on the development of theoretical background. The focus is more specifically on the application of theory for specific purposes. Training for this occupational level tends to involve the acquisition of job-specific technical tools with little or scant attention paid to the acquisition of school tools. In situations where technical curricula are offered within the institutional confines of community colleges or colleges of applied arts and sciences which offer a broad array of curricula ranging from university transfer, liberal arts, technological, technical, job entry, and preemployment, the opportunity for refining those skills required for participation in the spiritual reproduction of society exists even though they are not part of the required technical curriculum.

In these institutions, technical theory and to some degree social theory are acquired by learners and applied in laboratories with the assumption that upon entering the occupational world after completion of a curriculum, the acquired skills are transferable. In this context, the educational process is viewed as a transitional one between the worlds of nonwork and work. Systems like apprenticeship and cooperative work study represent somewhat of an anomaly in that in these approaches, school and work are more deliberately linked and more closely fit with each other so that the idea of transition is replaced with the notion of a community in which the school is embedded.

Post Secondary Vocational Education in the Nonformal Setting

The most visible nonformal settings for learning are found in business and industry. Estimates of expenditures for business and industry sponsored vocational education vary from one to two and a half times greater than that of the entire post secondary offerings by educational institutions (Eurich, 1985). The bulk of these programs are offered in the urban milieu, leaving the rural sector vastly underrepresented. Small businesses not associated with regional or national corporations may not be able to afford to send rural employees to urban training locations.

Despite its prominence, business and industry do not constitute the only source of nonformal training. Public organizations such as hospitals, the military, government organizations, crown corporations, public utilities, and nongovernmental organizations account for a vast amount of training opportunities, the magnitude of which continues to expand. The basic mode of training in the nonformal setting is through continuing education as opposed to preservice, with the training delivered on an ongoing basis and focused mainly on the organization's needs.

While most of the training opportunities found in the nonformal setting are situated within businesses, industries, and the various public sector organizations just discussed, other less recognized nonformal sites also exist. Nonformal learning settings located in the familial, religious, recreational, and aesthetic social institutions provide learning opportunities that transcend the narrow job-specific focus of the more recognized employment settings with an emphasis on those skills required for the ongoing development of society.

In these settings, the theory acquired in the formal setting is enhanced and applied. What makes these settings in post secondary vocational education different from secondary is that here the nonformal setting, in the case of the more recognized ones, is concerned with occupational and employment skills. In secondary vocational education the emphasis is more on social rather than technical skills. Still, the aesthetic, recreational, artistic, and other institutions are sites for advancing and applying social theory and thus direct post secondary vocational education toward not only the technical but also the social skills necessary for the intellectual and spiritual reproduction of society.

Post Secondary Vocational Education in the Informal Setting

Rural people work in farming or extractive industries, the small business community that supports these industries, or the public or social services provided by the municipality. These occupational sites present unusually rich opportunities for learning in that given the small size of operation, workers have the potential to experience the operation in its entirety. For instance, as an individual working in a rural small business situation may, through day-to-day experience with all the various aspects of the business and its relationships to the rural setting, develop an understanding of the community unavailable through any other means. The same could be said for those working in local government or hospital situations. The key point here is that the easy total accessibility of the rural community holds enormous potential for learning when the three settings for learning are connected.

The informal learning settings that are connected to the occupational sites of small communities are exceptionally rich. Due to the smallness of the community, job holders on a day-to-day basis interface with the majority of societal institutions. Although opportunities to acquire occupational skills could be seen to be less rich than the urban counterpart, the day-to-day interface presents unprecedented opportunity to enhance and modify social theory necessary for the spiritual reproduction of society. Individuals can creatively modify theory by taking the enhanced understanding gained through acquisition in the formal setting and the practical application acquired in the nonformal setting reframe the problem in the informal setting. Because the informal setting by its very nature is often contiguous with the other settings it is a prime site for the actualization of creative learning impulses.

COMMUNITY-BASED LIFELONG VOCATIONAL EDUCATION

The opportunity that rural people have to experience virtually all social aspects of their community combined with their close proximity with nature has an enormous potential for shaping vocational educational offerings in both the occupational and social dimensions. This potential has yet to be recognized and actualized by the vast majority of rural educators. The key to unlocking this potential is for educators to view the community as a *metaschool* composed of formal, nonformal, and informal settings for learning. Educational institutions, the hospital, the farms, the mines, the local small businesses, and "the school of hard knocks" become the structures of vocational education. The *metaschool,* in addition, provides a configuration of learning sites that accommodates the occupational as well as the social dimensions of vocational education.

For those actually implementing a community-based lifelong vocational education program, it is helpful to view program as occurring in the community-at-large level, at the institutional level within which a given program is offered, and at the individual program level itself (Thomas, 1964). By looking at the community-at-large in terms of its various social institutions such as education, family, industry, government, sport, and others, it becomes possible to see each of these as vocational learning sites, each of which has its own overall impelling motive that sets the stage and the limits for learning. Upon these stages individuals learn to identify and enact a goal directed course of action within the confines of the general motive of the institution. This goal directed action always occurs in the context of a specific set of circumstances within a given social institution. It is at this level of learning that the individual is able to bring to bear creative solutions that reflect the uniqueness of any specific practice situation and the practitioner's capacities (Wertsch, 1985).

Each of the institutional sites for vocational education and learning has its own motive in terms of its societal function. The educational institution is an exception in that it strives to provide instructional opportunities focused on learning for learning sake. It is from this site that learning can most easily be viewed as the motor for the intellectual and spiritual reproduction of society. Here the technical and social theory to be applied in the occupational and broader social setting can be explored without the constraints of practical application found in other institutional learning sites. In the context of the educational institution, learners are introduced to the role of vocational education in society. They can be provided with an opportunity to understand the reciprocal rural-urban relationships and the intellectual and spiritual reproduction of society. As part of this educational process they can learn to make the transition from rural to urban life should they desire to do so. This being the case, it is logical that the overall coordination of these community located vocational learning opportunities or "programs" be coordinated through the educational institution. If rural vocational educators were to conceptualize an individual as learning in the community located sites of play (the informal setting for learning), schooling (the formal setting for learning), and work (the various nonformal settings for learning) it becomes possible to design vocational curricula that are community based and encompass the lifespan of individuals.

On the one hand, the rural worldview is one in which nature and humankind are seen to be reciprocally related. This perspective is supported by the functional architecture found in small communities as well as the day to day experiences with nature that rural dwellers are exposed to as they go about their work in the resource industries or the related service industries. This production oriented view, effective as it may be for carrying out the intellectual reproduction of society, tends to down-play change and insulate its holders from altering their perspective. On the other hand, urban dwellers are literally swimming in a sea of change as on a day-to-day basis they experience the constant reverberations of the spiritual reproduction of society that occurs in the metropolis. Because these societal processes and locations are paradoxically related as apparent opposites, vocational education for either of these sectors must preserve the given position while at the same time superseding it with a view that encompasses both. The challenge for vocational educators is to provide learning opportunities that constructively reflect this productive but tension-filled relationship.

CONCLUSION

As pointed out initially, the rural sector of society is concerned with the extraction and primary development of raw materials. The extractive and developmental processes employed in the rural sector, when compared to those employed in the refinement and use of materials in the intellectual reproduction of society that typically occurs in the urban sector, often require less complex forms of technical and social organization. This has contributed to the currently popular view of the relationship between theory and practice where theory is thought to drive practice. This imbalance of power tends to denigrate not only the extractive development process itself but as well the social roles of those engaged in the process.

If we were to recognize the equal importance of the contribution of the rural sector, an alternative view of the relationship between theory and practice becomes possible in which theory and practice are thought to mutually modify each other, intertwine, and produce a new emergent. This view would help to dissipate the current dissociation between the rural and urban sectors that inhibits the full articulation of the intellectual and spiritual reproduction processes of society.

In the rural sector, at the secondary level one finds the composite school as the predominant form with its somewhat restricted range of offerings providing a liberal or academic approach to education with an extremely limited range of technical subjects. In contrast, offerings at the post secondary vocational institutions vary in a similar fashion but with a wider range of offerings. In addition, it was observed, that abundant training opportunities exist outside of the formal institutions and that all levels of rural vocational education can be enhanced through the linkage of formal, nonformal, and informal settings.

When vocational education is conceptualized as encompassing both occupational and social competence, it becomes possible to draw upon the power of the multi-settings-for-learning view in a manner that not only offsets the inadequacies of the various rural vocational institutional offerings by linking theory and practice in a collaborative way, but that also utilizes potential learning opportunities in which competencies are acquired for the intellectual and spiritual reproduction of society.

The uniqueness of rural vocational education stems from its rootedness in a community that is by its very nature less complex than its urban counterpart and therefore settings for learning are more accessible to its members. In that rural society is less complex, those responsible for the planning and provision of lifelong vocational education opportunities have a stronger vantage point from which to visualize a constellation of lifelong vocational learning opportunities that incorporates a view of connected settings for learning and an occupational and social view of education linked to the intellectual and spiritual reproduction of society.

REFERENCES

Carr, W., & Kemmis, S. (1986). *Becoming critical.* London: Falmer.

Cremin, L. (1976). *Public education.* New York: Basic Books.

Eurich, N. (1985). *Corporate classrooms: The learning business.* Princeton: Princeton University Press.

Habermas, J. (1984). *The theory of communicative action, Volume I.* (Translated by Thomas McCarthy). Boston: Beacon.

Kosik, K. (1976). *Dialectics of the concrete.* Hingham, MA: D. Reidel.

LaBelle, T. J. (1982). Formal, nonformal and informal education: A holistic perspective on lifelong learning. *International Review of Education, 28,* 159–175.

Mirkovic, D. (1980). *Dialectic and sociological thought.* St. Catherines, Ont.: Diliton.

Schön, D. (1987). *Educating the reflective practitioner.* San Francisco: Jossey–Bass.

Thomas, A. (1964). The concept of program in adult education. In G. Jensen, A. A. Liveright, & W. Hallenback (Eds.), *Adult education: Outlines of an emerging field of university study* (pp. 241–269). Washington, DC: Adult Education Association of the USA.

Wertsch, J. V. (1985). *Vygotsky and the social formation of mind.* Cambridge: Harvard University Press.

CHAPTER 6

Special Education
DORIS HELGE

The purpose of this chapter is to provide a description of factors distinguishing rural individuals with disabilities from those in nonrural settings. A brief description is given of rural community lifestyles, values, and other social and cultural factors. The unique needs of rural families having members with special needs will be discussed, as will resources needed for appropriate services, considerations for service delivery, and model development strategies. Sample strategies will be given for providing services, increasing public awareness, and formulating rural family-professional partnerships. Preservice training needs and competencies will also be discussed.

THE UNIQUENESS OF THE RURAL COMMUNITY CONTEXT

Rural communities have distinct environments and unique strengths and weakness. Many rural areas still have a relatively high trust factor, close family ties, and a sense of community. Extended families are a resource to programs. Rural citizens typically evidence a willingness to volunteer and to help those with disabilities. Rural subcultures vary tremendously. They range geographically from remote islands and deserts to clustered communities, and economically from stable classic farm communities to depressed lower socioeconomic settings and high-growth "boom or bust" communities. The array of rural service programs ranges from isolated agencies or schools serving as few as one to ten children in a location 350 or 2,000 miles from the next nearest service agency, to programs located in small clustered towns or surrounded by other service agencies.

The problems of serving an individual with cerebral palsy in a remote area with no physical, occupational, or speech therapist, and

107

where 250 miles exists between that individual and the next cerebral palsied citizen, are quite different from problems encountered in a more clustered rural area, where the chief barrier to service delivery is administrative apathy. Obviously, location has tremendous implications for proximity to resources, especially highly specialized services such as physical or occupational therapy.

Figure 6.1 is helpful in conceptualizing the diversity of rural communities and service delivery systems (schools, health, mental health, and other services agencies). Each of the variables listed has individual ramifications for service delivery. For example, a rural school's administrative structure has implications for securing resources outside of the school. A district that is part of a cooperative can usually obtain the services of an occupational therapist more easily than can a single, isolated district.

Two key variables of service delivery are population density (Are there an adequate number of individuals with a given disability so that a rural community or service agency can "afford" to hire a specialist?) and topography (Does a mountain with untraversable roads at certain times of the year inhibit transportation of services?). Interaction of these two dimensions with that of "other community and district variables" further individualizes an area and its services. Change of one variable in any of the three dimensions further differentiates a given community from others. Because this is an open model, the number of possible types of rural communities is infinite. In fact, previous American Council on Rural Services (ACRES) research cataloged over 300 combinations when conducting on-site visits (Helge, 1984a). Thus, rural service delivery systems must be individually designed. Figure 6.2 illustrates issues differentiating rural and urban communities as they serve children with disabilities.

IMPORTANCE OF FAMILY INVOLVEMENT AND RURAL FAMILY-COMMUNITY PARTNERSHIPS

The involvement of families in educational and service delivery programs is essential for program success. Families are resources for program follow-through and can supply new information useful to teachers and therapists. Parents and siblings, through involvement, develop more realistic expectations for a disabled individual's achievement (Children Defense Fund, 1984). Effective family community systems increase the level of support for special education and related services in the rural community. Typically, long-term relationships are established because many rural service providers are responsible for a rural citizen with a disability for more than one year at a time. Persons with disabilities

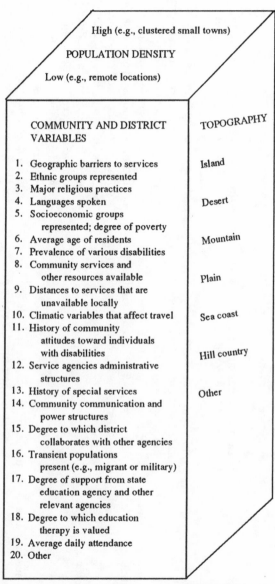

Figure 6.1 Dimensions of the diversity of rural community service delivery systems.

Issues	Rural	Urban
Transportation	Interagency collaboration hampered by long distances High costs Climatic and geographic barriers to travel	Problems primarily associated with desegregation issues or which agency or bureaucratic structure is to pay for transportation
Community structure	Sense of "community spirit" Personalized environment	Environment depersonalized except within inner-city pockets of distinctive ethnic groups
Geography	Problems include social and professional isolation, long distances from services, and geographic barriers	Problems posed by logistics of city (e.g., negotiating transportation transfers, particularly for wheelchairs)
Difficulties in serving specific disabilities	Low-incidence hardest to serve; integration of mildly/moderately handicapped students more acceptable than in urban schools	Adequate numbers of low-incidence handicapped children typically allow students to be clustered for services or for a specialist to be hired; urban environment frequently not attitudinally as conducive to acceptance of main-streamed mildly/moderately handicapped students
Backlog of need for assessment data	Results from lack of available services (specialized personnel, agency programs, funds, etc.)	Results from bureaucratic and organizational barriers
Communication	Mainly person to person	Formal systems (e.g.; written memos) frequently used

Figure 6.2 Issues differentiating rural and urban communities as they serve persons with disabilities.

110

Issues	Rural	Urban
Percent of U.S. population	Approximately 29%	Approximately 71%
Percent of school districts	Two-thirds (67%) classified as rural	One-third (33%) classified as metropolitan
Personnel turnover	Commonly 30% to 50% among special-ized personnel such as speech, physical, and occupational therapists; especially serious among itinerant personnel serv-ing low-incidence populations	More commonly involves program admin-istrators; teacher turnover less than in rural schools
Student body composition	Small numbers of handicapped students in diverse ethnic and linguistic groups pose difficulties for establishing "pro-grams" for bilingual or multicultural students	Typically has a wide variety of ethnic and racial groups
	Difficulties in serving migrant handi-capped students because of low num-bers and few appropriate resources	Open student populations pose challenge and service delivery complexities, but comprehensive multicultural programs are feasible
	Qualified bilingual and multicultural per-sonnel difficult to recruit	
	Appropriate materials and other re-sources typically unavailable or inappropriate	
	Religious minorities frequently strong subcultures	

Figure 6.2 Issues differentiating rural and urban communities as they serve persons with disabilities (*continued*).

Issues	Rural	Urban
Availability of community colleges & other adult learning agencies	Availability dependent on geographic location; transportation may be a problem for adults with some disabilities	Readily available
Availability of independent living centers and other services	Little availability in most rural areas, primarily due to sparse population of disabled adults; transportation frequently a problem	Available in major urbanized areas; transportation services for disabled typically available.
Approach of relevant professionals	Generalists needed to perform a variety of tasks and/or provide services to a variety of ages, handicapping conditions, and subjects	Specialists needed to serve as experts on one topic area or with one age group or disability
Educational service providers	Poor motivation; lack of educational goals and relatively low values for formal education	Discipline problems prevalent
Availability of technical resources	Advanced technologies less often available, particularly for client/student use	Modern technologies more prevalent than in rural areas and more available for use by clients/students
Service provider qualifications	Agencies frequently forced to hire unqualified personnel (e.g., schools frequently use temporary certifications)	Service providers and educators more likely to have advanced degrees with an appropriate specialization
Personnel recruitment and retention problems	More serious than in urban areas related to low salary levels, social and professional isolation, lack of career ladders, long distances to travel, and conservatism of rural communities	Problems regarding some types of professionals, but less than in rural areas; discipline, crime, violence, pollution, impact retention, etc.

Figure 6.2 Issues differentiating rural and urban communities as they serve persons with disabilities (*continued*).

Issues	Rural	Urban
Causes of funding and policy inequities	Rural advocates fewer in number and therefore less vocal; sparse populations facilitate policies ignoring rural problems	Separate but unequal services created by government policies and funding mechanisms facilitating areas with inadequate tax bases; existence of inner-city minority groups with little political clout facilitates unequal treatment for urban individuals with disabilities
Family expectations for adults with disabilities	Frequently adults withs disabilities are overprotected due to lack of role models of adults with special needs; independent living concepts not typically understood	Role models of adult disabled more readily available; families more accepting of the concept of independent living
Support groups for families	Generally not available	More frequently available.

Figure 6.2 Issues differentiating rural and urban communities as they serve persons with disabilities (*continued*).

usually feel more comfortable when there is a close working relationship between spouses/parents and service providers.

PROBLEMS RELATED TO RURAL FAMILY-COMMUNITY PARTNERSHIPS

The following problems were identified in a number of national studies conducted by the American Council on Rural Special Education (Helge, 1984a, 1984b, 1988). These factors frequently inhibit family-community involvement in rural areas:

• Persons with disabilities are frequently not identified, particularly those with mild and moderate disabilities. This is partly because of the rural norm of "taking care of one's own." It is also because rural Americans inherently dislike the labeling of individuals.

• Personnel qualified to assess the needs of adults with disabilities and prescribe appropriate adult education/training experiences are unavailable to many rural areas.

• Integrated adult independent living centers are typically unavailable. The concept of independent living is frequently not understood by rural families, many of whom have low expectations for an adult with disabilities. Role models of adults with disabilities are frequently lacking.

• Rural service providers tend to "make do" when given inadequate resources. Their innovativeness is to be applauded. However, sometimes they settle for less than needed.

• Rural schools and other agencies usually do not have enough enrollments of individuals with low-incidence disabilities to gain funding for segregated special education services or teaching specialists. They typically also have no other available services or support staff. Mainstreaming individuals who need major adjustments in classroom curricula, materials, or activities, may be particularly difficult for service providers serving large numbers of nondisabled persons.

• Rural community mores and values are different from those of nonrural areas. Many rural family members are reluctant to become involved with schools and other agencies because they view professional personnel as authority figures.

• The penchant for independence that is characteristic of many rural families contributes to a reluctance to depend on outside agencies. It is sometimes difficult for professionals to understand and approach them.

- Rural families operating farms may view problems as cyclical and expect them to change from year to year or season to season. This perspective can make it difficult for them to accept a chronic disability.

- Rural communities have much higher poverty levels than nonrual areas, and rural service agencies serve greater percentages of individuals with disabilities.

- Rural communities and schools contribute greater percentages of their local resources for education, medical, and social services. However, rural services cost more than similar services in urban areas because of expensive factors including transportation requirements and scarce professional resources. Even though rural populations increased somewhat during the last decade, their tax bases did not. Consequently, many services have inadequate funding.

- The increasing economic problems of rural areas have greatly elevated family stress. Problems that in the past were rare (e.g., chronic depression, suicide, substance abuse, spouse or child abuse) are increasing rapidly. Poverty leads to further isolation of the family.

- Many rural individuals and parents are unaware of their rights as per rehabilitation, vocational education, special education, and integrated college experiences.

- Most rural communities lack family resources such as spouse/parent support groups or programs.

- Some professionals view parents as adversaries and fear the roles of parents as lobbyists for child rights.

- Vast distances between schools, agencies, and homes, sometimes combined with inclement weather or impassable roads, impede family and staff travel. Transportation is also expensive and time consuming for rural parents who must drive long distances so that family members can participate in a quality program.

- Adolescents leave home at unusually early ages in many rural areas. Parents may lack ownership or responsibility for such children and the children may lack successful role models.

- The expenses of medical attention and specialized equipment are almost impossible. Day care can cost as much as $18.00 per hour for children with highly specialized needs.

- Quality respite and day care is frequently unavailable, and the constant strain of caring for a disabled individual can cause families to break up.

- Lack of various types of qualified medical and educational specialists and difficulties recruiting and retaining such personnel present difficulties in appropriately caring for at-risk individuals, transitioning technology-dependent family members back into the local community, and assuring continued service delivery.

- Low educational levels of many rural parents/spouses and lack of local area specialists inhibit follow-through concerning medical recommendations. Many spouses/parents in economically depressed areas have low motivation, suffer from alcoholism, or have other disabilities.

- Geographic isolation and population sparsity contribute to problems obtaining appropriate medical and social services.

- Revenue shortfalls, inflation, and other funding problems experienced by numerous states and impoverished rural communities have added to funding difficulties.

- Personnel recruitment and retention difficulties are a major problem. Standards for hiring rural personnel are typically lower than standards in nonrural areas. Emergency hiring is usually rampant.

- While rural service providers, including educators, applaud the national impetus toward excellence, certification guidelines are felt to be too specialized for rural programs (Helge, 1984a). Mandating that one or more areas of specialization occur in training is particularly difficult when most rural service providers work with a variety of low-incidence handicapping conditions and ages.

- Training programs generally do not consider special rural needs and circumstances. Most trainees are not trained specifically to work with rural communities, parents, social groups, and communication and power systems.

- Particularly when community agency personnel work on a part-time basis with schools or colleges, unsatisfactory working conditions may include lack of an office or a consistent and quiet place to work with teachers, students, and their families.

- Fewer educational services and other opportunities for lifelong learning are available in rural areas. A rural adult with a disability will typically have a lower income level and higher tuition and service costs. Yet that individual will typically lack financial assistance and public transportation. Colleges and other schools may have inflexible residency requirements, inconvenient scheduling of classes, requirements that part-time students pay full-time fees, traditional classroom instruction and testing, and lack handicapped transportation and accessibility.

● Itinerant staff are frequently faced with difficulties related to lines of accountability, long distances and times traveling, heavy caseloads, professional isolation, inadequate staff development, and inadequate communication with rural families.

Funding inadequacies, difficulties in recruiting and retaining qualified staff, geographic isolation, transportation difficulties, family involvement, professional isolation, needs for staff development, low-incidence disability populations, resistance to change, interagency collaboration, support services, and negative or lethargic attitudes of agency personnel and communities toward individuals with disabilities—all are significant problems in rural areas. These are compounded in areas of cultural and ethnic diversity, particularly when providers are serving transient populations such as migrant families.

PROBLEMS RELATED TO PERSONNEL RECRUITMENT AND RETENTION

National studies have consistently noted that rural special educators and other service personnel are more difficult to recruit and retain than are nonrural personnel (Helge, 1984a, Benson, Bischoff & Boland, 1984). Rural cultures are also a factor in that greater percentages of rural personnel vacate rural positions because of social and personal growth limitations than do so because of incompetence.

Rural personnel shortages constitute the most acute special services staffing deficiency because special services personnel have not been trained to adjust to the demands of remote, isolated, or culturally distinct rural areas. The difficulty is not the problem of preparing sheer numbers of personnel, but of preparing individuals who are willing and capable of working in areas which impose disincentives. These disincentives range from poor housing and low salary levels to rural conservatism. National data has indicated that lack of adequate social opportunities, frustrations caused by rural culture shock, and lack of acceptance by a rural community are sometimes more likely to be responsible for personnel attrition than are professional frustrations such as low pay or long distances to services, materials, and other instructional resources (Helge, 1984a).

Special service personnel in rural areas frequently find themselves being "all things to all people" and must have a broad range of generalizable skills. For examle, many rural school systems and colleges have not been able to recruit or afford full-time specialists such as those needed to work with the multihandicapped. Persons trained to work with individuals with moderate learning disabilities may find themselves having also to fulfill a variety of roles with multihandicapped students or students with low-incidence handicaps such as vision or hearing impairment.

Rural special services personnel must be prepared to work with various categories of handicapping conditions, including low-incidence handicaps. Because of scarce professional resources in rural America, personnel preparation programs should teach students to identify and use existing resources. Lasting change in rural areas cannot be accomplished unless change models are consistent with local community culture and value systems. Thus, curricula should teach students about local community systems and encourage understanding of successful service delivery models which are consistent with local rural community values.

Program strategies must provide for procedures to conduct follow-up evaluation of classroom training in actual teaching environments. Practicuums, internships, and job placements should be included. Field personnel should be involved in analysis of the skills of students trained by the rural preservice curricula.

Competencies for a core curriculum to train rural special services personnel have been defined, field-tested, and published (Helge, 1983). They serve as a foundation for rural preservice training modules that have been developed and field tested by a consortium of over 200 universities. These competencies include:

• Students will demonstrate an understanding of the context of a rural service delivery system and its environment.

• Students will demonstrate an understanding of differences involved in serving individuals with disabilities in rural and in urban environments.

• Students will demonstrate knowledge concerning the state of the art of rural service delivery.

• Students will demonstrate knowledge of effective service delivery models for rural individuals with disabilities (including low-incidence handicaps such as severely emotionally disturbed, hearing impaired, and visually impaired).

• Students will demonstrate an awareness of alternate resources to provide services to rural individuals with disabilities and skills to identify alternate resources.

- Students will demonstrate skills in working with parents of rural individuals with disabilities.

- Students will develop skills in working with citizens and agencies in rural communities to facilitate cooperation among schools and service agencies to serve individuals with disabilities.

- Students will demonstrate an understanding of personal development skills (a) for their own professional growth, and (b) to build a local support system in their rural environment.

- Students will develop skills in working with peer professionals from rural environments.

A number of creative preservice strategies are currently in practice in some universities having rural service areas. Examples include:

- Students living in the homes of rural individuals with disabilities while enrolled in internships or practica;

- Unique professor-student feedback and support systems while students are practice teaching in remote rural areas (e.g., mailing cassette tapes or interacting by video discs or satellite);

- Unusual statewide efforts to recruit university students interested in preparing for rural teaching (e.g., Utah State Education Agency efforts to identify potential recruitees at the high school level and refer them to university preparation programs for follow up);

- Transporting university students, faculty, and classes to remote rural areas where university faculty demonstrate master teaching skills; and

- Other field-based training models involving preservice students spending intensive periods of time living and working in rural communities and having dual supervisors (university faculty and staff of the collaborative field agency or school) for their preservice training.

CONSIDERATIONS FOR SERVICE DELIVERY PLANNING

Just as urban models are not appropriate for rural communities, there is no one rural service delivery model for the great variety of rural subcultures. It simply cannot be assumed that a practice effective in remote Wyoming ranching territory will be viable on an isolated island, in part of a cluster of New England seacoast towns, or in an agricultural migrant camp. Instead, service delivery models must be individually designed for the rural community and service delivery systems in which it will be implemented.

Each of the fifteen factors in this section must be considered by those designing a rural service delivery system. Most importantly, the interrelationships between them must be assessed. For example, areas with equivalent population densities should plan in significantly different ways if one service delivery system is surrounded by mountains with relatively untraversable roads all winter, while the other is located in a flat agricultural area with mild winters.

Population Sparsity

The population per square mile is significant for the model planner. Although a rural area is by definition relatively sparsely populated, services must be planned in a dramatically different manner for small clustered townships than for remote islands, vast rangelands, or in the isolated bush villages of Alaska. This is important in determining whether students with similar learning needs are available to be clustered for services and in assessing proximity to services.

Distance From Individual to Services Needed

Assuming a service exists, the planner needs to know the distance from the individual to the service location or from the itinerant staff member to the person. Knowledge of the actual travel time will assist in determining whether a service or professional should be transported to the student or vice versa.

Geographic Barriers

Absolute distance from potential services to a student is frequently complicated by geographic barriers such as mountains, untraversable roads, or the necessity of taking ferries or small planes. In some areas of the Northeast and Northwest, roads do not exist. Personnel must either travel by light plane, ferry, or snowmobile, or even detour through Canada, to reach the rural service area. Because the U.S. government owns and prohibits travel through large areas of several Western states, personnel in these states must frequently travel an extra two or three hours to reach their service destinations.

Climatic Barriers

In areas with severe climates or seasonal problems such as heavy spring flooding, it may be relatively unimportant (and highly frustrating) to planners that a qualified professional or program is located only an hour's distance from the individual. Persons with disabilities suffer when program continuity is frequently disrupted by weather-related problems. Administrators also experience difficulties with planning or implementing longitudinal goals for an individual.

Language Spoken in the Community

Just as primary languages spoken by an individual with a disability must be considered when designing an individualized education program, the primary language of the rural individual and the family also has relevance for selecting appropriate personnel, especially itinerant staff who visit rural communities with lifestyles and cultures different from their own. It is also extremely important to the administrator who is considering clustering persons for services.

Cultural Diversity

Besides the most readily recognized ethnic cultures with which service planners try not to interfere (knowing that disrupting family life interferes with the effectiveness of services), unique rural subcultures must be considered. Research has clearly indicated that some federal and state service requirements, though well intentioned, were written without extensive familiarity with various rural cultures. Implementing the requirement that written parental permission be obtained, for example, is particularly difficult in some rural-based cultures having no written language.

Similarly, some rural-based subcultures have no concept of the terminology of special services (e.g., learning disabilities). Some religious cultural minorities also have beliefs and traditions that are at variance with school traditions, such as religious holidays that conflict with a school calendar of services. Planners must also be aware of unique community and parent expectations for the success of family members with disabilities. Handicapped citizens who belong to transient rural subcultures (such as migrant and military populations) also provide unique challenges for the rural services planner. These include tracking such persons to ensure program continuity.

A relatively new phenomenon facing many rural planners is the "boom or bust" syndrome prevalent in states that develop energy resources. Some administrators, faced with "overnight" doubling of their client population because of temporary influxes of community workers, find that by the time they locate resources to provide services, their populations have significantly decreased.

Economic Lifestyles of the Community

Rural communities, particularly those with relatively nondiversified economies, tend to schedule their lives around the requirements they face as they attempt to make a living. Service delivery planners should be aware of total community priorities and events that might influence or even interfere with service delivery. Examples include individuals who are absent during periods of agricultural, fishing, or timber "harvesting" or during seasonal festivals in resort communities.

Community Communication and Power Structures

The service delivery planner who ignores the existing communication and power structures of a rural community will probably not succeed. Typically, information systems are more potent than those that are formally outlined. Informal rules often have significant ramifications. For example, they may affect such issues as who, in reality, assigns duties to the itinerant specialist, confidentiality of data, and the person to whom service deliverers feel accountable.

Ages of Persons Served

The planner should ascertain the ages of individuals to be served in the local program and in any adjacent communities or systems in which collaborative services are being considered. America still has many service agencies in which one service provider is responsible for a wide range of ages. Studies have shown that such a situation entails a greal deal of stress associated with burnout (Helge, 1984b). Thus it behooves the administrator to attempt to group individuals in similar age groups if at all possible. Exceptions, of course, are made when developmental age is more critical than chronological age and with some adult populations.

Type and Severity Levels of Disabilities

The level of severity of a disability frequently determines whether or not an individual can receive services within a mainstreamed setting. Some types of disabilities tend to be more prevalent in some rural subcultures than in others. Areas with colder temperatures tend to have more hearing-impaired citizens, and poor migrant cultures tend to have greater concentrations of mentally retarded children because of inadequate nutrition, health care, and prenatal care. Designing services for such unique groups of individual requires specific actions by the planner.

History of Services Provided

Past services to individuals with disabilities in a particular service area are closely linked not only to available funding and awareness of federal and state regulations, but also to community attitudes. In rural communities, key power sources (whether the judge, the school board chair, or a wealthy farmer) have pervasive influences on services.

Rural citizens are typically unimpressed by what they are told they "have to do " for citizens with disabilities. In contrast, they are highly motivated to provide appropriate services when the initiative is theirs. Adept administrators understand and plan to use such inherent rural community attributes, particularly when attempting changes. In rural communities having a unique ethnic heritage, it is possible and important to plan new services that will be palatable to the native heritage and as much as possible preserve the community's self-determination and identity. It is not surprising that isolated rural communities whose only choice in the past has been to send their disabled students to communities or cities with dissimilar cultures have resisted change—and sometimes even the concept of special services.

Currently Available Resources

While federal regulations require that appropriate services be available to each child in the "least restrictive environment," the law does not state how such services are to be delivered. Despite their reputation for inflexibility, rural citizens have, out of necessity, long tended to be creative problem solvers. The model planner should assess all existing resources. The resulting catalog of current resources should include intraschool and external facilities, equipment, and so forth. The planner should then identify and take advantage of the "hidden" resources endemic to rural America such as its sense of volunteerism and community spirit.

Relationship of Governance Systems to External Resources

A service agency that is administratively part of a cooperative or has access to a state's educational or rehabilitation service district typically has greater resources available to it than does one where the majority of external resources must come from a centralized state education agency. This is particularly true when the isolated agency is located a great distance from the state headquarters or when geographic or climatic barriers exist.

Cost Efficiency

When feasible, the planner should assess costs of alternate systems of providing a given service. The fiscal realities of rural service delivery systems must be considered. However, the planner will typically not be faced with evaluating monetary tradeoffs between equivalent alternatives. It is more likely that he or she will have to present a need and request funds from a supervisor, a cost-conscious rural board, or a community organization.

The administrator should be knowledgeable of budgetary accountability systems. Data gathering and subsequent presentations should consider cost efficiency in light of a varying range of potential effectiveness. The planner should address not only local expenditure per individual versus placement costs out of the area, but funding alternatives. The planner should also be prepared to answer questions concerning the percentage of the local agency contribution for salaries, transportation, consultants, and equipment.

Expertise and Attitudes of Available Personnel

The planner must not only note the grade levels and types of disabilities that existing personnel are prepared to serve, but also their flexibility in serving as generalists (i.e., serving several types of disabilities) or as specialists. Formal as well as information training must be considered, and attitudes of personnel toward serving individuals with various disabilities are equally important. The planner may need to structure staff development opportunities designed to guarantee that citizens are served by personnel who respect them and are comfortable with their specific disability.

Dealing With Interrelationships and Combinations of Factors

The importance of understanding and considering the interrelationship of all fifteen of these factors cannot be overemphasized. Combinations of factors are critical and should be weighted more heavily than single-factor barriers to service delivery.

It is difficult to design an effective service delivery model when a rural agency has multiple cultures or when, for example, the disabled individual resides in a sparsely populated area 150 miles from essential services. The task is even more difficult when the person's culture differs significantly from that of the nearest service area, when service delivery is inhibited by geographic or climatic barriers, or when the community's power structure has low expectations for the success of such an individual.

The planner should identify which of the fifteen variables are problematic, select those that appear to be most important, and address those variables first. Problems that can be quickly ameliorated (e.g., by linkage with technological or other resources available through the state or by gaining the understanding and support of the local power structure) should be. Usually, the planner can merely acknowledge factors that are unchangeable, such as spring flooding, when designing the service delivery plan.

MODEL DEVELOPMENT

After considering these factors, the planner is ready to develop a workable service delivery model. There is no such thing as a pure model for rural service delivery. Rather, eclectic approaches are the rule, and numerous variables must be juggled (such as cost versus intensity of need or availability of alternate services).

Technological advances are greatly improving the options of the local rural agency. For example, it is no longer necessary to choose between hiring a specialist or a generalist if a generalist can use satellite instruction (or some other technology) to supply specialized instructional content.

Variables of a service delivery model that must be manipulated so that the resulting eclectic model has a "fit" are as follows:

- Types of educational services and classes
- Scheduling of services and classes
- Fees charged for services and classes
- Financial assistance available
- Type of classroom instruction
- Testing/assessment services
- Equipment
- Facilities
- Staff development program
- Transportation system
- Staffing for services
- Family involvement and training
- Child care assistance available
- Community involvement and support
- Governance system
- Interagency collaboration

Figure 6.3 illustrates the process of designing a rural service delivery model. Factors that can present planning problems but cannot be controlled by the model designer are termed "givens." Factors that can be manipulated by the planner are labeled "variables." The planner can create an appropriate service delivery model by recognizing givens and

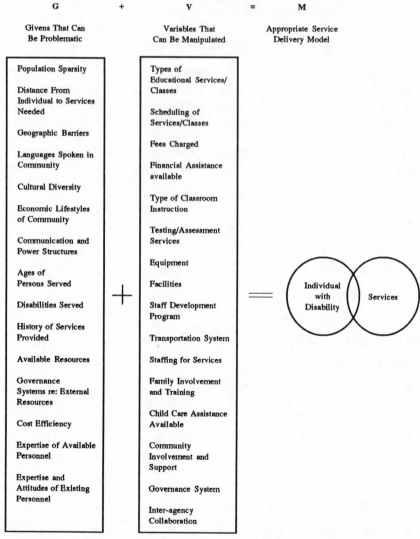

Figure 6.3 Consideration of "givens" and manipulation of "variables" in the creation of an appropriate service model.

controlling variables. For example, low-incidence disabilities vary greatly from one area to the next because of population and environmental influences. Thus, in one area, a given model may be used to serve citizens who are cerebral palsied or deaf. In another very sparsely populated area, the model may be adapted to serve the only moderately retarded individual in that particular community.

STRATEGIES INVOLVED IN SUCCESSFUL SERVICE DELIVERY MODELS

The following narrative illustrates resources, strategies, and models designed to assist rural citizens with disabilities. The strategies and models recognize that it is essential to identify and use the predominant norms and cultures of rural communities. Successful programs in rural areas literally grow out of the communities themselves.

Creating Flexible Educational Options

Community agencies, clients with disabilities, and their families must be involved in the design of lifelong learning experiences. For example, community colleges, universities, and G.E.D. programs should be approached regarding increasing flexibility in residency requirements, and class scheduling, location, and fees. Instructors should be trained in alternative teaching and testing approaches. Frequently, regional or other local agencies can assist in creating barrier-free environments. They can also help families understand the importance of lifelong learning and the potential for client success. Living centers or other resources in the state/region can be of great assistance in educating family and community members, as well as working with clients (Richards, 1990). Successful programs will respect adult learner autonomy and accommodate adult lifestyles and responsibilities (American Association of State Colleges and Universities, 1989).

Recognizing Rural Economies and Educational Levels

Effective programs will also address the limited economy and educational levels of many rural areas. Program planners will implement strategies designed to empower the local area and its citizens, provide extra education to citizens with low educational/performance expectations for those with disabilities, and provide family counseling and other support services for the disabled individual. The need for frequent face-to-face contact and a social orientation in the local community will be recognized, and community education programs will assist in preserving traditional folk art and practices (McCannon, 1985.)

Using Non-Service Agency Personnel

Discussion/support groups led by adults with disabilities or parents of handicapped children are generally more successful than those led by professionals. Rural programs frequently find that a public service announcement made by a person stating that he or she is not affiliated with the agency and would like to visit with and possibly assist others, is particularly successful. Advocacy and support groups may originally meet on their own and later can become an integral part of the agency's feedback system.

The involvement of siblings and extended family members is an asset. This practice also frequently encourages reticent parents to become involved. Families should be involved in designing unique program strategies (e.g., rural orientation and mobility markers).

Messages concerning support groups and other resources can be sent to isolated rural communities via persons who frequent such areas on a regular basis. Such individuals may include mail carriers, utility meter readers, bookmobile personnel, public health workers, and county extension workers. Agency personnel should work cooperatively with persons from other agencies who visit families or provide services to those with disabilities. For example, home health agents or county demonstration workers can assist with delivering messages, building support, and conducting follow-through services.

Meetings can be arranged of parent groups with diverse foci to encourage them to share personal achievements and ideas and occasionally to have joint projects. Joint advocacy projects are more effective than those of single parent groups.

Local physicians should be informed which spouses/parents are willing to work with others who have children with disabilities. It is especially helpful for spouses/parents newly experiencing emotions such as shock, grief, and hostility to have others available who understand these emotions. This is a particularly effective technique in rural areas where spouses/parents (and sometimes physicians) know which families have children with disabilities. Local physicians should be educated regarding the needs of families with members who have disabilities. Physicians should be trained to inform families regarding community resources that are available to them.

Social Ties

Rural families are frequently reticent to become involved with the authority figures of schools and other agencies regarding a spouse, child, or sibling's program. Thus, it is essential that service providers and administrators establish a positive rapport with family members. This sometimes occurs via a one-on-one discussion between service providers and family members regarding the strengths and weaknesses of a disabled individual's performance. It is frequently useful to precede such a discussion with social contacts. In fact, rural agencies host nonthreatening social events or meetings preceded by a meal. Free babysitting is also an established part of such events in several rural areas. Such amenities increase family willingness to share valuable information with agencies and to follow up educational instruction within the home setting.

Service providers who are respected community members have the most success with family members becoming actively involved with their program. Even itinerant staff who only visit a community once a month can express a sincere interest in community events and problems. This is especially true if they talk with the key communicators in the community (ranging from postal clerks and gas station attendants to school board members).

Home visits, after sufficient rapport has been established, are invaluable. Typically, itinerant staff, practicum students from regional universities, or others who accept invitations to visit or stay in client's homes while traveling learn a great deal about the real strengths and stresses of the family and generate the most success for the special needs program. Because of this, many programs plan for mobile instructional vans to travel through isolated regions. Generally, this also increases the commitment of the professional.

Meeting Other Family Needs

It is critical to truly listen to families and respond to their stated needs even if those are not on the professional's agenda (e.g., adult literacy or drug education for family members). Respite care or babysitting "checks" can be provided to parents for four to five hours of care. These can be donated by volunteers or by other parents of clients, establishing a parent-to-parent support system. It is especially helpful to establish one central location or phone number for families to call for help and one community intake form for all agencies. Responsive service may include traveling clinics and/or a community focus which would bring a consultation team to a community office. Compliance tracking by agencies is also helpful to clients, particularly those who are confused or nervous about dealing with education and service delivery systems. It is also helpful to define roles for professionals to take in helping families with their financial problems.

Family support groups should have an understanding that starting small and being patient about group growth will be a profitable long-term strategy. Family members and clients should be taught communication skills so they may effectively and assertively present their needs to communities and other agencies and professionals. This is particularly true in families of a minority ethnic background, migrant parents, and/or those who are illiterate. This should be done, if possible, by a person who is from a similar background.

Identifying and Using Local Power and Communication Sources

Parents and professionals should look within the community for communication, finances, transportation, and other resources. Informal community structures should be explored to identify the community person or persons who get things done.

By nature, rural America is based on informal structures and communication systems. Such systems should be used to spread the word. In locating power sources, it is critical to use the media for free public service announcements and to try to identify people "behind the power." Examples of such people are business or social colleagues, well-respected individuals who attend the local churches, cooperative extension workers, the gas station attendant at the one regional gas station who therefore talks with everyone who comes through the community, and spouses of community leaders. These people can be essential in gathering support for quality services. Such key communicators and power sources must be given opportunities to really get to know some of the families so that they can become advocates. As mentioned earlier, bookmobiles, county extension workers, public health workers, meter readers, and other transporters and communicators can be essential in information dissemination.

Regional and local corporations or outreach businesses should be approached for use of their equipment and staff, corporate donations, and so forth. Corporate tax deductions can be an incentive. Frequently, an important incentive in a rural area is to let companies know that the informal grapevine as well as formal articles in the local newspaper will be used to describe their helpfulness.

Parents and disabled adults need a neutral place to meet, accessibility to meetings, and practical information preferably given by a parent or disabled adult. Assertiveness training regarding asking for help is essential in many rural communities. Clients and parents are also needed on agency boards for the important input that only they are capable of giving.

All possible rural community resources should be used, particularly those that are informal and involve excellent communicators. This may include the local garden club, the Grange, the Welcome Wagon, or, in larger communities, a Lion's Club. Churches and bars are generally also important communication institutions in rural areas.

Technology

Technological devices can be as simple as a CB radio (capable of serving several families in clustered rural areas) or a telephone answering machine. Answering machines offer clients and families options of listening, at their convenience, to progress reports and appeals for follow-through.

Instructional assistance at home can be coordinated with television broadcasts or telecommunication systems and supplemented by mobile vans or itinerant staff visits. Video or cassette tapes can be mailed to clients for instructional use, or to educators for critique. Teacher visits and/or counseling via telephone, audio conferencing, or teleconferencing can be supplemental.

Family/Community Communications

"Communication books" can be sent home with clients on a daily or periodic basis. Such books offer advice for at home followup, reports of progress, etc., and can be responded to by family members and clients. Agency newsletters (even a one-page mimeographed sheet) should contain articles or suggestions made by families and a recognition that family support is crucial.

ACRES Rural Family-Professional Consortium

The ACRES Rural Family-Professional Consortium links rural families and professionals with services that may be of help to them. The consortium enhances rural family-professional involvement and links families with valuable resources and information. A Rural Parent Resource Directory was developed by the consortium and is available from ACRES headquarters (American Council on Rural Special Education, Western Washington University, Bellingham, Washington; 206/676-3576). The consortium also collects information on fathers' support groups and resources, collects information on available resources and strategies for ethnic minorities and other culturally diverse groups, and reviews and evaluates university course work that concerns rural families. The consortium meets each year at the ACRES National Rural Special Education Conference.

Curriculum for Physicians Defining Their Role With Individuals With Disabilities

The American Academy of Pediatrics, from 1982 to 1984, developed a model sixteen-hour training curriculum for practicing physicians. The curriculum underscored the physician's multiple roles as medical caregiver, counselor to the client and families, consultant to community agencies and schools, advocate, and concerned professional. The curriculum is available through the American Academy of Pediatrics headquartered in Evanston, Illinois.

State-Funded Intermediate Education Units (IEUs)

This administrative structure uses regional specialists who provide technical assistance and consultation to local district personnel. Some IEUs are designed specifically to provide special education services and others are designed to provide all specialized services that are difficult for small school districts to provide (e.g., comprehensive vocational education). IEU personnel generally provide services only to other professionals. This pattern is sometimes varied to demonstrate an effective technique or to train a professional to deliver the service independently in the future.

Some IEUs have centralized media and materials centers with extensive options for checkout, and some states incorporate mobile material centers. Generic specialists at the local level are sometimes supported by specialized regional consultants dealing with specific types of disabilities. This type of model is responsive to rural remote areas when consultant responsibilities are aligned by geographic region versus an entire state. The planner adapting this model for a particular area would want to design safeguards so that a generic specialist did not become too dependent on a regional specialist. This would prevent inadequate services or a lack of services in the absence of the regional specialist.

Statewide Networks of Itinerant Specialists

The small, rural state of New Hampshire has implemented a system to serve students with the low-incidence disabilities of hearing and visual impairments. This system is operated by contract with a private firm that hires consultants to provide services to blind and deaf students in remote rural areas with no specialized local personnel. These consultants also train local personnel to deliver followup services until they return. Items from an extensive media and materials center are taken to the local program for use when the consultants are absent, and are varied and updated as needed. This is an important resource for rural clients and families.

Model to Identify Scarce Resources

Other isolated rural areas have identified and optimally used every possible resource within their community. They have found that using community personnel as resources has created a side benefit of additional community support for their program.

Although the model varies from community to community, the following basic components are consistently present:

1. A needs assessment is completed at the local program level, as well as in each individual classroom or therapy center.

2. A resource survey is conducted of all program personnel, listing skills and competencies that could be shared with others. Data on potential community and parent resources is an integral part of the resource base. Community facilities and equipment are included in the resource data bank.

3. A manual card-sorting or computerized retrieval system is used to link identified resources and needs. This linkage may include having one service provider, uncomfortable working with a certain disability, interview another service provider with skills in this area. It may also include using students (e.g., high school students in a child development class), as extra manpower by having them assist a service provider with followup motor skills activities for those with severe physical impairments. Other programs have used unemployed certified volunteers in the classroom or therapy center. Isolated resort communities have actively recruited the assistance of long-term visitors. Volunteers provide services ranging from tutoring children to furnishing transportation. They reduce staff development costs by managing a program while a service provider engages in inservice, peer observation, or other relevant activities.

The legalities and protocol of the model are individualized for the particular area in which it is incorporated. However, in all cases, an evolving foundation of community resources is estabished. Community support for the program is enhanced in each location because citizens become integrally involved in programming.

Models Incorporating Advanced Technologies

The use of advanced technologies as a tool for serving remotely located individuals with disabilities is rapidly growing in popularity. For example, a variety of systems have been used to send instruction to isolated service providers inadequately trained to work with citizens with low-incidence handicaps. Model design ranges from consultant-teacher communication by satellite to remote inservice vans bearing computers programmed to teach specific subject areas to families or clients. Less expensive models include television instruction and exchanges of video tapes.

Technological approaches will be limited more by the imagination of the service planner than by the cost of equipment. Alternate types of advanced technologies are becoming increasingly available. Many programs have found human service agencies willing to collaborate in service delivery, especially when highly specialized equipment is not used by the agency on a full-time basis. Likewise, many rural businesses have been willing to share equipment. Adept administrators have been able to borrow by emphasizing advantages to local businesses, such as enhancement of their community images and potential tax write-offs.

Models Using Paraprofessionals

Trained paraprofessionals are frequently used by rural programs when certified personnel are unavailable. Paraprofessionals support certified staff conducting classroom or therapy activities. Tutoring activities might range from academic or psychomotor curriculum activities to counseling regarding improvement of social skills or work with parents. Paraprofessionals might also conduct follow-through exercises assigned by a speech, physical, or occupational therapist or assist with adapted physical education exercises.

An essential ingredient in the effective design of a paraprofessional model is appropriate training and careful observation of performance. Trained paraprofessionals are frequently teamed with family and community volunteers. Paraprofessional personnel are usually paid staff members, although sometimes they function as volunteers. Most rural paraprofessional programs have assumed that paraprofessionals will function as generalists. Their specialized tasks are generally limited to supervised follow-through activities assigned by speech, occupational, or physical therapists.

SUMMARY

Traditional models and strategies designed to provide a continuum of services to citizens with disabilities are inadequate for rural areas. The uniqueness of the rural community context requires service delivery and models distinctly different from those of nonrural areas. Family involvement and interagency collaboration are essential for successful service delivery. Because of the tremendous diversity in rural areas, there is no one rural service delivery model. There are, however, a number of community and agency characteristics that a model designed must consider. The planner may then appropriately control variables such as usage of personnel, transportation systems, and parent, extended family, and other community involvement to design an individualized model viable for the clients, family, community, and service agencies.

REFERENCES

American Association of State Colleges and Universities. (1989). *Assisting at-risk youth. A guide to programs at public colleges.* Washington, DC: Author.

Benson, A. J., Bischoff, H. G. W., & Boland, P. A. (1984). *Issues in rural school psychology* (Survey Report). Philadelphia: National Association of School Psychologists.

Children's Defense Fund. (1984). *Building health programs for teenagers.* (Washington, DC: Adolescent Pregnancy Prevention Clearinghouse.

Helge, D. (1983). Increasing preservice curriculum accountability. *Teacher Education and Special Education, 6*(2), 137–142.

Helge, D. (1984a). The state of the art of rural special education. *Exceptional Children, 50*(4), 294–305.

Helge, D. (1984b). Models for serving rural students with low-incidence handicapping conditions. *Exceptional Children, 50*(4), 313–324.

Helge, D. (1988). Serving at-risk populations in rural America. *Teaching Exceptional Children, 20*(4), 17–18.

McCannon, R. (1985). *Serving the rural adult: A demographic portrait of rural adult learners.* Manhattan, KS: The Action Agenda for Rural Postsecondary Education.

Richards, L. (1990, March–April). ILRU insights. *The National Newsletter for Independent Living*, p. 3.

CHAPTER 7

Higher Education

DOUGLAS M. TREADWAY

The United States has more than three thousand colleges and universities, and about one out of three are located outside of metropolitan areas. Proximity to rural residents, however, does not automatically mean that a given institution will perceive itself as a "rural" institution. Even though they are located in rural communities, a number of U.S. colleges do not have service to rural people and their communities as an expressly stated focus of their institutional mission.

A discussion of the relationship of rural higher education institutions to their host environment is timely as rural communities across North America and indeed across the world are experiencing accelerated forces of change. Rural families, schools, and businesses are stressed in both the economic and the social dynamics of an emerging global society. As they look toward higher education for support and assistance in the years ahead, we must ask the question: will they be served or neglected by our rural institutions?

While it is increasingly difficult to generalize about the nature of rural communities, some trends can be broadly applied to the rural context, not only in North America but across the world today. First, there continues to be a global-wide shift of populations from rural to urban centers. Since 1985 over one-half million people per year have been leaving rural America to move to the cities. This continues a 100 year period of outmigration which some demographers claim will not plateau until we reach complete reversal of the nineteenth century population distribution in the United States.

Of those involved in outmigration, young people make up the majority. Wherever one travels in the United States or abroad the same pattern is observed of young people leaving for the opportunities for higher education and careers afforded them in the cities. By the same token, the people left behind are aging as a population. For rural schools, both secondary and postsecondary, there is a profound economic impact of the continuing outmigration trend in that to the extent the product of the education institution goes out of the community their return on dollars invested in those people is never recovered. Rural schools are preparing young people for urban employers and urban communities, not their own. And yet, the rural community must bear the burden of the cost of that education and training.

In the 1970s many people predicted a "rural turnaround" which never materialized. Now the question is not posed as if the United States will reverse the long-standing trend of outmigration, but whether or not it can be effectively interrupted through a period of "revitalization." Today one can find a number of articles and presentations with the theme of "rural revitalization" (Gudenberg, 1985; National Governor's Association, 1988; Rural Development News, 1987; Treadway, 1988; Western Governor's Association, 1989). The theme starts with the premise that the holes creating the leakage of people out of rural towns can be somehow plugged with economic development in the broadest sense, which includes a major emphasis upon a better educated or trained nonurban work force.

Through the 1980s, government, industry, and higher education partnerships were formed in many U.S. states as well as other countries for the purpose of stimulating rural economic development. It is too early to determine whether or not these activities will produce the desired results. Some examples of initial success look very promising. Policy makers are placing a major emphasis upon the role of higher education as both a stimulus as well as an ongoing response mechanism to fuel rural revitalization (Western Governor's Association, 1989).

To summarize the rural context today, it is diversifying, less agriculturally oriented, diminishing in population, aging, less educated, less technology oriented, and less well off economically than its metro-based counterpart sector. This context sets into position a number of issues for rural educators.

CURRICULUM AND URBANIZATION

The first question to be explored is: do postsecondary institutions serving rural populations develop curriculum which is distinctly rural or otherwise modified for a rural audience as contrasted to a metro audience? Most observers agree that along with the century-long process of outmigration there has been a companion trend of "urbanizing" rural America (Amato, 1980; Cosby, 1980; Treadway, 1984). In the age of mass media and the industrialized nation, most Americans relate more to urban ideas, standards, and models than they do to rural ones. The products people buy, the entertainment they pursue, the courses of instruction they enroll in are all configured on an urban bias or mass media bias. Indeed, in some contexts an actual antirural bias is evident which prevades culture, politics, and the media (Reich, 1983).

Some argue that the major purpose of education in rural areas is to emancipate rural people from old ideas and values and to bring them into the contemporary urban-oriented world (Amato, 1988). Another version of the sentiment is that the purpose of rural education is to prepare people for successful outmigration. Certainly the vocational education movement was based in large part on the need to train people with farming backgrounds to be able to perform skills needed in the growing industries of the cities. The land-grant universities which were established to bring agricultural productivity to rural people now spend much of their resources on research and professional training with an urban bias. The majority of graduates from research universities do not return to work in small towns or predominately rural areas. A review of the professional schools shows very few examples of specific intentions to prepare people to serve in rural communities. Only a limited number of rural practitioner programs exist for health professions and a few more for rural education and human services. Most programs, even those found in rural schools, are either generic or urban-oriented.

The majority of community colleges state their primary purpose as that of preparing their graduates for transfer to four year colleges and universities. As a result we find few examples of community college curricula which have been designed specifically with contemporary rural issues in mind. One exception is the Native American tribal community colleges which are involved in Indian-controlled programs in economic development, community health, and cultural awareness within the reservation setting (Seronde, 1986).

Vocational/technical colleges or programs within community colleges do have in some instances curriculum which has been designed with rural business and industry in mind. With an aim to produce graduates who possess the skills necessary to function specifically in nonurban businesses, technical education on campuses as well as continuing education at the work site are often rural-specific in nature.

Most rural colleges and universities offer public service and noncredit adult education programs which are usually short-term and cover a specific topic. To the extent the topics deal with rural issues, one can find a number of examples of such activities across the country which would seem to support rural awareness and development (American Association of State Colleges and Universities, 1988).

During the twentieth century, the developed countries of the world experienced three distinctive shifts in their economies and prevailing social and educational paradigms. At the turn of the century most were still predominately agricultural and moving toward industrialization/urbanization. In the mid-1950s the so-called Information Society began to appear and as we enter the twenty-first century some futurists are describing the 1990s and beyond as entering the Knowledge Society or the New Learning Age. As rural people and their institutions have moved from agricultural to industrial to information age societies, the role of mass media and the rapid generation of new knowledge offer both promise and challenge. Whatever the distinct and compelling needs of rural communities now and in the future, they will need to be dealt with from a new set of assumptions which urbanization has brought forth and mass media is reinforcing wherever people live.

To deny rural students a curriculum which is contemporary and indeed global is to do them a major disservice. At the same time, not all rural problems are best solved using urban models and approaches. In addition, the values which have been associated with small and rural communities remain important for the shaping of the future. These include a strong work ethic, a spirit of cooperation and volunteerism, a respect for the conservation of the environment, and the importance of family and community. There are also traditions and cultures whose origins are distinctively rural in nature due to the ties to the land and an agrarian heritage. American and Canadian Indians speak and write often about their values and traditions within a distinctively rural perspective. In an article titled "Rural Education from a Native American Perspective," Jacques Seronde (1986) wrote: "The educational curricula emerge from the earth herself, from the first Teacher" (p. 11). The same holds true for immigrants from across the globe who came to North America from rural backgrounds and traditions which they cherish to this day (Vinz & Tammaro, 1988).

It is the thesis of this writer that rural people require and deserve a curriculum in higher education which is both appropriately urbanized and globalized and at the same time includes major elements which are rural-specific. To the extent that this blending and accommodation are not taking place, our institutions are not as relevant to the changing rural condition as they ought to be.

INSTRUCTION IN RURAL CONTEXT

As a rule, instructors in rural-based colleges and universities do not approach their teaching tasks in any way which would significantly distinguish them from their urban counterparts (Manno, 1989). This is largely because most still employ the lecture and discussion methodology and most adopt the same textbooks for college level courses as do urban-based faculty.

What is different is the student, not the instructor. The rural traditional age learner (eighteen to twenty-two years old) who has attended a small high school has typically not received the breath of opportunities as a student from a large and/or metro area school. On the other hand, it has been documented that students from small schools often have a better command of the so-called basic skills (Campbell, 1985). It may be that size of high school attended is a major determinant of differences among students at the time they enter college. However, no longitudinal evidence suggests that after successful mastery of the first year or so of college, that rural students do any worse or better than metro students.

It remains true that growing up in the metro cities and affluent suburbs and contrasting these experiences with growing up in non urban small towns elicit differences and comparisons. Urban youth arriving at rural colleges describe themselves as often bored and rural youth arriving at urban universities often say they are overwhelmed. It is a matter of degree based on their different frames of reference. It is not a matter of total lack of familiarity. The mass media brings rap to small towns and country music to the urban cities.

Instructors accommodate to the learners when a majority are from rural and small school backgrounds. At Southwest State University in rural Minnesota, all students take a minimum of two courses in rural studies as a graduation requirement. Some teacher education programs have rural education courses or practica, such as Western Montana College and Kansas State University. Instructors observe that today's students from rural backgrounds do not understand their own rural context with respect to economic, cultural, and political realities (Hubel, 1988). With only 3 percent living on farms, for example, most rural students do not have an understanding or appreciation for the role agriculture plays in the global economy nor of the many careers available in agribusiness, food, and agricultural sciences. Rural students lack knowledge of their history, their ethnic origins, and the changing nature of rural society across the world.

Lack of differentiation in teaching methods as well as content of the curriculum needs to be challenged. Schools serving rural populations ought to include major sections of rural-specific content in their courses of study for all students. Students preparing for professional careers should also have instruction in the differences of being successful in a small town versus a city. Instructors can also take advantage of a number of instructional methods in addition to the lecture method when teaching in a rural context. These will be discussed in more detail in the following.

RURAL LEARNING TRANSACTIONS

Should the *content* of higher education in the rural context be differentiated in the future, if it is not generally so today? The answer from this writer's perspective is yes, it should. Should the *methods* be changed as well? The answer here is a qualified yes, depending upon the learning objectives.

If the growing gap between the economies of rural and metro communities is to be reversed (or even stabilized), if the quality of life in rural areas is to be maintained or improved, then people who will bring about such results will need to have the tools of understanding and accomplishment relevant to those objectives as part and parcel of their higher education.

Studies have shown that the number one reason for dissatisfaction and/or poor job performance of school teachers in rural settings is their inability to relate to the small community context (Olson, 1986). While not as frequently documented, the same may hold true for all professional groups as they leave higher education and begin their work in a rural community, particularly one which is small in size. It would greatly aid especially the traditional age learners if their courses in history, economics, psychology, and sociology had specific content to help with developing a conceptual framework for the small and rural community. In terms of methodology, field studies and internships greatly assist in making real the concepts as well as offering some practical trial and error experience without the consequences of full-time employment.

Beyond the issue of successfully coping with the induction period of becoming a professional in a small community, is the other concern that future college graduates need to become agents of change on behalf of rural communities. In order to participate in learning events and interventions which empower rural people to redirect their local destiny toward renewed prosperity, and to protect or reclaim their areas' natural resources, graduates of the future must have a number of tools at their disposal. These would include: understanding of the changing global economy, the role of small business in that economy, the role of agriculture and natural resources and of technology transfer in stimulating rural development, the strengths and assets of small towns in the changing society, modern communications technologies, and rural-specific demographics with particular reference to poverty, literacy, health, and other rural concerns.

Within the global rural condition, the ethnic origins, traditions, and mores within small communities can be passed on to succeeding generations and even enriched through worldwide communications, including university international exchange. At the same time, newly emerging worldwide networks of people to people across nations and cultures can highlight a world community where what we have in common is also very important. When rural people from different nations and cultures meet, they seem to have an instant common bond which higher education can build upon.

While traditional age students and adults older than twenty-five years have much in common as to their being influenced by mass society, when it comes to their learning needs, goals, and outcomes, there may be decided differences among rural people. First, older students have made more of a commitment to live and work in the nonurban context, provided of course that they can earn a sufficient income. This writer's own conversations with a broad range of high school age students have revealed that the majority perceive opportunities for employment as well as desired lifestyle to be more attractive in the cities than in the rural areas. Most youth in rural colleges are not looking at their education as preparation for rural-based career opportunities. On the other hand, most of the placebound older students are.

The outmigration motivation for young people is fueled by their own sense that rural people are somehow second class citizens and by the antirural bias of many of their instructors, counselors, and in many cases their parents as well. Parental influence persists as the single most powerful factor in shaping the values and attitudes of youth. Farm families in particular show increasing concern that their children not be tied to the agricultural economy, which they view as increasingly precarious. They actively encourage in many instances their youth to pursue educational and career goals which lead them away from farming or even small town life. Colleges of agriculture across the country report that declining enrollments are fostered to a great extent today by active parental advice not to pursue agriculture as a career, despite an urgently growing need for agribusiness, agriculture, and food science professionals worldwide.

It is difficult for educators to redirect attitudes and values which parents ingrain in their offspring. To the extent parents are experiencing, or have experienced, severe economic hardship and they associate such problems with life in rural society, they will naturally and understandably seek to influence their young to take a different path of opportunity. Such influence, along with the antirural bias of the media which characterizes rural life as backward and lacking in sophistication, uninteresting, socially and intellectually isolated, may profoundly shape the young college student's outlook and disposition to a degree which may not be changeable.

By contrast, older students who remain in rural communities and attend full or part time a college in that setting, report a strong desire to remain, contribute, and participate in the revitalization of their communities. As these individuals populate rural classrooms in increasing ratios to younger students, we can forsee the possibility of them serving as powerful role models. If the nontraditional learners are strongly motivated toward rural educational goals, and if instructors and counselors share this agenda, it is likely that younger students would be positively impacted by such a potentially powerful combination of experiential forces. Even if their short-range career and maturation goals propel them toward urban areas, the seeds of positive rural images can bear fruit with maturity and a good number might return to rural towns to raise their families, develop their careers, and contribute to community betterment in the future.

Thus, attending to the expressed needs of older students for curriculum and methodologies which are directly relevant to the rural context is not only appropriate but may also address the potential for younger students to reconsider living in rural locations.

As rural outmigration continues and in some places even accelerates, the clock is moving too rapidly for us to place all of our emphasis upon the college population. Those adults who are currently employed and not attending college ought to be the number one priority for higher education's programs and services. There is an urgent need to develop rural entrepreneurs who can establish new small businesses as well as participate in the technology transfer of applied research designed to assist rural firms to be more competitive in the global market. Companies seeking to enter or expand in rural industries require a highly trained work force. Upgrading the existing rural work force and management/ leadership cadre is of utmost importance if rural firms are to keep pace with the transformation of American industry taking place in the metro areas and abroad. Continuing education for the professions in education, health, and human services and the credential development of the underprepared are also high priorities on the rural higher education agenda.

PROGRAMMING ISSUES

Institutions which have service to rural people as a significant thrust of their mission statement have major tasks ahead as they approach the twenty-first century. Starting with the premise that all of higher education is losing ground in its response to a changing world, the rural context evokes some particular challenges.

First of all, in our mass society the information and training needs of the rural and urban resident have a broad common base. In one small town of less than 2,000 residents this writer conducted an adult education needs assessment and received over 400 requests for different topics to be addressed. This community had no college within commuting distance. Prioritization into a handful of classes to conform to an outreach/circuit rider model of extended education is a difficult if not impossible task, and the information needs are growing dramatically.

Second, in the emerging information society, mere collection of bits of information through courses is becoming increasingly obsolete as an instructional mode. The majority of rural as well as urban learners are becoming able users of advanced communication and information retrieving/processing technologies. The stereotype of rural learners being less technologically oriented than urban adults has no basis in truth whatsoever. If they know what question to ask and how to access the sources, they can obtain what they need with little or no instructor intervention. Where telecommunications devices and computers have been made available to learners in rural areas, adaptation has been almost instantaneous. If by the year 2020 there will be the capacity for human knowledge to be doubled every thirty days or less, then the organization of information into courses as now practiced is clearly heading for obsolesence at an accelerated rate.

Information is power. Rural people can be empowered by their ability to access, process, and use information to solve their local problems. Therefore, programming for rural learners should stress the acquisition of information and communication skills more than the information memorization which is now emphasized. The methodologies involved in programming should render the rural learner more independent rather than instructor dependent. The learner should also cultivate skills in being a collaborator of active learning as a member of a learning team. The rural learner needs to understand team approaches to problem solving, something which has always been part of the rural community and which needs contemporary models to fit new opportunities.

Planning for programming should necessarily involve the rural learner as a direct participant. The idea of shipping a "canned" program out to rural people is not a workable solution. Learners must be viewed as resources both in the planning and the carrying out of educational activities. This fits into the notion of lifelong learning, where the formal educational experience models the later self-directed learning of adults in rural society.

Major efforts are underway in the United States and Canada to reach rural learners (both on and off campus) with telecommunications or *distance learning systems*. The potential is great to provide access across large geographical regions where populations are insufficient for on-site instruction. For the most part, institutions using distance learning systems are not reshaping the content or the instructional methodology for rural audiences. Instead standardized courses taught in the lecture format are being taped or broadcast by interactive television systems to distant locations. Some high cost studio television courses have been produced and tapes made available as course supplements and/or instructional motivation aids, but they contain little or no rural-specific content.

A number of principles for educational practice should be reviewed when considering the use of distance learning systems for rural areas. To begin with, telecommunications should be viewed as tools and not ends in themselves. Second, the design of curriculum transmitted at a distance should take into account the needs of rural learners as referenced in the previous section. Modules can be prepared which supplement the main body of content being broadcast. Local adaptation can be facilitated by the method of presentation. Using rural examples in presentation as well urban and/or large scale examples is also called for. Readings and other supplementary materials should offer options for rural learner needs.

The rural community itself should not be overlooked as a major resource when designing distance learning experiences. Learning activities and assignments which call for the students to actively explore their own community histories, problems, resources, and other unique features will greatly help toward meeting student needs. Interest levels and credibility of productions are also enhanced by doing some of the video and audio recording out in the rural towns, emphasizing business, cultural, and educational locations.

While there has been a tendency in the past two decades to offer unimodal distance learning systems, in the future it is the multimodal approach which will bring the most favorable results for rural populations. By combining the technologies of audio and visual recordings with FAX machines and microcomputers (with modem), every home, school, and rural business is a potential learning center for distance learning systems (Czech, 1989).

In addition to offering combinations of mix and match technology for rural learners, it is essential also to vary the other learning activities: participation in a near-to-home small group, independent study and research, field studies, group problem solving and simulations, and on-the-job training or internships.

By adapting the curriculum to rural learner needs and providing modern telecommunications mixed with other learning strategies, educators today and in the future have unlimited opportunities to reach, serve, and empower rural people through higher education.

ADMINISTRATION AND RURAL INSTITUTIONS

Instruction, programming, and the learner's direct involvment are constantly interacting components of rural higher education systems which require administration. Such administrative organization should follow from and be shaped by a new rural learning and teaching agenda, rather than to impose a structure apart from the dynamics of the new agenda.

Special populations require special educational interventions and strategies, wherever they reside. The fact that illiteracy continues in rural America to the extent it does should be a major concern of university administrators and faculties alike. Inequities in the opportunities for jobs, education, and health care among the rural poor persist as a condition of rural life despite many years of state and federal programs aimed at combating these problems. Higher education must renew its commitment to being an effective partner in addressing these entrenched conditions.

Providing university services and programs to rural areas requires a clear understanding of the unique nature of the problems facing rural communities and a firm belief in the self-determination of rural peoples and their right of ownership and participation in the planning of education agendas. One way in which higher education institutions involve rural learners is through advisory councils, either for the entire institution and its outreach mission or for specific academic and public service programs. Focus groups and needs assessments are also devices for planning and review involvement of rural citizens, whether they be current students or not. The use of alumni organizations is growing as a way of following up on graduates and of soliciting ideas for curriculum and service delivery from people who live and work in rural communities and who are committed to a particular institution.

Some rural communities have extension centers or coordinating centers where local people can have a say in what is taught in their area as well as how and when. Administrators should encourage such local bases of operation, even though they add to the complexities of organization in some instances.

In an age of systems, whether we talk about financial aids, career development programs, or educational media, for the most part our systems are contrived on a large scale model for profitability as well as efficiency. The systems in use in higher education have been most often developed by large institutions with extensive resources and increasingly by urban based corporations. Certain assumptions about time and distance may be built into these systems, their scheduling, and administration, which hold distinct disadvantages for rural students.

Administrators themselves are likely to have received their education in a program or institution which did not adequately, if at all, differentiate for them the challenges of administration in the rural context. They may lack both the understanding and the sensitivity to render their organization's behavior more responsive to rural concerns.

In those institutions and community settings with highly active rural citizens and enlightened university administrators, a number of effective organizational and curricular reforms have taken place. Institutions which are accepting responsibility to become partners with rural communities, industry, and government, are finding a high level of receptivity and involvement toward needed reforms. Those who establish policy as well as those who administer rural higher education institutions must themselves enter into a period of learning and re-orientation to the contemporary rural situation.

COLLABORATION WITH COMMUNITY-BASED ORGANIZATIONS

State and federal elected and appointed officials are increasingly concerned over the fragmentation which exists between higher education and other organizations endeavoring to provide educational and economic development services to rural communities. Vocational and community colleges and regional and research universities are for the most part not coordinated in their activities of distance learning/outreach or rural development. Community-based organizations sometimes become frustrated when higher education institutions bypass them, duplicate their services, or otherwise fail to integrate them into what they are attempting to accomplish. Some community-based organizations serve as brokers of educational opportunities and do so with varying degrees of success depending upon postsecondary cooperation. Rural citizens complain that it is difficult to obtain the programs and services they require due to the fragmented and often limited duration activities of higher education. When we add in the vast array of public and private organizations involving themselves in one way or another in pursuit of economic development, the frustration and confusion are only amplified.

One reason for the lack of collaboration with community-based organizations is the funding of higher education based on enrollments rather than on programs or services. There are few if any incentives for active cooperation and resource sharing between universities themselves or between universities and other agencies and organizations. Another consideration is that for many postsecondary institutions the faculty and administrators who provide services to rural people are not themselves placed in positions of responsibility sufficient to command the necessary budget allocations or organizational decisions.

Cooperative extension in the land-grant university system has been a long standing model, but today it has difficulty posturing itself as a first line priority for funding in the university. Regional colleges have programs at the periphery of their academic or public service mission but only a limited number seem to place such programs as the first or even second tier of institutional priorities for their budgets. Some community colleges and technical schools may be closer to the rural people through boards of governance and more concentrated public pressure which help assure their responsiveness to local needs.

Given the scarcity of resources and the many unmet needs of rural areas, effective strategies for collaboration are needed between all sectors of the education and public service communities. High schools, technical and community colleges, universities, and community-based organizations need to learn how to cooperate and share resources through consortia and other joint power agreements. This collaboration should be evidenced in economic development programs as well as the delivery of distance learning programs.

CONCLUSIONS

Today nearly 100 one room schoolhouses still exist in the state of Montana. Many look the same as they did at the turn of the century, but inside are computers, professional teachers, and a broad array of modern instructional resources. The land-grant universities and the normal schools were also established at the turn of the century. Some of their original buildings still stand, but regional colleges and research universities are a far cry from their beginnings as to their mission and priorities. The one room schoolhouse illustrates that change can occur without abandoning the essential structure of rural education. In the fervor to urbanize our institutions, the higher education community however, has lost any focus on the distinctive needs of rural learners and their communities. Similarly, the complexity of a changing global economy has shaken the foundations of extension and public service programs which are no longer the effective tools of rural development they once were.

For more than two decades, the concept of lifelong learning has been widely discussed in the United States. Participation in adult education is growing in both urban and rural areas. The National Center for Education Statistics reports that between 1975 and 1981 participation in adult education increased 34.4 percent in rural areas and 21.2 percent in urban areas (McCannon, 1985). The data also showed a significant disparity, even with the increase, between rural and urban participation with 27.6 percent of the total population enrolled in rural versus 74.4 percent in the metropolitan census districts.

At this point in time higher education is offering too little too late to rural America. It is as if we have bowed to the inevitability of what one writer described as "irretrievably lost frontiers" (Amato, 1988). Rural residents have been shortchanged in recent decades, and the time to improve learning opportunities for rural Americans is now. As older learners, attending both full time and part time, increase in numbers at our rural colleges and universities, administrators and faculty should utilize these learners as in-house consultants for designing new curricula as well as instructional delivery systems which are responsive to their needs and the twenty-first century (American Association of State Colleges and Universities, 1989).

Through increased learner involvement in both the design and delivery of lifelong learning activities, the unique needs and values systems of the diversified rural populations will be taken into account. The best kind of education is one that rural learners have helped plan, execute, and evaluate. With a heightened degree of learner involvement, and the commitment from institutional leaders to advancing the rural agenda to a high priority, the stage can be set for major new initiatives to take place. It will be necessary to evolve new strategies for partnerships between rural higher education, business, government, and industry. The preponderance of small businesses in rural areas does not lay a base for employer sponsored lifelong learning programs which stimulate the high degree of participation in urban communities. Public policy and funding arrangements need to consider this.

Above all we must formulate a new paradigm for how we approach the task of lifelong learning in rural America. The essential features of the new paradigm are as follows:

1. Purging the antirural bias with the same intentionality that we address gender and racial stereotyping

2. Creating a vision of a revitalized rural people in a global society

3. Re-tooling our institutions in ways which treat the rural human and natural environment as living laboratories

4. In cooperation with state and federal agencies, eliminating the fragmentation and competition involved in rural development and education and forming new alliances and systems designed to maximize effectiveness with well-planned strategies of collaboration

5. Fostering a climate of entrepeneurial risk taking and problem solving—seeking long-term restructuring of rural higher education and the economy as contrasted to short-term patchwork solutions

6. Assuring equity to rural students, both in the quality of education offered and in the relevancy of choices available to address their community needs and aspirations

The mission of higher education moving into the twenty-first century is to strengthen our rural population and to help dispel their isolation, reduce their poverty, link them to the new global economy, and sustain the values that historically have placed rural people at the center of our democratic way of life.

REFERENCES

Amato, J. (1980). *Countryside: Mirror of ourselves.* Marshall, MN: Southwest State University Press.

Amato, J. (1988). *Education for outmigration.* Speech delivered to the Minnesota Press Club, Minneapolis, MN.

American Association of State Colleges and Universities (1988). *Directory of economic development programs at state colleges and universities.* Washington, DC: Author.

American Association of State Colleges and Universities. (1989). *The revitalization of rural America.* Washington, DC: Author.

Campbell, A. (1985). *Components of rural school excellence.* Washington, DC: National Rural Education Forum, U.S. Department of Education.

Cosby, A. (1980). The urban context of rural policy. *The Interstate Compact for Education, 14*(3), 14–19.

Czech, D. (1989). Fax, TV and the remote classroom. *T.H.E. Journal,* (April), 24–29.

Gudenberg, K. (1985). *Toward an American rural renaissance.* Mississippi State University: Southern Rural Development Center.

Hubel, K. (1989). *Rural education: A special report.* Fergus Falls, MN.: Communicating for Agriculture, Inc.

Mann, B. (1989). *Rural education: A changing landscape.* Washington, DC: U.S. Department of Education.

McCannon, R. (1983) Serving rural adult learners. In C. Kasworm (Ed.), *Educational outreach to select adult populations* (pp. 15–29). New Direction for Continuing Education, no. 20. San Francisco: Jossey-Bass.

National Governor's Association (1988). *New alliances for rural America: Report of the task force on rural development.* Washington, DC: Author.

North Central Regional Center for Rural Development. (1987). *Rural Development News,* 11(2), 1–9.

Olson, J. (1986) *Review of teacher education programs effectiveness.* Denver: Western Interstate Commission on Higher Education.

Reich, R. (1983). *The next American frontier.* New York: Times Books.

Seronde, J. (1986) Rural education from a Native American perspective. *Educational Considerations,* 13(2), 10–11.

Schuh, E. (1986). Revitalizing land grant universities: It's time to regain relevance. *Choices,* (2nd Quarter), 6–10.

Treadway, D. (1984). *Higher education in rural America: Serving the adult learner.* New York: College Entrance Examination Board.

Treadway, D. (1988). Higher education and rural development. *Northwest Report* (Report No. 6). St. Paul, MN: Northwest Area Foundation.

Vinz, M., & Tammaro, T. (1988). *Common ground: A gathering of poems on rural life.* Morehead, MN: Decotah Territory Press.

Western Governor's Association. (1989). *A time of challenge . . . a time for change: The role of higher education in the rural west.* Denver: Author.

CHAPTER 8

University Extension
JOHN T. PELHAM

The focus of this chapter will be on the role of extension in the lifelong educational process of Americans in rural areas. It will trace the context within which extension was founded and the unique contributions it has made to education for rural citizens. The elements of extension programs will be identified, as well as how they relate to various aspects of the lifelong learning process, and how these have changed to reflect changed needs and opportunities. Finally, we will look into the future of extension programs for rural audiences and describe the kinds of changes that may be needed in organizational affiliations, programs and services offered, and funding sources.

HISTORICAL CONTEXT

In absolute terms and relative to their urban counterparts the quality of life for "rural people" in the late nineteenth and early twentieth centuries was not good. Rural people were predominantly farmers who were subject to the exigencies of weather, inadequate and inconsistent production input sources, and a lack of research-based information to aid them in production and marketing decisions. The social and geographic isolation of rural people was problematic. The lack of electricity, running water, cooking and heating fuel, and news and information were a part of that legacy. Rural isolation was negative in terms of quality of life.

Inadequate formal and informal educational opportunity was also a legacy of life in rural America in that era. More often than not, transportation and life on the farm were deterrents to full-time, long-term participation in education. The level and permanence of funding created problems in getting and keeping quality teachers and modern educational materials.

The relative inequality of rural life in this period was interwoven with the availability and affordability of a host of goods and services. Transportation services, public utilities (including electricity), and public information and entertainment sources were needed to add to the quality of rural life.

On the other hand, rural people were both independent and interdependent. They shared a strong work ethic and placed a high value on family, particularly the extended family. Because of the lack of paid services, they valued volunteerism. While "book learning" was suspect, gaining practical knowledge was highly valued. They did not expect a great deal from government. As we shall see, this combination of needs and attributes gave rise to a profound educational movement that was to sweep the countryside beginning in the second decade of the 1900s.

Responding to the Challenge

Against this backdrop, a host of movements to improve rural life began in 1862 with the passage of the Morrill Act creating the land-grant college system. Time and space does not permit a detailed recount of this profound educational movement. Among a host of excellent reviews are Rasmussen (1989), Sanders, et al. (1966), Sanderson (1988), and Stefferud (1962).

Unlike other institutions of higher education, the land-grant colleges were created to "promote the liberal and practical education of the industrial classes in the several pursuits and professions in life" (Sanders, et al, 1966, p. 425) as opposed to perpetuating the more traditional, elitist system of education imported from Europe and dominated by liberal and professional schools of the eighteenth and nineteenth centuries. This education of the "children of the common man" was to include, but not be limited to, branches of learning related to agricultural production and the mechanical arts and sciences.

As the popularity of the land-grant system grew and the colleges expanded, it became obvious that the knowledge base being created and taught on these campuses had practical and far-reaching consequences for a broad array of people across the country, particularly rural people. They needed useful and practical information to help them solve problems they experienced in their farm and home operations, to help relieve their isolationism, and to improve the educational inadequacies they and their children experienced.

In the two decades around the turn of the century, an off-campus educational movement began in rural areas. Aimed at bridging the communication and educational gaps, the movement took several forms, including farmers' institutes which were established in twenty-five states,

Iowa State University faculty using trains to transport information and promote corn production techniques throughout the state, and boy's and girl's club work which originated in Clark County, Ohio, by A. B. Graham, a local school superintendent. By 1904, his idea had become a federation of rural school agricultural clubs, a forerunner of the 4-H Club movement.

These movements proved that cooperation between schools, the farmers' institutes, the agricultural colleges, the U.S. Department of Agriculture, and private enterprise could produce an educational movement more powerful than any one of the organizations could develop independently. As educational outreach from land-grant schools gathered momentum, a series of actions gave rise to formalizing the movement. Beginning in 1903, Seaman A. Knapp put together the first known example of demonstration teaching, combining the efforts of local businessmen, farmers, and the land-grant system in an educational program to demonstrate the value of new agricultural methods. His efforts to fit needs and resources were so successful that farmer-operated demonstration farms were established in several counties in east Texas. The first county agent, W. C. Stallings, was appointed in Tyler, Texas, on November 12, 1906. By 1910, demonstration work was being conducted in 455 counties in twelve southern states, employing 450 agents.

These movements to enhance off-campus education were not totally oriented to agriculture. In establishing the Country Life Commission in 1908, Theodore Roosevelt appointed two people, Kenyon Butterfield, president of Rhode Island State College and Liberty Hyde Bailey of the New York State College of Agriculture, as two of its leading members. These gentlemen had been active in farmers' institutes and other early efforts to communicate the results of agricultural research to farmers. Rasmussen (1989) writes that their orientation toward extending the knowledge base of the university to practitioners influenced the findings and recommendations of the commission:

> The commission found there was widespread recognition of the need for redirecting rural schools. The commission called not only for change in the schools for young people, but also for continuation schools for adults. People must be reached in terms of their daily lives or welfare, which, for farm people, must be in terms of agriculture and of life on the farm. The commission recognized that the extension work carried on by some of the colleges of agriculture was helpful, but it was on a pitiably small scale as compared with the needs. In every agricultural college extension work, without which no college of agriculture can adequately serve its state, should be coordinated with both the academic and the experiment and research branches. (p. 44)

The commission called for the establishment of a national system for extension "so managed as to reach every person on the land in its state, with both information and inspiration. . . (and) designed to forward not only the business of agriculture, but sanitation, education, home making, and all interests of country life" (Rasmussen, 1989, p. 44).

Finally, the commission recommended what has become a central tenet for extension work when it reported:

> Care must be taken in all the reconstructive work to see that local initiative is relied upon to the fullest extent, and that federal and even state agencies do not perform what might be done by the people in the communities. The centralized agencies should be stimulative and directive, rather than mandatory and formal. Every effort must be made to develop native resources, not only of material things, but of people. (Rasmussen, 1989, p. 45)

For five successive years beginning in 1909, bills were introduced in Congress to establish a national system for extending the land-grant colleges to the people. Finally, a bill introduced by South Carolina Congressman A. F. Lever and Georgia Senator Hoke Smith was adopted and became law on May 8, 1914. At its signing President Wilson called it "one of the most significant and far-reaching measures for the education of adults ever adopted by the government . . . to insure the retention in rural districts of an efficient and contented population" (cited in Rasmussen, 1989, p. 48).

In its most important aspects, the bill carried the provision for cooperative funding and administration for extension by federal, state, and local levels of government. Additionally, it provided that federal funds would only be provided to states for purposes which Congress intended, namely: "To aid in diffusing among the people of the United States useful and practical information on subjects relating to agriculture and home economics and to encourage the application of the same" (Rasmussen, 1989, p. 49).

The educational work inspired by this act was intended to focus on instruction and practical demonstrations in agriculture and home economics for persons who were not enrolled in the land-grant colleges. Field demonstrations and publications were among the prescribed methods.

Armed with a mandate and a budget, land-grand universities began to establish extension services in the states, empowering local people to make decisions about their educational needs and priorities. The emphasis was on a nonformal educational organization which was responsive to the needs of local people. Local citizens comprised extension boards, were actively involved in raising local funds to support extension work, and gave leadership to the effort.

EXTENSION EDUCATION: LIFELONG LEARNING FOR RURAL CITIZENS

Two conceptual descriptions of lifelong learning will form the focus of this discussion. First, lifelong education can be described as a process involving participation in a series of formal, nonformal, and informal educational activities throughout an individual's life. A review of the extension educational programs and activities at local, state, and national levels suggests that programs exist for people throughout the lifespan. Prenatal care education for expectant mothers affects the preborn; early childhood education programs for new parents assist them in early socialization activities for young children; 4-H youth programs develop the life skills of young people ages six to nineteen; adult educational programs covering almost every topic available within the land-grant university are available for adults; and extension gerontology specialists are focusing educational programs on elderly audiences and those who care for them.

Another description of lifelong learning deals more with methodology and conceptual focus. It more clearly distinguishes university extension from its formal and nonformal educational peers and it forms the theoretical basis for the discussions in the remainder of this chapter.

Knowles (1978, p. 165) describes the history of education up to the first quarter of the twentieth century as "a process of cultural transmittal" and the role of teacher as that of "transmitter of information." Alfred North Whitehead (1931, p. viii–xix), in a speech at Harvard in 1930, contended that major cultural change is occurring at a rate so rapid that it is shorter than the life span of individuals; hence, "our training must prepare individuals to face a novelty of conditions."

Education, thus, becomes a process of preparing people for continuing inquiry and searches for knowledge; hence, the practice of "teaching" changes from information transmittal to learning facilitation and self-directed resource. Teachers take many different forms and are relevant to learners throughout the life span.

Extension education emphasizes learning, not for learning's sake, but for application to living. Indeed, extension literature abounds with a variety of principles which scholars like Knowles and Whitehead would find compatible with their concept of lifelong education. A few of the more common are adapted as follows:

1. Extension provides informal, noncredit education conducted beyond the classroom, for all ages.

2. Extension provides practical, problem-centered, situation-based education.

3. The extension educational process begins with helping people to identify and understand their needs and problems and to use technology and information in solving them.

4. The subject matter used by extension teachers is more practical than theoretical and is intended for application to solve problems.

5. Application of the subject matter requires changes in both mental and physical behavior.

6. Participation in extension programs is voluntary and is available to a large and heterogeneous audience.

7. Extension teaching uses a variety of methodologies, but emphasizes the demonstration form of teaching.

8. Extension values cooperation and partnerships with other agencies in the mutual conduct of their business to benefit local citizens.

9. Extension relies extensively on local leadership in both program planning and implementation.

It is not enough to know that extension was and is a major factor in the lifelong educational process for rural Americans. The concept of lifelong education presupposes a system that commits to changes in content and methodology as the population it serves changes. As Knowles (1962) so appropriately points out:

> As the needs of rural people changed, so did the extension program. Before and during World War I the emphasis had been primarily on improving farm production. Following World War I, with the problem of production diminishing in importance, the emphasis gradually shifted to problems of marketing and conservation. (During the depression years) the Extension Service was called on to manage state and federal emergency rural relief and farm programs. By 1950 only about the one-third of the efforts of county extension workers were directed toward more efficient production of crops and livestock, about one-fourth to providing services to rural organizations and training volunteer leaders, and much of the balance toward improving social relationships, helping people make social adjustments, and developing cultural values among rural people. (pp. 90–92)

Extension proved that it was an educational organization that had the *ability* to change rapidly and the *commitment* to do so. Included in this change was an increasing emphasis on the extension of the total university, not just colleges of agriculture and home economics.

This change has not been easy. It almost always generates resistance. Traditional constituencies have not felt they get back as much as they give up; new constituencies don't always accept extension with the open arms of traditional audiences. University colleagues outside the cooperative extension framework are sometimes slow to take up the commitment to this different educational concept and delivery system. Decision makers who have control of traditional funding bases can't always expand their resource commitment to include these new opportunities for service. New sources of funding are easily identified but not so easily tapped. In all too many cases extension educators themselves are often slow to change due to inertia, fear, inadequate training, or lack of understanding of extension philosophy.

FROM COUNTY AGENT TO TECHNICAL CHANGE EXPERT

Extension continues to change; however, there are some "unchanging suppositions" which contribute to the uniqueness of extension and which make change necessary and possible: individual empowerment, citizen involvement in program determination, variety of teaching methods, availability of the total university subject matter base, and coordination and cooperation within the university and with other agencies.

Extension has often been described as constantly changing its content, its methodologies, and/or its audiences. Ratchford (1984) traces some of the more important changes in extension during the period from 1948 to 1983:

1. Strengthening the tie of extension to the academic base

2. Broadening extension's program areas beyond agriculture, home economics, and 4-H

3. Increasing the visibility and involvement of extension in a variety of social issues

4. Strengthening extension and agencies

5. Encouraging greater use of mass media and other delivery methodologies

6. Increasing emphasis on leadership development and volunteer leader training

Recently, a dramatic increase in extension involvement in the area of public policy education has occurred. Norman and Williams (1989) report that public policy educational programs can create new energies for both extension staff and local lay leaders and can assist extension staff in revitalizing skills and values aimed at involving people in the process of learning, provide them with more confidence in their leadership role in the community, and help local citizens develop opinions and make choices about critical public policy issues. Such programs are engaging extension audiences in discussions regarding such issues as family and youth, environment, community infrastructure, agriculture, and social and economic development. Extension's role in these programs has been to provide process expertise and to link subject matter expertise from the university.

Extension staff have some insecurities about walking the fine line between telling people what to think as opposed to how to think. In the truest sense of the Knowles definition, however, that is the appropriate role for the "teacher" in lifelong education.

THE NEW FACE OF EXTENSION—ISSUES-BASED EDUCATIONAL PROGRAMMING

One of the most pervasive and substantive changes that extension has experienced is one in which it is currently engaged—issues-based programming.

In a recent publication by Dalgaard, Brazzel, Liles, and Taylor-Powell (1988), the following characteristics of issues programming were identified:

1. Defining problems based on multiple contributing factors rather than a single cause

2. Shifting from a disciplinary to a multidisciplinary/collaborative focus on problem solutions

3. Shifting from single agency to multiple agency cooperative approaches to problems and concerns

4. Decreasing emphasis on "solving problems" and increasing emphasis on prevention technologies

5. Increasing involvement of scholars and disciplines outside the traditional sources which colleges of agriculture and home economics provide

6. Increasing emphasis on developing and enhancing coalition building skills

7. Increasing use of "medical models" that bring specialties to a situation for their unique contributions to problem solving

As extension units throughout the country have struggled and in varying degrees converted to this new way of extension education, we have seen interesting changes in definitions of audiences, methodologies, and program focus and content.

Audiences for Issues-Based Programming

Tactics for identifying relevant audiences for issues programming differ from those used in more traditional programming. One may speak of primary, secondary, and perhaps tertiary audiences which evolve out of detailed studies of many issues. For example, in dealing with youth issues the primary audience is the youth themselves, while secondary audiences may include families and other groups which work directly with youth to prevent and ameliorate problem behavior. Tertiary audiences may include regional and state levels of organizations and governmental units which promulgate policies and provide statewide support for programs which ultimately impact on the first and second levels of audience. It should also be pointed out that starting with the issue, as opposed to a program, forces us to look beyond the existing traditional users of extension programs.

Educational Methods Critical to Issues Programming

Tradiitional "teaching" methods are not consonant with issues-based programming. Methodologies are necessary which encourage and enhance "learner" involvement at all stages from issue identification to prevention/intervention/solution program implementation. Examples of two such methodologies evolve from a recent extension-sponsored program in Missouri.

On October 10, 1990, a satellite conference was conducted focusing on the health care delivery problems facing rural Missourians. The conference, featuring expertise from the university, state department of health, private practice, and a private school of osteopathic medicine, was downlinked into more than 90 percent of the rural counties in Missouri. In those local sites, coalitions of care deliverers, local volunteers, elected leaders, and consumers were involved in hearing the experts talk about the breadth and degree of health care delivery problems. More importantly, local groups were facilitated in discussions of their local health care delivery concerns, had opportunity to address questions via telephone to the panel, and were encouraged to commit to continuing local discussions to address the issue further. State extension program personnel, in turn, have committed to serve as a contact point for community groups with need for technical expertise/support which might be available from somewhere within the university system and/or state governmental agencies.

Hence, distance learning and coalition development and management are seen as two important methodologies, or technologies, in issues-based programming. Others include environmental scanning, focus groups, and increased use of computer technology.

Issues programming forces us to design delivery methods to fit the needs and characteristics of diverse audiences and the specific implications of the issue. Differences in audience groups, stages in clientele development, and the environments in which clientele are located are among the factors which should be considered in the selection of appropriate methodologies.

Focus and Content of Issues Programming

The rural health example above is indicative of the challenge which issues-based programming has provided extension. More than any time in history, such issues as substance abuse, adult and youth literacy, teenage pregnancy, rural human services delivery, water quality, economic development, sustainable agriculture, and quality of life for the elderly are part of the extension focus. Throughout the country, examples of how extension is addressing these and others have encouraging implications for the efficacy of this change in direction.

Job Training and Assistance for Farm Families

In cooperation with the Job Training Partnership Act (JTPA) Michigan State University extension developed a comprehensive program of counseling, training, and placement for farmers making or contemplating a transition to new occupations. A feature of the program was that it enabled the families to support their existing farm or start a new life off the farm.

Leadership Training for Public Issue Involvement

The Family Community Leadership (FCL) program, jointly sponsored by the W. K. Kellogg Foundation and the National Extension Homemakers Council, provides leadership training for people to become effectively involved in the political process and in identifying and resolving public issues affecting families. In almost every state in the nation, local organizations and communities have been strengthened through the efforts of this program.

Strengthening Families for Early Childhood Socialization

In Wisconsin, "Family Times" teaches families to set goals, assess strengths, and develop skills and attitudes to strengthen parent-teen bonds. The program, designed as a prevention model for at-risk behavior, has been adopted in whole or modified in a number of other states with excellent acceptance by local parent-youth groups.

Enhancing Water Quality

An extension-led group in a rural Missouri community sponsored a multicounty water quality seminar. Now, more than three years later, committees within the community are still addressing issues raised through their participation and a five-year plan for enhancing overall environmental quality has been implemented.

Solid Waste Disposal

West Virginia University Extension Service has made a commitment to work on solid waste management which has included educating solid waste leaders, public awareness programs, and encouraging an environmental ethic of improved stewardship of natural resources. Audiences ranging from local solid waste authorities to youth and homemakers groups have been involved in a host of activities and projects.

Issues-based programming has made extension and the land-grant university aware that they do not have all the answers to all the issues. They have found that they are among several players. As a result, new skills are developing in interagency collaboration, networking, being both a catalyst and a participant in coalitions, playing both facilitator and program deliverer roles as necessary, and searching for unique opportunities for interagency funding sources.

IMPLICATIONS FOR EXTENSION

This chapter has chronicled the changing lifelong educational needs of rural audiences and the evolution of extension practices to accommodate those changes. What of the future? Without doubt, we will continue to experience changes in the lifelong educational needs of rural audiences. We will briefly mention some of those changes and project some implications of those changes for extension.

Projections of this nature are probably best left to the futurists. Changes which may be occurring in one sector of the rural community may be nonexistent or already passed in other sectors; while in others, they may never happen. Thus, it is imperative that rural educators become familiar with environmental scanning and focus group techniques and employ a variety of futuring strategies for determining specific kinds of changes happening and anticipated in the future. Those caveats aside, there is evidence to predict the following kinds of changes in rural society which have direct implications for extension:

1. *Geographic and cultural isolationism, which once characterized rural societies, will largely be erased by the year 2000.* This change has both positive and negative consequences. Access to a host of human services delivery systems, including education and health care, along with greater access to retail trade centers has a number of very positive consequences. On the other hand, many of the social ills which were once considered "city problems" now, and will in the future, impact rural constituencies.

   Extension has credibility with rural constituencies and has access to the educational resources of the land-grant institutions in the states. The linking of the entities will create an even more challenging role for extension, particularly as rural needs extend even further beyond the traditional outreach arm of agriculture.

2. *In many parts of the country, the rural population is becoming increasingly elderly, whether from out-migration of young or in-migration of retired elderly.* The impact has been a significantly changed audience with much different needs.

   Again, extension can provide a much needed link to resources of the university such as medicine, physical therapy, housing, social work, and nutrition. By networking with other care provider organizations, extension can catalyze programs to address the unique needs of these audiences in a locality-specific manner.

3. *The changes which agricultural production and producers will go through will be profound.* The widening gap between the few producers who produce the large majority of our food and fiber products and the vast majority of producers who produce a relatively small proportion of our product will get greater. Likewise, their needs for educational programming will become increasingly diverse and divergent. For the large farmer, needs will increasingly be oriented toward international marketing, computerized technology and records keeping systems, and systems management. The small farmer will increas-

ingly need help in identifying income supplement opportunities and niche marketing techniques and opportunities.

Extension agricultural leadership has a tremendous challenge in addressing this bi-modal agricultural structure which is far different from the traditional family farm dominated structure of the past. For example, the juxtaposition of computer-assisted marketing decision-making programs alongside programs for marketing produce from subsistence farmers will require the best minds from agriculture and other disciplines.

4. *Rural communities will increasingly need trained paid and volunteer leadership to remain viable.* The future of many such communities as places to live and make a living will be more dependent upon the quality of their leadership than any other single variable.

This is not so much a new role for extension, but a re-commitment to a role which has been deemphasized in many state organizations and, in many others, replaced by community economic development efforts. Both leadership and economic development are necessary and extension has the history and expertise to catalyze both.

5. *Family viability will become increasingly problematic as rural societal demands become more complex.* Such changes as the "ruralization of social concerns" and the economic and social demands imposed on two wage-earner families, early childhood educational needs, techniques for effectively balancing work and family demands, and the needs for education/vocatonal skill development and economic development all evolve out of this complex of change issues.

This area has probably involved as much extension concern and attention as any other in the recent past. Undoubtedly, the future will require more. A large question looms—can extension leadership realign an increasingly large share of its resources to address these issues in the face of increased demands from agriculture and others sectors? National 4-H Council President Richard J. Sauer, among other leaders, says we must (Sauer, 1990).

It is interesting to note the relationship between these changes and what is being projected as the programmatic, organizational, and re-source developmental needs for the future viability of extension. Much of the leadership in identifying the transition of extension to better meet the lifelong educational needs of our changing society has been done by a futures task force (Futures Task Force, 1987). Of the thirty-two recommendations of that task force, the following are particularly important as we consider the role of university extension in addressing the lifelong learning needs of rural Americans:

1. The compelling issues facing people must drive the system. These issues must constitute the basis upon which all decisions regarding programs, training, delivery methods, funding, and audience selection are made.

2. The system must transcend the former boundaries of program areas and disciplines to delivery issue-oriented educational programs.

3. Over time, extension should place more emphasis on limited term, issue-oriented interdisciplinary teams.

4. The extension system should have access to and utilize all appropriate expertise related to relevant issues from throughout the land-grant university.

5. Extension leadership should review alternative funding sources, including grants, subcontracting with other agencies and user fees.

6. A nationwide network should be established to better serve the high technology needs of agriculture, including emphasis on problem solving, producer education, and education for professionals.

7. Extension must create a system that will be a recognized source for applied research-based data and programming that the entire spectrum of community, family, and youth organizations may utilize in decision making and program design to deal with major societal issues.

8. Extension must assertively address the emerging and critical issues and needs of families through educational programs which improve the overall quality of life and contribute to the development of human capital.

9. Extension should enhance its adult and youth volunteer and leadership development programming efforts.

10. The extension system should use the most effective and efficient communications methods for program delivery.

As extension changes to meet the needs of a changing rural society, it is important to do so from the historical perspective of the context through which it has developed. It has always been oriented toward empowering clientele to address and solve their own programs, utilizing the educational resources of the university. There is no reason for that underlying tenet to change. In fact, if extension is to maintain a viable role in meeting the lifelong educational needs of rural as well as urban societies, that must be the continuing focus.

REFERENCES

Dalgaard, K. A., Brazzel, M., Liles, R. T., Sanderson, D., & Taylor-Powell, E. (1988). *Issues programming in extension* (Joint publication of ES-USDA, ECOP, and Minnesota Extension Service). St. Paul: University of Minnesota.

Futures Task Force to the Extension Committee on Organization & Policy. (1987). *Extension in transition—Bridging the gap between vision and and reality.* Washington, DC: Author.

Knowles, S. (1962). *The adult education movement in the United States.* New York: Holt, Reinhart and Winston, Inc.

Knowles, M. (1978). *The adult learner: A neglected species* (2nd ed.). Houston: Gulf.

Norman, C., & Williams, R. (1989). Futures oriented public policy education. *Journal of Extension, 27,* 9–10.

Rasmussen, D. (1989). *Taking the university to the people—Seventy-five years of cooperative extension.* Ames: Iowa State University Press.

Ratchford, C. (1984). Extension: Unchanging, but changing. *Journal of Extension, 22,* 8–15.

Sanders, H. C., Arbour, M. B., Bourg, T., Clark, R. C., Fritchey, F. P., & Jones, Jr., J. H. (Eds.). (1966). *The cooperative extension service.* Englewood Cliffs: Prentice-Hall.

Sanderson, D. R., Beard, R., Cyr, L., & Griffin, C. (1988). *Working with our publics: Understanding cooperative extension: our origins, our opportunities* (Module 1 of a series on in-service education for cooperative extension). Raleigh: North Carolina State University.

Sauer, R. J. (1990). Youth at risk: Extension's hard decisions. *Journal of Extension, 28,* 4–7.

Stefferud, A. (Ed.), (1962). *After a hundred years—The yearbook of agriculture 1962.* Washington, DC: U.S. Department of Agriculture.

Whitehead, A. N. (1931). Introduction. In W. B. Donam, *Business adrift* (pp. viii–xix). New York: McGraw-Hill.

CHAPTER 9

Rural Community Adult Education

MICHAEL W. GALBRAITH
DAVID W. PRICE

Adult education whether in rural or urban areas, has always been carried out by a variety of agencies and organizations with a plethora of purposes and with and for many different kinds of people. Within this conceptual framework, adult education characterizes and contributes to the dimensions of vertical (birth to death) and horizontal (linking education and life) integration aspects of lifelong education (see Chapter 1). The vertical and horizontal integration of education with life is only realized through the capacity of individuals to make life a sustained and cumulative process of educational interactive episodes. The community, therefore, can serve as the fundamental locus of lifelong educational practice (Galbraith, 1990). As the vessel in which life is contained and the medium through which living occurs, the whole of the community's physical and social resources and the dynamics of intracommunity interaction and change are the field of the educational environments. The community through its interaction with educational providers, adult educators, and learners, then, is a principal focus within rural community adult education practices.

The purpose of this chapter is to examine the concepts of community, rurality, and community adult education, and to discuss various organizational frameworks within adult education and the types of programs and providers associated with each that affect rural adult leaders. The chapter concludes with a brief discussion concerning the future of rural community adult education.

CONCEPT OF COMMUNITY

The field of community studies has over the years yielded an impressive number and variety of operational definitions of community which

169

include social interaction, common ties, and locational criteria as definitive of the concept (Warren, 1978). The emphases of human interaction and relationships within places, and commonalities in interests, values, and mores, are frequently cited attributes of "community," as well as in the casual use of the term such as "sense of community," and "community interests," and so forth. It is primarily the locational emphasis and geographic connotation of community to which we refer in our discussion of rural community adult education programs since it is largely within this geographical context that the resources and provisions for lifelong education practice are realized. However, other nongeographical criteria of the term merit some particular attention (see Chapter 1). Brookfield (1983a) suggests that, aside from the familiar locational expression of community, there are "communities of interest" and "communities of function" which may supersede geographic boundaries. Communities of interest are those groups of individuals bound by some single common interest or set of common interests. This category is wide ranging, including leisure interests (hobbies, sports, and various recreational interests), civic and special political interests (better government, improved health care, pro-life or pro-choice concerns, environmental protection) as well as including the communities of interest formed around particular spiritual and religious beliefs and affiliations. Communities of function are those groups identified by the function of major life roles, including vocational and professional (teachers, attorneys, mechanics, street workers, small business operators, farmers), as well as other major life role functions such as those of homemaker, student, and parent. As is readily apparent, communities of interest, communities of function, and geographic communities intersect and overlap.

Another typology of the concept of community is derived from the field of educational marketing. Besides the geographic concept of community, demographic and psychographic communities exist. Demographic communities are those groups bound by common demographic characteristics such as race, sex, age cohort, religion, and occupation. It is not uncommon to speak of "the black community" or "the elderly community." Psychographic communities are those formed by commonality of value systems, social class, lifestyle, special interests, and hobbies. A psychographic community, for example, may be the "yuppy community," the "gay community," or the "baseball community."

Nonlocational conceptions of community bear special consideration in community adult education practice on two particularly salient points. First, it is precisely these nongeographic features of community through which formal, nonformal, and informal adult learning is facilitated, and by which adult educational programs often are designed.

These concepts of community derive from and address the needs and interests of the adult learner. Clientele needs and interests-based programming have been a hallmark of community adult education since its inception as a professional practice (DeLargy, 1989). So persistent and integral has been the notion of meeting the needs of learners that it has become a shibboleth in the rhetoric of the field. Second, the nonlocational conceptions of community transcend geographic boundaries, calling attention to the fact that while community adult education relies principally on the geographic concept of community, the extra-community patterns of interaction impact markedly on community-based programs. So profound is this impact that some community adult educators find it productive to dismiss altogether the geographic and locational emphasis of community and to focus solely on the commonalities of interests, concerns, and functions of people in operationalizing the concept (Roberts, 1979). Although we contend that the geographical emphasis is the single most definitive feature of the concept of community for the practice of community adult education, these other dimensions cannot be dismissed or regarded as irrelevant. Indeed, to do so would rob the concept of certain emotive and practical qualities that are particularly germane to lifelong education in rural America (Galbraith & Price, 1991).

RURALITY AND COMMUNITY ADULT EDUCATION

Although there is little agreement among academics and governmental agencies as to just what qualitative and quantitative features constitute rurality (DeYoung, 1987; Ilvento, Fendley, & Christenson, 1988; Rios, 1988; Van Tilburg & Moore, 1989), it is generally acknowledged that rural areas in North America are characterized by low population density, a limited resource base in human as well as financial capital, a lack of specialization and diversity, a tendency toward relative isolation, and closely knit homogeneous communities (Amato, 1980; Barker, 1985; McCannon, 1983, 1985; Whitaker, 1982). Bunce (1982) and DeYoung (1987) suggest that rural should be viewed as a unique subculture in which a unified group is sharing common characteristics, attitudes, values, and motivations. Consequently, Van Tilburg and Moore (1989) suggest that "educators can approach rural adult education by drawing on the cultural traits that bind all rural adults together" (p.539). Unfortunately, common bonds and cultural traits among rural adult learners are not easily identified. Rural and urban learners are, in fact, quite similar in their characterization by sex, age, reason for participation in adult education, subjects enrolled, type of provider, number of courses taken, and source of payment (Galbraith & Sundet, 1988, 1990; McCannon, 1985; Sundet & Galbraith, 1990). However, formidable contrasts do exist within the rural adult education milieu. It is these elements of the rural environment that present special problems and considerations to rural community adult education providers not generally attendant among their urban counterparts. Given smaller adult populations and greater distances between potential clientele and service centers, the participation rates for specific adult and community education services may be lower, resulting in an overall higher cost of providership. Compounding the problem, many adult and community education providers are dependent partially, if not wholly, on financing from local governmental units (municipal, county, and school districts). Lower tax bases in rural areas mean fewer revenues on which to operate public services of all kinds, including those for adult learners, if governmental units are able to provide them at all. Additionally, the availability and quality of complementary services such as libraries, community colleges, and vocational-technical schools, are often times limited in rural areas, further frustrating the work of community adult education programmers who are dependent on a supporting network of related community services. The lack of diversity and specialization in human capital which is typical in small rural communities presents the educational programmer with a smaller resource base from which to draw in recruiting instructors, volunteers, and other resource people in the development and provision of needed community adult education programs. The relative isolation and homogeneity of rural community people and their general lack of exposure to diversity in lifestyles, ideas, and values may also present special problems in the development of effective community adult education programs. Program development in community adult education extensively relies on the determination of local educational needs by local client groups and community leaders. Where the scope of vision of local people is limited to a relatively narrow and homogeneous set of life experiences, greater gaps may exist between their felt needs and perceived opportunities and the actual or real needs and opportunities of their community.

The foregoing conditions of the rural community environment suggest certain distinct approaches and considerations for the practice of community adult education in rural areas. Of particular merit is the value of interagency cooperation. The coordination and integration of community adult education program development and delivery by various providers in rural communities can potentially reduce provider costs, and enhance community-wide adult education impacts. Interagency cooperation in the assessment of community needs through periodic community-wide surveys, for example, can serve as a way to identify and prioritize community needs and interests in a wide range of community functions: civic, recreational, educational, spiritual, economic, social, political, and so forth. Perceived needs-based data derived from such surveys, along with demographic and economic data gathered from various community sources, can be shared among agency providers. Similarly, cooperatively developed community resource inventories, including a community-wide skills or talent bank, can be shared among and productively used by various providers in the community. Other areas of interagency cooperation include collaboration in the development and use of computer-based data such as mailing lists and locally generated demographic data, and shared meeting facilities and resource persons. While important, given the resource limitations of rural communities, the cost savings to providers may not be the most valuable gains to be realized through this interagency cooperation. Rural providers can effectively leverage previously unrealized community educational resources by initiating community-wide interagency cooperative efforts. When providers whose central purpose is community adult education (community school, county extension service, or public adult basic education center) cooperate with institutions whose adult educational functions are noncentral or auxiliary (church organizations, civic and service clubs, private industries, libraries, chambers of commerce, or local business associations), it enhances the educational functions of all these community institutions with educational potential. Such concerted efforts develop and strengthen the horizontal community adult education infrastructure in the rural community, thereby creating an interrelated network of institutional providers. When such developmental efforts are intensified over time, they can effectively transform an educationally resource-poor community into one rich in lifelong education opportunities and functions (Galbraith, 1990).

TYPES OF PROGRAMS AND PROVIDERS

Various frameworks and classifications have been developed that attempt to capture the essence of the adult education delivery system (Apps, 1989; Darkenwald & Merriam, 1982; Schroeder, 1970). The most recent framework developed has been by Apps (1989) in which he identifies four provider categories: tax supported, nonprofit, for profit, and nonorganized. He bases his frameowrk "on the assumption that adult learners have choices for learning opportunities" (p. 279) and that learners can engage in deliberate and nondeliberate learning within all four categories. Tax-supported agencies or institutions may consist of adult public schools, four-year colleges and universities, community and technical colleges, cooperative extension, the armed forces, libraries, or museums. The nonprofit category would comprise religious institutions, health institutions, community-based agencies, service clubs, voluntary organizations, professional associations, and worker education programs. Correspondence schools, proprietary schools, private tutoring, publications, business and industry human resource development programs, and conference centers are examples of for-profit providers. Apps's fourth category is concerned with nonorganized learning opportunities such as those experienced through the mass media, work setting, family, travel, and recreational and leisure-time activities. While many of the specific providers may not be housed or easily located in rural America, an abundance of the providers mentioned are present and do provide educational opportunities to the rural adult learner.

In an effort to understand and connect the concepts of community and adult education, Brookfield (1983b) has proposed a three-fold typology of community adult education according to characteristic approaches employed by providers. These are adult education *for, in,* and *of* the community. Although the conceptual typology advanced by Brookfield is not specific to the rural practice of community adult education, programs and providers of all three types are found to operate in rural America. The three-fold typology suggested by Brookfield can easily be identified within Apps's framework of providers mentioned above.

Adult Education for the Community

This classification has as its central feature a consumer-oriented, market sensitive modus operandi. Specific programs are designed and delivered in response to perceived clientele interests within a specified agency service area. Programs *for* the community tend to be formal courses, workshops, seminars, or short courses; and program content is wide ranging, depending on the availability of resource persons, cost-effectiveness and marketability. In the context of lifelong education, such approaches contribute to the satisfaction of the ongoing expressed and felt needs and interests of learning activity oriented community members.

Programs and Providers

One of the more prevalent examples of rural adult education *for* the community is the publicly sponsored community school. Responsible for addressing community educational needs and interests through the public school system, its programs provide a broad spectrum of courses and workshops for adults. Class offerings will often include technical and occupational related courses (computing skills, beginning real estate), leisure and recreational courses (angling, home horticulture, various arts and crafts classes), family and personal improvement (parenting, family finance, stress management, auto repair), and personal enrichment topics (foreign languages, various music classes). Classes are typically offered during evenings and weekends in public school facilities and are taught by local community members interested in sharing their particular skills and talents through part-time teaching. The community school program in the United States is most often financed through a mix of state and local monies, and coordinated by a professional community school director employed by the local school district. Community school programs in Canada are more likely to be locally financed, and sponsored by non-profit agencies such as community development corporations and economic development groups, rather attached to public schools (Delargy, 1989).

A prominent feature of the rural community adult education landscape is the U.S. Cooperative Extension Service (CES). Mandated by Congress since the 1913 Smith-Lever Act, the CES links the resources of state land-grant universities with the educational needs of adults in rural communities. Programs are carried out by professional and paraprofessional staffs through county extension centers, involve a variety of formal, nonformal, and informal educational approaches, and address clientele-identified needs in the principal areas of agriculture, home economics, and community resource development. Many specific extension service projects and efforts characteristically reflect programmatic approaches *in* and *of* the community rather than *for* the community as here indicated. However, taken as a whole and given the organization's pervasive and historical commitment to locally determined needs, the agency is first a provider of adult education *for* the community. This may shift. As a result of several pressures including fiscal austerity, increased concern for accountability, and demographic and socioeconomic changes, the CES nationwide is at present undergoing a fundamental transition in its mission and approaches to serving rural America. At the heart of the change is a shift away from a primarily locally driven needs determination and reactive mode of program development and toward a national and regional issues-based approach to educational needs and pro-active mode of program development (see Chapter 8). This may signal as well a shift from educational programming *for* the community toward an emphasis on adult education *of* the community.

Municipal recreation departments, especially those situated in medium sized rural communities, also provide a variety of leisure and recreation adult educational programs for the community. Educational services may include adult swimming classes, classes in various sports (tennis, angling), nature studies, and arts and crafts workshops and courses. Programs are typically supported through a mix of course fees and municipal revenues.

Senior citizen centers or older adult activity centers are another source of adult education programs for the rural community. Established and financed primarily through state funds, senior centers host a variety of services, including adult educational programs in the enrichment, self-improvement, and skill areas. Public health agencies and rural hospitals, in addition to their primary role as health care providers, in many communities offer adult health-related educational programs for the community.

State and regional colleges and universities also contribute to the educational opportunities for rural adult learners within their specific community locale, especially the community college (Treadway, 1984). The community college has since its inception, served as a principal provider of adult education for the rural community (Cohen & Brawer, 1982; Sullins & Atwell, 1986; Van Tilburg & Moore, 1989). In addition to its academic collegiate functions, many community colleges offer a wide variety of noncredit adult education workshops, courses, and seminars depending on expressed community interests. Community adult education programs through the community college are usually subsumed under the rubric community services and administered by a professional community services coordinator. Shearon and Tollefson (1989) predict that this function of the community college will continue to expand during the 1990s.

Private and nonprofit educational institutions also provide education for the community. For example, the Adult Learning Center in Nashua, New Hampshire, is a private, nonprofit corporation organized to provide relevant educational programs for disadvantaged and undereducated area residents. Its programs include ABE, GED, ESL and life skill classes, vocational programs that deal with computer literacy, resume construction, and word processing, as well as career planning and counseling. In addition, higher educational programs exist that are primarily organized and operated for a specific population within a rural community or region. In Stilwell, Oklahoma, the Flaming Rainbow University primarily serves Cherokee Indians and other low-income and educationally underserved people of rural northeastern Oklahoma. Its programs are life-centered with a curriculum designed to incorporate job and life experiences, community and tribal involvements, and a cross-cultural environment.

Adult Education in the Community

This second type of community adult education identified by Brookfield (1983b) seeks to encourage, support, and enhance the educational dimensions of community efforts and activities as they emerge in the natural course of community life. In this mode of practice the community adult educator serves as a resource person, encourager, and process facilitator for the educational dimensions inherent in the activities of various community groups (Jeffs & Smith, 1990). The practitioner often times serves to catalyze valuable learning processes among group members, that might otherwise fail to emerge, in the context of ongoing community group efforts. The community adult education practitioner becomes immersed in the life of the community and seeks to fit into and influence the natural learning processes of individuals and groups. This approach to the community is referred to by one analyst as justified community infiltration (Polsky, 1978) and is strongly recommended by the findings of Canadian adult learning researcher Allen Tough (1983). This approach to community adult education recognizes and focuses professional attention on the vast and largely unrecognized portion of adult learning occurring in the natural course of individual and community life (Brookfield, 1983b). Adult education *in* the community, however, is not limited to group work but also includes practices that support and enhance the self-initiated and self-guided learning efforts undertaken by individual community members, by providing such learners, for example, with resource information and materials, advice, and educational consultation. Whether in the group or individual context, the important distinction between this mode of practice and other forms of community adult education is that community members themselves control all determinations of content, format, and duration of the educational episodes in which they engage (Brookfield, 1983b). As is apparent, this category typically incorporates nonformal and informal adult education practices. Also included are those formal community adult education practices that use the community environment as a learning resource or laboratory, wherein program participants study various aspects of community life and functions. Site visits to local institutions (industries or governmental offices, for example), personal interviews with community members, windshield surveys of local neighborhoods followed by group discussion and analysis, and in-classroom presentations by local experts are some techniques exemplifying this form of community adult education. In the context of lifelong education, programs of adult education in the community contribute greatly to the dimension of learning how-to-learn. Whether in the informal and nonformal educational modes characteristic of community group efforts and individual self-directed learning projects, or in the more formal class using the community as a laboratory, participants develop knowledge, skills, attitudes, and other competencies for learning from and in their community environment. The horizontal dimension of lifelong education is emphasized and strengthened.

Programs and Providers

To describe programs and providers of adult education practice *in* the community is an ambiguous and illusive task. Few, if any, agency providers conform wholly to this community adult education form, but rather, a myriad of community-based providers incorporate, somewhat unevenly, education in the community into their broader educational agendas. From the previous discussion three distinct manifestations of adult education in the community are noted:

1. Education through infiltration and influence of community action groups

2. Community as learning resource for organized adult education classes

3. Support for self-directed learning

The technique of infiltration and influence is most often associated with community organization and development practitioners and agencies. Although their efforts are properly classified as education for the community, given their usually heavy agendas of preconceived notions of community deficiency, much of the work in this field of community practice emphasizes supportive and enabling educational functions with group participants engaged in community action efforts (Morris, 1970; Rothman & Trotman, 1987). Thus, the infiltration and influence approach is seen in the work of community development specialists employed by the Cooperative Extension Service, rural community workers for the federal and state supported Community Action Agencies, church and community workers associated with rural ministries, economic development specialists employed by chambers of commerce in medium sized rural communities, and a host of other rural community-based organizations and practitioners. The use of the community as a learning resource for organized classes is, unfortunately, an all too infrequently used adult education method (Brookfield, 1983b). Such approaches, however, do find occasional application through the community service course offerings in rural community colleges, community schools, and county extension service programs. A County Extension Homemakers Council in Howell County, Missouri, for example, sponsors an annual local government day in which members of the extension's homemaker clubs countywide visit various offices of city and county government to hear informal presentations by local officials on the functions and operations of their offices. The visitations are followed by a group meeting led by an extension educator in which participants discuss and critique their experiences. Similar programs sponsored by county extension centers have taken community members to local manufacturing plants, specialized farm operations, and other rural community institutions. Support for the self-directed learning efforts of rural community members include, among other things, the provision of informational brochures, guides, books, and videotapes on a variety of subject areas, and the provision of advice and educational counselling. Rural libraries and their staffs have traditionally served as important resources for self-directed learners (Neehall & Tough, 1983), as have CES county extension centers and staffs and their practical bulletins on topics ranging from parenting skills to farm water supplies to repairing leaky faucets. Commercial noneducational institutions also contribute to the informational demands of adult self-directed learning projects. Many building supply and hardward retailers, for example, display racks of free fliers that help people with various home repair and building construction projects. The retailers themselves offer customer advice on such projects. Similarly, financial institutions, medical, dental, and optometry offices, and various other public and private institutions serve as learning resources for adults interested in gaining awareness, knowledge, and skills in particular subjects highly relevant to their daily lives. Recognition of the value to community adult education of such commonplace learning resources present in the community, and potentials for their enhancement, has been emphasized in the research and writings of community adult educators such as Brookfield (1983a, 1983b), Galbraith (1990), Hiemstra (1972), Knowles (1984), and Tough (1982).

Adult Education of the Community

In the third type of community adult education practice identified, program approaches are strongly prescriptive (Brookfield, 1983b). The community is viewed by the provider as deficient or lacking in certain features or qualities, be it effective leadership, self-reliance skills, esprit de corps, or economic viability. A gap between what is and what ought to be is perceived by the provider. Educational programs, then, are geared to address the deficiencies and narrow the gap. Several community adult educators use the concept of community health to describe such desired community qualities (Brookfield, 1983b; Lackey, Burke & Peterson, 1987); while others have used the terms "good community," "competent community," and "community well-being," (Lackey, Burke, & Peterson, 1987, p. 2). In a 1987 article, Lackey, Burke & Peterson propose essential attributes of a healthy community as consisting of certain "(1) attitudes and values, (2) capacities, (3) organization and (4) leadership" (p. 3).

Programs in this category are distinctive in their normative approach to the community. Whereas adult community education practitioners of the other two types respond to or engage in the expressed and felt community needs and naturally occurring movements, the practitioner of adult education *of* the community designs programs on the basis of his/her own perceptions and values of what constitutes a healthy community, and the attitudes and competencies desired of community members. According to Brookfield (1983b), "this avowedly prescriptive notion of community adult education is close to the classic tradition of citizenship training in which a vigorous, democratic society is seen as being dependent on the development of certain informed critical faculties among its members" (p. 157). This prescriptive approach to community adult education is not unlike the ideals of lifelong education in the rural community, which itself can be viewed as a prescription for a healthy community.

Programs and Providers

One of the most prominent forms of the professional practice of adult education *of* the community is community development. Although a great many definitions of community development are advanced in the literature, most emphasize an educational process dimension (Hamilton & Cunningham, 1989). Essentially, community development is an adult educational process whereby participants gain the attitudes, skills, and knowledge empowering them to achieve their mutually determined goals of community improvement and problem resolution. This particular form of community adult education practice is referred to by other names: "community education for development" (Compton & McClusky, 1980), "locality development" (Rothman & Tropman, 1987), and "community resource development" (Phifer, List, & Faulkner, 1980); however, "community development" appears to be the most widely accepted and durable of the appellations. Community development providers serving rural areas in North America include the Cooperative Extension Service, rural local governments, state agencies of community and economic development, and a variety of nonprofit organizations. The specific task accomplishments of community development projects vary widely, but some in recent years have included retail business development in economically declining rural towns, the establishment of new occupational avenues for displaced farmers and displaced homemakers, and the restoration and preservation of rural community historical sites. One rural nonprofit community development organization of singular recognition is the Highlander Research and Education Center in New Market, Tennessee. Established in 1931, and particularly noted for leadership training in the southern labor move-

ment of the 1930s and on behalf of civil rights in the 1950s, the Highlander Center has addressed issues of rural social justice through community adult education for nearly sixty years (Glen, 1988). Current
programs of the Highlander Center include environmental issues and
economic development (Highlander Research and Education Center,
1987).

In addition to the Highlander Center, other community-based organizations are found within rural America that contribute to the specific
educational, community and personal development of its adult learners.
For example, the Dungannon Development Commission (DDC) in Dungannon, Virginia, was formed in 1979 by fifty townspeople in an effort to
improve the Dungannon community. The DDC promotes the development of business concerns, cooperates with the town of Dungannon,
engages in housing production to improve living conditions, and works
with a nearby community college in maintaining community-based
classes for the rural community. Another example is the Federation of
Southern Cooperatives located in Epes, Alabama. It operates the Rural
Training, Research and Demonstration-Farming Center which also serves
as the headquarters for the total economic development movement in the
South. The federation's mission is to formulate and implement a comprehensive rural economic development strategy. It serves 30,000 families
organized in 120 cooperatives in various rural communities.

From this discussion of rural adult community education it is possible to generate various images. Some of these images will be about the
providers of education; others will be directed at the adult learner or
adult educator; still others toward the educational topics, agendas, and
purposes. Each holds as its primary focus educational opportunities for
learners to engage in deliberate and nondeliberate learning. The goal is to
enhance the intellectual, social, political, recreational, and professional
aspects of their lives. The interactions of community, rurality, education
provider, adult learner, and adult educator contribute to the development, structure, and implementation of effective rural adult community
education programs. Rural America holds this great potential for its adult
learners.

THE FUTURE OF RURAL COMMUNITY ADULT EDUCATION

If rural communities accept the idea that education is a function
reserved for childhood and adolescence, then the concept of lifelong education and the dynamic dimensions and opportunities that it presents will
be lost. Galbraith and Sundet (1988) found in their study that used a key

informant analysis that the rural culture seems to dictate that the function of education is more formal in nature. Education is not perceived as a lifelong process that accepts informal and nonformal mechanisms throughout adulthood as being valid and meaningful education. The need exists for rural America to understand the vertical and horizontal integration of lifelong education and the potential it holds for the development of effective community adult education.

Hesser, Spears and Maes (1988) suggest that rural adult education can address some of the persisting social and economic concerns that now confront the rural community. Community adult education can help reduce the marginality that rural America now holds as it relates to the disproportionate amount of economic and institutional resources. Through social and political intervention, rural adult education can increase its level of empowerment by raising the national consciousness toward rural America, by developing strong ties with the state and federal government policy and decision makers, by constructing a solid economic development plan that would keep the "rural investment of resources local" (p. 12), and by developing the human resource potential. Lifelong education must play an important role in the future success of the social, political, economic and educational aspects within the rural community. It calls for rural adults to engage in social and political activity and to understand that an educated populace can reduce the barriers that confront and inhibit the development of human potential. Emery (1988) and Bailey and Hesser (1988) say that educational outreach and institutional cooperation are essential. However, the cultural and community dynamics must always be understood and in the forefront of the thinking as linkages between learners, agencies, and institutions are developed.

In addition, future forms, content, and value of rural community adult education will be shaped by various societal trends. Chief among these are demographic changes, technological changes—especially communications technologies—and the growing degree of complexity of society itself. The aging of rural America suggests that the culture will give way to an older and more mature society and with it an increased demand in the educational marketplace for formats, methodologies, and content geared to the unique characteristics of adult learners. Cohen and Brawer (1989) and Sullins and Atwell (1986) indicate that the increase in adult community members will place greater demands on the community service functions of the community college. Other institutions of higher education must also reevaluate their missions, goals, and delivery modes if they are to effectively serve the rural adult learner and the community (Treadway, 1984). Institutions must view themselves as providers of formal as well as nonformal educational opportunities for all adult learners within their delivery system. They must respond to the professional as well as the paraprofessional who seeks a response to professional and personal needs such as continuing education, certification, licensure, stress management, caregiving to older parents, displacement from agricultural occupations, unemployment, and the rural crisis in general. The demographic changes influence the demands placed upon all community adult education providers, thus calling out for greater interagency cooperation among educational, religious, social, and human service providers. Rural adult educators can play an important role in the coordination and development of these linkages.

New technologies and the advent of the so-called information society also will markedly impact rural America. Conditions of relative isolation and access to economic resources, which had traditionally constrained and largely defined rural society, are dissipating as new communications technologies give rural adults access to many of the commercial and cultural features of urban and metropolitan communities (Black, 1986). Economic development in rural areas, largely confined to extractive industries and highly dependent on transportation considerations, may increasingly be based on an information economy enabled by communications rather than transportation. The development of "footloose enterprises," in which geographic location plays no part, will open the doors of opportunity to various forms of economic activity and entrepreneurship in rural areas. An example of this type of enterprise is the development of an 800 number service in which an 800 number is called for information or the purchasing of various products. The caller doesn't know or care where that call is actually being received. In the case of ordering merchandise or services (such as airline tickets) through the 800 number service, orders are then "faxed" to the various manufacturers or service providers to be completed. As telecommunications technologies build and enhance new extracommunity patterns of interaction, not only will rural-urban relationships change, but ties among rural areas throughout North America will develop. Already, computer mediated communications projects, such as Big Sky Telegraph at Western Montana College, offer residents of rural communities the opportunity for international dialogue and information exchange, virtually free of cost to them. Computer mediated communication technology offers enormous potential for enhanced dialogue and information transfer among both learners and institutional providers of community adult education. It creates opportunities for interagency cooperation and for the development of new modes of learning in the community environment. All told, the demands for information-age adult learning in rural areas may be as important in the next fifty years as a practical knowledge of agriculture has been to many rural adults in the past fifty. Communication technology and the changing nature of society to an information-oriented one will certainly require new thinking and action by adult educators with futuristic insight and vision. Its impact will affect the social, political, and educational dimensions of the rural community (Dillman, 1985). Technology and its relationship to rural America is examined in more depth elsewhere in this book.

The increasing complexity of society itself and the multitude of public issues born of it—driven by the rapidity of socioeconomic and technological change—will also impact adult learning needs in the rural community. There is growing concern that large numbers of adults will become eclipsed, unable to keep up and comprehend the nature of the complex social issues affecting their lives and communities (Wellborn, 1982). The future will bring a greater demand for community adult educational efforts, especially community development approaches. People need to understand and influence through collective action changes that impact their communities and their lives (Phifer, List, & Faulkner, 1980). Institutions of higher education, community schools, human service agencies, religious institutions, business and industry, libraries, and other community, social, and political action agencies must begin to recognize the benefit of cooperative ventures and the strength they can generate through such linkages. At the center of this cooperation is education and the potential it holds for empowering individuals to solve rural problems and building strong communication and sociopolitical networks. The future of rural America depends on many factors and facets; education is a primary player in the scenario.

CONCLUSION

Through community adult education and effective leadership, the opportunity to create lifelong learning communities for rural America holds great promise. Perhaps at the center of this optimism is the hope and persistence that rural America has always demonstrated throughout history. This chapter has examined the aspects of *for, in,* and *of* adult community education and the potential each has toward contributing to a bright and productive future for rural adult learners and their communities. Adult educators must help educate the various "communities" within the rural community to the potential that formal, informal, and nonformal education holds toward solving personal, professional, social, and political problems and concerns. It must be viewed as a lifelong process with all individuals contributing to the identification and resolution of such issues, problems, and concerns.

REFERENCES

Amato, J. (1980). *Countryside: Mirror of ourselves.* Marshall, MN: Southwest State University.

Apps, J. (1989). Providers of adult and continuing education: A framework. In S. Merriam & P. Cunningham (Eds.), *Handbook of adult and continuing education* (pp. 275–286). San Francisco: Jossey-Bass.

Bailey, G., & Hesser, J. (1988). Rural professionals: An untapped audience for continuing education. *Continuing Higher Education Review, 52*(1), 41–48.

Barker, B. (1985). Understanding rural adult learners: Characteristics and challenges. *Lifelong Learning: An Omnibus of Practice and Research, 9*(2), 4–7.

Black, J. (1986, October). *Reducing isolation: Telecommunications and rural development.* Paper presented at the Conference on Research on Computer Conferencing. Guelph, Ontario.

Brookfield, S. (1983a). *Adult learners, adult education and the community.* New York: Teachers College Press.

Brookfield, S. (1983b). Community adult education: A conceptual analysis. *Adult Education Quarterly, 33*(3), 154–160.

Bunce, M. (1982). *Rural settlements in an urban world.* New York: St. Martin's Press.

Cohen, A., & Brawer, F. (1989). *The American community college* (2nd. ed.). San Francisco: Jossey-Bass.

Compton, J., & McClusky, H. (1980). Community education for community development. In E. Boone and Associates, *Serving personal and community needs through adult education* (pp. 227–249). San Francisco: Jossey-Bass.

Darkenwald, G., & Merriam, S. (1982). *Adult education: Foundations of practice.* New York: Harper & Row.

DeLargy, P. F. (1989). Public schools and community education. In S. Merriam & P. Cunningham (Eds.), *Handbook of adult and continuing education* (pp. 287–302). San Francisco: Jossey-Bass.

DeYoung, A. (1987). The status of American rural education research: An integrated review and commentary. *Review of Educational Research, 57*(2), 123–148.

Dillman, D. (1985). The social impact of information technologies in rural North America. *Rural Sociology, 50*(1), 1–26.

Emery, M. (1988). Three models for improving access for rural adults with community connections. *Continuing Higher Education Review, 52*(1), 21–27.

Galbraith, M. W. (Ed.). (1990). *Education through community organizations.* New Directions for Adult and Continuing Education, no. 47. San Francisco: Jossey-Bass.

Galbraith, M. W., & Price, D. W. (1991). Community adult education in America: An overview. *New Horizons in Adult Education, 5*(1), 3–18.

Galbraith, M. W., & Sundet, P. A. (1988). Educational perspectives of rural adult learners: A key informant analysis. *Journal of Adult Education, 17*(1), 11–18.

Galbraith, M. W., & Sundet, P. A. (1990). Comparative analysis of barriers to participation in rural adult education programs. *Proceedings of the 31st Annual Adult Education Research Conference* (pp. 89–94). Athens: University of Georgia.

Glen, J. (1988). *Highlander, no ordinary school, 1932–1962.* Lexington: University of Kentucky Press.

Hamilton, E., & Cunningham, P. (1989). Community-based adult education. In S. Merriam & P. Cunningham (Eds.), *Handbook of adult and continuing education* (pp. 439–450). San Francisco: Jossey-Bass.

Hesser, J., Spears, J., & Maes, S. (1988). Action priorities for rural adult education. *Continuing Higher Education Review, 52*(1), 11–20.

Hiemstra, R. (1972). *The educative community.* Lincoln: Professional Educators Publications.

Highlander Research and Education Center (1987). *Highlander Review—'87.* New Market, TN: Author.

Ilvento, W., Fendley, K., & Christenson, J. (1988). Political definitions of rurality and their impact on federal grant distribution: The case for the Farmers Home Administration. *Journal of the Community Development Society, 19*(1), 1–20.

Jeffs, T, & Smith, M. (Eds.). (1990). *Using informal education: An alternative to casework, teaching and control.* Philadelphia: Open University Press.

Knowles, M. (1984). *The adult learner: A neglected species* (3rd ed.). Houston: Gulf.

Lackey, A., Burke, R., & Peterson, M. (1987). Healthy communities: The goal of community development. *Journal of the Community Development Society, 18*(2), 1–17.

McCannon, R. (1983). Serving rural adult learners. In C. Kasworm (Ed.), *Educational outreach to select adult population* (pp. 15–29). New Directions for Continuing Education, no. 20. San Francisco: Jossey-Bass.

McCannon, R. (1985). *Serving the rural adult: A demographic portrait of rural adult learners.* Manhattan, KS: The Action Agenda for Rural Adult Postsecondary Education.

Morris, R. (1970). The role of the agent in the community development process. In C. L. Cary (Ed.), *Community development as a process* (pp. 171–194). Columbia, MO: University of Missouri Press.

Neehall, J., & Tough, A. (1983). Fostering intentional changes among adults. *Library Trends, 31*(4), 543–553.

Peterson, M. (1986, August). *Marketing community development.* Paper presented at the meeting of the Community Development Society, Carbondale, IL.

Phifer, B., List, F., & Faulkner, B. (1980). History of community development in America. In J. Christenson & J. Robinson (Eds.), *Community development in America* (pp. 3–17). Ames: Iowa State University Press.

Polsky, H. (1978). Community needs assessment—Another viewpoint. In C. Klevins (Ed.), *Materials and methods in continuing education* (pp. 85–86). Los Angeles: Klevens.

Rios, B. R. (1988). *Rural—a concept beyond definition?* (Report No. EDO-RC-09). Las Cruces, NM: New Mexico State University, ERIC/CRESS. (ERIC Document Reproduction Service No. ED 296820)

Roberts, H. (1979). *Community development: Learning and action.* Toronto: University of Toronto Press.

Rothman, J., & Tropman, J. (1987). Models of community organization and macro practice perspectives: Their mixing and phasing. In F. Cox, J. Erlich, J. Rothman & J. Tropman (Eds.), *Strategies of community organization* (pp. 3–26). Itasca, IL: Peacock.

Schroeder, W. (1970). Adult education defined and described. In R. Smith, G. Aker & J. Kidd (Eds.), *Handbook of adult education* (pp. 25–43). New York: Macmillan.

Shearon, R., & Tollefson, T. (1989). Community colleges. In S. Merriam & P. Cunningham (Eds.), *Handbook of adult and continuing education* (pp. 316–331). San Francisco: Jossey-Bass.

Sundet, P. A., & Galbraith, M. W. (1990, April), *Adult education as a response to the rural crisis: Factors governing utility and participation.* Paper presented at the annual meeting of the American Educational Research Association, Boston, MA.

Tough, A. (1982). *Intentional changes: A fresh approach to helping people change.* Chicago: Follett.

Treadway, D. (1984). *Higher education in rural America: Serving the adult learner.* New York: College Entrance Examination Board.

Van Tilburg, E., & Moore, A. (1989). Education for rural adults. In S.

Merriam & P. Cunningham (Eds.), *Handbook of adult and continuing education* (pp. 537–549). San Francisco: Jossey-Bass.

Warren, R. L. (1978). *The community in America* (3rd. ed.). Chicago: Rand McNally.

Wellborn, S. (1982, May 17). Ahead, a nation of illiterates. *U.S. News and World Report,* pp. 53–56.

Whitaker, W. (1982). *The many faces of Ephraim: In search of a functional topology of rural areas.* (Report No. RC 014 680). Orono: University of Maine. (ERIC Document Reproduction Service No. ED 242459)

CHAPTER 10

Special Interest Organizations
WILLIAM S. GRIFFITH

Special interest organizations address concerns of the rural society. As is the case in urban areas, these organizations have been developed to serve the specialized interests of specific groups. The unique aspect of rural America is that the agricultural sector is now only a small percentage of the total rural population. Nevertheless, a large proportion of these rural organizations were established to serve the farming population. In this chapter some of the social, fraternal, and economic organizations found in nonmetropolitan areas will be discussed and their special relationship to the rural population will be examined. Some attention must be given to the relationship of the formal educational system to the nonformal one, since the latter is often confronted with the necessity of dealing with problems that may have been produced by the former. Finally, attention will be given to the kinds of adjustments that seem essential if the social, fraternal, and economic organizations of rural America and Canada are to make their most effective contribution to lifelong learning.

THE CHANGING RURAL POPULATION

Rural is definitely not a synonym for *farm* today because the proportion of rural residents engaged in farming has dropped from a majority to a small and still shrinking minority. Accordingly, those who examine the educational system of rural society are finding that while they may continue to consider the agricultural producers, placing primary emphasis on this small group is not appropriate if the purpose of the education is to serve the entire rural population.

Nachtigal (1982) developed a taxonomy of rural America based on the characteristics of the residents. The first category is described as the people left behind. They are below the national averages for almost all measures of the good life. For these individuals the basic socioeconomic problems are so overwhelming that an approach to remediation through education is not likely to be of any value. The second category can be thought of as traditional rural America with productive farms, well-kept homes and communities, a puritan work ethic, and a politically active population. These are agricultural producers and the professional people in the communities that service their needs. Such people are prepared to participate in education and to consider alternative ways of farming as well as living. The third category is found in communities in transition. In such communities the majority of the population are commuters who have moved to the rural area for recreation, for lower costs, and to provide a more attractive environment for their families than they can afford to enjoy in the urban areas. The development of adult education programs for the rural areas has tended to fit the interests of only the second of the three groups.

Killacky (1984) noted that "Between 1975 and 1981 rural participants in adult education grew from 4.3 million to 5.8 million" (p. 12). While the number of agricultural producers was decreasing, the number of adult education participants was increasing, possibly indicating the greater tendency of the commuters to seek adult education. The extent of commuter involvement in programs serving the farming people has not been established.

PARTICIPATION AND SPONSORSHIP

Rural learners find tuition costs and transportation problems difficult obstacles. The rural population on average is older and has a lower level of formal education than its urban counterparts. Although characteristics of rural and urban populations differ significantly, both have similar continuing education needs (Barker, 1985).

McCannon (1985) conducted a survey of 3,560 rural residents and found that 94.9 percent of the participants were not farm residents. The providers of the adult education programs for this audience are shown in Table 10.1.

Based on his study of the census data and a comparison of rural and urban adult education participants, McCannon (1985) concluded rural adults take part in adult education for occupational advancement and personal development. They are clearly not primarily interested in education for remedial or recreational purposes, if at all. Instead of being concerned with problems of subsistence, illiteracy, and elementary sanita-

Table 10.1   Types of Providers of Adult Education Courses
Participated in by Rural Adults

Type of Provider	Percentage Attracted
2-year College	17.3%
4-year College	16.5%
Business & Industry	13.9%
Vocational/Technical Schools	11.0%
Government	10.2%
Community Organizations	9.8%
Elementary & Secondary Schools	6.0%
Tutors	5.2%
Labor & Professional Organizations	4.0%
Other	4.1%
Other Schools	1.8%

(source-McCannon, 1985:ii)

tion, rural communities are facing more complex problems. Community life must adjust to rapid and far-reaching changes in the quantity and makeup of the population. People must learn how to bring the various groups together into one effective working group that is both well-informed concerning the nature of its problems and willing to undertake their analysis and solution. It is a challenge to the creative programmer of adult education to address such conditions rather than serving only the easiest to reach segment.

Spears and Maes (1985) examined adult education in rural communities and emphasized that no one educational provider seems best suited to provide services to rural learners. They identified characteristics of successful programs:

1. Each program responds to a specific need.

2. Each program is designed to fit the intended learners' expectations.

3. All programs are cooperatively planned with other agencies rather than being conducted under sole sponsorship.

4. Supporting advertising and printed materials are presented in concise and jargon-free language.

Treadway (1984) observes that rural adult educators seem to agree that social interaction is one of the primary motivators for adults to take part in education programs. Adult education is small towns tends to center around educational programs with social benefits to the community such as parenting classes, practical skills for farm, home or small business, health, nutrition, local history, culture, and arts. The problem seems to be that members from all three of the groups previously identified by Nachtigal do not seem to be equally willing to participate in programs.

The Illinois Agricultural Leadership Foundation conducts an annual agricultural leadership program to serve some thirty rural men and women, involving them in a series of twelve seminars, a ten-day travel seminar in the United States and a two-week international travel experience. The goals of the program are to: expand the participants' experience in the areas of professional improvement, communication, current issues, public affairs, government, and business and industry; provide educational experiences at the local, state, and national levels; and improve the awareness and understanding of issues involving the rural and urban sectors in a changing political, technological, and increasingly urbanized domestic and international society (Hone, 1984). Such programs are important because they offer the opportunity for an elite group of those who have a basic commitment to their rural communities to acquire insights and understandings that may greatly increase their capacity to provide essential leadership in not only maintaining but also strengthening their home communities.

Treadway (1984) notes that:

> In the Province of Alberta, Canada, Further Education Councils have been established to mobilize all available resources to offer coordinated, comprehensive continuing education courses to adults. These councils are composed of community volunteers, as individuals, and as representatives of organizations who offer courses in the community. (p. 22)

The eighty-five Local Further Education Councils serve to bring together the agencies providing all types of noncredit adult education. In the rural areas the councils include volunteers and individuals who are simply interested members of their communities. Provincial financial support is generally provided to serve as a stimulus and not the major source of income, for the entire system was predicated in 1975 on the idea that voluntarism was to be encouraged and provided with only minimal financial assistance. The level of support is intented to provide for approximately a half-time salary for a coordinator who is regarded primarily as a volunteer.

These coordinators are community members with a commitment to adult education whether or not they have had any formal training to prepare them for their work. In the past fourteen years there has been a move toward developing a higher level of professional performance on the part of the coordinators, who themselves have organized an association called the Company of Coordinators which helps new coordinators to learn how to do their jobs and provides in-service training for established coordinators. This organization works closely with the Ministry of Advanced Education in planning meetings and in working within the Alberta Association for Continuing Education.

The Local Further Education Councils were established primarily to stimulate the rural areas to initiate adult education programs that would draw upon the talents and abilities of the local people rather than having them continue to be dependent upon the program planning and need identification carried out by educational institutions. In the major cities, Calgary and Edmonton, large-scale adult education programs were already being provided by the existing educational institutions, but in the rural areas the small number of educationally oriented institutions and organizations seemed disinclined to take the initiative in developing programs utilizing local talent. Accordingly, volunteers were the foundation of the Local Further Education Councils in many of the rural areas and these volunteers were enthusiastic and ingenious in identifying both educational needs and the educational resources that lay outside of the established educational institutions. A measure of their success is that the membership of the Local Further Education Councils in some of the rural areas is now made up almost entirely of representatives of institutions that are providing programs.

Largely due to the work of the Local Further Education Councils, which have made adult education opportunities available where previously none existed, the rate of participation in adult education by the people of the Province of Alberta has increased from one in ten in 1975 to one in four in 1989. Today the system must deal with the need to become more entrepreneurial as provincial funding has been capped. Further, the business orientation is an influence that tends to move the system away from its voluntary, part-time basis to an approach that requires sophisticated managerial and financial skills. Although the level of participation has been positively influenced over the past fifteen years, the rate of increase appears to have slowed and future expansion may require the use of more professional prepared leaders who will stimulate a fresh approach to need identification and program planning, supplanting the natural tendency to offer the same menu to the same group of learners perennially.

PROGRAMMING TO SERVE THE HARD TO REACH

Jensen (1985) reported on an innovative rural program designed to cross ethnic barriers in home economics in southern Dona Ana County in New Mexico. Although the first three of the criteria she used to assess success are traditional for agricultural extension activities, the fourth is not: (1) Level of involvement of women; (2) Ability to adapt national and state programs to local economic and social conditions and needs; (3) Amount and quality of technology transfer achieved; and (4) Number of rural people able to remain on the land. Increasing rural people's ability to meet their needs while they remain in the rural community is infrequently identified as a goal in traditional extension work where technology transfer is often the dominant, if not exclusive, concern.

Jensen noted that the shortage of agricultural agents able to work in Spanish, the fact that the Farm Bureau was clearly Anglo-oriented, and that the children's clubs were gender segregated all detracted from the effectiveness of the educational efforts. In the northern part of the county greater success was achieved by the Spanish speaking home demonstration agent who reported reaching 80 percent of the farm families by organizing thirteen adult clubs and children's food, clothing, and gardening clubs; providing weekly newspaper columns in Spanish; helping Hispanic women obtain canning equipment and sewing machines; encouraging women to take an interest in the interiors of their homes; and promoting the sale of traditional handicrafts. Taking the education to the learners and presenting it in their first language facilitates learning.

Participation is the result of adults' becoming aware of a program, perceiving the relevance of the content to their life situation, and having the opportunity to take part. Traditional advertising techniques are often not effective in attracting the hard to reach undereducated adults in rural areas. Havercamp (1988) in an innovative problem-solving adult education program was able to win the confidence and inspire the active participation of farm families in Michigan who were concerned about their life situations. Through systematic study they determined that it would be possible to grow their products with less dependence on chemical agents and then to market such products to urban families who were interested in buying organically grown foodstuffs. The greatest value of the program as perceived by the leader of the effort was not the direct financial improvement in these families' life situations, but rather their increased self-reliance and ability to work together in deciding how to improve their agricultural plans and practices. The end result was not the solution of a single problem, but rather the acquistion of problem-solving skills that would enable them to face future problems with increased assurance and effectiveness.

Sullins and Vogler (1986), who examined barriers to rural adult education, regard the potential participant's disposition as an important obstacle. They concluded that the most serious of these was a "faulty perception" on the part of rural adults regarding the linkage between education and good jobs by family, peers, and the community (p. 11).

McDaniel, Severinghaus, Rude, Gray, and Emery (1986) examined the barriers to participation in adult education by rural residents in seven northwestern states and reported that geographical isolation, weather, class scheduling, family responsibilities, time constraints, and limited access to advanced instructional technology were obstacles, but most respondents were successful in overcoming them. The researchers found that the providers and the learners were in relatively close agreement concerning the existence of institutional, informational, psychological, personal/situational, and policy impediments to participation by rural adults. There was no question but that rural residents who wish to pursue systematically organized adult instruction face both more and different kinds of barriers from those encountered by urban residents.

Lidster (1978) examined community adult education in the Northwest Territories of Canada and identified five philosophical considerations to successful programming:

1. Start where the people are.

2. Accept the notion that people are, psychologically, anxious to learn about events happening around them and exploding in their midst.

3. Take the programs to the people instead of requiring the people to come to the programs.

4. People respond to learning situations which they see as reponsive to their own immediate situation.

5. Work in harmony and accord with other locally bound agencies and government departments.

Lidster saw as critical the importance of developing progams **only** if they address needs which have been expressed by the people of the community and **only** if the people are prepared to take ownership of the program from its inception.

FARMER'S ORGANIZATIONS

Rural organizations have traditionally been equated with farmers' organizations. These have played and continue to play a significant role in the adult education of one segment of the rural communities—the agricultural producers. Even though they have not yet accepted the ideal of serving more than the farm communities, because of their historical significance three of them are deserving of specific attention. The Grange, the Farm Bureau, and the Farmers Union have been instrumental in shaping rural communities and in influencing public policy in agriculture as well as in education. The big three farm organizations attract somewhat different members to programs that differ as well.

The Grange

The Grange is the oldest of the three major farm organizations which carry out programs of education in rural areas. In 1867 the founders of the Grange listed educating and elevating American farmers as a principal purpose for creating the organization. It has been called the great school out of school (Kreitlow, 1954). Strong interest in education is demonstrated in the local units' programs and in literature published in their state and national offices. An officer known as the lecturer is responsible for organizing the local unit's educational program. The duties of the lecturer include planning and directing the educational work of the local Grange; cooperating with other lecturers to exchange educational plans; encouragement of the appreciation of country life and satisfaction in rural living; and working to improve rural-urban relationships by promoting better understanding. There is not a clear commitment to welcoming into membership those who have no clear identification with agricultural production.

In 1886 the Juvenile Grange was established and in 1910 home economics education activities were authorized by the National Grange. They have worked on conservation projects as well as the establishment of circulating libraries (Kreitlow, 1954). Nevertheless, the focus is on the farm people and little is being done to enlarge the membership by seeking out individuals and groups who share many of the basic convictions of the Grange.

Much of the work of the Grange is political in nature, but even that can be viewed as educational. In fact, there has been a continuing effort on the part of the national and state leadership to encourage local units to emphasize their educational roles. Membership in the Grange is on an individual basis with anyone fourteen years of age or older eligible for membership. In the other two major organizations enrollment is on an entire family basis.

The Farm Bureau

The American Farm Bureau Federation is involved in a program of education related to legislation dealing with economic and educational matters. Its primary purpose is to promote, protect, and represent the business, economic, social, and educational interests of the American farm people and to develop agriculture. To achieve these intentions an ambitious program of education is essential. While the Farm Bureau was initially formed through the efforts of Cooperative Extension employees, the link between these two organizations has been weakened by administrative fiat from the federal government. Often seen as representing the farmers who are financially well established, the organization has not demonstrated any real interest in incorporating like-minded rural non-farm members.

The Farmers Union

The Farmers Union lists goals of peace, abundance, security, and freedom and emphasizes the necessity of providing an educational program to advance these purposes. The symbol of the Farmers Union is the triangle, with one side representing education and the other sides representing legislation and cooperation. The Farmers Union stresses that study is necessary before local units can take action on any problem. It has the reputation of being the most liberal of the major farm organizations. According to Kreitlow (1954) the farm families enrolled as members of the Farmers Union have as guides to their educational program local education directors, county education directors, and a director of education in their state office. The Farmers Union is viewed as being to the left in its political orientation and as such might have a greater opportunity to attract environmentalists and similar groups into its membership, should the leadership come to appreciate a need for such a change.

All three organizations have extensive publication programs to carry educational messages as well as other information dealing with members' concerns. There are, however, very limited efforts made to attract members from outside the agribusiness sector despite the dwindling number of farm families and their declining political influence.

THE ROLE OF COOPERATIVES

Historically adult education work in rural communities has not been restricted to the work of organized groups. Instead adult education has been used to organize groups to promote change and economic development. Insightful adult educators, such as M. M. Coady, have examined the life situations of the residents of their communities and have devised ways of using education to improve the conditions of people's lives through stimulating and facilitating the establishment and operation of cooperative societies.

Coady's approach in the Province of Nova Scotia was straightforward and effective with rural people of limited educational and financial
resources. From his base as an extension officer of St. Francis Xavier
University, he undertook a program of rural revitalization in the 1930s
that has received worldwide attention for its effectiveness. Coady followed a simple formula. First, he would convene a mass meeting of the
residents of a depressed farming or fishing community. Second, he would
speak to them eloquently, persuading them that they had within themselves the power to improve their lives and communities through scien-
tific study and informed action. Third, he would help to organize those
who were moved to act by forming study circles of twelve individuals
who had agreed to undertake serious study of some pressing problem that
they all faced. Fourth, he would provide the tutorial assistance needed to
enable the study groups to secure the information they required to develop a sound knowledge of their own problem situation and to figure
out possible courses of action they might take to improve that situation.
Fifth, he would assist the study groups in reaching a conclusion concerning the most feasible alternative and then to making a commitment to
perform the necessary work to implement the decision. This approach
proved effective with the rural people of Nova Scotia and could be used
more by rural adult educators today.

Coady (1980) described the initial mass meeting as:

> a kind of intellectual bombing operation. It must shatter the mind-sets of
> the people, engender an attitude of scientific humility, and bring them to a
> state of neutral which is the starting point for motion in the right direction.
> This is but the first step. If we break down, we must rebuild; if we con-
> found, we must encourage. Consequently, the second function of the mass
> meeting is to indicate to the subjects thus prepared the way they must
> subsequently follow. (p. 35)

The adult education efforts Coady carried out with his colleagues
were intended to result in the establishment of cooperatively owned economic institutions. Through the cooperative movement, various types of
organizations were established and programs begun. For example, the
cooperative at St. Andrews, Nova Scotia, found that its members were
having difficulty meeting their hospital bills. After some study, a contract
with St. Martha's Hospital at Antigonish was signed, providing for a
month's hospitalization and for a reduction in the cost of laboratory fees
as well for each family in the cooperative. In Reserve Mines, Nova Scotia,
a housing cooperative was successfully established by a group of miners
who had been studying housing in their study circle. In the construction
of the homes they learned a great deal about the process and by investing

their labor, which was becoming appreciably more skilled, they were able to reduce the cash cost of their homes. Their cooperative efforts resulted in significant improvements in their housing arrangements, but possibly more important, the experience had a powerful effect on the outlook of the miners and their families.

The cooperative movement in Nova Scotia produced cooperatives of many kinds including credit unions, cooperative fish-packing plants, consumers associations, and farmers' marketing associations (Coady, 1980). Throughout all these efforts adult education was the instrument that made it possible for those who previously had had no confidence in their ability to improve their own life chances to see that by disciplined study and working together they could, indeed, increase the quality of life for all.

The Federation of Southern Cooperatives Cooperative Education/ Rural Development Institute in Epes, Alabama, was established in 1971 to (1) meet the educational needs of individuals and communities that are starting or continuing cooperatives business ventures; (2) assist rural communities in the economic development process; and (3) offer training in skills that will enhance the development of cooperatives and rural communities. This program serves approximately 200 low income black rural residents annually (Hone, 1984).

Established cooperatives conduct a wide range of adult education activities including the use of mass media, board member training, staff development, organizing and assisting study circles, conducting educational meetings, and teaching about cooperatives. Kreitlow (1954) identified twelve such functions and acknowledged that others have enumerated at least twenty-five. Yet adult educators for the most part appear unaware of the valuable outcomes, both educational and financial, that can result from the founding and operation of cooperative societies.

RESIDENTIAL CENTERS

Rural residential centers for adult and continuing education can be found in various locations and are managed by a variety of institutions. As has been demonstrated in the adult education research literature, residential education is particularly effective in influencing the values and attitudes of learners because of the intensity of the experience, the concentration on a given topic, and the group support that is characteristic of such programs. Two of the most famous of these are the Highlander Folk School and the John C. Campbell Folk School, both located in the South. Probably no other adult education residential center has been the object of more argument and discussion than the Highlander Folk School in New Market, Tennessee. This institution "emphasizes empowerment through self-discovery, increased self-confidence, and improved self-concept" (Van Tilburg & Moore, 1989, p. 543). Although it is considered to be a rural education center, its programs have been aimed at improving the welfare of laborers, Southern black men and women, and other groups that have been historically discriminated against in American society, many of whom have applied their newly acquired skills in urban as well as rural settings. Accordingly, it might be concluded that although the Highlander Folk School is perceived as rurally oriented, its programs have addressed the problems of towns and cities more than they have rural reconstruction.

In 1925 Mrs. John C. Campbell founded the John C. Campbell Folk School as a community center located near Brasstown in the Appalachian mountains of North Carolina. Local people were involved in providing the land for the school, building it, and developing a working farm. Instruction is carried out without formal lectures or conventional textbooks. No examinations are given and no academic credits awarded. Evaluation is conducted primarily by the participants who recognize an increase in their skills and feel an increased sense of satisfaction with living. Although the Folk School has succeeded in teaching better farming methods, its greater contribution has probably been the awakening of the mountain people to the value of their own traditions (Department of Rural Education, 1960). This center is identified with the improvement of living for all rural people and is not dedicated to promoting social change other than through improving the self-image and financial conditions of its learners.

These residential adult education centers differ from the established educational institutions in that they respect the traditions and values of the rural communities and do not attempt to impose urban values and lifestyles on their learners.

FUTURE CONSIDERATIONS

In 1956 the Saskatchewan Royal Commission on Education reported that hundreds of voluntary organizations provide the bulk of continuing education in Saskatchewan. Although most of them were organized primarily to deal with problems rather than to provide education. To accomplish their objectives they have found it necessary to conduct adult education and it is clear that their total contribution to the objectives of continuing education is significant.

The birth and growth of voluntary organizations to pursue a common purpose or to solve a common problem reflect the social and political consciousness of people struggling to control their environment. Some organizations serve their purposes and fade away in a short time; others become permanent institutions with considerable influence. Citizens' organizations demonstrate by practical example what governments should do and, frequently, how they should do it (Saskatchewan Royal Commission, 1956).

Most rural organizations were established to solve practical problems. Economic interests have dominated the scene, but there are many organizations directed toward cultural enrichment and the creative use of leisure time. Enthusiastic volunteers have established community centers, art activities, and hobby facilities which are less directly concerned with formal education than with developing creative abilities. They are partly an expression of rebellion against the "spectatoritis" of modern mass entertainment media (Saskatchewan Royal Commission, 1956).

The amazing proliferation of such organizations is indicated by the fact that "One banker in a town with a population of about 600 informed this commission that over 150 organizations maintained accounts at his bank" (Saskatchewan Royal Commission, 1956, p. 284). New organizations are often created where an existing organization could serve a newly identified need by discarding outmoded activities. The problem of an excess of organizations that seems characteristic of adult education in Canada and the United States will become more troublesome unless some means are found to examine the situation and to improve coordination. The development of a community council where information can be exchanged and priorities assessed is one way of attempting to cope with a situation which has been recognized by thoughtful educators for many years.

The chief limitations of the voluntary organizations are related to problems of finance, insufficient study of social and economic issues, over-organization, and over-concentration on the leadership of relatively few citizens and a limited perspective of the common concern for lifelong education. If the enthusiasm and initiative of voluntary organizations are to be harnessed in the interest of lifelong education, then means must be provided so that priorities can be established, knowledge of programs shared, and activities coordinated around significant objectives (Saskatchewan Royal Commission, 1956).

R. Alex Sim (1988) believes that adult education has a major role to play in the regeneration of rural communities. But he doubts that tax-supported educational institutions will be inclined to reach into small communities or that they will offer courses that promote fundamental social change or deal with controversial issues. Regarding the centralization tendency as the main problem, he argues that even though the rural communities may now have many organizations, these are too often merely the local branches of distant urban-directed organizations. The way to revitalize rural communities, he believes, is to emphasize the creation of purely local groups without formal connections to groups in other places. The large-scale organizations with operations in many locations tend to require paid managers whose primary concerns are the perpetuation of the organization and the raising of fees, a part of which must go to the parent organization. Accordingly, he argues for the creation of "a new coalition of small or part-time farmers, small-town activists, concerned consumers and ecologically sensitive city people" (p. 152). Because of its inherent opposition to centralization, such a coalition offers the best hope of restoring the power of decision making to the communities. Sim concludes: "If a society, or an organization, for that matter, is too complex for intelligent, well-motivated citizens to understand, it is indeed too complex and should be dismantled bit by bit into intelligible, manageable units. One of these units is the community" (p. 181). Present organizational structures seem to divide rather than to strengthen community members and to separate rural from urban concerns.

The Appalachian Regional Steering Committee reported both a lack of public awareness of rural postsecondary issues and a lack of legislative support for rural concerns, with a resulting increase in the educational gap between rural and urban adults. Further, gaps persist within the rural community and too little effort is being made to improve communication among the sectors of the community. The committee believes that "the formation of a rural postsecondary education center is the most effective means to focus attention and gain support for the educational needs of the rural adult" (Sullins & Vogler, 1986, p. iv). Such centers might improve communication and cooperation among the multitude of organizations that may be dedicated to solving problems of one sector without considering the implications of the solution for other sectors. The urban public also has a stake in maintaining a vibrant rural economy lest the surplus of unemployed rural laborers migrate to the cities.

Hobbs (1986) argues for knowledge-based rural development depending heavily on adult education but not of the traditional variety. He claims that historically education has endorsed the notion that economic opportunity must be sought beyond the local community and that it is necessary to leave one's home community to find economic opportunity. He asserts that "The emphasis on training rural youth not needed on the farm for employment elsewhere has long been the most prominent feature of the nation's rural development strategy, although it was seldom labeled as such" (p. 3). Now, he believes, there should be a shift of skill training from the secondary schools to adult education programs, because an adult's need for a marketable skill is immediate. Furthermore, if rural development efforts are to succeed, there must be an analysis of both needed and available resources and a plan for making the most appropriate use of those existing resources in furthering development goals.

Commercial agricultural producers face increasing costs and continuing problems, a situation that suggests more farms will be liquidating in the future. Unless public policy makers address this situation and formulate both farm policies designed to cope with the farm debt burden and adult educational policies to assist rural communities in dealing with their problems, the future for agriculturally oriented rural communities will not be bright. A major public concern in both rural and urban areas ought to be whether the migration into urban areas by the families who operated the farms which were forced into bankruptcy is to be preferred to the provision of appropriate educational opportunities that will make it possible for the rural communities to absorb these human resources and prevent or reduce the extent of movement into the cities where opportunities are at a premium.

Socially significant lifelong education in rural communities is restricted rather than facilitated by the constant proliferation of associations that address the limited felt needs of disparate sectors of the community. While the Local Further Education Councils in Alberta and the Area Coordinating Councils in Illinois, which attempt to consolidate the providers of adult education in a specific geographical area, may constitute effective ways of achieving cooperative adult education, such groups need analysis and program planning. The lack of adequate evaluations of their effectiveness makes it premature to conclude that they offer the solution to the pervasive problem of fragmentation and loss of identity in rural communities. Adult educators may perceive a need to revitalize rural communities through education so that it will enrich, rather than deplete, the community's human and material resources, but at this point serious scholars of rural society and practical rural adult educators continue to face what appear to be insurmountable obstacles to the accomplishment of such worthwhile goals. Perhaps it is an opportune time to rekindle the spark of cooperative activity to rebuild rural communities, capitalizing on the diversity of its people and drawing strength from their commitment to the improvement of life their in the rural community. If it is such a time, then who has a greater opportunity to provide the vision and to lead the planning that will produce a rural renaissaance for the 1990s than those who aspire to be known as rural adult educators?

REFERENCES

Barker, B. (1985). *Rural adult learners: An emerging clientele for continuing education.* Paper presented at the Annual Conference of the National University Continuing Education Association, Louisville, KY.

Coady, M. M. (1980). *Masters of their own destiny. The story of the Antigonish movement of adult education through economic cooperation.* Antigonish, Nova Scotia: Farmac Publishing Co., Ltd. (Originally published by Harper & Row, New York, 1967.).

Department of Rural Education, National Education Association. (1960). *Improvement of rural life: The role of the community school throughout the world.* Washington, DC: National Education Association.

Havercamp, M. J. (1988). *Learning and involvement in the research discernment process by community members.* Paper presented at the Adult Education Research Conference, Leeds, England.

Hobbs, D. (1986). *Knowledge-based rural development: Adult education and the future rural economy.* Paper presented at the National Invitational Conference on Rural Adult Postsecondary Education, Airlie, VA.

Hone, K. A. (1984). *Serving the rural adult: Inventory of model programs in rural adult postsecondary education.* Manhattan, KS: The Action Agenda Project.

Jensen, J. M. (1985). *Crossing ethnic barriers in the Southwest: Women's agricultural extension education, 1914–1940.* Paper presented at the symposium on the History of Agricultural Education, Athens, GA.

Killacky, J. (1984). *Furthering nonformal adult education in rural America: The rural free university and three traditional providers.* Las Cruces, NM: New Mexico Center for Rural Education.

Kreitlow, B. W. (1954). *Rural education: Community backgrounds.* New York: Harper and Brothers.

Lidster, E. L. R. (1978). *Some aspects of community adult education in Northwest Territories of Canada, 1967–74.* Yellowknife, N.W.T.: Department of Education.

McCannon, R. S. (1985). *Serving the rural adult: A demographic portrait of rural adult learners.* Manhattan, KS: The Action Agenda Project.

McDaniel, R. H., Severinghaus, J. B., Rude, T., Gray, W. H., & Emery, M. (1986). *Barriers to rural adult education: A survey of seven northwest states.* A report of the Northwest Action Agenda Project. Pullman, WA: Washington State University.

Nachtigal, P. M. (Ed.). (1982). *Rural education: In search of a better way.* Boulder: Westview.

Saskatchewan Royal Commission on Agriculture and Rural Life (1956). *Rural education.* (Report #6). Regina, Sask.: Queen's Printer.

Sim, R. A. (1988). *Land and community: Crisis in Canada's countryside.* Guelph, Ont.: University of Guelph

Spears, J. D., & Maes, S. C. (1985). *Postsecondary and adult education in rural communities.* Paper presented at the National Rural Education Forum, Kansas City, MO. Washington, DC: Department of Education.

Sullins, W. R., & Vogler, D. E. (1986). *Barriers to rural adult education: A report of the Appalachian regional steering committee.* Blackburg, VA.: Virginia Polytechnic Institute and State University.

Treadway, D. M. (1984). *Higher education in rural America: Serving the adult learner.* New York: College Entrance Examination Board.

Van Tilburg, E., & Moore, A. B. (1989). Education for rural adults. In S. B. Merriam & P. M. Cunningham (Eds.), *Handbook of adult and continuing education* (pp. 537–549). San Francisco: Jossey–Bass.

CHAPTER 11

The Rural Public Library

BERNARD VAVREK

In the United States, 80 percent of the 10,000 public libraries are located in rural and small towns. While the definition of rural may vary—the Center for the Study of Rural Librarianship tracks both the U. S. Bureau of the Census definition of a place fewer than 2,500 people as well as a limit up to 25,000 residents—there is no mistaking the economical and educational bargain provided by America's public libraries. In many ways, this library is a type of cultural K-Mart as seen by the variety of its services. The purpose of this chapter is to describe the layers of educational and informational services provided by the typical American rural public library and how these contribute to the opportunities for lifelong learning.

THE COMMUNITY INFORMATION CENTER

It is not just trendy to label the public library as the *community information center*. While some public librarians have not enabled their institution to measure up fully to this holistic goal, the public library is frequently the only educational institution located in the small and rural towns of America. It provides the only opportunity many have for accessing information. Community information commits the library to be a clearinghouse of all types of data relevant to clients' needs including that of local government. Indeed, it is a reasonable expectation that the public library will have available information pertaining to the decisions of local fiscal authorities, copies of ordinances, minutes of town meetings, and so forth. In this same relationship as a community information center, archival collections of local newspapers can be found, frequently on microfilm or some other micro-format. In towns or counties with a historical society, the public library often has a working relationship with that institution to provide relevant local information that may not be directly owned by the library. From the client's viewpoint, it is important to understand that the library cooperates with other local community agencies to secure information. Additionally, sometimes resources are available from other libraries within the state or throughout the country.

On the matter of networking with other community agencies, library educators are presently attempting to prompt librarians into a mode as community leaders, particularly in places with few structured efforts toward community development. While assuming this leadership post is a relatively new concept for the local librarian, progress is being made. Being a vital part of the community's organizational political structure is also in the best interest of the library. A recent study of rural library clients, conducted by the Center for the Study of Rural Librarianship, discovered that clients who are members of community organizations have greater informational needs than those who do not belong and more often use the library to satisfy those informational needs (Vavrek, 1990). Librarians and cooperative extension agents are also beginning or augmenting discussions of joint ventures. The key element for the consumer is to become aware of the library's ability to switch between local resources in an effort to locate the type of service requested. In some libraries, this service will be direct, that is, the library staff will physically locate the information needed and provide it to the customer. In other instances, library clients will be directed to the appropriate agency where the service is provided, in-house. To facilitate information access among local agencies (health, educational, family, and so forth) some rural libraries will maintain Information and Referral (IR) files. Data may be kept on index cards, computer printouts, or as a locally published document distributed widely within the community. The important element for the library client is that data is up-dated at regular intervals, ensuring accurate and timely information pertaining to local issues and services. It becomes a type of community yellow pages.

As suggested above, even the smallest library is usually a "slice" of a larger network—formally or informally. Through the growing ubiquity of communications interconnectivity such as FAX, the most remote outpost can provide a continuum of information to its client. This contingency hinges on the willingness of the client to ask questions that may transcend immediate perceptions of service, and the commitment of the staff to make known the library's layers of information in an intelligible fashion. This latter matter is sometimes found to be lagging. Actually the difficulty relates to the variety of educational/informational products and services available in the typical rural library and the fact that customer's needs are selective rather than "wholesale." For example, someone who regularly accesses the library exclusively for the decisions of local government may be oblivious to the full-range of books, magazines, and services that are also available—until these are needed.

Through networks of libraries the futility of the "micro-library" being unable to collect an adequate portion of what is required is buttressed by resource sharing and directed access. While a sense of frustration may sometimes result from the exact piece of information not being available locally, this is potentially offset by the ability of the local librarian to retrieve information through a system approach. Interlibrary cooperation is a highly effective service in all states.

THE LIBRARY AS A MEETING PLACE

Consistent with the library's role as the community information center is its utilization as a meeting place for programs (those sponsored by the library as well as activities facilitated by others) and social events of all types—from card playing to square dancing. Programming is a highly significant activity of the typical rural library particularly because it may have the only meeting space available in the community. While there is a growing array of programs offered that interest adults—everything from tips on financial investments to health clinics on lowering cholesterol—the bulk of public library programming is typically organized for children. This, in a majority of cases, consists of storytelling or similar of activities. These programs are often so popular that children and parents sometimes overwhelm available facilities. Seeing queues of eager children has skewed the perception of the library's image. Some adults, particularly males, think the library is intended for women and children. In any event, programs are an integral part of the modern public library. Basic adult literacy services, which are particularly significant programming activity of the modern public library, will be discussed later in this chapter.

LIFELONG LEARNING THROUGH BOOKS

If a word association test were conducted asking individuals how they conceptualize the public library, undoubtedly the category *book* would dominate the field of responses. This is not surprising in that the public library movement in the United States has been largely driven by using books as an anchoring product (Harris, 1975).

Parenthetically, it is ironic to note that the American Library Association, while wishing to broaden the bookish image of the public library to include a more ubiquitous concept of information, continues to use as one of its sustained public relations efforts a retinue of celebrities— Oprah Winfrey, Paul Newman, Sting—on a series of glossy posters which have one common theme, reading books. So old images are difficult to shed. Even micro-libriaries, which today have a variety of resources from which to choose, often appear to emphasize books. This latter comment may seem like a contradiction, but as much as some librarians would like to diversify the resources which they have available, they are limited by funding. The typical public library's annual total budget is approximately $81,000. In communities under 2,500 people, annual budgets are closer to $15,000 (Podolsky, 1989). Even with considerable imagination, these annual budgets do not stretch very far.

Notwithstanding limited budgets, both adults and children can usually find a wide array of paperbound and hardbound books available even in the smallest library. While the tendency may be toward collections of nonfiction titles, the public library's treasures represent the classification of knowledge from philosophy to history. The typical micro-library has a collection of approximately 25,000 volumes. Further, through interlibrary cooperation and statewide card systems, clients have access to books—whether for research or leisure reading—from unseen repositories. Some libraries rent current bestsellers, at nominal fees, to ensure reader access to items currently listed in the *New York Times Book Review* or similiar sources.

Books for children and young adults are usually available in the typical rural library in considerable abundance. Still, budgetary restraints frequently affect all levels of readership. Among the creative ways of overcoming limited financial resources in the purchase of books is through targeted memorial donations. For example, upon a child's birthday, a book would be placed in the library acknowledging the donor's contribution with a bookplate—as a type of living memorial. Likewise, librarians encourage people to purchase books in memory of a friend or neighbor. Those futurists who forecast a paperless society and the absence of books guessed badly. Circulation records in most libraries give tacit proof to the continuing popularity of the library as a repository for books and similar reading materials. Time spent reading has continued to escalate from within most levels of society notwithstanding the popularity of television, personal computers, and video stores (Purto, 1989). Videos have become an important new adjunct activity for public libraries. This will be discussed in more detail later in this chapter.

SOURCES OF NEWS INFORMATION

In addition to the popularity of books, newspapers also provide prominent levels of information in the typical public library. In the survey of rural public library clients referred to earlier in this chapter, news information ranked only second in importance to that of leisure books as a priority need (Vavrek, 1990). It is not surprising to find, for example, a morning crew of clients (often the retired members of the community) frequenting the library early enough to help receive the delivery of local and national newspapers. Incidentally, these morning newspaper readers probably include the town's opinion leaders to whom news information is a particularly important facet of daily life. Whether or not this library stop occurs before or after visiting the local breakfast meeting place is a reflection of individual community habits.

Most libraries are able to maintain some retrospective collections of the actual newspapers, but usually bulky papers are preserved on microfilm. With the use of microfilm reader/printers, hard copies of newspaper pages may be produced for further study, whether for the amateur genealogist or for one who is looking for a long-lost zucchini recipe that was published two years ago by the Civic Club.

Genealogical interests are particularly strong in most public libraries and especially so in small communities. As a consequence of this local enthusiasm, librarians frequently create the only extant index to the community's newspaper by creating a scrapbook of news clippings. Articles comprise those of historical importance to the town including obituary notices. These items are usually organized into subject files from which an index is generated. This latter mentioned index may then be transferred onto 3x5 cards or electrionically filed with the use of a personal computer. Interestingly, local newspaper publishers frequently will rely on the library to index subject access to their own publications, and to facilitate the situation may provide free subscriptions to the library as a way of saying "thanks."

Beyond the presence of local news, the adult client can usually expect to find nationally syndicated newspapers available in the public library representing cities of regional importance as well as those papers of national prominence such as the *Washington Post, Wall Street Journal, USA Today,* and *The New York Times.* For these publications, printed indexes facilitate utilization. Libraries that provide online information access may subscribe to Mead Data's electronic file of *The New York times* which allows full-text retrieval of the news 24 hours after the printed version of the newspaper is produced.

MAGAZINES AND ONLINE INFORMATION

In addition to the newspaper as a genre of current information, magazines as a type provide another resource useful for timely data. Consumers familiar with online searching may not conceive of accessing magazine data other than in an electronic format. But while visions of electronic libraries may seem to be a natural extension of our information society, a majority of rural/small libraries are unable to fiscally provide this "bonus" information service. This is mentioned to the reader to soften the frustration level when the amenity of online searching is unavailable. Glossbrenner's book describing online services is the most complete manual of its type, and it is recommended to the reader for a general orientation to electronic data services and for direct use in those 10 to 15 percent of the nation's rural libraries where electronic information access is available (Glossbrenner, 1985). Depending on the community library, the costs of online retrieval may be subsidized by the library or the client will be expected to pay for the search.

Today, online information retrieval is available from a wide-variety of resources, everything from Grolier's *Academic American Encyclopedia* to the full-text of the *Harvard Business Review.* Electronic access is being discussed along with the library's magazine collection because of the strong influence of the two concepts together. Perhaps it is useful to provide some additional commentary on electronic services before returning to the more realistic situation observable in rural libraries. The personal computer or terminal appropriately connected provides a window of information from suppliers such as BRS, Dialog, and COMPUSERVE. Some random examples of available databases are: *ABI/INFORM, Arts and Humanities Search, Books in Print, Computer Database, Current Contents, Dissertation Abstracts Online, Exceptional Child Education Resources, Medical & Psychological Previews, Merck Index, Medline, Pais International, Pollution Abstracts, Social Work Abstracts, Sport Database,* and *Zoological Record.* While most of these products are oriented toward bibliographical access (author, subject, title identification), the growth of full-text delivery is high on the typical consumer's wish list. The issue of relative costs cannot be easily discounted because in addition to the expense of purchasing hardware, database use begins from the inexpensive, $12/hour for *ERIC* (Educational Resources Information Center) documents to the more expensive *Hazardline* at $102/hour. Electronic access is not close to being foolproof and contrary to the typical notion, it is no more current than the frequency with which it is updated. Old information is untimely, whether in printed or electronic format. It must be readily admitted, however, that the most experienced reference librarian cannot compete with the computer's ability at retrieving isolated tidbits of information. The reference librarian's role excels in all other instances that require an integration of different types of data from an eclectic number of resources, which is typical of most library inquiries.

The H. W. Wilson Company, Bronx, New York, noted since the beginning of the twentieth century as the preeminent publisher of bibliographical tools such as the *Nineteenth Century Reader's Guide,* the *Reader's Guide to Periodical Literature,* today provides a gateway of services to the library client. Through *Wilsonline,* one has access to informational tools such as the *Social Sciences Index* and *Humanities Index,* and a bridge to other bibliographical vendors. The *Magazine Index* is another popular guide to the library's magazine collection.

In a practical sense, it is important for the consumer to be aware that, when available, computerized access to remote data bases is usually facilitated by a library staff person. This individual is usually responsible for conducting the actual search. The logic behind this approach is that it allows a person experienced in online retrieval to expedite locating information for the client. Efforts by bibliographical vendors to simplify online access continue, but a natural language approach is still in the offing. While some customers of the rural library may feel frustrated at a less than personal hands-on approach to online searching, library routines and practices are organized to save the client time and money. Implicit to the online search and really any information seeking in the library that involves a staff person is the reference interview. This technique promotes a "structured" dialog between the customer and the library staff person to ensure that both parties are cognitively considering the same concepts. For example, the question: "Do you have a magazine dealing with stamps?" is actually discovered to be: "I'm attempting to identify the car depicted on this stamp. Can you help me?" If the reader is wondering what difference is created by this previous example, it is a matter of search strategies. In the original question, the client requests a magazine because it is envisioned to be a likely solution to the inquiry. The "real question" is not for a periodcal relating to stamps, but rather for a handbook dealing with cars. The reference interview helps everyone save time.

Before continuing with additional illustrations of how technology is transferring America's rural libraries, it is important to keep the perspective that only one in five small libraries actually provides a semblance of electronic online service. The intriguing and confounding thing for rural librarians is that with changing rural communities new rural people (the "come-heres" as they are known in Virginia) expect the same services that they previously utilized in their former metropolitan location. Everyone connected to the library, it is hoped, will make an effort to support needed services. But while the public library is catching up to the information age, the lifelong learner may more typically expect to find modest collections of magazines and indexes to these publications available in paper format. Space limitations usually preclude much of a historic collection of magazines to be available locally—usually no more than five years worth of accumulation. If not through online access, interlibrary cooperation will enable the library's users to request resources from other institutions.

THE DYNAMICS OF CD-ROM TECHNOLOGY

Compact discs, which enabled the lifelong learner to enjoy the quality of music recordings as never before, have developed from an audiophile's delight into a storage device for textual data. The CD-ROM (compact disc read only memory) facility has the potential to transform the micro-library into the Library of Congress. Well, maybe not Congress's library, but geographical remoteness has definitely been abridged by the availability of resources at the local level that previously could only be obtained locally, that is, through online access. At the present time, there is an exciting and growing array of CD-ROMs available. Among these are some of the same databases that were previously mentioned as being available online, as *ERIC* (a key resource in the lifelong learning process), *Academic American Encyclopedia,* and so forth. The beauty of **CD-ROM is that diskettes** may be searched endlessly without the need **to pay for telecommunication** and database charges that otherwise would **be involved in the online** search process. The disadvantage, once again, is that **the micro-library** cannot always afford the cost of the hardware and the subscription or purchase price of the compact disc alternative.

In what may be an indication of the growing cost-effectiveness of compact disc technology, a brief article in the *The New York Times,* entitled "CD-ROM for the Common Man," describes the availability of a personal computer from Headstart Technologies Company that includes a compact disc drive as part of the computer's basic setup. The cost is approximately $2000 and bundles the following CD-ROM programs as part of the deal: *The New Grolier Electronic Encyclopedia; Microsoft Bookshelf* that includes the *American Heritage Dictionary, Roget's Thesaurus,* the *World Almanac, Bartlett's Familiar Quotations, The National Directory of Addresses and Telephone Numbers,* thirty computer games, and more. This computer will also permit the operator to listen to audio

CD discs in the same drive intended for CD-ROM data discs with the sound coming through headphones instead of the computer's speaker system (Lewis, 1989).

LEARNING WITH GOVERNMENT PUBLICATIONS

One of the most important types of publications available in the typical rural library is often underused not only by clients but librarians as well. There is something "mysterious" about the publications produced by governments (local, state, national, and international), perhaps it is related to the distrust that some individuals manifest in anything relating to governmental action. This is unfortunate because these documents are usually primary sources of information, provide timely data, and most often are less expensive than commerically printed publications. As an aside, because government publications are usually not registered for copyright since they are owned by all citizens as taxpayers, they are often reissued bearing the imprint of some for-profit company. The tendency here is for the information to be the same, but at a higher price when compared to the government's issuance.

The U. S. Government Printing Office (GPO) is touted as the world's most prolific publisher. A publication of the USDA describing 100 ways of preparing fresh pumpkin, a timely research report pertaining to the Solar Max satellite issued by NASA, and a document explaining the changes in rural education are individual examples of the range of subjects examined by what are collectively referred to as government documents. Keeping competitive with the variety of subject areas which comprise government documents are the formats in which they are produced. Maps and atlases, books, periodicals, photographic slides, charts, floppy disks, and computer tapes are some examples of the ubiquitous nature of these publications. A flyer from the Department of Commerce describes the availability of the *State and Metropolitan Area Data Book, 1986*, on CD-ROM, another aspect of the compact disc trend that is developing.

To facilitate access in most rural libraries, the client can expect that available government publications will be organized in any of the following methods. They may be shelved along with the book collection using the prevailing classification system, usually the Dewey Decimal Classification. Sometimes they are kept in a separate section of the library or in a file using what is called the Superintendent of Document's Classification, which may look odd since it is an alphanumeric nomenclature (for example, LC.1, as opposed to the Dewey approach which is basically comprised of numbers—912.73). The third technique, which is probably found most often, is that government documents will be simply treated as pamphlets and placed into a vertical file cabinet called the Vertical File, and organized alphabetically by subjects. In the argot of the library world, the Vertical File refers to the pamphlet collection. Parenthetically, there is a published index to pamphlets, which will include some government publications, called—not surprisingly—the *Vertical File Index*. While the pamphlet approach at organizing documents is not the most convenient, it nevertheless ensures some relatively logical location for like things. The reader should be sensitive to this pamphlet approach even if the library staff person forgets to suggest it. In general, pamphlets present a very important resource to the lifelong learner because of the variety of items which are available and the endless number of subjects covered. Further, in a small library the Vertical File tends to be a catch all for oddments which don't fit neatly in other places. Whether or not these publications appear banished should not diminish their potential usefulness.

The above guidelines should make it easy to locate government documents physically in the library. The available card catalog will list documents shelved as books, and in libraries with a substantial and separate collection of these resources, the *Monthly Catalog* is the most complete index issued by the Government Printing Office. This publication will typically be available in most medium-sized rural libraries. Some librarians who cannot afford to purchase it may prepare a homemade index in card form. Beyond the availability of documents locally, library users are again reminded that through interlibrary cooperation access to the holdings of other repositories is possible. This is particularly true with government publications. The existence of depository libraries, established originally in 1876, ensures the availability of resources within each region. Depository libraries exist for state, federal, and international publications. The most common type of depository is that established within congressional districts, intended to ensure access to federal documents. Historical collections of documents are usually available, and in the event that a client's educational and informational needs are not met regionally, a hierarchy of depository libraries exists within the United States. Ultimately, the National Archives or the Library of Congress can provide the greatest historical collection of federal documents.

In addition to the library and/or depository approach, the library client should be aware that a considerable number of government documents—regardless of the level at which they are published—are available for the asking. Remember, we subsidize these publications as taxpayers, in fact, to keep ourselves informed about our government.

While this last comment sounds a bit circular, nevertheless, it is a function of a free society. Incidentally, it is also an aspect of a country that has a well-developed booktrade. In any event, the lifelong learner can frequently obtain documents simply by requesting them from the issuing agency. This does not include the GPO, which is only authorized to sell documents. But congressional committees, independent agencies and special commissions usually have gratis copies for distribution. Addresses of these "agencies" may be located in a source such as the *Congressional Directory*. One's success rate will be improved by requesting those items which are distributed without charge, although "it doesn't hurt to ask" is a useful approach to take. For priced items, it may be helped to contact local state representatives for state publications and members of congress or senators for federal publications. The *Monthly Catalog* is a good source of available titles. Additionally, government documents are identified in newspapers, professional literature, and so on. Sometimes, elected representatives will send lists of available publications to the home.

Local publications frequently present the greatest level of difficulty in relation to identification and access, since there is no standard nomenclature. They are, nevertheless, enormously important because they provide information that cannot be found elsewhere. In libraries where a collection of these local publications cannot be found, prompting the public librarian might be of value.

VIDEOS: THE NEWEST OVERLAY OF INFORMATION

The information explosion has been extended by the addition of the hottest item in town, the videocassette recording. Historically, libraries have offered clients film and other forms of visual presentations, but with the availability of VCRs in over half of the homes in the United States, it is not suprising that the public library is in the video market. It is important to note that local videocassette collections may not include the popular *Rambo* type recordings but rather may emphasize how-to-do-it titles. The typical rural library probably will have a mix of popular movies and educational recordings. Further, some libraries will loan the recorder as well.

THE REFERENCE LIBRARIAN

To ensure that libraries may be utilized fully, the client may normally expect to find a reference librarian available to assist with informational needs. In a small library, the reference person may also be the chief storyteller or government documents specialist, among other jobs. Not all individuals wish to be assisted, so the self-help approach is equally "tolerated." Enlisting the reference librarian should shorten the time needed to arrive at the same spot, educationally speaking. Essentially, the role of this person is to explain the library and its services to its constituents. This same staff person can also assist with obtaining materials through interlibrary loan.

Physical support for assisting the reference staff person and client can be found in the form of a collection of resources that includes encyclopedias, dictionaries and indexes. Additional resources can be identified in a source such as that by Haurer et al. (1987). These items tend to be organized conveniently in the library enabling quick consultation to occur. It is important to remind the lifelong learner to ask specific questions without the perceived need to show any form of library familiarity.

OUTREACH SERVICES

While it may be surprising because of costs that the typical library would provide services aimed at a constituency beyond the walls of the library, these programs are most important, nevertheless, to the modern library. This chapter will consider three such services: literacy activities, bookmobile delivery, and books by mail. Literacy support, while not necessarily a programming service literally provided outside of the library, is being considered here both because of its importance to the lifelong learner and its significance to explaining the role of today's library as it attempts to provide nontraditional services.

Literacy Activities

Approximately thirty million adults in the United States are unable to read at a functional level. The enormity of the problem grows when we also consider those learning English as a second language and the young adults failing basic skills in some of today's schools. Most often the library's position will be supportive of the literacy activities of other groups, such as literacy councils—although this will vary from place to place. In this helping capacity, the library may provide training space (remember, in many communities there are limited public meeting facilities), training manuals, and high-interest low-level books for perfecting one's skills. In some communities, the library staff will take an active part in the literacy training and act as tutors. Regardless of the strategies utilized, the greatest challenge facing literacy providers in rural areas is the difficulty of recruiting students. Adults who have spent their lives secretly compensating for their reading inabilities are loath to suddenly reveal their inadequacies to the world. This is particularly true in small towns where keeping secrets is a challenge. The lifelong learner, in need of skill improvement, is encouraged to contact the local library whether for direct remedial services or for referral.

Literacy for the workplace is another aspect of today's overall training efforts. Because of the inability of some workers to demonstrate those skills required for today's job market, remedial action has been taken by literacy providers aimed at organizing compensating efforts. Sadly, while the national press has made us aware of American workers who, for example, are unable to manage automated equipment or interpret assembly-line oriented manuals, society is also confronted with people who cannot use even simple math skills in the workplace. In rural areas particularly, the lack of a trained corps of workers is seen as a major obstacle to recruiting industry. And, conversely, communities that have successfully attracted new corporations into the local economy, point to the availability of qualified workers as one reason for this success.

Public libraries have attempted to deal with needs of the workplace by providing students with tutorials relating to math skills along with basic adult reading materials. Recently, the Kellogg Foundation established Educational Information Centers (EIC), a national effort to provide public libraries with basic computer hardware and software oriented to such things as job skills, preparing resumes, and writing business letters. Another innovative project directed at workplace skills has been organized by WPSX-TV along with the publisher, Prentice-Hall. This Penn State University based project is entitled Workforce Basic Literacy Skills. It will ultimately provide both math-oriented and basic adult reading tutorials via television on PENNARAMA, a Pennsylvania based system of educational cable stations that broadcast throughout the state. In the near future, this exciting project with its training tapes and accompanying manuals will be available nationally.

The Mobile Library—The Bookmobile

In many rural areas, the concept of the library reaching beyond its physical boundaries becomes a necessity. Presently, there are approximately 1,000 bookmobile installations in the United States attempting to reach their readership. This number includes independent rural libraries and urban libraries which provide service to nonmetropolitan areas.

Two features distinguish bookmobile services: their highly personalized nature and the convenience provided. Because of the remoteness of some stops, the mobile library and its staff play a social role in addition to providing needed information. There are closely guarded rumors alleging that the newest books in the library are often spirited away and somehow appear on the bookmobile shelves waiting for an already identified client. Staff persons are often rewarded with cookies and similar treats for their mediating efforts as they travel from stop to stop. Direct door-to-door service is sometimes provided, although determining the location and frequency of stops is based on demography of the service area. Typically, in addition to home stops (which might be included particularly for the elderly), the bookmobile travels to public and private schools, apartment complexes, and shopping malls.

The bookmobile—particularly for those removed from any other type of library resource—can be viewed as a total service outlet. Interestingly, bookmobile services often include storytelling hours and film showings in addition to a core collection of books, magazines, and references. Some mobile libraries provide direct communications between the vehicle and the headquarters library, which provides the ability to answer in-depth reference inquiries or to reserve a book to be delivered the next time the bookmobile is in town. A typical bookmobile has approximately 2,500 books and 11 magazines. A personal computer may be used for circulation control or data base access.

Books-By-Mail

Books-by-mail operations work in the following fashion. Brochures or catalogs describing recently acquired (or classic) books are mailed to clients within the service area of the library. Tear-off coupons are provided, enabling the consumer to identify those items which are of interest. The coupons are mailed back to the library, and requested books are then posted to clients. Depending on the library, postage costs may either be provided by the library or shared with the consumer. Some books-by-mail operations also include a mail-in reference service. A library with a bookmobile service usually doesn't have books-by-mail delivery.

The library's choice of delivery systems is most often a matter of relative cost. For example, several years ago the State Library of Maine abandoned its bookmobile operations in favor of books-by-mail. Research conducted by the Center for the Study of Rural Librarianship has demonstrated that when consumers are faced with multiple library alternatives—use of the headquarters library, bookmobile, or books-by-mail,—access tends to be selective rather than involving all three layers. While some consumers have no choice because of their remote locations, it appears that library clients develop their own preferred strategies of access.

CONCLUSION

Our society is described as a culture based on and comprising information. While the choices are many, those living in rural America have more limited possibilities when accessing this infrastructure of information. The public library is a quiet but powerful institution that not only provides the lifelong learner with a university of alternatives, but also protects a democratic form of government. Still, educational pursuits can sometimes be minimized or unappreciated by conservatively oriented rural people. The tendency is to applaud the self-reliant approach as opposed to the institutional. The public library offers both options. Through its collection of local information, books, magazines, and videos, the community library provides a wealth of resources at a discount price. It is the best bargain in town!

REFERENCES

Glossbrenner, A. (1985). *The complete handbook of personal computer communication.* New York: St. Martin's Press.

Harris, M. H. (1975). *The role of the public library in America: A speculative essay.* Urbana-Champaign, IL: University of Illinois, Graduate School of Library Science.

Haurer, M. G., Murray, R. C., Dantin, D. B., & Bolner, M. S. (1987). *Books, libraries, and research.* Dubuque, IA: Kendall Hunt.

Lewis, P. H. (1989, November 28). CD-ROM for the common man. *The New York Times,* p. C17.

Podolsky, A. (1989). *Federal-state cooperative system for public library data.* Washington, DC: National Center for Education Statistics and the National Commission on Libraries and Information Service.

Purto, R. (1989). I love a good story. *American Demographics,* 11(7), 36–39, 54–55.

Vavrek, B. (1990). *Assessing rural information needs.* Clarion, PA: Clarion University of Pennsylvania, College of Library Science, Center for the Study of Rural Librarianship.

CHAPTER 12

Churches and Religious Education

PAULETTE T. BEATTY
BARBARA P. ROBBINS

Given the dramatic changes and the technological advances that are bringing us into the twenty-first century, we might ask: Just how is it that the rural church has prevailed across time when other aspects of American life have disappeared? How is it that the rural church seems relatively unchanged when so many other facets of life in this country have made dramatic shifts in value and life style? The church, in fact, has become in many rural settings the central institution in the life of the community.

With the advent of the 1990s, we witness an acceleration of a consumer-oriented society, a radical restructuring of the family, a work force technologically unprepared for the future, and other such perplexing societal problems as substance abuse, homelessness, poverty, pollution, and political upheaval. What portends in the immediate future of the church for rural religious bodies placed in isolated communities with a crumbling infrastructure and an economy that can no longer find security in agriculture or related areas of employment? Problems of this nature make survival more tenuous for who choose to remain in rural communities. What message lies in the regular gathering of a group of small town residents as they worship and learn together? What are they learning, and just what sort of projected future might we envision for the educative role of the rural church as an institution?

We will address the question of the continued vitality of the rural church during the first portion of this chapter. Second, we will explore the current educational mission of the church in rural America. This exploration will highlight features characteristic of rural church education. It will address specific areas such as the goals and functions, the programs and content, the processes employed in the delivery of the educational programs, the participants, and the leadership. It will further identify hallmarks of truly exemplary educational efforts at the congregational level. In the third section of the chapter, we will identify some of the ongoing concerns experienced in the delivery of rural church education and describe some of the adaptive strategies and emerging practices which are shaping education in the rural church. Lastly, we will summarize by pondering those ways in which the rural church is intimately involved in the advancement of the concept of lifelong learning and pose a challenge for the future if the full potential of rural church education is to be realized.

THE RURAL CHURCH IN A ERA OF CHANGE

Just as we recognize the dynamic shifts that have taken place in rural communities in recent decades, so too we acknowledge that the church, while remaining a symbol of stablility, has experienced transitions of its own.

The number of local congregations in rural settings has not altered appreciably; although, there has been a shift with fundamentalist congregations increasing and mainstream congregations decreasing somewhat, even though the latter still dominate the rural scene. Baptist, Methodist, and Lutheran denominations have a greater percentage of rural members than do most other denominations, while only about 2 percent of Jews and 20 percent of Catholics currently live in rural America. Further, there is more diversity in church membership: congregations are older, women outnumber men, congregations tend not to be racially or ethnically mixed; and congregational size ranges from 10 to 500 (Hassinger, Holik, & Benson, 1988; Rogers, Burdge, Korsching, & Donnermeyer, 1988).

Insight into the rural religious community in recent decades provides possible clues regarding its current status and vitality. Changes in program and internal organization of rural churches have been truly modest. According to Hassinger, Holik and Bensen (1988), rural congregations remain, in essence, local institutions, "of limited reach, with their attention focused inward upon congregational programs and activities" (p. 105). Primary attention is given to "programs of worship, instruction, and fellowship for their own members" (p. 146). These churches have remained oriented to, and dependent upon, the immediate locale. They function as primary groups. Apparently, they serve as buffers for the local religious congregations as external influences, be they denominational or societal, are encountered.

Even though the complexion of the rural church in America has been changing, there has been a continuity of purpose which the church has fulfilled. Researchers have addressed the multiple functions of religious groups and the importance of their contributions (O'Dea & Aviada, 1983; Chalfant, Beckley, & Palmer, 1987). Beatty and Robbins (1990) described the practical embodiment of the educative role and functions of the church in current practice. They suggest that when the church stands with individuals in all of their life events, when the church helps individuals discover meaning and order in life, when the church helps individuals shape basic belief systems in light of a spiritual tradition, when the church provides guidance for the critical examination of societal values, when the church helps individuals affirm themselves as part of a religious tradition, and when the church helps individuals accomplish developmental tasks of human growth and maturation, then these functions are well served.

A PROFILE OF RURAL EDUCATION IN THE CHURCH

In an effort to address the central topic posed by this inquiry, namely, what are the educational intitiatives of rural education in the church, the authors invited religious leaders from ninety-three denominations and religious groups, as identified in *The World Almanac and Book of Facts* (Hoffman, 1989), to respond to a series of questions:

In what ways are rural educational programs in your denomination different from their urban counterparts?

What goals and functions guide your denominational efforts in rural education?

What are the most prevalent programs or content areas in your denominational efforts as they are implemented in rural congregations?

What methods, techniques, devices, and locations are most frequently used to deliver your rural educational services and programs?

How would you characterize those who typically participate in your educational progams?

How is organizational leadership provided and developed for the educational ministry of the rural church?

What are the hallmarks of excellence which serve as standards for practice in the delivery of rural church educational programs?

Responses gleaned from both mailed survey questionnaires and telephone interviews from over forty denominational leaders form the basis for the following discussion. The responses reflect a wide diversity of denominational input and geographic dispersion.

Characteristics of Rural Church Education

The question regarding differences in rural educational programs and their urban counterparts elicited quite a range of responses. Even though a number of recurrent themes emerged, quite a few of the respondents' comments seemed to contradict each other. Certainly, this could be due in part to differences among the various denominations. It may in fact reflect the variability that exists in the delivery of rural educational programs; or for that matter, it may be a function of the variability that exists in the delivery of any educational program. Many respondents were unable to identify any significant differences between their denomination's urban and rural educational programs, claiming that since the curriculum is the same, any variations would be of the same order as those found between any two congregations. Other respondents indicated that since they were serving primarily either an urban or suburban constituency, they had not become aware of, or sensitive to, any differences between the programs based solely upon location along the rural, suburban, urban continuum. Still others indicated that nothing is being done on the denominational level to differentiate rural or urban educational programs, and so it was assumed that no significant differences existed. Lastly, quite a few leaders perceived differences in the delivery of educational programs based upon the size of the congregation and consequently of its educational program regardless of whether it was located in a rural, suburban, or urban setting.

In sight of the above discussion, we will share with you the recurrent themes which did emerge from our inquiry, and leave to you the interpretation as to whether these themes serve to "uniquely define" the phenomenon of education in the rural church. A number of subtle differences did emerge. These could be considered differences of degree rather than of kind. These differences related to program emphasis, program structure, and program participation.

The emphasis of rural church educational programs: is oriented toward the practical, is centered in family concerns, is focused principally upon issues in the immediate world of the rural community, is loyal to the concept of community identity, is responsive to local community needs, is tied to unique traditions within the local congregation, is imbued with a sense of religious tradition, and is committed to the doctrinal teachings of the denomination.

The structure of rural church educational programs is characteristically described as: informal, involving direct face-to-face interactions, with high levels of personal engagement, in small learning clusters, with frequent intergenerational groupings, in strong primary group orientation, and with integration into the fabric of the congregational life. There is relatively little emphasis placed upon formal and extensive planning for educational programs, and also relatively infrequent use of electronic instructional media or other structured instructional materials. Educational programs tend to be conducted by local congregations functioning independently as self-contained entities, with little interest in collaborating with other neighborhood churches, and in relative isolation from other denominational congregations in the region or at a higher denominational level.

The participation in rural church education programs can be described from several perspectives. Since congregations are typically small, the size of educational programs is also small; however, they involve a cross section of the entire congregation. Additionally, with the aging of America, and especially rural America, rural congregations are increasingly faced with meeting the needs of a progressively older constituency. And although, in many respects, the differences between urban and rural are changing, one would typically find a somewhat less educated membership, and a membership somewhat less oriented to the printed word. Further, since most congregations are fortunate in having even a single full-time professional religious leader, shared lay leadership in many facets of the congregational life, and especially in the educational enterprise, is very pronounced.

Goals and Functions

In all instances, the central function of education at the congregational level is described as conveying the doctrine of the particular denomination. Further, as part of this central religious education mission, there is a sense of the relevance of the gospel to today's world and of the necessity for responding to community needs. A representative from the Episcopal Church says:

> The goal is to make the local congregation a more effective ministering presence in the community in which it resides. This is to be done by transforming it from being a community gathered around a professional minister into a ministering community.

A similar sentiment is expressed by a representative of the Church of the Nazarene: "Our primary objective is to prepare our members to engage their religious faith in practice and behavior that demonstrates their relationship to God through Jesus Christ."

Programs and Content

Almost without exception, most of our conversations related to locally delivered programs at the congregational level. Invariably, religious leaders spoke of programs related to the spiritual growth and development of the membership. From a canon of the Episcopal Diocese in Oklahoma we find a response which captures this broadly held conviction:

> It's really a back to the basics approach. Familiarity with the Scriptures and the history and traditions of the church is not merely a way of preserving the past. These are the tools for envisioning how God is at work in the midst of life bringing about sacred work of redemption, reconciliation, and servanthood. By learning our own story, we are prepared to go out and interact with the story of the rest of creation.

The religious education director of the Greek Orthodox Archdiocese of North and South America speaks to the importance of fidelity to and identity with one's tradition: The educational program of the Greek Orthodox parish is "largely aimed at trying to retain its identity in the larger religious community, and in the civic community at large." From the director of the Jewish Living and Learning Network, United Synagogue of America, the Conservative tradition, we find content relating to life cycle events, especially in terms of understanding Jewish tradition, namely, Bar and Bas Mitzbahs, births, weddings, and funerals. Teachings also center upon the importance of prayer and its role in Jewish worship, learning the traditional melodies, and cultivating a daily life of prayer. Although our respondents spoke repeatedly of the logical outgrowth of the core religious message as ministry within the community, relatively few programs have this broader scope. In one instance, a minister in the Christian Church has occasional programs on stewardship and environmental concerns. Examples of community outreach as a component or outgrowth of religious education is cited by a representative from the Episcopal Diocese of Oklahoma.

> In the places where "Total Ministry" or "Mutual Ministry" is most successful, the local congregations are turning away from a survival and dependency mentality towards an outward looking and pro-active involvement in the life of the local community. For example, one local congregation will initiate a community-wide educational program on AIDS when an 8 year-old boy in the school system has been diagnosed positive with the HIV virus. Another congregation launches a Walk-a-thon for the hungry. Still another uses their small old vicarage as emergency housing for the homeless.

In addition, programs and the related content in rural communities go well beyond that provided at the congregational level. The delivery of formal schooling in rural settings, including preschool, grade school, high school, and higher education, has been identified as a specific initiative of a number of denominations. Denominational officials of the Wisconsin Evangelical Lutheran Synod indicate that rural area religious education

occurs in large part through their elementary school system. A denominational level religious educator with the United Church of Christ indicates
that "for over 35 years the church has been developing schools in
Appalachia and in Fort Collins." Within the United Methodist denomination, it is asserted that: "There is a trend toward providing education in
the preschool, and historically attention has been given toward week-day
school at the elementary level." A representative of the Presbyterian
Church of the U.S.A. speaks eloquently:

> Our denomination has maintained historically a primary emphasis in pro-
> viding higher education, full liberal arts colleges, in rural settings. In addi-
> tion, education at the secondary school level has also been emphasized.
> Both higher and secondary educational opportunities have been directed
> toward educationally disadvantaged segments of our population. Racial
> and ethnic minorities, and economically deprived regions such as Appala-
> chia and communities bordering Mexico have been targeted.

Methodology

Little mention was made of educational programs conducted by
and for individuals outside of the small group setting. A representative of
the Church of Christ, Scientist, describes an individualized, self-directed
component as an integral complement to collective study opportunities,
suitable for both rural or urban settings:

> Their members study daily a Bible Lesson-Sermon, consisting of passages
> from the Bible and the denominational textbook. To read through this Bible
> Lesson-Sermon typically takes an hour, and Christian Scientists often spend
> much more time exploring it or other passages and subjects of spiritual
> interest. Each church also provides a public reading room in which Bibles,
> Bible commentaries, and denominational literature are available for study
> or to be borrowed or purchased. These reading rooms provide a quiet
> haven for study and prayer.

Most respondents mentioned small group settings. From the Office
of Alternative Education of the Christian and Missionary Alliance
comes a program typical of that frequently reported to us. Their educational program routinely includes: "Sunday Schools and special meetings which always use church facilities and ordinarily consist of lectures
with discussion, and, only occasionally, the use of a video." A leader
within the Church of God, headquartered in Cleveland, Tennessee, enu-
merates a variety of approaches for the delivery of educational programs: "Sunday Schools, Kid's Crusades, Vacation Bible Schools, Children's Church, Seminars, Conferences, Conventions, District Rallies,
Youth Camps, and Revivals." The Wisconsin Evangelical Lutheran rep-

resentative describes the activities frequently encountered in their denominational group educational events. There would be a utilization of group methods, discussion, perhaps the telling of a story, an exploration of applications to the member's lives, and subsequent comparisons of the various applications. Their tradition is moving away from the use of lecture and lay leaders are learning to encourage participation through discussion. As with other denominations, they have their own publishing house for producing religious materials. They also have a media library available for local congregations, and most especially, this respondent was pleased to report the existence of a substantial publication fund available to local congregations to develop appropriate materials at the local level. Hence, their church is supportive of innovative practice and curricular/methodological exploration. And in a final example, provided in a project report by the Director of the Jewish Living and Learning Network, we learn of the success of small group experiences even in the absence of a rabbi:

> We have, in the past year, purchased approximately 40 hours of high quality Jewish content video. These videos are now circulating in 30 communities in our region. According to the reports we have received, the average attendence in communities where these videos are shown is about 8 people per location. This means that every month, approximately 240 rural Jews are watching an hour of Jewish content video programming.

Participants

In response to our question concerning how the religious leaders would describe those who participated in the educational programs offered in rural settings, a number of observations were offered. Again, from the Church of the Nazarene we catch a glimpse of the diversity that is represented in the rural community.

> Rural churches serve clientele that are as sophisticated and worldly-wise as those of an urban or suburban church. The only differences are matters of degree. Progressive rural churches adapt their delivery systems to the context in which they exist. Conservative rural churches, like the Church of the Nazarene, combine a world-encompassing mission of gospel proclamation, with programs geared to training, educating, and developing believers.

An Episcopal Church representative brings into focus a very exciting facet of the rural educational scene.

> Not long ago, when one heard the term "Christian Education", you thought immediately of children and Sunday School. Not so any longer. The arena which is seeing most of the action these days is that of intergenerational and adult learning. At first, the effect was to recruit select

individuals for specific training in certain ministries, but increasingly, programs are being developed for all members of the congregation.

A spokesperson for The United Synagogue of America describes the participants in his programs from the Maine, New Hampshire, and Vermont region as individuals who were raised in the Jewish tradition, who moved away from their urban roots into rural settings within the last twenty to thirty years, and who until they started to raise their families, did not feel the absence of their Jewish traditions, their synagogues, or the guidance and instruction of their rabbis. Now they are hungering for what they had laid aside. A representative from the United Church of Christ mentions that, in a number of rural congregations, the education level of the members is not at a par with what is found in most suburban or urban settings. Several additional conversations have also highlighted this lower educational level and the fact that many members in their rural congregations are not oriented to the printed word. Most respondents identify their constituencies as belonging to the "graying" majority in rural settings. A representative of the Church School Department Educational Ministries of the American Baptist Churches of the U.S.A. sees a growth in black and hispanic membership within this denomination. Other respondents have commented on the changing complexion of the membership and of the participants in educational programs. This has been attributed to seasonal variations associated with agriculture and migrant families as well as vacationing patterns of senior citizens leaving the harsh winters of the northern states and moving temporarily to the sunbelt. In Texas, these winter residents, affectionately referred to as "snow birds," create fluctuations in program needs of the churches. One representative of the United Methodists speaks of the tradition of "independence" characteristic of lifelong residents in rural communities. Consideration of the educational implications for each of these groups, and others not identified, becomes crucial if programs are to meet real needs of real people.

Leadership

In the rural setting the issue of leadership and leadership development is most crucial in insuring the survival and continued vitality not only of the rural church but also of its educational role. Although rural efforts may seem impractical, if not prohibitive in terms of monetary and staff outlay, all traditions must find some mechanism for meeting the leadership needs of their rural congregations. Some are creating innovative ways of involving rural laity in facilitating educational programs and in managing other ministries of the church. Yet other denominations are identifying ways to give rural congregations access to a professional religious leader, whether priest, minister or rabbi. Our discussion will highlight the initiatives being taken to meet the leadership needs, both from the perspective of the professional religious leader and the perspective of the lay leader.

More and more denominations are unable to provide a full-time minister or priest for every single rural congregation. In our conversation with a representative from the American Baptist Churches in the U.S.A, she spoke of their institution of "yoked parishes," in which one pastor serves more than a single congregation. We also learned that the Christian and Missionary Alliance is benefiting where, in some regions of the country, previously retired priests and ministers have moved back into pastoring, or have assumed other leadership responsibilities in rural settings. Further, given the small size of a number of local congregations, ministers are serving in that role on a part-time basis, while working elsewhere in the community to provide a livelihood for themselves and their families. Yet another avenue for expanding the ranks of the professional church leader for the denomination has been found in those individuals making midlife career shifts into the ministry. All these developments have begun to ease the problem of a shortage of ministers for some rural congregations. Some denominations are reluctant to consolidate the many small rural congregations into a single larger regional congregation, except as a last resort. In some instances regional clergy are made available to rural congregations in order to enable special skills and expertise to be accessed as needed. In the Presbyterian Church of the U.S.A., seven congregations in Maine have formed into a consolidated parish which functions through a leadership team while at the same time respecting the identity and individuality of each of the local congregations.

A denominational level leader from the Church of Christ says his denomination conducts an annual conference specifically for rural clergy and the Evangelism Division also gives some attention to the unique needs of rural ministry. Much more frequently, we hear of conferences and workshops focused upon the needs of the pastor in small, though not necessarily rural, congregations. Regional networks provide support to local clergy, though they do not necessarily focus upon educational issues.

Although virtually all leaders with whom we were in contact discussed the centrality of lay leadership development, especially in rural settings, we typically find that leadership development programs and curriculum have been developed without specific reference to rural, suburban, or urban settings. One resource is a catalog of continuing lay training opportunities within the Church of the Nazarene. It details four specific training programs under the general category of leadership development.

These include a program for children's workers, one for youth workers, one for adult workers, and one for chairmen of Christian Life and Sunday School. The catalog also identifies thirteen specific training programs under the rubric of lay ministry development. It is instructive to focus briefly upon the continuing lay training of adult workers. In that section of the catalog we read:

> The world around us demands that our workers continue to learn and grow. The world is also telling us that ministry to adults will be the cutting edge of the church over the next 25 years. Among other things, population projections and estimates tell us that the focus of Christian ministry at the end of the 1900's and into the 21st century must be upon the adult.

Certificates are offered for basic, intermediate, and advanced lay training reading program. Once advanced status has been attained, encouragement is offered to go beyond these levels and seek further opportunities for growth. Virtually every denomination is involved in preparation of volunteer lay leaders for the educational mission of the local congregations.

Hallmarks of Excellence

Five recurrent themes were identified by our respondents although, frequently, these hallmarks identified were offered with the caveat that they could equally apply to educational programs in urban settings. Nevertheless, church leaders would look for these hallmarks as standards for excellence in rural educational programs. Leaders spoke of the necessity for the educational program to be comprehensive, to be rooted in the local community, to be carefully planned, to meet developmental needs, and to be fully participatory.

The general coordinator of training for the Church of the Nazarene addresses the issue of comprehensiveness quite concisely when he emphasizes that:

> The educational mission of any church is three-fold: training, facilitating skill development or enhancement; educating, providing orientation to values distinctly Christian; and developing, facilitating personal Christian growth. This means that a Christian education program provides instruction in Biblical literacy as well as practical faith development, and training in skills consonant with good churchmanship. This ambitious task is achieved through a structure that provides opportunity to address the full agenda.

Another hallmark of excellence, repeatedly identified by church leaders, relates to an educational program rooted in the local community.

Rural educational programming must: be sensitive to issues within the rural community; be involved in the life of the community; be built around a core program but flexible enough to respond to local needs and perspectives; and be marked by a high community consciousness and outreach of a personal nature.

A number of leaders have captured some of the challenges associated with planning educational programs in rural settings. The director of Christian education and training for the Episcopal Diocese of Olympia in Washington has provided a most insightful elaboration of this hallmark of excellence. She writes:

> A truly outstanding rural church considers the following components in planning educational programs. It takes into account the stewardship of people's time as well as money; it makes choices about the number of programs people are asked to participate in and the quality of those events. It is clear about the purpose of any program; whether it is to bring the family together, to encourage spiritual journeys, to work through an issue of faith, or to deal with issues of conflict. It plans as carefully for a small group of people as it would for a large group so that each person is valued and the time spent is evidence of that value. It listens to the concerns and cares of the members of the congregation and provides practical educational programs which will enhance the members' skills in meeting the crisis events of life. It challenges, with love, the tendency to be insular and parochial, without overloading the information so that people are immobilized. It seeks opportunities to play together, as well as take learning seriously.

In considering the next hallmark of excellence, religious leaders focused upon programs addressing the developmental needs of local congregations, as individuals, as family units, and as a community of faith. The Greek Orthodox Archdiocese of North and South America, both in written response and in a sample newsletter, mentions the necessity for intergenerational programming focusing upon the centrality of families. Others emphasize the success of educational programs which consider the developmental needs of every age group, particularly those concerned with issues of older adulthood. Responses suggested that churches are actively involved in dealing with parenting concerns and other aspects of the family life cycle. For example, a Church of God respondent describes "family training hours every Wednesday, quarterly seminars and conferences for adults, and ongoing programs for singles, youth, and senior citizens." Exemplary programs demonstrate flexibility in responding to people's needs.

The final hallmark describes a truly exemplary program as highly participatory. In a telephone interview, a staff member from the Board of Christian Education in the Cumberland Presbyterian Church observes that: "consistent Sunday School participation of all members of the congregation" is certainly one measure of excellence and is characterized by a high level of intimacy and direct, interpersonal interaction. Additional responses point to the importance of this participation as a precursor to Christian action in the community or to congregational involvement in evangelistic outreach. One benefit of a strong participatory process is the formation of committed lay leadership teams who in turn become proactively involved in, and responsible for, a dynamic educational program.

In summary, hallmarks of a truly exemplary educational program include being comprehensive in scope, being rooted in the community, being sensitively planned, being responsive to developmental needs, and being highly participatory.

CURRENT CHALLENGES AND ADAPTIVE STRATEGIES

One of the most interesting facets of our dialogue with denominational leaders related to the challenges which they face on an ongoing basis. They spoke earnestly of their rural educational programs, some of the unique here and now problems, and the adaptive strategies used in facing these challenges.

Current Challenges

As denominational leaders spoke with us, a number of challenges to the delivery of rural educational programs surfaced. Two fundamentally different types of concerns existed. One type of concern related to the access and management of resources in fulfilling the educational mission of the rural church. A second impediment to the full flowering of the educational mission of the rural church concerned the presence of certain value sets within the membership of local rural congregations. Both of these concerns will be addressed.

Effective educational programs require resources. The most frequently identified resource deficiencies are associated with finances, facilities, personnel, and materials. The financial resources for rural congregations are extremely limited and need to be dispersed to meet the total needs of the congregation, of which education is only a part. Consequently, most educational programs are conducted on a very small budget. In many very small congregations, the sanctuary is the only available gathering place for the congregation. This greatly restricts what might otherwise be dictated methodologically for a given educational program. The lay leaders are volunteers. When the demands are great, the resources are few, and no relief is in sight, volunteers burn out. The same has also been said of the priest, minister, or rabbi. Instructional equipment and nonprint materials are both in short supply. Equipment such as audio and video cassette recorders may exist in the homes, but not all rural congregations have a budget that can afford such equipment for instruction. Print materials are limited to those procured through denominational headquarters or to those which are teacher made. Most curriculum materials have been developed from a large congregational model and contain few strategies appropriate for small homogeneous groups or heterogeneous intergenerational groups. Further, they rarely help to focus upon unique issues of concern to the rural constituencies: educationally, generationally, ethnically, socially, economically, or culturally. Many at the denominational level are concerned that staffing restrictions at that level make adaptations to curriculum difficult, if not impossible, even though the need is there. Further, there appears to be an absence of leaders at the middle management level, representing a significant deficiency. This could account for the communication gaps which seem to exist between the local and denominational levels.

The second type of concern which echoed throughout many of our interviews related to value sets encountered within the members of the rural congregations. Although not all of these value sets are present in all congregations, they are values to be dealt with as educational programs are implemented on the local level. First, the historic reliance of the laity upon the clergy for many leadership functions frequently interferes with lay members assuming responsibilities in the educational program. In many instances it makes people less ready to accept leadership from peers in the congregation. Second, the increasing orientation of youth and adults to the stimulation of television and radio as a source of much of the information from the outside world places the church at a strategic disadvantage in competing with the media for attention. Third, there is a sense of disconnectedness from the denominational headquarters, a sense of remoteness of being out of touch. Much of what is communicated downward does not get read, much less adopted, at the local level. Fourth, there is an orientation to conduct all religious business, including education, within the local congregation. This creates additional demands when material resources are limited, or when certain areas of expertise are not available locally. Fifth, frequently, lay leaders in rural settings have little tolerance for the type of careful planning that is required for an educational program to be consistently and effectively provided to the membership. Sixth, education is, frequently, not highly valued among members of the rural congregation. Seventh, the spilling over of urban values constitutes an increasing challenge facing rural church educators. In sum, values are necessary considerations in the delivery of educational programs.

Adaptive Strategies

Adaptive strategies relate most closely to resource management concerns. Few solutions were offered to the conflicts between rural value sets and the effective delivery of educational programs.

What adaptive strategies are either in place or on the horizon to assist in dealing with limited resources? Increasingly, programs are being conducted in homes and alternate sites when rural church facilites are not adequate. The creation of new organizational structures and linkages on an extra-congregational level is resulting in regional ministries which enhance access to critical leadership skills. Increased incidence of dual-career, mid-career, and retirement career ministries help ease the strain of a limited professional pool. Increased attention to the training of lay volunteers for educational ministries is occurring both in regional workshops and in individual adaptations. Denominational leaders charged with fostering education at the local level are beginning to look at needs unique to the various rural communities in which they function, and how those needs impact their educational mission. The result is an increase in participation in independent home study, reading programs, and monitoring. Curriculum material development is enhanced: by funds established to foster the design of teacher-made materials, by methodological adaptations to small group settings, by informal library rotation systems, by the design of curriculum applicable for intergenerational groupings, by the development of home-study options, and by the establishment of audio and video lending libraries. On the horizon, we see capabilities to engage in distance learning and learning-by-extension.

A number of these creative, adaptive strategies may also address some of the challenges presented by value sets as discussed earlier.

THE RURAL CHURCH AND LIFELONG LEARNING

In summary, those who speak of education and the rural church are speaking of a rich diversity of experience that is difficult to capture in sweeping generalizations. As Beatty and Hayes (1989) addressed the issue of diversity in the field of adult religious education, we are impelled to address it again in the review of the total spectrum of rural education for youth as well as for adults:

> Diversity is one of the most characteristic hallmarks of adult religious education as a field of practice. Diversity exists in the institutions involved,

purposes espoused, programs delivered, methodologies employed, learners attracted, and leadership provided. Yet, even in the presence of this diversity, one finds an array of similar concerns and challenges that confront the professionals as they approach their singular task of facilitating learning. (p. 397).

The rural church in today's world, through its educational mission, provides a model for fostering both the concept and the reality of lifelong learning as it reaches into the lives of individuals, shapes their experience of community, and facilitates their response to the emerging needs of the larger society. When education in the church impacts the three overlapping worlds of individuals, of the learning community, and of the social environment, lifelong learning becomes an integral part of the faith experience.

Insofar as educational programs meet individuals at teachaable moments, lifelong learning is facilitated. This occurs when learning opportunities are shaped to: meet the developmental needs of individuals across the life span, meet the diverse needs of all of the segments of the local congregation, provide a forum for dialogue regarding dilemmas of an uncertain and rapidly changing environment, shape value systems anchored in the sacred, assist the individual in realistic assessment of self-identity and esteem, create ability to transcend every experience, and enable the individual to formulate a sense of meaning and purpose in life. Insofar as the church does all these things, learning has the potential to reach the individual and to capture teachable moments in the life of the individual. There is, consequently, the possibility of learning across the life span to permeate every dimension of human growth.

Insofar as the educational mission of the rural church fosters a community of learners, lifelong learning is facilitated. In the congregational context, this happens when the following occur:

• Primary group relationships are fashioned.

• Participants are involved in the design and implementation of their own learning experiences.

• The social climate provides a sense of caring and being cared about.

• Individuals are valued and uniqueness is affirmed.

• The lay community commits itself to a shared agenda for learning.

• The local congregation accepts responsibility for the educational undertaking rather than leaving it to professionals.

• Both participation in and leadership of the educational program is widespread.

- Participants in the learning community are genuinely concerned with the lives of the members.

- A sense of corporate responsibility is prevalent.

- Members of the learning community have extensive and ongoing relationships and frequent contacts with each other.

Insofar as the educational program of the rural church activates the learning community to proactive involvement in the larger context of society, lifelong learning is fostered. This occurs when congregational choices are made concerning outreach ministries and when commitments of resources to, and personal engagement in, outreach extend beyond the congregational frame of reference. This occurs when individuals move beyond their own needs and immediate concerns to address needs and concerns of other groups and individuals.

Those charged with the delivery of religious education in rural church systems are, today, already enhancing the basic quality of life for individuals, learning communities, and the social milieu of the rural community. They face continued challenges in confronting the issues that will arise in an increasingly "secular, pluralistic, multicultural, technologically driven, mobile, impersonal, and aging society" (Beatty & Hayes, 1989, p. 407). The concentration of energy, creativity, and commitment that has fostered the success and staying power of rural congregations and their educational programs holds within it a message that begs to be communicated. Herein lies one of the greatest untapped resources available to religious educators.

If one aspiration could be expressed for the advancement of lifelong learning in the rural community, it would be that all individuals engaged in furthering education in the church commit themselves to dialogue and sharing. People must share their ongoing concerns and the adaptive strategies which are working in rural settings. They must share, most especially, those successful educational practices, those hallmarks of excellence, which so effectively encourage lifelong learning.

REFERENCES

Beatty, P. T., & Hayes, M. T. (1989). Religious institutions. In S. B. Merriam & P. M. Cunningham (Eds.), *Handbook of adult and continuing education* (pp. 397–409). San Francisco: Jossey-Bass.

Beatty, P. T., & Robbins, B. P. (1990). The educative role of religious institutions. In M. W. Galbraith (Ed.), *Education through community organizations* (pp. 29–36) New Directions for Adult and Continuing Education, no. 47. San Francisco: Jossey-Bass.

Chalfant, H. P., Beckley, R. E., & Palmer, C. E. (1987). *Religion in contemporary America* (2nd ed.). Palo Alto: Mayfield.

Hassinger, E. W., Holik, J. S., & Benson, J. K. (1988) *The rural church: Learning from three decades of change.* Nashville: Abingdon.

Hoffman, M. S. (1989). Headquarters, leaders of U.S. religious groups. In M. S. Hoffman, (Ed.), *The world almanac and book of facts* (pp. 592–593). New York: World Almanac, An Imprint of Pharos Books, A Scripps Howard Company.

O'Dea, T., & Aviada, J. O. (1983). *Sociology of religion* (2nd ed.). Englewood Cliffs: Prentice-Hall.

Rogers, E. M., Burdge, R. J., Korsching, P. F., & Donnermeyer, J. E. (1988). *Social change in rural societies: An introduction to rural sociology* (3rd ed.). Englewood Cliffs: Prentice-Hall.

CHAPTER 13

Educational Needs of Rural Women

VICKI LUTHER
MARIAN TODD

Carol realized that she had to find full-time work when her husband, who drove a log truck, was laid off. The newspapers were full of stories about the downturn in the housing market and the possibility that the logging industry might never recover. Her husband soon left the family to take a long-distance trucking job and Carol was left behind to "hold the family together." When she heard about the community college program that would train her as an LPN, she decided that it was an investment of her time that would pay off for her entire family. When she began the program, she had no idea what the sixty mile drive would mean in the winter or what it was like to have more homework to do than her kids did. She was on the verge of dropping out when another woman from her church decided to try the same program and from then on, Carol had help with driving, homework, and even babysitting.

Besides the support from her church, Carol heard about a special program that the County Agent put on for women in transition. She went to the first class expecting to feel uncomfortable but soon realized that all the women in the group were recently divorced or widowed and had problems very much like her own. As she continued to attend the classes, she discovered her talents and felt good about her ambitions. When she decided to try part-time work at a nursing home in a neighboring town, she got help with the job application and preparation for the interview from her class.

This chapter is intended to describe the changing educational needs of rural women. Remarkable changes have taken place in the lives of rural women and families, requiring a variety of responses on the part of educational service providers. A final section will present recommended design considerations as a framework for the development of programs targeted at rural women.

The viewpoint is essentially focused on rural and small town situations. While differences in the regions of the United States can be signifi-

241

cant, there are, however, some basic similarities in the experiences of rural women whether they live in New England or the Pacific Northwest, the farm towns of the Midwest or the Southeast. These similarities are, of course, defined by parameters set by such immutable factors as distance, weather, and geography. Dynamic forces such as tradition and culture change also greatly influence the way that rural women live out their lives.

CHANGE AND RURAL COMMUNITIES

It has long been a cliché in American parlance that small towns and rural areas constitute the heart and soul of the country. The mythology of rural life represents an ideal that began in the eighteenth century vision of Thomas Jefferson's yeoman farmer (with wife and family) who would settle the frontier and develop a uniquely American version of spirituality and democracy. The development of the popularly held image of rural America is a topic worth study in itself, but there can be little argument that it is an image combining both idealized virtues as well as negative stereotypes.

While the popular culture holds that rural Americans enjoy an enviable quality of life with simple, hardworking, and honest folks as neighbors, these same rural Americans are thought to suffer from inferior schools, poor health care, limited job opportunities, and so forth.

Rural communities have felt the impacts of this two-sided image in American popular culture as a double-edged sword. On one side, many Americans believe in protecting what seems like an idealized lifestyle but, and perhaps more significantly, many Americans also see rural communities as unable to cope with the impacts and demands of rapid change.

The definition of a rural community has itself undergone an interesting and significant change in the last ten years. Traditional land use and geographic definitions of community are based on the importance of location and economic transactions.

In other words, in order to survive, a community must be in the right place (at the junction of a river or highway) and have certain economic transactions taking place (a bank, for example or a certain level of retail trade) in order to maintain vitality (Isard, 1960).

Today, many communities have weathered the extreme economic turbulence of the 1980s through leadership and attitudes that have redefined small rural communities into retirement centers, bedroom communities for commuters, and recreational and tourist attractions. Research on healthy small towns and counties describes this change in survival focus (Wall & Luther, 1990; John, Baties, & Norris, 1988).

It is, of course, the rapid and fundamental changes in all aspects of life that have most deeply affected rural communities and rural women and families. Not only have changes in attitudes and economics had an impact on work life, but change has occurred in all aspects of everyday life as well.

If the role of farm women, for example, is reviewed historically, the impact of mechanization following World War II can be seen as one of the important trends that changed women's status. Once valued as full and very necessary partners in a family farm operation, women were among the labor sources replaced by machinery and so relegated to a smaller and less important role.

Another more recent example is the growing number of single parent families in rural communities. As heads of households and most often lacking child support from absent or ex-spouses, single mothers are among the many rural women entering the work force in record numbers (Haney, 1982).

Not only are rural women entering the work force, but they are exploring many nontraditional jobs, including aspects of agriculture, logging and coal-mining (Trent & Stout-Wiegand, 1987). Interest stems from the fact that these traditionally male occupations are often the highest paying jobs in a rural area.

Rural women are today facing a different future than did their mothers a generation ago. Technology has changed rural isolation; television and telephones have connected town and country in new and dramatic ways. Increased participation in activities that range from women's team sports to elected offices has and will continue to gradually change the experiences of rural women.

This is not to minimize the constraints of tradition and limited economic freedom at work in rural America, but the circumstances and demands of rural life *are* changing because of economic and social trends. This means that the educational needs of rural women are no longer based on traditional roles as homemakers or parents in a nuclear family.

OBSTACLES FACED BY RURAL WOMEN

Rural women face personal, interpersonal, community and institutional obstacles to change. At a personal level, women are socialized to discount themselves, their accomplishments, and their abilities. The omission of women's domestic work from computation of the gross national product is a primary instance of social attitudes which help shape women's self-concepts in this negative way. Conceptually limiting productive activity to paid work ignores the economic impact of housework, community service activities, and work that women perform on farms and in other rural family business (Haney, 1982).

As women respond to changes in rural communities today, lower self-esteem will have a variety of effects. Rural women may be less likely to view their skills as marketable skills without further education. Farm women's intentions to move to off-farm employment under circumstances of financial stress have been found to be tied to their level of higher education (Albrecht, Murdock, & Schiflett, 1986). This type of self-limitation is often reinforced by employers who require women who have been out of the paid work force to obtain training and experience before they are hired (Butterwick, 1988). Women in these situations may benefit from programs which help build self-esteem and confidence for new endeavors, as well as programs which enable them to reassess the knowledge and skills which they already have.

Because societal factors may be the source of a woman's negative personal self-image, it is important for women to realize that others share the same problems. The opportunity to identify and take action with other women collectively has been shown to be an important emancipatory process (Butterwick, 1988). Women are then able to recognize and work together to change societal factors which contribute to their individual problems. Barriers to such collective action for rural women include factors such as geographic isolation and traditions of mutual support to cope with rather than change adverse conditions.

Other personal obstacles faced by rural women involve particular skills. While there are regional differences, many rural women experience illiteracy as a personal obstacle to growth. The lack of basic reading skills may be complicated by other conditions. Responsibilities of early motherhood for example make it difficult for some women to take steps to learn these skills.

The Information Age brings new personal challenges to rural women. A hypothetical computerized farm of the twenty-first century (McGrann, 1984), for example, depends on women trained in the subject matter of computerized tools including accounting, economics, and finance. Educational opportunities need to be provided for women to improve and to remediate in areas involving math and science (Cheng, 1988). Whether on or off the farm, rural women as well as men need such skills in today's technological society.

When rural women are able to overcome personal obstacles to growth, they are often then faced with an array of interpersonal difficulties. Women's roles may change from partner to provider, from mother to supervisor, from farm-based to town. More women in rural areas are now finding themselves alone, due to such factors as more common divorce and separation due to economic dislocation. Many women who have always been homemakers are now responsible for their own and often their children's support.

The family emphasis is strong in rural life, and in many cases the family is still there but it is restructured. Both men and women are struggling to discover ways to handle these new relationships for the rest of their lives. As women assume new roles, major issues may emerge in relation to childbearing, home and family maintenance, and family life.

In traditional rural communities, early childbearing is a common expectation. Women who decide to delay childbearing have reported marital and family conflicts as a result (Haney, 1987). For women with children, rural communities in many cases do not provide child care and preschool and after-school services which are now needed by more families. The traditional rural emphasis on self-reliance can make it difficult for a woman, now employed outside the home, to gain acceptance for a decision to obtain help with domestic work such as housecleaning.

A husband or children may have difficulty in adjusting to the woman's new activities. The woman experiences double jeopardy when she, as the traditional caretaker, assumes responsibility for easing their adjustment. Practically speaking, programs for rural women should also respond to the needs of the men and children in the lives of these women to help all those involved to adjust to the gender role changes (Haney, 1987).

Women's roles in the community are also changing. Psychologist Jean Houston has observed that "there is no turning back from the fact that women are now joining men in full partnership in the domain of the human agenda" (Houston, 1989, p. 25). In the changing rural context, women are emerging as community leaders. This change-in-process might be illustrated in the example of a traditionally all-male economic development corporation in a northern state which has received invaluable help toward their goals from a female state legislator and recently hired a woman as their executive director. To minimize obstacles in this changing community context, possible differences between men and women in leadership styles and paths to leadership need to be understood.

The recent election of a woman governor and appointment of twenty-four women to top administrative positions in Vermont provided a golden opportunity for a study of women's pathways to leadership and leadership styles (Cheng, 1988). This study showed that there was in fact no one pathway to leadership; that women's career paths are nonlinear, contextual, and interwoven with personal concerns. Their leadership styles also reflected a process of relatedness, with decisions made being more contextual and connected to other agencies of government and networks. This study concluded that educators serving women need to be aware of and value women's ways of knowing and recognize that women make sense of education, work, and intimate relations in a contextual, connected way.

Educational institutions which serve rural women may present obstacles by ignoring women's special needs and abilities or by reinforcing traditional attitudes and roles. This can happen despite the stated intention of the program. One study looked at a reentry program for women which established a woman-centered approach to updating and acquiring new skills and increasing self-confidence and self-esteem (Butterwick, 1988). The study found that this women-centered program supported the status quo in terms of employment level and gave the women contradictory messages. For example, the trainers emphasized that the reentry women had much to offer with their human and personal skills, and at the same time lectured women on how to answer the phone. Institutions are challenged to recognize the capabilities of rural women in all aspects of their programs, including both design and implementation.

Perhaps the most significant long-range development that has affected educational opportunities, rural communities, and especially the women who live in them is the conflict between the cost of services and the ability of service providers to deliver. It simply costs more to provide fire protection or cable television adult education classes to several hundred taxpayers in a remote community than it does to provide the same services to a suburban neighborhood.

This friction between the delivery of services and an economy of scale is a major influence on the type of education opportunities that are now and will be available to rural citizens in the future. And it is a friction that has an especially serious impact on the program development targeted at rural women.

RESPONSES TO CHANGING NEEDS

Responses to the changing educational needs of rural women have come from a variety of sources including community-based groups and women's organizations as well as educational institutions. Several insightful and innovative examples will be described, not necessarily as models for replication, but to stimulate thought and further innovation in educational opportunities for rural women.

In rural areas across the nation, the federal Carl Perkins Act has supported vocational education programs for single mothers and displaced homemakers which address some of the personal obstacles faced by these women. These programs are often a building block toward other efforts on the part of women who are not yet ready for school or employment because of personal obstacles such as low self-esteem. Personal support provided in these programs might include assertiveness training and self-assessment. Once a woman enters a training or retraining program, support may include assistance with transportation, child care, and tutoring.

Some programs for single mothers and displaced homemakers have addressed the problems of pay equity and job availability faced by rural women by encouraging women to learn skills for nontraditional jobs (M. Hathaway, personal communication, January 1990). By training for jobs traditionally held by men, women may enjoy better placement and wage potential.

Programs in rural areas which provide training in literacy skills are seldom targeted specifically to women. However, in many cases the clientele are largely women. Programs such as "Mommy and Me" in Mississippi and "Happy Hearts" in Kansas have linked adult literacy with preschool activities. This provides both convenience and motivation for young mothers (J. Spears, personal communication, October 1989).

A computer literacy program in Idaho served primarily women although it was not originally directed at women. This predominance of women in the program was attributed to lower technology anxiety on the part of women, and to the inconvenient schedules of men who work in the mills and woods. As with reading literacy, some of the women were motivated to gain computer skills in order to be more effective parents as well as to improve their own job skills. Program instructors tried to be aware of math anxiety and to include math instruction as it was needed. Women reported using their computers on the farm and in the home for correspondence and bookkeeping as well as in business (M. Emery, personal communication, December 1989).

Easy access to information can be an important first step to employment or continuing education. A Job-Education Fair cosponsored by a local Commission on the Status of Women and community action agency in Lancaster County, Nebraska, has proved to be a popular and effective special event for low-income, unemployed, and underemployed women. The project was begun in 1983 as a job fair. An education component was added in 1987 in response to participants who expressed strong interest in going back to school. The fair is now held three times each year to provide information on job-seeking skills and educational opportunities. In recent years, the fairs have included forty-five minute individual career counseling sessions and on-site tours of schools and agencies the day after the workshop. A phone survey of participants in 1989 showed that more than half had either found employment, were continuing their education, or both (Lincoln Journal-Star, 1989).

Programs of the Cooperative Extension service have addressed problems of stress experienced by farm families during periods of change. The Managing for Tomorrow program was developed by the Extension Service in Nebraska in 1984 in response to the need for financial planning by farm and ranch families created by the farm financial crisis of the early 1980s. The goal of the program was to help families gather, organize, and analyze information to make informed financial decisions about the future of their operation. The program focused on the family as a management unit, and involved goal setting as an integral part of the financial planning process. Families undertook a guided process of developing business and personal goals. This approach of family decision making for personal as well as financial goals provided an opportunity for families to develop mutual adjustments to change. Significant numbers of the families made changes in the interface between family life and the farm or ranch business as well as in business management (Florell, Green, Rood, Bitney, & Fox, n.d.).

The national Extension program, Family Community Leadership, also provides an educational framework in which participating families might make adjustments to the changing rural environment. This program offers leadership workshops preparing participants for involvement in public policy decision making. One objective of the program is to involve women to lead in public affairs on family-related issues. Evaluation results have shown significant positive change in the lives of participants (Hill, n.d.).

Rural women are recognize as leaders and supported and encouraged in leadership in a variety of ways. Grassroots organizations of rural women such as Women Involved in Farm Economics (WIFE) have been successful in making changes in rural policies at state and national levels. Such organizations have focused on problems specific to rural women such as inheritance laws and banking practices and on issues which affect rural life in general such as federal policies in agriculture. The meetings and conferences of grassroots organizations such as WIFE provide rural women with the personally empowering experience of collective action.

The work of the Land Stewardship Project in Minnesota provides another example of women learning through the exercise of leadership on rural issues. Women who are active in the Land Stewardship Project feel that farm women play a major role in decisions made on the farm and are often the ones who raise the concerns about chemical fertilizer and pesticide use. Based on their concerns about family health and wise use of land, these women play an important role in pushing for changes in toxic chemical use on the farm (Land Stewardship Project, 1989).

In today's context of change, rural educational institutions are challenged to involve women in planning the programs which will meet their evolving needs. A focus group technique was used for an assessment of the continuing education needs of rural women living in the Moberly Junior College district in Missouri. Two small groups of women from a local free cooking school and from area Extension clubs were asked to respond to a set of questions about needs and obstacles to meeting these needs. The focus group technique elicited qualitative information that would have been largely missed by other survey methods. Personal contact and the participant's exposure to public relations information were valuable side effects of the focus groups (Lee, 1982).

Personal, interpersonal, community, and institutional problems often overlap, and educational programs may respond at more than one level. The Women's Opportunity and Resource Development, Inc. (WORD) and the Montana Women's Economic Development Corporation (MT WEDCO) are programs which address the needs of rural women at several levels (Todd, 1989). WORD is a Montana corporation started by women with many years of experience in women's education and service programs. Broad areas of interest for WORD are education and employment for women. This includes cultural events and radio and video programs on women's issues. WORD also conducts a welfare reform project, Options Unlimited, funded by the Montana Job Training Coordinating Council.

Through an Entrepreneurial Training Project (ETP), WORD began providing skill training programs and technical assistance, promoting self-employment opportunities. ETP staff also developed a four-month micro-business Incubator Without Walls training program which combines group workshops and individual consultation. This program provides the group identification, mutual support and technical assistance functions of a business incubator, without the physical facility of an incubator.

WORD began planning the Montana Women's Economic Development Corporation in 1987. By 1988, the planning group had established that there was an expanding need in Western Montana for small business technical assistance and capital services among unemployed and underemployed Montana women. Financial support and technical support were identified including financial, legal, management, and marketing professionals willing to volunteer to assist MT WEDCO staff.

In January 1989, MT WEDCO began operations and now offers classes through the Incubator Without Walls program in Missoula, and one-on-one counseling in business finance, marketing, and general business operations. A loan guarantee program, funded by the city and county of Missoula, is available in that county. In their second year, MT WEDCO will expand statewide with basic support services provided locally by three rural displaced homemakers programs. MT WEDCO will use telecommunications to provide technical assistance with business plans and marketing research to these remote locations.

CHARACTERISTICS OF SUCCESSFUL PROGRAMS TARGETING RURAL WOMEN

The examples described in this chapter highlight programs that have successfully responded to the needs of rural women in ways that enhance educational opportunities for the participants. These examples are, in fact, the "best practices" of the providers of educational services. Such programs share the following characteristics.

Grounding in the Accepted Assumptions About Adult Learners

Successful programs for rural women incorporate the assumption that the participant's life experience is a valuable basis from which to proceed. This means that experiential techniques are used whenever possible (Knowles, 1984).

Rather than designing educational opportunities that are subject-centered, these successful programs use a problem-centered approach and recognize the importance of timing and readiness on the part of the adult learners.

Finally, these programs are based on an emphasis of improving self-concept among learners that is especially important for rural women in transition from a traditional cultural role to a new and perhaps risk-laden life change.

Problem-solving Approach to Learner Needs

Rural women participating in any learning project will encounter obstacles such as those already discussed as well as additional circumstances that will evolve. The best programs are those in which staff assumes a problem-solving role in relation to the obstacles encountered by participants.

Flexibility as a Standard

The more flexible the structure of an educational opportunity, the more likely it will be able to fit into the limits of a participant's life.

Innovations based on distance learning and telecommunications technology hold great promise for rural program delivery. Such mechanisms as correspondence courses, mentoring matchups, internships, individualized coursework and time lines, and requirements that can be tailored for an individual situation are all examples of such flexibility.

Avoiding Competition for Resources

Many times programs that serve women will be placed in competition with one another. Successful programs develop strategies that maximize combined resources rather than creating win-lose situations. For example, rather than forcing an institution to choose between funding a program for elderly widows or a teen parenting class, program designers need to explore ways in which both needs might be met such as combining the elderly women as mentors for the teen parents in something like a "foster grandmother" program.

This list of characteristics of successful education oportunities for rural women is by no means exhaustive. It is intended as a discussion point for the assessment of current educational opportunities and a possible source of evaluation criteria. These characteristics might also be considered in the design of any new programs targeted at a rural population.

SPECIAL DESIGN CRITERIA FOR RURAL WOMEN'S PROGRAMS

There seem to be, however, several design considerations that are especially important for rural women's programs. Among these are context and the impact of change on the learner.

Context for a rural woman as an adult learner means the community at large, the smaller community of family, and finally, herself. The community at large represents the burden—and sometimes security—of tradition and accepted behavior. It is typical for a rural woman to be moving against the stream of accepted behavior when she takes on a learning project, whether it is learning a new job skill or trying out a new interest. She may be the first in her family to go back to school or be far removed from the acceptable age for a student in her community. And self-concept cannot be overemphasized as a necessary and integral part of program design.

The impact of change on the learner is another important design criteria. When a rural woman engages in a learning project, she may not be prepared for resistance from spouse and family. She may not realize that learning causes changes in behaviors and that her behaviors in one role (wife, mother, daughter, etc.) may change if she learns new skills, attitudes, and self-concepts.

This aspect of the impact of participation can often be addressed by designing support group or discussion opportunities for participants as part of a training program or class. Often simply talking about how the "folks at home" are dealing with the participant's new schedule, activities, language, ideas, and so on can be very helpful. In fact, one successful program recommends that such discussion or support groups also be offered to family members as a means of adjusting to and supporting the new behaviors of the participant.

WOMEN AS AGENTS OF CHANGE

While participation in educational programs has implications for the families of participants, there are also potential impacts on rural communities. In recent research, women in leadership positions in rural communities seem to be more accepted, at least in those communities that are coping well with change (Wall & Luther, 1990). The need for increased involvement of women in community development projects has also been strongly suggested (Stoneall, 1983).

It seems obvious that the rural community that survives the dramatic social and economic changes at work in our country will be the community that develops every possible competitive advantage including the emerging leadership of female citizens.

With this in mind, a final design consideration for the development of educational opportunities is to focus on a contribution to the community. Educational opportunities that simply retrain rural women so that they might relocate in urban areas or channel women's economic activity into business development that takes resources away from the community are, in the final sense, self-defeating.

In fact, many parallels can be seen between the overlooked and often hidden lives of rural women and the discounted and inferior status of rural communities in the national scene today. Both offer a wealth of history, experience, and strength that represent a tremendous resource.

It is possible to design programs that encourage women to expand their participation in the community, to become the new and emerging leadership of the community as it struggles into the future.

CONCLUSION

The woman whose story opened this chapter experienced several obstacles. Carol was faced with the problem of distance from educational opportunities, attitudes towards working mothers, and lack of employment history. Each of these obstacles might be offset in the variety of innovative programs which have been described.

Changes in societal roles and economic realities create impacts in the lives of rural women and their families. Innovative institutional responses to women as lifelong learners can overcome obstacles and enhance the individual and community's ability to cope with change.

REFERENCES

Albrecht, D., Murdock, S., & Schiflett, K. (1986). *Farm financial stress and level of off-farm employment.* Paper presented at the Annual Meeting of the Rural Sociological Society. Salt Lake City, UT.

Butterwick, S. (1988). Re-entry for women: This time it's personal. *Proceedings of the Twenty-ninth Annual Adult Education Research Conference* (pp. 25–30). Calgary: University of Calgary.

Cheng, B. (1988). A profile of selected women leaders: Toward a new model of leadership. *Proceedings of the Twenty-ninth Annual Adult Education Research Conference* (pp. 49–54). Calgary: University of Calgary.

Dillman, D., & Hobbs, D. (Eds.). (1982). *Rural society in the U.S.: Issues for the 1980's.* Boulder: Westview.

Easton, S. (1988). Overcoming barriers to education for rural adults: A consideration of public policy proposals. *Proceedings of the Twenty-ninth Annual Adult Education Research Conference* (pp. 103–108). Calgary: University of Calgary.

Florell, R., Green, J., Rood, D., Bitney, L., & Fox, J. (n.d.). *Managing for tomorrow: Participant views of a financial management educational program.* Lincoln: University of Nebraska.

Florin, C. (1989). Women find new options, forge new roles in rural America. *Earth Matters: Journal of Faith, Community and Resources, 38* (1), 6–12.

Haney, W. (1982). Women, In D. Dillman & D. Hobbs (Eds.), *Rural society in the U.S.: Issues for the 1980's* (pp. 124–135). Boulder: Westview.

Haney, W. (1987). Entrepreneurship: An economic opportunity for women. *National Rural Entrepreneurship Symposium.* Knoxville, TN. Southern Rural Development Center.

Hill, D. (Ed.). (n.d.). *Revitalizing rural America program ideas resource book.* Madison: Cooperative Extension System.

Houston, J. (1989). The rise of the feminine. *Women of Power, 12,* 25.

Isard, W. (1960). *Methods of regional analysis.* New York: Wiley.

Job-education fairs winning combination. (1989, November). *Lincoln Journal-Star,* p. 6F.

John, D., Batie, S., & Norris, K. (1988). *A brighter future for rural America?* Washington, DC: National Governor's Association.

Knowles, M. (1984) *The adult learner: A neglected species* (3rd ed.). Houston: Gulf.

Land Stewardship Project (1989). Farm women play a major role in transition to sustainability. *The Land Stewardship Letter, 7*(4), 1 & 7.

Lee, J. (1982). *Using new methods to determine continuing education needs of rural women.* (ERIC Document Reproduction Service No. ED 233 131).

McGrann, J. (1984). *Computerized farm of the 21st century.* Paper presented at the Rural Sociological Society 47th Annual Meeting, College Station, TX.

Stoneall, L. (1983). Bringing women into community studies: A rural midwestern case study. *Journal of the Community Development Society, 14*(1), 17–29.

Todd, M. (1989). *Eco-feminism as a force in planning and development.* Unpublished masters thesis, University of Nebraska, Lincoln.

Trent, R., & Stout-Wiegand, N. (1987). Attitudes toward women coal-miners in an Appalachian coal community. *Journal of the Community Development Society, 18*(1), 1–14.

Wall, M., & Luther, V. (1990). *Clues to rural community survival* (6th ed.). Lincoln: Heartland Center for Leadership Development.

CHAPTER 14

Rural Education and Minorities
RAY BARNHARDT

Special considerations come into play when racial, ethnic, or religious "minorities" are factored into the rural education equation. Since diversity is an inherent feature of any environment in which a particular segment of the population comes to be identified as a minority, attention will be given to the particular and unique ways in which diversity is manifested in rural communities, and to some of the consequences of such diversity for educational planning, policy making, and program development. Of particular concern will be the underlying political, socioeconomic, and cultural considerations that contribute to and derive from the identification of part of the rural population as a minority. The chapter will conclude with a discussion of ways in which educational institutions serving the lifelong needs of a rural community can be more appropriately designed and operated to accommodate cultural diversity.

Rural communities in America are not microcosms of their urban cousins. Differences in scale, in population density, in geographic dispersion, in economic structure, in social organization, in political outlook, and in many other aspects of day-to-day existence, combine to distinguish life in a small rural community from life in a large urban center. All of these differences must be taken into account in the development of educational programs. Policies, programs, and structures designed to meet the needs of the population in a large urban industrial center are not likely to be well suited to the needs of a small rural farming community (Nachtigal, 1982).

In addition, there are also implications for the ways in which differences are situated. Urban communities often reflect great diversity of socioeconomic composition within their boundaries, while rural communities tend to be relatively homogenous internally, but can reflect considerable socioeconomic diversity from one community to the next. The educational planning and policy-making implications of the rural/urban distinctions are greatly magnified by these differences between rural communities, many of which involve differences in socioeconomic status. It is to these latter differences, which often lead to de facto classifications of social, ethnic, racial, cultural, and economic minority populations, that much of this chapter will be directed.

MINORITIES IN RURAL CONTEXTS

The notion of "minority" can mean many things and is highly relative in its application. In some cases, minority groups are defined along ethnic or racial lines (black, Hispanic, Native American, Meti), while in others they may be distinguished on the basis of religious affiliation (Amish, Hutterite, Mennonite) or by position on the economic ladder (Appalachian poor white, migrant). But whether or not a person is in fact a minority at any point in time depends on many other circumstances as well. In the context of a reservation, Indian tribal members constitute a political and cultural majority and presumably, can shape their own policies and programs. In the larger state and national political arena, however, they are a minority and are subject to many constraints that are imposed from beyond their jurisdiction as a tribe. A group of migrant farm workers may originate from a home community in which they are the dominant political force when they are in residence. While on the road and in the fields, however, they are often in a subservient status and are subject to political and economic forces largely beyond their control. For the members of any group, it is this lack of political influence or sense of local control and self-determination that gives meaning to the notion of being a minority. For the purposes of this discussion, therefore, "minority" will be taken to refer to any group of people that hold a unique identity and/or position outside the social and political mainstream.

Given such a definition, one of the most critical variables that must be considered when examining the implications of public policy on a minority population is the power structure of the community in which it is situated. If the members of the population in question constitute a political majority in the community, their ability to shape the policies and programs that impact their lives is much greater than if they are a minor element in the power structure. Determination of such a political status cannot be based on numbers alone, however, because many other historical, cultural, and economic factors influence the level of participation in political affairs on the part of any group of people. Blacks in the South, for example, have only recently begun to exercise the level of political influence that their numbers would warrant. Appalachian poor and migrants, like blacks, have long been subject to economic exploitation by a small but powerful political system which has been able to keep the majority of the population in a politically marginal role. To overcome such exploitation, one of the first and most critical arenas that minority groups have sought to utilize has been education, for it is through education, formal and nonformal, that the political consciousness of a people can be activated and brought to bear on the policies and programs that impact their lives (Darnell, 1980).

To the extent that the majority of the population of a rural community is composed of a relatively homogenous "minority" population—for example, the majority are black, Chippewa, Amish, or Hispanic—there is going to be considerable diversity of need and perspective from one community to the next. Furthermore, the various rural minority populations in the United States and Canada tend to be clustered by region, such as a preponderance of blacks in the South, Hispanics in the Southwest, and Native Americans in the Northwest and Plains areas, with Amish, Hutterites, and Mennonites centered in the Midwest and southern Canada. How a particular minority group or community positions itself and is perceived in the surrounding social, economic, and political environment depends on many variables, ranging from past history to current economic opportunities and population composition. Any educational initiative from within or outside a community must take all of these variables into account, along with many less tangible considerations, such as differences in cultural values, lifestyle, and world view, if it is to have any likelihood of succeeding. Policies for one minority group, community, or region may or may not be appropriate for another.

EDUCATION ISSUES FACING RURAL MINORITIES

It is apparent that the needs of rural minorities present some unique challenges to the development of appropriate educational services in their communities. While rural minority communities share some characteristics in common with other rural communities (small scale, geographic isolation, low population density), as well as some characteristics in common with their urban minority cousins (low socioeconomic status, political marginality, cultural differences), many of these characteristics require differential treatment in the rural minority context, along with the qualities identified previously that distinguish one rural minority community from the next (Nachtigal, 1989). Some of the most critical variables that differently impact the educational opportunities of rural minorities are socioeconomic status, locus of control, level of community participation, and cultural appropriateness of instruction.

Socioeconomic Status

The most influentiaal factor that shapes the educational experience of minority communities is their socioeconomic status vis-à-vis the larger society in which they are situated (Arends, 1987). To the extent that a community has control over the social, political, and economic forces that define its existence, it is able to shape the educational experience to reflect its needs and wishes. Thus, the Amish have gone so far as to take the state to court to protect their religious prerogatives with regard to who teaches their children and how long they are required to attend school. They have established and maintained an independent social, religious, and economic position from which they have been able to define their sustaining educational needs and establish appropriate mechanisms to meet those needs on a community-wide and lifelong basis.

Other rural minority communities have not fared so well, however. Many Native American tribes have been historically subject to the oversight of the federal government, and until recently have had little direct control over the educational and economic policies that impacted their lives and communities. Lacking such control, Indian people have had little incentive to see formal education as being in their best interests. At the same time they have managed to resist pressures for assimilation and have maintained their own informal educational processes to protect and pass on many of their cultural beliefs and traditions from generation to generation. It was the federal Indian Self-Determination and Educational Assistance Act of 1976 that finally made it possible for Indian people to take control of the programs and services in their communities and re-shape them to their own ends.

One of the biggest impediments to the development of an active minority community role in education has been the long history of economic exploitation. Whether it originated with oil drilling on the reservation, coal mining in Appalachia, sharecropping in the South, or migrant labor on the vegetable and fruit farms of the West, the legacy of exploitation continues to be reflected in the high levels of poverty and stifled aspirations imbedded in the homes and communities of the people who have been the victims. The steps necessary to overcome the sense of powerlessness that accompanies such exploitation often begin with education in one form or another. Rosa Parks sat in the front of the bus after participating in a civil rights workshop at the Highlander Center in Tennessee. Cesar Chavez sought early on in his organizing efforts to improve the educational opportunities for migrant farm workers. One of the first concerted political actions of the congressionally created Alaska Native Corporations was to obtain legislative action to dissolve the state-operated school system and create in its place twenty-one locally controlled school districts. In each of these instances, education was the lifeline to a sense of community and a stimulus to political action, but only because the initiative came from within the minority communities themselves.

From a socioeconomic standpoint, many rural minority communities are not unlike third world countries coming out from under colonial domination. They are seeking to assert themselves and carve out a future of their own making, reflecting the cultural values and traditions that give them distinction as a minority. For the educator, this means working *with* minority communities from a posture of facilitator and resource person, rather than in the all-too-prevalent role of outside authority or benevolent benefactor imposing their will *on* the community. For policy makers and community activists, it means shifting the emphasis from externally defined solutions to human resource development within the communities, and letting each community set its own course for development (Sher, 1981, 1983).

Locus of Control

The way educational services are organized can have a major impact on how responsive they are to the needs of diverse populations. One characteristic that distinguishes formal education from nonformal education is the locus of control and decision making with regard to the content and processes involved. Formal education tends to be much more constraining in the degree to which local communities can exert influence over what occurs. Schooling is subject to a wide array of externally imposed laws, rules, regulations, accreditation standards, certification requirements, curriculum guidelines, testing criteria, and graduation requirements, not to mention tradition, conventional wisdom, and institutional inertia. To bring schooling processes in line with minority community wishes, on even a relatively minor change in curriculum offerings or the school calendar, can often require enormous amounts of time and energy to negotiate through the multiple layers of bureaucracy that protect the status quo of the formal educational system.

Nonformal education initiatives, on the other hand, have very little in the way of externally imposed constraints and thus can be readily shaped to meet the particular needs of a community. Adult literacy programs, cooperative extension service, health and nutrition workshops, 4-H clubs, leadership development initiatives, voter registration campaigns, and so forth all illustrate the potential of locally oriented and implemented community educational endeavors. For rural minority communities, such initiatives, unburdened by the structure of the formal educational system, provide the latitude to create educational opportunities that take into account the cultural inclinations and aspirations of the people being served. Nonformal education can thus provide a valuable complement to the services offered by the formal system.

Another factor that determines how susceptible educational services are to minority community concerns is the size of the community or institutions involved. In general, the larger an institution, the more rigid and bureaucratic it is likely to be, and the harder it will be to get it to make localized accommodations. On the surface, this would indicate that institutions in small rural communities would be more flexible and able to adapt to the special needs of the populations they serve. This is not always the case, however, because rural institutions have had a tendency to model themselves after their larger urban counterparts, and the persons working in these institutions often come out of training programs oriented to large scale systems (Sher, 1977). This orientation to the large scale "one best system" has been the basis for much of the pressure to consolidate small rural school districts into larger institutions, but consolidated school districts generally have distanced schooling from minority populations, rather than improve the opportunities available to them. For the same reason, many American Indian tribes have taken over the operaton of their schools from the federal and state-operated systems and established tribally oriented institutions. Small, locally run schools have a better chance of responding to the needs of a minority community than schools imbedded in a large bureaucracy.

Level of Community Participation

Local control of an institution by a particular minority community does not in itself ensure that the institution will be sensitive to the cultural beliefs and practices of that community. The high expectations of more than one community have been dampened when the operational version of their attempt at a more culturally appropriate educational program turned out to be little different from the program it was intended to replace. It would be easy to attribute such a lack of cultural adaptability in institutions to the fact that most professional level positions associated with educational programs are held by people from outside the minority community, and thus cultural innovations are constrained by the imposition of a Western/Anglo monocultural perspective. Such an interpretation, however, neglects to take into account the reality that similar frustrations have also been experienced in situations where minority people have held professional roles and have made a deliberate attempt to respond to the wishes of the minority community. This would indicate that cultural biases can reside not only in the individual occupying an institutional role, but in the very structure of the institution as well.

While people in professional roles, through their own deliberate action, can function as institutional gatekeepers, there are many other less obvious ways in which institutions can present unintended structural barriers to the accommodation of rural minority community concerns and perspectives (Weise, 1989). Such barriers may exist in any feature of an institution in which there is potential for different cultural beliefs and practices to influence the attitudes and behavior of institutional participants. This includes implicit behavioral routines, such as the way people are expected to communicate and interact with one another, and the way decision making and leadership are exercised. It also includes explicit institutional routines, such as recruitment and selection procedures, the way time and space are structured, and the criteria and techniques used to judge people's performances.

It is possible to reduce some of these institutional barriers by training nonminority personnel to recognize how institutional policies and practices favor some people over others, and encourage them to develop practices that take cultural diversity into account. Such an approach does not, however, address inequities in the distribution of power in the institution, nor is it the most effective or efficient means of building cultural sensitivity into institutional practices. Minority people, with appropriate training and the opportunity to bring their unique perspective and skills to bear, are generally in a better position to break down institutional barriers to minority participation, because they have inherent within them the necessary cultural predispositions. They must also, however, have the incentive and support to take culturally appropriate initiatives in the restructuring of institutional practices, or they will simply perpetuate the inequities built into existing practices.

Bringing professional responsibility for the delivery of educational services to the level of the minority community is a critical step if those services are to reflect local cultural considerations. In doing so, however, new kinds of demands are placed on the role of the professional, which require a familiarity with and sensitivity to features of the local cultural system that few people from outside the system are likely to develop. It becomes imperative, therefore, that minority people assume those roles and decision-making responsibilities, and be given the latitude to introduce their own *modus operandi* in response to the needs and conditions in the community. Efforts to achieve "cultural fit" may require changes in institutional features ranging from the simple rescheduling of daily activities to a rethinking of the very function of the institution. Persons fully immersed in the cultural community being served are in the best position to recognize and act upon the discrepancies between instiutional and cultural practices that interfere with the performance of the institution.

While moving the control of services closer to the community and bringing minority people into decision-making and professional roles are critical and necessary steps toward transforming rural programs and services into more culturally sensitive institutions, those steps in themselves are not sufficient to achieve the equity of services that is needed. In addition to possessing all of the bureaucratic and political skills necessary to maintain a Western institution, the minority community must also understand how the institution can be made to fit into the minority world without subverting essential features of that world. When such a transformation of existing institutions is not possible without losing more cultural ground than is gained, the minority community must also have the skill to build new kinds of institutions that can respect and sustain the biculturalism that is inherent in the contemporary minority experience. The innovative kinds of social, political, and educational institutions that have grown out of minority community initiatives, such as the Highlander Education and Research Center in Appalacia, the Farm Workers Union in California, and the native art cooperatives across Canada and Alaska, all reflect the strength and cultural spirit of the minority communities from which they emerged.

Cultural Appropriateness of Instruction

One of the biggest challenges that schools serving minority populations face is bringing the educational experiences provided by the school in line with the social, cultural, and economic aspirations of the community it serves. To the extent that the cultural fabric of the community being served is different from that out of which the school was constructed, some kind of accommodation is going to have to be made on someone's part if the two are to come together in a mutually productive manner. Most often the community and students are called upon to make the adjustment, but increasingly, as minority people take on more influential roles in the schools, they are making an attempt to meet the students halfway. These efforts have been particularly evident in minority communities where a second language is spoken and schools attempt to incorporate the local language in the curriculum.

While it is not often easy, it is possible for a school to provide an integrated educational program that builds on the local cultural environment and indigenous knowledge base as a foundation for learning about the larger world beyond (Barnhardt & Tonsmeire, 1988). Learning about one's own cultural heritage and community need not be viewed as supplanting opportunities to learn about others, but rather as providing an essential infrastructure through which all other learning is constructed. It is often a reality of today's existence that cultural minority students have a foot in more than one world, so their education needs to reflect the symbiotic and synergistic potential of that existence.

The school cannot do the job alone, however. The most critical factor in the success of any educational effort is its initiation from the cultural community being served and the strong, sustained, and unequivocal support provided by representatives of that community. Without such commitment and persistence, innovative initiatives are likely to fall by the wayside within a few years. The parents and school board members must take an active interest in the education of their children, both in and out of school. The values and skills to be taught in school should mirror those encouraged in the home and the community. Education is a community responsibility, with the school serving as one player, albeit a key one, in the process. That which is expected of students and the school should be reinforced in explicit ways by the parents and the community. Parents should be active participants and contribute their indigenous knowledge and expertise to the school (Barnhardt, 1990).

A cultural system is more than the surface or visible attributes of the language, arts and crafts, eating habits, or subsistence practices of the people who sustain it. Being Hispanic, or Amish, or Eskimo, or black, also means a way of thinking, a way of seeing, a way of behaving, a way of doing things, and a way of relating to the world. Education must take all of these aspects of minority cultural existence into account if it is to be truly culturally appropriate.

RURAL EDUCATION FOR CULTURAL DIVERSITY

Socioeconomic status, locus of control, level of community participation, and cultural appropriateness of instruction must be considered in the design and provision of educational services for rural minority populations. To the extent that such factors require special attention, we must find ways to formulate more sensitive policies and construct more appropriate institutions, so that we can bring the necessary attention to bear on the issues that have been raised. The remainder of this chapter will examine some of the policies and practices that can enhance an institution's ability to accommodate cultural differences: participatory decision making, a decentralized authority structure, a distributive communication system, and a loosely coupled organizational framework.

Participatory Decision Making

As indicated earlier, a minority perspective in decision making can come about only through the presence of minority people in the decision making arena. To be truly responsive to minority concerns, an institution must not only reflect an awareness of minority cultural values and practices, but must also convey an attitude of respect for those values and practices. This must be done in such a way that minority people feel a sense of ownership with regard to the institution and see it as incorporating their traditions and perpetuating their interests. So long as the institutional decision-making processes are in the hands of nonminority decision makers (regardless of how well-intentioned), minority people are going to feel shut out as equal participants. But it is not enough to invite a token minority representative to "bring a minority perspective" to the decision-making arena, or to hire a token minority employee to integrate the staff and appease the critics. Nor is it enough to have minority people in professional or supervisory roles using conventional bureaucratic-style criteria to perpetuate Western institutional values. Such gratuitous avenues of participation are too easily subverted by the weight of Western bureaucratic machinery and do little to counteract the cultural distance between Western-style institutions and minority people.

To develop a sense of institutional ownership, minority people must feel they are a part of the action and are a party to decision making from top to bottom, beginning to end. They must be on the delivery end of institutional services, not just on the receiving end. If such a transformation is to take place, institutions must adopt a participatory approach to decision making, whereby everyone that is affected by an institution, whether as producer or consumer of institutional services, has an opportunity to influence the way the institution operates. This requires multiple avenues of access to the decision-making process, so that people can contribute in a manner consistent with their relationship to the institution and with their style of participation and decision making. It also involves a horizontal distribution of power, so that all of the decision-making authority is not vested in a top-down hierarchical structure. Participatory decision making is at the heart of any institutional or educational process which seeks to strengthen the degree of control that people have over their lives (Barnhardt, 1982).

Increased minority participation in institutional decision making can be achieved through a variety of mechanisms. These range from the establishment of affirmative action programs that strengthen minority presence in existing institutions, to the creation of new institutions, where minority people sustain their cultural community through their own system of educational and service institutions. Other options include contracting with minority institutions to provide services to minority people; establishing minority councils to oversee minority interests; employing minority elders to advise in areas of cultural and spiritual significance; and creating minority units within existing institutions through which minority people can manage their own affairs. It is through mechanisms such as these that minority people can begin to wield the power needed to shape their own destiny. It is not enough to be the beneficiaries of benevolent institutions. Minority people must be full and equal participants in the shaping and operation of those institutions.

Decentralized Authority Structure

Participatory decision making is empty rhetoric without a decentralized authority structure. In the content of building institutional respect for diversity, bigger is not better. If institutions are to be responsive to differences in cultural beliefs and practices, they must be scaled and situated in such a way that they can interact with the client community on local terms (Barnhardt, et al., 1979). The larger the system and the more distant the decision making is from the clientele, the greater the demand for comformity to institutional norms, and the more difficult it is to accommodate diversity. Conversely, the closer the system is to the people being served, the fewer the bureaucratic constraints and barriers that tend to interfere with peoples access to the system, and the greater the opportunity for diverse points of view to be heard and acted upon. The functional units of an institution must be small enough to allow for a personalized approach to services, so that local styles of communication and interaction can enter into the decision-making process, and so that services can be structured to fit the cultural norms of the client community.

One of the most common approaches to decentralization is to distribute authority over certain aspects of institutional services to regional or branch offices. Such a move can be a signficant step toward decentralization, but if the local authority is still tightly controlled by a distant central office, it may achieve no more than to add another layer to the institutional bureaucracy. If decentralization is to increase participation in decision making, it must include the establishment of local bodies to whom local or regional authorities are answerable. Whenever possible, representatives of the client community should have a direct voice in policy making and personnel and budgetary decisions. Client participation in the selection of key personnel is especially critical, so that local considerations can be taken into account, and so that the persons selected feel a sense of responsibility to the client community.

Another important consideration in institutional decentralization is the criteria for definition of a service area. Typically, decentralized service areas are structured along the lines of established political boundaries or geographical regions. Such criteria do not always coincide with traditional minority kinship and tribal structures, however, and as a result, tend to interfere with rather than enhance minority participation in decision making. Any attempt to establish a decentralized system sensitive to the needs of minority people must begin with a framework that minority people themselves use to organize their lives. For some services, this may mean a community-oriented system. Others may require a regionally oriented structure. Whatever approach is used, it should fit into the natural authority and decision-making structure of the community or region to be served. In those situations where institutional services are to be decentralized to better serve both minority and nonminority, it may be necessary to establish a dual system with different criteria for service areas for each group.

Once again, it is important to recognize that the structure of an institution is a crucial factor in determining how effectively and equitably the institution can perform its functions. A decentralized structure, scaled to fit into the cultural and organizational framework of minority communities, will make an institution more accessible to minority participation, and thus increase its potential to serve minority needs.

Distributive Communication System

A key ingredient for any properly functioning decentralized, participatory institutional structure is an effective communication system. If minority people are to be active participants in economic, community, or institutional development, they must have already access to information related to the development, and they must be able to convey their own views in culturally appropriate ways. This requires a system of communication that provides multiple and diverse avenues for people to participate in, and contribute to, the development process. Institutions must encourage a free flow of information into and out of their decision-making structures. This can be accomplished through formal and informal channels, including participatory committees, community meetings, newsletters and other regular publications, and various kinds of community consultantships. The important thing is that communication processes be distributed throughout the community so that everyone is well informed, and so that people can use their natural communication patterns to get their views across.

A large-scale, centralized, top-down communication structure is of little use in furthering local participation, whereas a distributive network that links people together with one another and with the institutions serving them, can greatly enhance the quanity and quality of participation (Wallace, 1979). If institutions are to be responsive to minority interests, they must establish a communication system that taps into minority communication patterns and encourages two-way dialogue.

Loosely Coupled Organizational Framework

Another characteristic necessary for institutional systems to be able to respond favorably to the cultural diversity reflected in minority issues is that the various components of the system be loosely coupled, so that the system can maintain a flexible, adaptive, and open-ended posture in response to diverse demands. A rigidly structured centralized system will have considerable difficulty responding to the variations in social, cultural, economic, political, and historical circumstances that exist in rural minority communities. Along with decentralized administrative authority, it is important, therefore, that there also be sufficient latitude to adapt institutional structures to the particular circumstances in each community or service area. It is not necessary, for example, that each local unit of a dispersed educational agency adopt the same framework for the delivery of services. As long as there is general agreement on the functions to be performed and on the outcomes upon which effectiveness is to be judged, each unit should be encouraged to adapt its structure and services in response to local conditions, rather than be required to maintain a standardized bureaucratic framework. Different means can be used to achieve the same ends.

Demands for institutional uniformity arise from notions of cultural universality and bureaucratic efficiency. While such notions may be applicable to situations of cultural homogeniety, or in relation to functions of a strictly mechanical nature, they are not well suited where human behavior is a significant variable. In such situations, it is necessary to maintain a flexible and adaptive institutional framework that can respond to a varied and changing human environment (Conklin & Olson, 1988). This requires personnel who are sensitive to cultural variations in behavior and possess a repertoire of skills for organizing diverse interests and efforts so that they fuse into a coherent collective endeavor. The person in such a situation functions less as a bureaucrat and more as a coordinator and mediator, leading by example and consensus rather than by decree. It is essential for educational policy makers and practitioners to recognize, therefore, that the characteristics of the individual who occupies a role, the way the role is defined by the institution in which it is situated, and the posture of the institution in relation to the populations it serves, are all factors that influence the ability of the institution to respond to cultural diversity.

SUMMARY

Many factors must be considered when attempting to devise policies and practices that address the unique needs of rural minority populations. Qualities such as scale, density, dispersion, composition, and perspective shape the way educational services are influenced by and have bearing on a particular population, when that population is labeled "minority". It is also of critical importance to take into account factors such as socioeconomic status, locus of control, level of community participation, and cultural appropriateness of instruction. These factors, more than anything else, determine the effectiveness of schooling in minority settings.

To the extent that a rural community or educational institution is serious about finding ways to respond to the educational needs and aspirations of minority constituencies, special consideration will need to be given to the structure of the social, economic, and political dynamics that define the relationship between the institution and the minority population being served. Some of the institutional qualities and practices that can be most instrumental in facilitating a productive and mutually beneficial relationship are participatory decision making, a decentralized authority structure, a distributive communication system, and a loosely coupled organizational framework. If implemented appropriately, institutional features such as these will be of benefit not only to minorities, but to all segments of the population being served.

Minority people in rural communities are seeking ways to bring educational institutions and services more in line with their particular interests and aspirations. The issues raised in this chapter reflect just a few of the considerations that come into play when educational institutions attempt to respond to minority concerns. Some of the issues raised apply to urban settings and nonminority populations as well, but the distinctiveness of rural minority communities, one from another as well as from urban communities, calls for a distinctive response. As we create more open and adaptive educational institutions and services to respond to the needs of rural minority communities, we will have improved the lifelong educational opportunities for all of us.

REFERENCES

Arends, J. H. (Ed.). (1987). *Building on excellence: Regional priorities for the improvement of rural, small schools.* A report to the National Rural Schools Task Force by the Regional Educational Laboratories. Washington, DC: Council for Educational Development and Research.

Barnhardt, R., *et al.* (1979). *Small high school programs for rural Alaska.* Fairbanks: University of Alaska, Center for Cross-Cultural Studies.

Barnhardt, R. (Ed.). (1982). *Cross-cultural issues in Alaskan education* (vol. 2). Fairbanks: University of Alaska, Center for Cross-Cultural Studies.

Barnhardt, R., & Tonsmeire, K. (Eds). (1988). *Lessons taught, lessons learned: Teachers' reflections on schooling in rural Alaska.* Fairbanks: University of Alaska, Center for Cross-Cultural Studies.

Barnhardt, R. (1990). Two cultures, one school: A case study. In *Rural Education Task Force Report to Ford Foundation.* Manhattan, KS: Kansas State University Rural Clearinghouse for Lifelong Education and Development.

Conklin, N. F., & Olson, T. A. (1988). *Toward more effective education for poor, minority students in rural areas: What the research suggests.* Portland: Northwest Regional Educational Laboratory.

Darnell, F. (1980). Education and local development in rural minority communities. *Proceedings of OECD International Seminar.* Fairbanks: University of Alaska, Center for Cross-Cultural Studies.

Nachtigal, P. (Ed.). (1982). *Rural education: In search of a better way.* Boulder: Westview.

Nachtigal, P. (Ed.). (1989). Rural schools and community development. Special issue of *Noteworthy.* Aurora, CO: Mid-Continent Regional Educational Laboratory.

Sher, J. (Ed.). (1977). *Education in rural America: A reassessment of the conventional wisdom.* Boulder: Westview.

Sher, J. (Ed.). (1981). *Rural education in urbanized nations: Issues and innovations.* Boulder: Westview.

Sher, J. (Ed.). (1983). Do we want standardized rural schooling. Special issue of *Phi Delta Kappan,* 65(4), 252–283.

Wallace, J. (Ed.). (1979). *The national seminar on rural education: Conference report.* Las Cruces, NM: Eric Clearinghouse on Rural and Small Schools.

Weise, J. (1989). *The relationship between personal, school, and community characteristics and teacher turnover in Alaskan Rural Education Attendance Areas during 1987–89.* Unpublished doctoral dissertation, University of Oregon, Eugene.

PART THREE

RESOURCES AND FUTURE PROSPECTS FOR RURAL LIFELONG EDUCATION

CHAPTER 15

Resources for Rural Lifelong Education

JACQUELINE D. SPEARS
GWEN BAILEY
SUE C. MAES

As is evident from the previous chapters, rural lifelong education shares the diversity that is characteristic of adult education. From the formal institutions sustained by tax dollars to the community organizations created through the interests and energies of local citizens, a rich tapestry of educational providers is woven into the very fabric of rural community life. This richness reflects the diversity of rural communities as well as adult learners. Different histories, cultures, values, resources, and needs give rise to a wide range of educational efforts.

Having been provided an introduction to these educational efforts, the reader may now want to pursue several in more detail. This chapter is designed to provide a departure point for such inquiries. For the past six years, the Rural Clearinghouse for Lifelong Education and Development (formerly known as the Action Agenda Project) has collected information and maintained a network among the many educational providers. In sharing this information, we ask the reader to keep two points in mind.

First, the list is not exhaustive. Space considerations alone do not enable us to include all the resources available. Moreover, interest in rural communities has grown substantially. As we write, efforts to understand the link between educational resources and rural development are underway and will undoubtedly yield a number of useful resources. We have tried to select materials that are relatively easy to acquire and that lead the reader to yet other resources and networks.

Second, the reader is encouraged to explore resources across several of the educational providers. Rural environments appear to present a similar set of challenges and opportunities to educators, regardless of the level or structure of the institution. Limited resources also encourage institutions to broaden their mission or activities. Rural community colleges, for example, often find more in common with rural community based organizations or private colleges than with urban community colleges.

Resources are presented within three broad categories: rural schools, higher education, and nonformal education. Within each category, four types of resources are reviewed:

1. Clearinghouses/Centers: groups which function primarily as collectors/disseminators of information.

2. Programs: ongoing activities of schools, colleges, or nonformal providers that are unique or especially illustrative.

3. Organizations/Associations: membership organizations which support networking and professional development.

4. Publications: journals, newsletters, books, monographs, and videotapes.

This chapter presents a brief overview of the various resources. The appendix offers a complete list.

RURAL SCHOOLS

Despite a past dominated by criticism and punctuated by consolidation, rural school districts continue to endure—today serving about one-third of the nation's children. Rural schools are often endowed with strong community support and more flexible organizational structures, leading some to propose that rural schools offer a laboratory in which to explore educational change. Yet rural schools have remained isolated— often from one another as well as from an educational system reluctant to understand the role local context plays in the way schools should be run. Interest in rural schools has grown, however, and the resources we now share are significantly expanded beyond those available a decade ago.

Clearinghouses/Centers

The single, most comprehensive resource for rural schools is the ERIC Clearinghouse on Rural Education and Small Schools (ERIC/ CRESS), housed in the Appalachia Educational Laboratory in Charleston, West Virginia. One of a network of federally supported educational document collection and dissemination centers, ERIC/CRESS solicits documents on economic, cultural, social, or other factors related to educational programs and practices for rural residents, American Indians, Alaskan Natives, Mexican Americans, and migrants. Materials are available through the ERIC/CRESS offices or through some 700 participating libraries and educational service centers.

A more recently developed resource has been the regional educational laboratories. Created to link educational practice with research, the laboratories have devoted varying levels of attention to rural practice. The most sustained efforts have been the Rural Education Project at the Mid-continent Regional Educational Laboratory (McREL). A three year block of funding has drawn all the laboratories into work specific to rural schools, however. The appendix includes a summary of the work undertaken by each of the laboratories and the most recent contact for the rural projects.

Programs

States themselves can be valuable resources. State educational agencies sometimes support rural projects. A number of universities maintain rural education centers which support networking efforts among rural educators and focus university resources on rural school needs. Examples include the National Center for Smaller Schools at Texas Tech University or the Rural Schools Program at Cornell University. ERIC/CRESS has compiled a list of these centers in its *Directory of Organizations and Programs in Rural Education.* The regional educational laboratories should also be able to supply a list of efforts in the various states.

While space will not allow us to include the many special projects currently supported by universities or local schools, several are worth mentioning by way of illustration. Going far beyond the concept of a university based rural education center, the University of Alaska's College of Human and Rural Development has placed eight regional field centers throughout the state. Collectively these centers offer a complete program in teacher education, using technology to link the learners and faculty. Responding in part to the need to recruit native Alaskans into teaching, the centers offer postsecondary and inservice educational opportunities to isolated populations.

Groups in North Carolina, Georgia, and South Carolina have recently formed the REAL Enterprises Federation to promote the use of school-based economic enterprises as part of the rural school curriculum. The nonprofit organizations help schools create school-based businesses. Once developed, these businesses are "spun off" and become community businesses, offering rural communities a strategy for local economic development and rural schools a motivating educational experience for their youth.

A more recent program explores the capacity of telecommunications to support information exchange and networking among rural educators. One room schools in Montana are linked to an electric bulletin board, the Big Sky Telegraph, maintained by Western Montana College. The bulletin board supports electronic mail, computer conferencing, a software preview loan library, and a lesson plan database.

Organizations/Associations

A number of national and state organizations support rural educators. The National Rural Education Association (NREA) is the most visible national effort. The association hosts an annual conference, sponsors a Teachers Forum and Research Forum, and works to influence federal policy on behalf of rural schools. Several educational associations have rural divisions or special interest groups. The American Educational Research Association has a Rural Education Special Interest Group; the National School Boards Association supports a Rural and Small District Forum; and the American Association of School Administrators (AASA) includes a Small Schools Committee.

At last count, thirteen states had statewide organizations. These vary from parent groups created in response to consolidation threats to state affiliates with NREA. Most sponsor annual conferences and many disseminate newsletters which focus on promising practices or state issues. The *Directory of Organizations and Programs in Rural Education* (Rios, 1986) includes a complete listing of these groups.

Several organizations support rural special education. The American Council on Rural Special Education, one of several rural efforts under the umbrella of the National Rural Development Institute at Western Washington University, hosts an annual conference and publishes a journal devoted to rural special education. *Counterpoint,* a publication of the National Association of State Directors of Special Education, has been dedicated in its efforts to include information specific to rural programs. And finally, New Jersey has organized a rural special education coalition to support networking and advocacy needs among its rural districts.

Publications

Many of the organizations use newsletters, journals, or occasional publications as a strategy for sharing information. For the most part, the newsletters disseminated by the regional laboratories are not restricted to rural education. But two of the labs, the North Central Regional Educational Laboratory (NCREL) and the Regional Laboratory of Educational Improvement of the Northeast and Islands (NE/IS), routinely distribute excellent packets specific to rural education. Most of the associations also publish newsletters specific to rural practice. Information on the availability and frequency of these newsletters is included in the organizational descriptions found in the appendix. Most are free to members.

Journals devoted to rural education range from informal to formal, with *The Country Teacher* offering a delightful forum for rural teachers to reflect or share tips and *Research in Rural Education* providing a more formal publication for researchers. The other journals are more field based, offering a balance between research and practitioner based analysis. All are excellent resources, refreshingly free of the jargon often present in scholarly work.

Both quantitative and qualitative approaches characterize research in rural education. The more traditional, quantitative research explores urban-rural differences in student outcomes, measures factors associated with teacher retention or administrator satisfaction, or examines the issue of fiscal equity. The various journals and dissertation abstracts are excellent sources to this work. The field is also blessed with a number of fine case studies. Efforts by Gjelten (1978), Peshkin (1978), and Nachtigal (1982) illustrate the power of the case study in describing rural school practice from within the context of the local culture. A number of journal articles provide excellent overviews of both types of research, the most recent of which is a review by DeYoung (1987).

A number of monographs explore effective practice, resources available to rural schools, and issues important to the field. NREA collaborated with McREL to identify exemplary programs and practices (Jaquart & Newlin, 1988), many of which would appear to be adaptable to urban schools, while AASA supported the collection of practices specific to the problems posed by rural schooling (Lewis, 1981). More recent monographs have explored the role of rural schools in community development, ranging from the case studies developed by Stoddard, Wall, Luther, and Baker (1988) to the blueprints shared by McREL (1989). Spears, Combs, and Bailey (1990) broaden these visions to include examples which illustrate the role of rural schools in lifelong learning and social services. Spears, Oliver, and Maes (1990) document rural school practices with regard to multicultural education.

In exploring the many resources available, it helps to keep several points in mind. First, conflicting perspectives exist. One explores rural education from within the framework of existing educational practice, while the other examines features specific to rural environments. To the extent that theoretical frameworks in education are often derived from urban or suburban practice, conventional research can fall victim to introducing an "urban bias" into its assessment of rural schools. Consolidation battles can be traced to this research, as can research agendas or funding priorities dictated by urban school problems. Case studies and programs developed in rural settings are, thus, extremely important to creating a more balanced view of rural schools.

Second, the term *urban bias* can be misleading. Originally used to describe the bias that emerges when educational researchers create frameworks from studies in urban and suburban schools, this term often implies to many that urban schools are faring better. In reality, inner-city schools face many of the same frustrations as rural schools. Both share the need for research and policy that is more context sensitive.

Finally, while conflicting perspectives continue to exist, researchers and practitioners are beginning to understand how to support rural school reform. The final chapters in Nachtigal (1982), closing papers in Stern (1989), videotapes available from McREL (1989), and the paper by Killian and Byrd (1988) document the growing body of knowledge surrounding strategies that support educational change in rural environments.

HIGHER EDUCATION

While not as numerous as rural schools, rural colleges and universities exist in substantial numbers. A mosaic of vocational-technical schools, community colleges, private colleges, regional universities, and outreach programs offered by comprehensive universities serve rural populations. For the most part, this segment finds itself caught in a world of increased demand but decreased resources. As rural communities make the transition to more diversified economies, their citizens find themselves in need of postsecondary education. But as state economies lag and enrollments increase, state legislators and higher education coordinating boards begin to wonder who will pay—especially for the increased costs associated with reaching dispersed populations.

Clearinghouse/Centers

The single, most comprehensive resource for rural postsecondary education is the Rural Clearinghouse for Lifelong Education and Development, housed in the Division of Continuing Education at Kansas State University. An outgrowth of the Action Agenda Project, the Rural Clearinghouse maintains a network of rural adult educational providers, collects and disseminates information on effective rural practice, and advocates rural needs with policy makers and educational associations. It supports a searchable database on rural issues, association activities, and exemplary programs. Special projects enable the Clearinghouse to research specific topics, such as innovative rural postsecondary programs, literacy practices in rural areas, the role of community colleges in rural economic development, barriers to adult access in the Northwest and Appalachia, and education's response to the farm crisis. Information is disseminated through monographs, conferences, and a newsletter.

The ERIC system supports two clearinghouses which collect documents of interest to rural practitioners. The Clearinghouse on Adult, Career, and Vocational Education is located at Ohio State University and the Clearinghouse on Junior Colleges is housed at the University of California at Los Angeles. Like the ERIC Clearinghouse for Rural Education and Small Schools, these groups maintain a document retrieval system available at their centers and through participating libraries and education service centers.

Programs

Prior to the work of the Action Agenda Project, relatively little information on rural postsecondary education had been collected. With support from the Fund for the Improvement of Postsecondary Education, the Action Agenda Project and the Western Interstate Commission for Higher Education released a directory of model programs designed to reach rural populations (Hone, 1984). A number of other efforts to collect and disseminate information on rural programs have followed, leaving us with far more examples than we could possibly include. The few programs included in this chapter illustrate some of the adaptations needed to improve rural access. Other examples can be found in the monographs listed in the appendix.

Programs in rural settings are more successful when they respond to locally determined needs. Thus, institutions have to be prepared to build rather than simply deliver courses. The Rural Education Centers at the University of Alaska accomplish this by using regional councils to guide program planning. The Dental Hygiene Mobile Program uses an advisory committee of local citizens, health professionals, and dentists to define the programs at each community site. Academic standards are maintained, but not through standardization of programs.

Distance, dispersed populations, adverse weather conditions, and increased costs are constant barriers to rural access. Programs at the College of Great Falls (Montana) and California State University at Chico illustrate the use of technology. The program at Great Falls combines videotapes with periodic audio conferences, enabling the students to complete much of the course work at times convenient to their schedules. The use of microwave technology enables California State University at Chico to deliver live, one-way video, two-way audio instruction to sixteen remote sites. The Dental Hygiene Mobile Program moves a complete dental hygiene laboratory to community college sites around the state.

The Washington/Alaska/Montana/Idaho (WAMI) Program coordinated through the University of Washington Medical Center illustrates a multistate cooperative designed to share educational facilities but not drain states of their human resources. Students studying to be primary care physicians complete one year at the University of Washington campus and then the other two years in their home state, thus protecting the linkages that will enable them to establish a practice in their home state when medical school is completed. The program has been successful in increasing the number of physicians establishing practices in rural communities in participating states.

Finally, the Center for Rural Pennsylvania illustrates one strategy for focusing a broader array of university resources on rural needs. The center undertakes research in a broad range of rural issues, not simply agricultural production. In addition, the center is governed by a board whose membership includes state policy makers, increasing the chance that knowledge gained will make its way into the process of formulating policy. These and other institutional adaptations are important to increasing rural access to the educational resources of the state.

Organizations/Associations

While there are a large number of organizations and associations serving higher education, relatively few maintain active rural efforts. The National University Continuing Education Association (NUCEA) maintains a Division of Rural Continuing Education, and the American Association of State Colleges and Universities has a Committee on Agricultural and Rural Development. Both groups support rural sessions at conferences, distribute information through newsletters, and offer leadership to projects specific to rural institutions. The Commission on Small and/or Rural Community Colleges in the American Association of Community and Junior Colleges (AACJC) has taken an active role in collecting and disseminating information about rural practice, most recently in the form of a monograph that describes rural community college involvement in economic development, literacy, use of technology, and so forth. The American Association for Adult and Continuing Education (AAACE) has no rural division but involves rural educators in units across the entire association. The Cooperative Extension Service Unit and Continuing Education for the Professions Unit are especially involved with rural issues.

The need to stimulate economic growth in rural areas has led to a number of initiatives specific to rural practice. The first of these was a university forum sponsored by Continuing Higher Education Leadership

(CHEL), a project within NUCEA. While the forum was organized around the theme of continuing education leadership, the challenges explored were those being induced by economic change (CHEL, 1987). More recently, the Western Interstate Commission for Higher Education (WICHE) and Western Governors' Association (WGA) have explored the link between higher education and rural development. WGA commissioned a study of how effectively university public service has served rural communities and the potentials for strengthening that linkage. WICHE sponsored a workshop on higher education and rural development in conjunction with the Five State Legislative Conference in 1989.

Publications

The field of rural postsecondary education is still relatively new. While a rich literature exists in cooperative extension, traditionally the nonformal provider in higher education, the issue of rural access to formal programs has not received much attention. A study by Willingham (1970) first proposed that willingness to pursue postsecondary education depends on proximity to an institution, concluding that rural and urban inner-city regions both face more limited access. Research into barriers to adult access to formal education eventually led to interest in rural populations as a special case (Darkenwald, 1980), and "place-bound" was added to the list of situational barriers adults face. The farm crisis and collapse of other natural resource based economies have increased interest in improving rural adult access to education.

No single journal and relatively few books address the topic of rural postsecondary education. The book by Treadway (1984) is the most comprehensive source, surveying the range of programs needed in rural areas as well as institutional, state, and federal policy issues. For the most part, journal articles are relatively scattered. *Continuing Higher Education Review* and *The Community, Junior and Technical College Journal* devoted entire issues to rural postsecondary education and offer convenient references.

A number of excellent monographs are emerging from the field, many of which are building a clearer picture of rural practice. Hone (1984) provided the first comprehensive look at rural postsecondary education. Sullins, Hoerner, and Whisnant (1987) offer a closer look at programs in the Appalachian region. A directory of programs developed to respond to the farm crisis (Spears, 1987a) explores the diversity of programs created by the specialized needs and personal values of rural adults struggling to deal with events over which they had little control.

Interest in the link between education and economic development has led to several excellent inventories. Work in the Northwest (Emery,

1987) offers a taxonomy as well as sketches of programs in that region. WICHE (1989) profiled twenty-two programs in conjunction with its legislative workshop on the link between higher education and rural development. Thomas (1989) produced a series of excellent profiles of rural community college programs. Several publications explore the needs and characteristics of rural adult learners as well as the barriers they face in gaining access to postsecondary education. McCannon (1985) examined the rural cohort of NCES data on participation in adult education and completed augmentation studies at several sites to create a picture of rural adult learners. Two monographs (McDaniel, 1986; Sullins, Vogler, & Mays, 1986) and a series of papers (Easton, 1988; 1989) explore barriers to rural adult access. All have drawn their research framework from the adult education literature, leading to some overlap in the barriers identified.

Finally, a number of monographs can best be called issue pieces. The series of proceedings dating back to the 1981 National Invitational Meeting on Rural Postsecondary Education (Margolis, 1981) raise progressively more focused questions with regard to issues of access and appropriateness (Spears, 1986; 1987b). Interest in rural economic development has led to another series of papers. Hobbs (1987) explores the issue of education through the filter of *local* economic development, leading to a number of implications for educational practice. As mentioned earlier, Treadway (1988) explores guidelines which help define ways in which state colleges and universities can appropriately support local development efforts. The work summarized by the Western Governors' Association (1989) and WICHE (1989a) adds the perspective brought to the discussion by policy makers.

In exploring these programs and resources, it helps to keep several points in mind. First, issues in rural access to postsecondary education are shared with both rural education and adult education. Programs and policies in higher education share some of the "urban bias" features of public schooling. Added to that are the many ways in which higher education has not yet adapted to the situational barriers faced by adult learners. Both perspectives are needed to understand the barriers faced by rural adults.

Second, higher education sees individuals apart from their communities. It sees its role as the development of individual capacities regardless of whether those capacities are of value to the local community. Individuals who, by virtue of their values or circumstance, see themselves through their communities are simply not understood by the system.

And finally, economic development has been the first undertaking for which policy makers and educators have acknowledged urban and rural differences. Concerns with equity and access have stimulated some interest in rural postsecondary education, but the current interest in involving higher education in economic development appears to be a much more promising context within which to articulate the need to respond differently to adults in rural environments.

NONFORMAL EDUCATION

If higher education presents a mosaic of institutions responding to rural adult needs, nonformal education offers a crazy quilt of providers. Individual chapters have explored the primary nonformal providers—cooperative extension, community adult education, and libraries. In addition, churches and human service organizations have traditionally played an important role in rural areas, one that becomes more obvious in the wake of any crisis. A variety of nonprofit organizations have been and continue to be created, generally in response to issues missing or ignored in the political arena. These play a dual role, educating rural adults in an effort to build a political base while at the same time articulating those perspectives to local, state, and federal policy makers.

Clearinghouses/Centers

The single largest provider of nonformal education in rural areas is the Cooperative Extension Service. For the most part, however, its efforts have been directed at agriculture or other natural resource based economies. Four regional centers for rural development support the broader need for community and leadership development. The appendix includes a summary of the work underway at each center. In addition, the Rural Information Center extends the resources of the National Agricultural Library to elected and appointed officials, community development professionals, and volunteer leaders.

A number of national and regional centers support the work of other nonformal educational providers. The Center for the Study of Rural Librarianship, for example, offers leadership to rural libraries. The Northwest Iowa Regional Library publishes a quarterly newsletter, *Rural Library Service Newsletter,* that carries articles related to rural community needs, information resources for rural collections, and effective rural library management. The National Center for Small Communities, recently established within the National Association of Towns and Townships, conducts research and disseminates information useful to local government officials. In response to the severe economic problems being felt in most areas, some land-grant universities and/or state legislatures are establishing information clearinghouses to support local economic development efforts. Check with your state government or local university.

Programs

The rich diversity found in rural lifelong learning is reflected most clearly in the array of programs that emerge from grassroots concerns or foundation priorities. Education is so deeply embedded in our vision of democracy that grassroots efforts and special interest groups name education as their primary task. In addition, a number of foundations concerned with rural issues support special programs aimed at using nonformal structures to develop leadership or community organizing skills.

The reality of rural poverty has given rise to a number of projects whose mission is, in part, education. The Federation of Southern Cooperatives, for example, grew out of a concern for the loss of black, family-owned farms as well as for the poverty rate among farmers in the rural South. The federation encourages the formation of farmer cooperatives and then offers technical assistance and education needed to help the cooperatives succeed. The Highlander Research and Education Center evolved out of concerns for the poor in Appalachia. Efforts to empower local people through education have taken many forms, including participatory research in land ownership patterns and the development of an economic literacy curriculum.

A second category of projects has emerged from the trend toward large scale agriculture, which has given rise to grassroots organizations concerned with the demise of the family farm, the effect of large scale agriculture on the land and water resources, or both. The Center for Rural Affairs in Walthill, Nebraska, supports research and education efforts in sustainable agriculture, conservation techniques, leadership development, and rural community development. Other projects, such as the Land Stewardship Project, focus on society's use of natural resources. Projects often involve educating urban as well as rural people, as the Minnesota Food Association sought to educate urban legislators on rural problems.

A number of programs focus on rural leadership, human service delivery, and community development. Some, such as the Heartland Center for Leadership Development, integrate research on effective communities with leadership programs derived from that research. A number of rural leadership projects have been funded by the W. K. Kellogg Foundation and typically operate through land-grant universities. The Partnership for Rural Improvement at Washington State University, for example, explores collaborative relationships among communities and educational institutions. Tomorrow's Leaders Today in Iowa offers educational assistance to clusters of rural communities.

One corporation, Pioneer Hi-Bred International, Inc., offers a series of seminars to its employees. Called "Rural America: The Search for Solutions," this program illustrates a unique approach to community involvement, as the corporation attempts to improve the capacity of its sales force to offer informal leadership within the communities in which they work.

One final project bears mentioning because of its efforts to link formal and nonformal educational providers in a unique way. The Intermountain Community Learning and Information Services (ICLIS) project is a collaboration between libraries, extension service personnel, and universities. Taking advantage of modern technology, the project is exploring the use of rural community libraries as information centers for their communities. The libraries are being equipped to receive courses from land-grant universities and provide access to a wide range of database and electronic information services.

Organizations/Associations

Perceived differences between urban and rural practices have led to the creation of a number of rural-focused associations. The National Rural Health Association offers leadership in developing strategies for rural health care delivery. The National Association of Development Organizations offers information and technical assistance in rural/small town economic development. The Small Towns Institute supports community management and leadership development. The Rural Ministry Institute responds to the unique needs of rural churches. Finally, the Rural Sociological Association offers researchers a forum specific to rural cultures.

Other groups support research and dissemination activities helpful to policy makers as well as rural practitioners. The National Governors' Association explored rural communities that continue to thrive despite the economic downturn, offering insights helpful to communities as well as to the policy makers served by the association. The Rural Coalition organizes task forces to research issues in five areas: agriculture, American Indian, natural resources, rural economy and development, and military issues.

Finally, groups such as the Association for Community Based Education (ACBE) and Community Transportation Association of America (CTAA) illustrate organizations that serve broader alliances. ACBE serves educational organizations whose goal is to empower community members. These organizations emerge where substantial populations are either underserved or ill-served by conventional institutions, often minority populations within urban settings or rural populations. CTTA, formerly known as Rural America, evolved from efforts to study rural transportation problems. The elderly, disabled, or poor encounter some of the same barriers, leading to an association that responds to more than just rural populations. These alliances are promising, in part, because they sidestep traditional rural-urban confrontations.

Publications

Nearly all the centers and associations disseminate newsletters and occasional news journals. They range from the relatively informal styles used by the Association for Community Based Education or Rural Coalition to the magazine format used in *Western Wire,* published by the Western Rural Development Center. The type of information included also varies. Most include news briefs and membership news from the organization. The *CBE Report* includes fund raising sources and a calendar of proposed deadlines. The *Center for Rural Affairs Newsletter* reports and reviews pending legislation. *Visions from the Heartland* includes stories from successful communities. Because the information is current and presented concisely, these newsletters are one of the more productive ways of keeping up with current projects and approaches.

Journals support the work of the primary nonformal providers. The *Journal of Extension* serves as the professional journal for the Cooperative Extension Service. *Human Services in the Rural Environment* provides a forum for mental health, health care, and social work professionals. A number of journals deal with rural community or economic development, most notably *National Resources and Rural Development* and *Small Towns.* For the most part these journals are field based, offering examples of successful programs or articles that explore effective practice. The single most comprehensive journal is *Rural Development Perspectives.* The others become more specialized in the segment of nonformal education they serve.

Books and monographs offer a rich but not very predictable resource. For the most part, these publications emerge from funded projects and are consequently more episodic. Some, such as the *Catalogue of Catalogues* developed by John Christenson (1988) at the Traverse des Sioux Library System or *Community Education and Economic Development* by Emery, Horton, and McDaniel (1988) offer information helpful to one specific provider. Others, such as Brown (1985), Jackson and Chaudhuri (1989), and Office of Rural Development Policy (1984) offer information on programs or funding sources. A number of monographs offer community groups strategies or processes to use. Hustedde, Shaffer, and Pulver (1984) offers a step-by-step process by which communities can explore their economic health. Luttrell (1987) provides a workbook for examining a community's economic life.

Some of the most powerful monographs have emerged from case study work. The National Governors' Association used case studies to identify keys to success and implications for state and federal policy makers (John, Batie, & Norris, 1988). Wall and Luther (1987) completed a similar study in Nebraska. In an excellent review of the process of creating jobs through agricultural diversification, Stark (1988) shares strategies used, lessons learned, and resources available to guide similar efforts. These types of publications are valuable to community groups as well as to nonformal educational providers.

For the most part, nonformal educational providers in rural areas find themselves directly engaged in individual or community action. The character of the programs, associations, and publications reflects this perspective. Journals tend to be more field-based. Newsletters and monographs explore programs or strategies that are working. Programs focus on offering information such that it results in action. These complement the more research-based approaches common in the other two sectors of rural lifelong learning, empowering communities to act despite the uncertainties of current knowledge.

SUMMARY

A rich tapestry of educational providers supports rural lifelong learning. From early childhood education to continuing professional education, formal institutions work to ensure rural access to educational opportunity. Their labors are complemented by the nonformal providers, organizations often committed to translating knowledge into action on behalf of rural people or communities. This chapter has reviewed many of the resources that better define these providers and their role in rural lifelong learning. Those interested should explore the appendix, which includes an expanded list of resources and contacts.

REFERENCES

Brown, H. (1985). *Keys to successful funding: A small town guide to community development block grants and other federal programs.* Washington, DC: National Association of Towns and Townships.

Continuing Higher Education Leadership Project (CHEL). (1987). *Chal-*

lenges for continuing higher education leadership: The transformation of rural America. Washington, DC: National University Continuing Education Association.

Christenson, J. (1988). Catalogue of catalogs. Mankato, MN: Traverse des Sioux Library System.

Darkenwald, G. G. (1980). Continuing education and the hard to reach adult. In G. G. Darkenwald & G. A. Larson (Eds.), Reaching hard to reach adults (1–10). New Directions for Continuing Education, no. 8. San Francisco: Jossey-Bass.

DeYoung, A. J. (1987). The status of American rural education research: An integrated review and commentary. Review of Educational Research, 57, 123–148.

Easton, S. M. (1988). Overcoming barriers to education for rural adults. A consideration of public policy proposals. Paper presented at 29th Annual Adult Education Research Conference. Syracuse, NY.

Easton, S. M. (1989). Barriers to education for rural adults in 13 Western states. Paper presented at Rural Education Research Forum. Reno, NV.

Emery, M. (Ed.). (1987). Education and the rural economy: A directory of educational models for economic development. Manhattan, KS: Action Agenda Project.

Emery, M., Horton, D., & McDaniel, R. (1988). Community education and economic development: Activities in the field and potential new models. Pullman, WA: Washington State University.

Gjelten, T. (1978). Schooling in isolated communities. North Haven, ME: North Haven Project for Career Development.

Hobbs, D. (1987). Knowledge based rural development: Adult education and the future rural economy. Manhattan, KS: Action Agenda Project.

Hone, K. (1984). Serving the rural adult: Inventory of model programs in rural adult postsecondary education. Manhattan, KS: Action Agenda Project.

Hustedde, R., Shaffer, R., & Pulver, G. (1984). Community economic analysis: A how-to manual. Ames, IA: North Central Regional Center for Rural Development.

Jackson, G., & Chaudhuri, K. (1989). National directory of community based adult literacy programs. Washington, DC: Association for Community Based Education.

Jaquart, M., & Newlin, J. (1988). Rural school source book: Exemplary programs, practices and resources for rural educators. Aurora, CO: Midcontinent Regional Educational Laboratory.

John, D., Batie, S. S., & Norris, K. (1988). A brighter future for rural America? Strategies for communities and states. Washington, DC: National Governors' Association.

Killian, J. E., & Byrd, D. M. (1988). *Teachers' perspectives on what promotes instructional improvement.* Paper presented at the Annual Meeting of the American Educational Research Association, New Orleans, LA.

Lewis, A. C. (1981). *Creative ideas for small schools.* Arlington, VA: American Association of School Administrators.

Luttrell, W. (1987). *Claiming what is ours: An economics experience workbook.* New Market, TN: Highlander Center.

Margolis, D. (1981). *The Kansas City initiative: Proceedings of the National Invitational Meeting on Rural Postsecondary Education.* Manhattan, KS: Action Agenda Project.

McCannon, R. (1985). *Serving the rural adult: A demographic portrait of rural adult learners.* Manhattan, KS: Action Agenda Project.

McDaniel, R. (Ed.). (1986). *Barriers to rural adult education: A report of the Northwest Action Agenda Project.* Pullman: Washington State University.

McREL. (1989). *What's noteworthy: Rural schools and community development.* Aurora, CO: Author.

McREL. (1989a). *How to organize rural school clusters.* Aurora, CO: Author.

Nachtigal, P. M. (Ed.). (1982). *Rural education: In search of a better way.* Boulder: Westview Press.

Office of Rural Development Policy. (1984). *Rural resources guide: A directory of public and private assistance for small communities.* Washington, DC: Author.

Peshkin, A. (1978). *Growing up American: Schooling and the survival of community.* Chicago: University of Chicago Press.

Rios, B. R. (1986). *A directory of organizations and programs in rural education.* Las Cruces, NM: ERIC Clearinghouse on Rural and Small Schools.

Spears, J. D. (1986). *Proceedings 1985: Four regional conferences.* Manhattan, KS: Action Agenda Project.

Spears, J. D. (Ed.). (1987a). *Education's response to the rural crisis: Model programs in the midwest.* Manhattan, KS: Action Agenda Project.

Spears, J. D. (1987b). *Proceedings 1986: National invitational conference on rural adult postsecondary education.* Manhattan, KS: Action Agenda Project.

Spears, J., Combs, L., & Bailey, G. (1990). *Accommodating change and diversity: Linking rural schools to communities.* Manhattan, KS: Rural Clearinghouse for Lifelong Education and Development.

Spears, J., Oliver, J., & Maes, S., (1990). *Accommodating change and diversity: Multicultural practices in rural schools.* Manhattan, KS: Rural Clearinghouse for Lifelong Education and Development.

Stark, N. (1988). *Growing our own jobs: A small town guide to creating jobs through agricultural diversification.* Knoxville, TN: National Association of Towns and Townships.

Stern, J. D. (Ed.). (1989). *Rural education: A changing landscape.* Washington, DC: U.S. Department of Education.

Stoddard, S., Wall, M., Luther, V., & Baker, K. (1988). *Schools as entrepreneurs: Helping small towns survive.* Lincoln, NE: Heartland Center for Leadership Development.

Sullins, W. R., Volger, D. E., & Mays, S. B. (1986). *Report from the Appalachian regional steering committee on rural postsecondary education.* Blacksburg, VA: Appalachian Action Agenda Project.

Sullins, W. R., Hoerner, J. L., & Whisnant, W. T. (1988). *Increasing rural adults' participation in collegial programs: Exemplary programs.* Blacksburg, VA: Appalachian Action Agenda Project.

Thomas, M. (Ed.). (1989). *A portfolio of community college initiatives in rural economic development.* Kansas City, MO: Midwest Research Institute.

Treadway, D. (1984). *Higher education in rural America.* New York: College Entrance Examination Board.

Treadway, D. (1988). *Higher education and rural development: The next frontier.* St. Paul, MN: Northwest Area Foundation.

Wall, M., & Luther, V. (1987). *20 clues to rural community survival.* Lincoln, NE: Heartland Center for Leadership Development.

Western Governor's Association (WGA). (1989). *A time of challenge . . . A time for change: The role of higher education in the rural west.* Denver: Author.

Western Interstate Commission for Higher Education (WICHE). (1989). *Higher education's response to rural needs: Selected model programs.* Boulder, CO: Author.

Western Interstate Commission for Higher Education (WICHE). (1989a). *Evolving partnerships: Higher education and the rural west.* Boulder, CO: Author.

Willingham, W. W. (1970). *Free access higher education.* New York: College Entrance Examination Board.

CHAPTER 16

Future Prospects for Rural Lifelong Education

MICHAEL W. GALBRAITH

The concepts of lifelong education and community are complex and multidimensional. Within this complexity lie the richness, potential, and hope for the continuation of learning in the rural American community. Educational providers that contribute to this lifelong learning opportunity stress the validity of formal, nonformal, and informal learning. The knowledge, skills, and attitudes thus gained will assist youth and adult learners in shaping the social, psychological, intellectual, economic, political, and leisure aspects of their lives.

The contributors to this book have stressed that the rural American community and culture holds a viable alternative to the urban American ideology of living, learning, and work. Incorrect assumptions, major misjudgments, and inappropriate efforts that permeate the rural community movement today have left a legacy of problems, attitudes, and social policies that are misinformed and misguided. Creating a dynamic rural lifelong educational environment can only occur if the uniqueness of the rural American culture, character, and heritage is interwoven into the design. Understanding the present and future potential for lifelong education and learning in rural America must be put in context of the rural culture.

If we accept the proposition that the rural American community is unique and that to understand the educational issues we must address the rural community as a subculture (DeYoung, 1987; Van Tilburg & Moore, 1989), then the construction of the future prospects for rural lifelong education must also be structurally and substantively unique and different from those put forth for urban and industrialized communities. Trying to predict the shape of a rural American lifelong education society may prove fruitless. It does allow us, however, to recognize the present as

291

a time of transition and to cope with this reality of inevitable change. Change itself requires people capable of adapting to shifts in the ideology of schooling and lifelong education and the implications this holds for the rural community. The nature of educational changes has resulted in a shifting paradigm from education that is only valid through formal settings, such as schools and colleges, to one that recognizes the necessity and value of education that is obtained through nonformal and informal settings as well, such as community-based organizations. Implicit in this is the belief that educational opportunities should exist for people of all ages, that all organizations (formal and nonformal) in the community take responsibility for facilitating such educational opportunities, and that the community should be the locus of planning and conducting educational activities.

Within these three implications, several things can be concluded. One is that the word *lifelong* should be taken literally to mean education and learning throughout the entire life span. This draws on the elements of the vertical integration component of lifelong education as suggested in Chapter 1. Second, all forms of education and learning, whether in formal, nonformal, or informal settings, should be embraced. There are no limitations on what is learned, by whom, for what reason, or the mechanism utilized in obtaining the education. Third, it calls for a new configuration and philosophical basis for bringing into existence a cooperative network of educational and community-based organizations that are concerned with the continuous educational development of individuals within the community (Peterson, 1979a). This can only be accomplished within the specific context of the rural community and through an understanding of the horizontal integration dimension of lifelong education (see Chapter 1). Cremin (1976) stresses the need to recognize the multiplicity of individuals and institutions that educate individuals and suggests that "education must be looked at whole, across the entire lifespan, and in all the situations and institutions in which it occurs" (p. 59).

Can the above scenario become a reality in rural America? Galbraith and Sundet (1988), in a research study concerned with continuing learning for adults, found that "apparently in this environment, the culture dictates that education is a function of childhood and adolescence, not a lifelong process" (p. 15). However, the contributing authors and the various topics in which they have written about suggest great hope for a conceptually sound lifelong education scheme within the rural American community. The foundation is laid for the construction of rural lifelong education. The primary question is whether or not rural American communities are willing to adapt to change. Will rural Americans be willing to educationally, philosophically, socially, and psychologically change to make lifelong education a viable alternative to the present state of affairs?

In examining the future prospects for rural lifelong education, some trends and factors that influence the need for lifelong education will be discussed. The aims and priorities of lifelong education will also be examined as well as how they relate to new directions and schools of thought concerning dispositional change, school and lifelong education curriculum, and the role of professional educators and life educators in rural America. Finally, the benefits of lifelong education will be discussed in the context of the rural American community.

TRENDS AND FACTORS

From a broad perspective, the concept of lifelong education can be examined through various trends, factors, and pressures that influence it. While there are numerous influences, several of the most salient ones that contribute to the growth of lifelong education will be briefly discussed.

Shifting Orientation from Youth to Adult Population

Upon until the first half of the twentieth century, the American society had more youth-aged individuals than adult-aged ones. After the 1950s the median age crept up to around age 21. Going into the last decade of this century the median age is nearly 31. By century end it is projected to be 36.4. The National Center for Education Statistics predicts that by the year 2000, the largest age group will be 30 to 44 years of age, with a rising curve for 45 to 64 years old. What this suggests is that American society is now dominated by an adult population that is growing steadily older. In terms of older Americans, at the turn of the century only three million Americans, or 4 percent of the total population, were 65 years or older. Today those older than 65 comprise nearly 12 percent of the total American population, with those 85 years and older experiencing the greatest expansion (Rosenwaike & Logue, 1985). By the year 2000, older Americans will represent 13 percent of the population in the United States (American Association of Retired Persons, 1987) and 12 percent in Canada (Pitman, 1984). The life expectancy has and continues to increase at a steady rate and with it comes social, educational, and psychological implications for the need for lifelong education.

The increase in the life span has provided a litany of new experiences that affect our lives as a result of rapid change. Transmitting the culture through education is no longer a viable perspective as the culture with its constant changes is shorter than the life span of the people experiencing such changes. Individuals can no longer rely on what they learned in school settings to carry them through life. A constant examination of the present state of knowledge must be made to determine if it is viable and adequate to carry them into the future years.

As Daryl Hobbs discussed in Chapter 2, a population shift exists in rural America. Young people are exiting the rural community after the schooling years for the urban area in search of work, social, and leisure experiences. What remains in many rural communities is an adult population that is constantly getting older. However, this shift from a youth to a maturity orientation provides the necessity for continuous learning as it relates to health, familial, social, political, economic, recreational, and human relation issues. The shift to an older population suggests it will be imperative that individuals use nonformal and informal educational resources in their lifelong educational pursuit. Rural people need continuous information about the changing nature and future of agriculture, land use, water, forestry, the elderly, rural youth, social and human services, health care, the labor force, women, the disadvantaged, and the use of natural resources. Adequately dealing with these issues and the changing future depends upon the ability of this shifting population to see the necessity of lifelong education as it affects their individual, social, economic, and political lives.

The Influence of Technology

If any one thing has transformed society and contributed to the knowledge explosion, it has been the increasing sophistication and influence of technology. Technology affects the social, educational, communication, political, economic, and recreational aspects of community life. It is present in our homes, schools, and places of work. Technology has transformed communication, medicine, transportation, and other similar parts of society (Naisbitt, 1982; World Future Society, 1988). The technological age is an economic, social, political and intellectual reality. For example, the prediction of Toffler (1980) a decade ago that society would move into an era in which communication technology would replace transportation has become a reality. The satellite transmission allows people to engage in learning activities from almost anywhere in the world. Technology, particularly in the rural community, provides a means for breaking the bonds of isolation. It allows for the possible development of concern for local, state, national, and global issues and problems.

Technology and the explosion of knowledge offers a profound opportunity to influence the nature of lifelong educational endeavors (Florini, 1990; Heermann, 1988; Lewis, 1989). Technology makes it increasingly possible to engage in the information age, provides hard-to-reach and homebound populations with learning options, helps to meet varied learning needs, and provides multiple opportunities for enhancing the formal, nonformal, and informal learning processes.

Various technologies contribute to the enhancement of lifelong education. Perhaps the most significant technological revolution has been the computer. Whether in a school, work, or home setting, the computer provides management and informational support. It assists learners in writing, word processing, graphing, problem solving, research, as well as in controlling and organizing information. Interactive video is another important technological advancement. This technology allows a learner to participate in a simulated conversation on the screen. Audio technology has also influenced lifelong education. Tapes are easily obtained and can be used for various formal and informal educational purposes. Telecommunication, the transmission and reception of messages over long distance, has contributed significantly to the opportunity for lifelong education (Lewis, 1989). An example of telecommunication, and how it can be adapted within the education environment, is teleconferencing. Teleconferencing "is designed as a substitute for face-to-face meetings and travel . . . and has the ability to transmit voices, and sometimes images, and allows for instruction . . . to rural and outlying areas" (p. 618). Its greatest asset is the potential for delivering informational and professional services almost anywhere—to the public school, to the corporate classroom, to the learning community resource center. Perhaps the most exciting component of the telecommunication system is the telecomputing opportunities. Personal computers are connected to various electronic data base retrieval information systems, such as CD-ROM, that make it possible to search for and retrieve topic information. In addition, telecomputing "makes possible the sending and receiving of electronic mail almost anywhere in the world and permits participation in both public and private conferences on a specific topic" (p. 619).

Technology has extended the opportunities to engage in continuous learning and to make learning as private and personal as one wishes. It has opened up avenues for the exploration of topics that are meaningful perhaps only to the learner. From it, groups of learners gain, whether in formal, nonformal, or informal settings, a richness in the quality and variety of learning programs. It reduces the isolation, and the excuses for not continuing learning, for people who have little or no way of participating in traditional learning experiences. In addition, technology provides alternative forms of instruction. Lifelong education has and certainly will continue to be influenced by technology and the many options it provides.

The Social Changes and Pressures

Social changes and pressures have made it imperative to increase the attention paid to their influences on lifelong education. A shift from a linear to blended life plan, a rising educational attainment level, the increase in credit and noncredit learning, career patterns, and mandatory continuing education are a few that presently affect society and influence the necessity for lifelong education. In all of the above changes, education, in general, is usually perceived as helpful in improving professional, personal, and social aspects of life.

Blended Life Plan

Until recently, particularly in industrialized nations, a linear life plan was the norm and the tendency was to separate education, work, and leisure. It was a life plan in which education was for the young, work was for the middle aged, and leisure was for the elderly (Cross, 1981). She contends that what is happening today is an adoption of a blended life plan in which "work, education, and leisure are concurrent, rather than alternating, at all points throughout life" (p. 12). For example, a twenty year old may decide to be a part-time student, part-time worker, and part-time vacationer. A forty-five year old may work fewer hours a week in an effort to leave more time for educational and leisure endeavors. The sixty year old may plan a gradual withdrawal from work activities to engage in some leisure and education experiences instead of accepting full-time retirement. "In other words", according to Cross, "the blended life plan would consist of a blend of education, work, and leisure throughout most of the years of life" (p. 12).

The blended life plan seems to be holding some credence since more post-secondary institutions are experiencing a substantial increase in the number of part-time students and a decline in full-time student enrollments. The workplace is experiencing an increase demand for professional part-time jobs by people who want to help raise children; are looking for a transition before full retirement; have a desire to return to school; or have a need to maintain flexible working hours so they can share home and child care responsibilities. A blended life plan seems to be slowly transforming society's way of looking at work, education, and leisure. Since education plays a major role within such a plan, new opportunities for all ages to participate in lifelong education exist.

Rising Educational Attainment Level

The overall educational attainment level in America has and continues to increase. In this country, nearly 85 percent of the people now complete high school. The expectation of this figure suggests a continuing rate of interest in education and the likelihood more people will continue education, in some form, beyond the secondary education years. Cross (1979) found that the more education people have, the more education they want and the more they participate in further learning activities. The probability exists that children of well-educated parents are likely to seek a good education themselves and as a result continue to participate in educational activities throughout their lives as well. Education is "addictive not only for individuals but for entire societies" (Cross, 1981, p. 15). According to a study conducted by the Center for Education Statistics (1984), certain groups of people were more likely to participate in adult education activities such as whites, persons with a college education, persons living in the western states, persons with above-median incomes, or persons working in executive, professional, or technical occupations. In addition, women were more likely to participate in adult education than men. As suggested in most research on participation, a positive correlation exists between a high level of educational attainment and the actual participation in continuing education activities.

Credit and Noncredit Learning

The shift in demographics, the influences of technology, the idea of a blended life plan, the rising educational attainment level, and the recognition that lifelong education participation is necessary—all have contributed to the increased participation in credit and noncredit learning. Some reasons why people participate in adult education activities are to gain general information or for personal, professional, or social reasons. The primary reason, according to the Center for Education Statistics (1984), relates to the world of work. Nearly twenty years ago, over half of all adult education courses were taken to get a job or to advance in a job. Today nearly two-thirds of adult education courses are taken for job-related reasons. It is important to note however that non-job-related courses continue to increase in real numbers as do job-related offerings.

While the number of job-related courses offered reflects a shift in participation patterns, it does not suggest that credit learning has outdistanced noncredit learning. In fact, the percent of adult education courses taken for credit toward a degree, certificate, or license declined from 55 percent in 1969 to 36 percent in 1984 (Center for Education Statistics, 1984). Noncredit courses, particularly those to meet a requirement for obtaining or renewing a license or certificate in a trade or profession, doubled during that same period. As will be discussed later, mandatory continuing education by various professions contributed to this tremendous growth.

The noncredit learning figures provided above do not take into account self-education activities that are planned and carried out by individual learners. According to Tough (1979), a pioneer in the study of self-directed learning, nearly everyone engages in some type of learning that is independent of institutional providership. He suggested that people get involved with "learning projects" in which they identify their learning needs and objectives, plan how they will reach the learning objectives, and determine through self-evaluation if the learning was successful. From this categorization of noncredit learning, it can be suggested that all people have the capability to design specific learning activities to reach their particular needs and do it quite successfully. Adults have the potential to be self-directed learners and to engage in education throughout their lives that help reach social, personal, professional, and recreational needs (Brockett & Hiemstra, 1991; Brookfield, 1985; Candy, 1991; Hiemstra, 1985; Knowles, 1975).

While elementary and secondary schools, two and four year colleges and universities, vocational institutions, and other credit-earning providers offer a significant amount of opportunity for generating credit learning, the majority of noncredit learning is facilitated through community-based organizations and self-education efforts (Galbraith, 1990a). The trend toward more learning providers and the emphasis on self-directed learning projects have greatly influenced the potential for individuals to engage in lifelong education.

Career Pattern Changes

Lifelong education participation is also affected by the changing nature of career patterns, which is quite evident in both rural and urban settings. Various factors contribute to this reality such as job obsolescence, increased participation of women, increased longevity, job competition, higher aspirations, and the social acceptability of change (Cross, 1981; Long, Apps, & Himestra, 1985).

Job obsolescence usually occurs because of technological advances or social changes that decrease the need for the present job. New skills and knowledge are required through human resource development activities that are either mandated by the employer or self-recognized and generated by the employee (Gilley & Eggland, 1989; Nadler & Nadler, 1989). According to Cetrone, Soriano, and Gayle (1985), a worker who stays in the labor force thirty years will need retraining or reeducation anywhere from three to six times. From this scenario, there is little reason to believe that the importance of lifelong education and training will diminish in the future.

Another factor is the increased participation of women in the labor force. Women between the ages of twenty and fifty-five have increasingly formed larger proportions of the labor force. For example, in 1970 women constituted 43.4 percent of the labor force while by 1985 it had risen to 54.5 percent and a projected 59.0 percent by 1995 (U.S. Bureau of the Census, 1987). This trend is a reflection of changes that are associated with "a longer life span, better health, few children and a longer delay of marriage and birth of first child" (Rice & Meyer, 1989, p. 551). Consequently, these factors keep women as active participants in the labor force and motivate them to seek more education for job upgrading and training.

The average worker today spends nearly forty years in the labor market. This increased longevity affects not only the choices about where to work but also the changing nature of the job itself. Rarely does any specific job not change over a lifetime. Thus additional education and training must offset this inherent obsolescence. Closely related to increased longevity are the factors of job competition and enhanced aspirations. Cross (1981) states that "increased job competition is generally believed to stimulate employers to raise educational requirements and workers to gain the competitive edge through further education" (p. 21). Opportunities to seek job advancement through further education is also recognized by many groups in society as a way obtaining the "good life." Thus aspiring to jobs that require additional education is highly acceptable to those who seek advancement. Lastly, it seems more socially acceptable to change career paths to something different and exciting than to remain forty years in the same job. Considering the nature of the changing job market, opportunities, and the increase in obsolescence, society expects a certain amount of movement in a person's career development activities.

Mandatory Continuing Education

One of the major reasons why certain professionals participate in continuing education at such a high rate is because it is required by either the state in which they reside or by the professional association in which they hold membership. Presently all fifty states use participation in continuing education as a basis for relicensing members of certain professions. A study by Phillips (1987) lists sixteen professions that are regulated in this way. Many more occupational groups fall under a professional certification requirement that is regulated by a professional association or by a certification agency independent of the professional association (Galbraith & Gilley, 1986). The purpose of licensure and certification is grounded in the belief that the public is protected from incompetent practitioners if they are required to participate in mandatory continuing education to update their skills and knowledge. Much debate surrounds the issue of mandatory continuing education such as voluntary learning versus compulsory learning and knowledge acquisition versus knowledge application in practice. The question that has not been answered adequately is whether or not mandatory continuing education makes professionals more competent and improved practitioners (Cervero, 1988).

The trend is toward more professions and occupational groups to be mandated to participate in continuing education or suffer punitive consequences by failing to meet the requirement. Long (1974) suggests that this trend stems from institutional pressures that are philosophical and practical in nature. Whatever the reasons for its continuation, mandatory continuing education has thrust numerous willing and unwilling learners into the mainstream of lifelong education.

AIMS AND PRIORITY GOALS

As defined in Chapter 1, lifelong education is a process of deliberate and unintentional opportunities that influence learning throughout the life span. This definition attempts to avoid the idea of institutionalization "simply because it is possible to see education on a number of levels of formalization and the educational process within a number of different social institutions" (Jarvis, 1987, p. 5). What aims and priority goals can bring about lifelong education in the rural American community? What is needed to establish an educative society in rural America that can utilize formal, nonformal, and informal modes of education to acquire new knowledge, skills, and attitudes throughout the life span? Such a framework should be grounded in a model of lifelong education that is contextually designed and specifically suitable for rural America. It should consist of the following aims and priority goals:

1. To develop a perspective of lifelong education that seeks to view education in its totality in which formal, nonformal, and informal patterns of education are accepted as valid modes of acquiring knowledge, skills, and attitudes.

2. To accept the notion that community is a natural setting for the lifelong education process.

3. To recognize that lifelong education can be utilized to liberate individuals from their social structures and allow them to become agents of change in society.

4. To construct new kinds of educational programs, involving new combinations of services and new organizational arrangements, in order to better meet identified needs of populations of learners.

5. To involve school organizations and community-based organizations in planning and implementing educational programs.

6. To recognize that structural reforms and substantive reforms must be treated as separate and distinct issues.

7. To assist youth and adult populations with varying educational levels to recognize the process and value of lifelong education to solve personal, professional, social, political, and recreational concerns.

8. To assist all rural individuals to become literate and functional in rural society.

9. To acknowledge both the potential for and the fact of excellence that exist in rural America.

10. To respect the primacy of local circumstances of the rural community.

11. To maintain high standards of practice in all educational programs.

12. To develop forms of thinking and acting that fit the situations that rural people find themselves in and maintain an active appreciation of, and engagement with, the social systems through which they operate and the cultural forms they use.

13. To assist youth and adults to become resourceful, autonomous, continuous, and critically reflective learners in all aspects of their lives.

14. To recognize the lifelong learning potential and educational opportunity that exist in the various facets of rural America.

Several things are implicit in the aims and priority goals listed above:

1. There should be an acceptance that all people of all ages have educational opportunities in which they can pursue.

2. All school and nonschool organizations within the rural community should take responsibility in planning and implementing lifelong education.

3. Various formal, nonformal, and informal modes of education are accepted and recognized as valid.

4. A new configuration of services and community organizations is called for to meet the diverse needs of all populations.

5. The concept of lifelong education can serve as a philosophical basis for bringing together the broad range of educational providers who are concerned with the continuous development of individuals and society.

6. A host of new life options can be available for learning, work, and leisure.

7. A new look at lifelong education public policy could lead to new social norms and cultural values (Apps, 1985; Cropley, 1977; Dillman & Hobbs, 1982; Galbraith, 1990a; Gross, 1977; Jarvis, 1986, 1987; Jeffs & Smith, 1990a; Long, Apps, & Hiemstra, 1985; Peterson & Associates, 1979; Sher, 1977, 1981).

Whether the aims and priority goals of lifelong education in the rural American community become a reality depends almost exclusively on the ability to change the educational, social, and political aspects that presently exist. What new directions need to be implemented to make it a lifelong educational community and what implications do these changes hold?

NEW DIRECTIONS

Numerous structural and substantive reforms must be realized if the rural American community is going to be transformed into a lifelong educational community. Foremost, rural America must begin to understand the conceptual foundation and the vertical and horizontal dimensions of lifelong education. The aims and priority goals mentioned above demand the acceptance and implementation of education and learning throughout the life span as well as connecting and integrating this education and learning across the various domains of life associated with rural society. Rural education must be viewed as an integrated network rather than unrelated, narrow, and discrete disciplines. Cropley (1977), Dave (1976), Dubin (1974), and Jarvis (1986) as well as others, concerned with the psychological and social aspects of lifelong learning, suggest that lifelong learners should strive to be cognitively well equipped, highly educable, and internally motivated.

Cognitively, lifelong learners should be familiar with a variety of disciplines and skills, acquainted with the structures of knowledge and not merely facts, skilled at adapting the tools of learning how to learn, and aware of the relationship between cognitive skills and real life. Lifelong learners should strive to be highly educable; possess varied learning strategies; be able to learn in a variety of individual and group settings; be equipped with basic learning skills; be able to understand nonverbal communication; be well equipped with basic intellectual skills such as reasoning, critical thinking, and reflection; be skilled at using many learning devices such as printed materials, mass media, programmed and technological materials, and networks; and perhaps most important be equipped with abilities and skills in identifying learning needs, setting learning objectives, developing activities to meet needs and objectives, and designing methods for evaluating the learning project. Lifelong learners should also be motivated to carry on a process of lifelong learning which requires them to be aware of the rapidity of change and its effects on social and political life, and on knowledge and job skills. They should be aware that formal schooling is only the beginning of learning for life and that they hold a personal responsibility to acquire new knowledge, skills, and attitudes. Lastly, lifelong learning demands a motivation and awareness that learning is the primary tool for personal and societal growth. Within this framework, implicit changes concerning the attitude and purpose of rural education are suggested. One of the more apparent implications of lifelong education and lifelong learning is that a shift in concept must occur from that of schooling to one of lifelong education.

It is out of the scope of this chapter to provide an indepth analysis of all the factors affecting the new directions of change. Three broad areas will be examined briefly: dispositional change, school and lifelong education curriculum, and professional educators and life educators.

Dispositional Change

Dispositional change suggests an examination of held assumptions, givens, behaviors, knowledge bases, and attitudes toward education and learning. It calls forth a need to be critically reflective and aware of the factors that influence a paradigm shift from schooling to lifelong education. It suggests that we struggle with the conceptual foundation and meaning of the vertical and horizontal dimensions of lifelong education, determine approaches for implementation, accept the validity of not only formal learning methods but nonformal and informal as well, recognize the availability and diversity of educational providers and opportunities within the rural community, and appreciate the benefits that lifelong education provides to the various aspects of life.

If lifelong education is to happen, the importance and influence of the rural cultural and social environment must be understood. A shifting from a static to a dynamic culture in which rural people have a say in decisions affecting their self-expression, individuality, home, social, work, and leisure activities is imperative. Cropley (1977) argues that perhaps the "most powerful environmental influence is provided by the framework of social institutions within which people live their lives—what is usually called their society or culture" (p. 106). Cultural expectations shape people's attitudes toward school, learning, society, and so forth. If the rural culture dictates that education is equated to formal schooling, then a disregard for nonformal and informal education is present. The rural culture, then, places less meaning and validity to such alternative mechanisms and approaches to fulfill educational ambitions. It is no easy task to change viewpoints of individuals who have acquired a set of common goals, aspirations, beliefs, values, and so on that hold great meaning, even if these viewpoints are misguided. Yet, lifelong education can only become a reality "when it is accepted by the people in the street; i.e., when it is absorbed into and becomes an integral part of their culture" (Cropley, 1977, p. 111). Through lifelong education, the rural culture holds the potential to foster a constructive educational reaction to the problems and dangers of the times, helping individuals to gain insight into cultural problems in their society, and develop feelings of control over their future as producers, consumers, citizens, and creators (Cropley, 1977).

Attitudes toward lifelong education must also be recognized within the family and work environment. Implementing a healthy disposition toward continuous learning throughout life can be instilled within the family unit. Skager and Dave (1977) suggest that within the family itself there is an important and significant educational process going on. It is the main learning environment for very young children. Within this family unit, crucial basic skills are transmitted as well as attitudes toward work, leisure, and learning. An enlightened family life has the potential to lay down a basic framework of emancipation of spirit, enthusiasm, and skill which will transform the whole life of the individual. In other words, the family environment can help shape an understanding of the importance of lifelong education and how it connects to the horizontal dimensions of life. Such a family environment also emphasizes cooperation between family and school. Parents become involved in parent advisory councils, strategic planning, and decision making.

Dispositional change must also occur within the work environment. The work environment must not be viewed as a place in which learning ceases. Lifelong education becomes a forging link between learning and work; the work place becomes a place of learning (Galbraith, 1990a; Marsick, 1987; Schön, 1983, 1987). The work environment is not only a means of economic reward, but also a mechanism for education that is carried into other dimensions of employees' lives. The private sector devotes great resources to human resource development programs. Carnevale (1986) estimates that $210 billion or more is being spent per year on formal and informal employer provided learning. These learning experiences for employees affect activities away from work in areas such as the use of technology, decision making, and interpersonal relations. Indeed, the work environment interacts in many important ways with the society, school, family, and individual. It can be an important link in the promotion of lifelong education as participants see work place learning as vital to the horizontal dimensions of community life.

The potential for realizing a shift from a schooling mentality to one of lifelong education must be harbored in the notion that rural Americans can change their dispositions and attitudes toward education and learning. It calls into being a critical analysis of how the cultural, social, family, and work environments can contribute to the extension of lifelong education. The ultimate aim in a disposition change would be to help rural America recognize what the adoption of lifelong education would mean to the various aspects of their culture and personal lives.

School and Lifelong Education Curriculum

A key notion in lifelong education is that it will occur both in and out of school. Since most of our learning experiences occur outside our formal school years, it is possible to talk about curriculum as not only school curriculum but also as lifelong education curriculum. The latter entails a curriculum for the very young who are not in formal school settings, a curriculum for adult learners, a curriculum for work, and a curriculum for life itself (Cropley, 1977). In essence, it is a curriculum that is concerned with education across the life span (the vertical dimension) and within the interwoven environments in which life exists at the moment (the horizontal dimension). This section will examine new directions in this expanded version of curriculum development.

The acceptance of lifelong education involves a dramatic curriculum change in elementary and secondary schools as well as in postsecondary educational institutions. Future curriculum changes will not advocate the abolition of schooling but will demand a conceptual reorganization of it as it is currently understood. Schooling in its broadest sense will need to offer an effective core of education that allows learners to acquire knowledge, skills, and attitudes needed for learning throughout the life span. The curriculum will be designed to offer multiple learning opportunities and an identified link to learning systems outside the school in the home, work, social, and leisure environments. Such a curriculum provides a connection to both the vertical and horizontal dimensions of lifelong education.

School curriculum must shift from the transmission of fixed knowledge to teaching the fundamental skill of learning how to learn (Smith, 1982). Cropley (1977) suggests that this means "there will be less emphasis on specialization in school curriculum, and that general and specialist education will move closer to each other" (p. 129). From this scenario, implications toward enhanced emphasis on communication skills, the mass media, and the interacting with peer groups emerge. It suggests that lifelong education must involve more individualized learning and instruction (Hiemstra & Sisco, 1990), more individual contacts between instructors and learners, and more individual and group work through learning projects, investigations, and inquiry exercises. A series of criteria for school curriculum in light of lifelong education has been developed by Skager and Dave (1977). They suggest that school curriculum should:

- regard learning processes as continuous, occurring from early childhood to late adulthood;

- be viewed in the context of concurrent learning processes going on in the home, community, place of work, and so on;

- recognize the importance of the essential unity of knowledge and the interrelationship between different subjects of study;

- recognize that the school is one of the chief agencies for providing basic education within the framework of lifelong education;

- emphasize autodidactics, including development of readiness for learning and cultivation of learning attitudes appropriate to the needs of a changing society;

- take into account the need for establishing and renewing a progressive value system by individuals, so that they can take responsibility for their own continuous growth throughout life.

The aim of the school curriculum in a lifelong education framework must be to assist learners to function under minimal supervision and to adapt to a changing society. It must foster the development of independence, self-reflection, and critical analysis in individuals. Knowles (1975) argues that the curriculum would shift from a content plan to a process plan. Classroom practice would emphasize productive thinking. Particular disciplines would then serve simply to provide the concrete materials upon which productive or creative thinking would act. Students will learn through analysis of the tactics and codes of knowledge how to create and explore alternative ways of thinking and acting as well as how to examine assumptions underlying their thoughts and actions (Brookfield, 1987). They will recognize that past learning can serve as a basis for the acquisition of future learning.

A lifelong education curriculum, in addition to the school curriculum, must also be recognized in the rural American community. Lifelong education recognizes that the early years lay down a basis on which later social and psychological development builds. Cropley (1977) suggests that "early educative experiences are crucial in laying the groundwork upon which later learning rests" (p. 124). The development of early education for very young children, that which is outside of the school setting, can foster cognitive and psychological development. According to Biggs (1973), it should provide a source of stimulation, foster a sense of identity, and provide an appropriate socialization experience. These kinds of skills do not require formal schooling but can be fostered by life itself which is a very important component of lifelong education. Early childhood education within the lifelong education framework advocates the development of skills for dealing with information and symbols, appreciates various modes of self-expression, nurtures curiosity and the ability to think, cultivates confidence in the ability to learn, fosters a sense of self-worth, increases the capacity to cooperate with others, and provides the basis for the development of intellectual tactics for organizing and reflecting upon experience. The mastery of language is the key skill. It enables children to organize and transmit their own ideas, desires, thoughts, and feelings. It permits very young children to move toward self-directedness, an important consequence that must be nurtured in early childhood so it can be continually fostered into adolescence and on into adulthood.

The examination of the influences of the work environment discussed elsewhere in this chapter implicitly suggests that the lifelong education framework also has a curriculum for work. Dubin (1974) states that this curriculum needs to foster personal initiative for continued growth and development. Gilley and Eggland (1989), Marsick (1987), and Schön (1983, 1987) suggest that this initiative for growth is fostered both by organizations that openly encourage professional upgrading and development and by the internal and external rewards that come with continuous learning. Dubin (1974) describes the characteristics of a work curriculum oriented toward lifelong education:

- Provision of tools for self-assessment

- Opportunities for self-assessment

- Establishment of an organizational climate fostering creativity

- Contact with challenging work projects that promote on-the-job solutions to problems

- Peer interactions promoting the exchange of ideas and information

As suggested in this book and elsewhere (Galbraith, 1990a), community-based organizations such as libraries, churches, business and industry, human service agencies, museums, social and fraternal organizations, and educational institutions hold the potential for creating a curriculum for work. This curriculum not only provides a more healthy environment for employees and employers but also assists workplace learners to extend such learning into other aspects of their lives outside the work environment.

Lastly, a curriculum for life itself must be considered if rural America is to embrace the realization of lifelong education. Lindeman (1926), nearly sixty-five years ago, stated that "education is life" (p. 6) and if education is life then "life is also education" (p. 9). A curriculum for life helps people develop a serious commitment to living a worthwhile and meaningful life which goes beyond just a means of existing. It helps them enjoy the spiritual, cultural, and emotional aspects of life, and not just the material dimensions. Cropley (1977) argues that such a curriculum "should emphasize that education involves more than simple intellectual knowledge . . . but it involves the idea that life itself is a major source of learning, and the view that one can learn about life, mainly through the process of living" (p. 128). Integration of the various aspects of living and learning constitutes the focal point for a curriculum for life itself (Griffin, 1983). This curriculum is closely related to the theory of learning how to learn in which individuals become able to apply thought to life itself; to use their knowledge; to exchange social and cultural experiences with others; to think critically about held assumptions; to exhibit alternative ways of thinking, acting, and behaving; and to recognize the great diversity of educational opportunities that exist within their lives.

School curriculum and lifelong education curriculum should not be viewed as separate and distinct entities, but as an interaction between the learning environments and the various aspects of people's lives. If rural America is to move in new directions toward lifelong education, there must be a recognition that curriculum is not synonymous with schooling. The learning society must associate curriculum with very young children, the work environment, and life itself. A lifelong education curriculum can become a reality only when the multifaceted components of the rural community recognize and accept the ideal as well as the practical aspects of lifelong education.

Professional Educators and Life Educators

This last section examines the new roles of professional educators and life educators in relationship to dispositional, school, and lifelong education curriculum change. Within this context, professional educators are those who instruct learners in formal settings such as elementary, secondary, and postsecondary educational institutions. Life educators facilitate learning in formal, nonformal, and informal settings such as the school, family, church, library, workplace, and the plethora of other community-based agencies and organizations. Life educators are concerned with learning throughout the life span in a variety of social and cultural contexts, in addition to formal schooling.

Professional Educators

Cropley (1977) suggests that the role of professional educators in a lifelong education-oriented curriculum has

> several major features involving their influence on the attitudes, on the motivational structures and on the cognitive skills of students. In the attitudinal domain, the lifelong education-facilitating teacher will help pupils to adopt a creative attitude towards new situations, in order to cope with them effectively and to experience satisfaction from such coping. In the motivational domain, the teacher's major task will be to arouse in pupils the desire to face change and novelty in order to come to grips with them and to profit from them, rather than to avoid them. Cognitively, the teacher's task will be to equip pupils with skill in gaining skills, as and when they are required. This will be achieved through the development of a feel for the structure and methods of knowledge, and through building an understanding of the sources of information that are available. (p. 132)

Professional educators in rural America must be able to cope with sparsity, utilize community resources, be creative and visionary, and maintain a learner-centered orientation. Professional educators must harbor an attitude and appreciation for learning across the life span as well as an ability to place learning within the cultural context of rural life. They should be less concerned with subjects and more concerned with learners and helping them learn how to learn. Professional educators should not simply impart knowledge but assist in creating environments that foster independence and self-directedness. The lifelong education model implies that professional educators themselves will have to be lifelong learners. In addition, they will engage in the process of lifelong education as co-learners and at times be identified in such roles as mentor, guide, facilitator, resource provider, and coordinator of learning. The teaching and learning process will be viewed as a transformational journey in which teachers and learners see their lives in motion and constantly changing (Daloz, 1986; Galbraith, 1990b). Lifelong education should be characterized as a democratic and collaborative endeavor whereby professional educators and learners are engaged in a mutual act of challenge, critical reflection, sharing, support, and risk taking. No one learner will have a monopoly on insight, and dissension and criticism will be regarded as inevitable and desirable elements.

Professional educators within elementary, secondary, and postsecondary educational settings must be prepared to engage in a transactional process, which is characterized by an active, challenging, collaborative, critically reflective, and transforming educational encounter, if lifelong education is to be fostered. Implications for such a process suggest that teacher preparation and instructional training programs must engage in a paradigm shift from a content plan and teacher-centered orientation to a process plan and learner-centered orientation. A transactional process developed by Galbraith (1991a, 1991b) for educators of adult learners also holds relevance for professional educators in elementary, secondary, and postsecondary institutions. Explicit in this work are important elements and principles by which professional educators can promote lifelong education.

As suggested by Galbraith, the most common elements of a transactional process are collaboration, support, respect, freedom, equality, critical reflection, critical analysis, challenge, and praxis. To incorporate these elements, both professional educators and learners must reconceptualize their roles, responsibilities, and purposes within the educational encounter. Brookfield (1987) states that this process at times may be uncomfortable and even painful because of the confrontation and challenge involved. The transactional process requires elements of truth and responsibility: truth about reality, values, beliefs, and knowledge bases; and responsibility for personal behavior and learning.

The process of praxis is at the heart of lifelong education and learning, whether in elementary, secondary, or postsecondary settings. Praxis is the process whereby: "Learners and facilitators are involved in a continual process of activity, reflection upon activity, collaborative analysis of activity, new activity, further reflection and collaborative analysis, and so on" (Brookfield, 1986, p. 10). Such a process allows professional educators and learners to culturally construct their learning and constantly self-examine their beliefs, values, and actions.

Another important feature of the transactional process is risk taking (Galbraith, 1991b). Risk taking suggests that we enter new and unfamiliar territory; that we do things that we are unaccustomed in doing for the sake of change and personal growth. Three types of risk taking exist within this process: risk of commitment, risk of confrontation, and risk of independence. The first type is a commitment to the ideals and actions of a transactional process. To submit to this process suggests that professional educators and learners run the risk of self-confrontation and change. The risk of confrontation is closely related to the openness to challenge held beliefs, values, and demonstrated actions. It is an act that assists learners to critically analyze why they think and act in the manner they do. It assists in recognizing any incongruence in their feelings, attitudes, thoughts, and actions. Perhaps the most important risk within the transactional process is that of independence. Independence suggests a shedding of the psychological dependence held toward the teaching and learning encounter. It suggests that educators and learners take responsibility for their own learning, individuality, and independence as well as take a leap toward self-direction. In doing so, the pleasure of intellectual freedom and the excitement of exploring new dimensions of thinking and acting are realized.

The transactional process for professional educators is important if lifelong education in rural America is to be implemented. Teacher preparation and instructional training programs can follow six guiding principles in the implementation of the transactional process that encourage new ways of promoting lifelong education in the formal setting (Galbraith, 1991b).

The first principle is that an appropriate philosophical orientation must guide the educational encounter. Elias and Merriam (1980) suggest that "philosophy raises questions about what we do and why we do it" (p. 5). It does not equip the professional educator with knowledge about what to teach, how to teach, or how to organize a program but instead is concerned with the why of education. Within this context, progressive and humanistic philosophies seem most appropriate and consistent with the transactional and lifelong educational process. Each is consistent with the ideals of responsibility, risk taking, mutual respect, challenge, collaboration, as well as promoting critical reflection and personal growth.

The second principle is to understand the diversity and variability of learners. Lifelong education demands that learners are understood from a holistic perspective, with consideration of their physical, social, psychological, ego, moral, and learning developmental directions. Another dimension within this principle is to recognize the various learning styles that each learner brings to the educational encounter. Learning styles are the ways that individuals prefer to engage and process information in learning activities. Professional educators can investigate learning styles from various perspectives such as cognitive, affective, or physiological (Claxton & Murrell, 1987; Cornett, 1983; Galbraith, 1987; Kolb,

1984). The important thing is to recognize the diversity of learners and their styles and then to utilize diverse learning methods and techniques that best fit a collaborative, challenging, and critically reflective educational encounter.

Creating a conducive psychosocial climate is the third principle. This principle suggests that learners need not only a good physical environment (adequate lighting and ventillation, colorful decor, appropriate temperature, and so on), but also a psychological climate that encourages collaborative relationships, mutual rapport, communication, trust, support, challenge, risk taking, friendliness, and encouragement. Such a climate can be encouraged and maintained by designing a planning process that mutually involves educators and learners in assessing learning needs, establishing learning activities, and developing evaluation strategies. Such an approach suggests to learners that they are important in the development of the educational encounter and that their perceptions and contributions matter.

Related to the third principle is principle four: professional educators must provide challenging interactions. This has as its primary purpose the development of learners who can think critically and reflectively. Egan (1986) suggests that challenge is the last most essential component necessary before an individual can develop alternative ways of thinking and acting. Appropriate challenges are those that call out for closure, while at the same time provide insight to how this new knowledge can be applied to the learners' lives. Professional educators should provide a "mirror" for learners to see themselves in a different way, to see how they have changed and developed as a result of their accomplishments through the process of challenge. Using strategies such as peer learning groups, critical questioning, critical incident exercises, role playing, and crisis-decision simulations can assist learners in questioning givens and examining the assumptions that form the foundation of their thoughts and actions.

Fostering critical reflection and praxis, the fifth principle, is paramount in the transactional process. Lifelong learning is comprised of both psychological and social constructs. When professional educators encourage learners to question and understand the nature of their knowledge, values, assumptions, ideologies, judgments, and behaviors in a broader context, they are helping learners to be critically reflective as well as fostering a sense of how these qualities are culturally and socially influenced. The primary consequence is that this promotes the development of critical thinkers who can identify and explore the assumptions under which they think and act. Incorporating the process of praxis means that curricula are not studied in some kind of artificial isolation, but that ideas, skills, and insights learned in the classroom are tested and experienced actively in real rural contexts. Critical reflection and praxis assist learners to interpret and question beliefs and actions from new viewpoints.

The sixth principle is encouraging independence. By incorporating the first five principles, professional educators are ultimately asking learners to become engaged in transformative learning that leads to independence, autonomy, empowerment, and self-direction. Independence allows learners to reinterpret, renegotiate, and recreate their perspectives which results in alternative ways of thinking and acting. It gives them an awareness of their learning process and a recognition of any self-imposed limits.

Life Educators

Up to this point the discussion has been on professional educators. Those who help individuals learn through the settings of family, workplace, and other community-based agencies and organizations are referred to as life educators. Professional educators may be life educators but not all life educators are professional educators. Life educators may have no formal teacher training and may not possess a professional educative role, but do play "an important role as part of the educative functions of life itself" (Cropley, 1977, p. 134). Their preparation comes through living and life itself, through on-the-job experiences, independent learning, collaborative efforts, and so forth (Galbraith & Zelenak, 1989). They assist in the implementation of the vertical and horizontal dimensions of lifelong education by helping individuals learn and development within specific cultural contexts. Life educators have the ability "to develop an appreciation of the culture encountered and ways in which interventions may be understood" (Jeffs & Smith, 1990b, p. 134).

Expanding the conceptualization of educator finds a large group of individuals engaged in helping youth through adults learn. Lifelong education suggests that everyone can learn and everyone has the potential of helping someone else learn. Rural America is comprised of numerous formal, informal, and nonformal educational providers. The question is whether or not individuals within this plethora of educational providers recognize that they hold the role of life educator. Some of these individuals are parents, fellow workers, peers, and social acquaintances. Life educators may be found in churches, social and fraternal organizations, business and industries, libraries, museums, university extension programs, human service agencies, schools, and other community-based organizations (Galbraith, 1990a). Whether with young children, adolescents, or adults, life educators can help learners experience the world around them as well as provide a foundation for connecting this experience to their social and cultural contexts. They assist people in dealing with and learning from the tasks of day-to-day living and at the same time provide encouragement to learners to take the responsibility for their own learning. The lifelong educator's classroom is the rural environment and the various dimensions of society that comprise it.

Everyone in the rural environment has the potential to be engaged in expanding learning opportunities as well as encouraging self-directed learning in others. What needs to be understood about facilitating learning if lifelong education and effective practice are realized, whether with young people or adults? How is the life educator's role conceptualized?

This latter question may be addressed more fully once parents, fellow workers, friends, and peers understand the multifaceted roles they play within the rural context of family, school, and community. At any one time, an individual is engaged in multiple life roles such as parent, worker, relative, volunteer, and community leader. In each of these roles, contact is made with a host of individuals at different physical, psychological, and social stages of life. Opportunities to help others learn something meaningful and important are constantly present. In addition to all the other roles, the role of educator must be added. Reconceptualizing what "educator" means in its broadest sense, and how it fits within the concept of lifelong education, must be understood and accepted.

The primary purpose of formal, nonformal, and informal education is to promote development and growth. The means by which life educators help bring this about vary depending upon the age of the learner. Life educators are engaged, to a high degree, in informal education, a form of pedagogy in which certain values and concerns are emphasized such as the self-worth of the learner, the importance of critical thinking, and the need to examine what is taken for granted (Jeffs & Smith, 1990c). Jeffs and Smith suggest that "informal education is a special set of processes which involves the adoption of certain broad ways of thinking and acting so that people can engage with what is going on" (p. 3). What life educators do is "contribute to the development of the context and conditions which allow the desired 'internal' change we know as learning to occur" (p. 7). In other words, they manage the external conditions that facilitate the internal change called learning (Brookfield, 1986). Life educators understand the need to develop forms of thinking and acting that fit the situations that individuals find themselves in, and understand the social systems through which people operate. They are sensitive to the possible range of learning styles and to the rural culture in which they are working. They are aware of the multitude of reasons why young people and adults engage in learning, and they understand the barriers, especially for adult learners, that deter involvement in educational pursuits (Galbraith & Sundet, 1990; Sundet & Galbraith, 1990).

For a dynamic future in rural education, the role of the life educator needs to be reconceptualized. What principles characterize effective practice? In discussing professional educators, an adaptation of the transactional process was detailed. In essence, most of the elements and principles examined also hold true for life educators if effective lifelong education is to be realized. An adaptation of Brookfield's (1986) six principles of effective practice forms a valid foundation for life educators who work with young people and adults. These principles provide a philosophical stance on which to build effective learning relationships and practices.

The first principle is concerned with voluntary participation. With the exception of formal schooling, most young children and adults engage in learning on their own volition. Life educators do not coerce, bully, or intimidate individuals into learning.

The second principle suggests that life educators and learners recognize that effective practice is characterized by a respect for each other's self-worth. Learners are made to "feel that they are valued as separate, unique individuals deserving of respect" (Brookfield, 1986, p. 13).

The third principle is concerned with collaboration. Life educators and learners should maintain a cooperative and collaborative spirit within the learning encounter.

The fourth principle maintains that effective practice places praxis at the heart of lifelong education and learning. As described above, praxis is the continual process of activity, reflection upon activity, collaborative analysis of activity, further reflection and collaborative analysis, and so on.

Life educators understand the need to foster a spirit of critical reflection, which is principle five. Brookfield suggests that effective practice aims to foster an attitude of healthy skepticism as well as to prompt in learners "a sense of the culturally constructed nature of knowledge, beliefs, values, and behaviors" (p. 17). To accomplish this, life educators must present alternative interpretations of learner's views.

The final principle is concerned with nurturing self-direction in learners. Learners must recognize the benefits of taking control and responsibility for their learning. As a part of this, life educators can assist learners with alternatives in their current ways of thinking, behaving, and living. Life educators can encourage learners to seek out and image alternative perspectives about things they believe and act upon.

These six adapted principles suggest that life educators must pay attention to the way they understand and implement assistance in the process of lifelong education. Effective practice depends upon their ability to identify and nurture the reconceptualized role of educator. It is critical that they see themselves as "educators" in a role that transcends the many social roles and boundaries in rural American life.

Up to this point this chapter has detailed the trends and factors that influence lifelong education, examined the aims and priorities, and suggested the new directions needed to bring about lifelong education in rural America. Critical to these new directions is a dispositional change, a reconceptualization of school and lifelong education curriculum, and an understanding about professional educators and life educators. These new directions may seem rather utopian, ideal and abstract to some. To others it may suggest that lifelong education is feasible if a reconceptualization of what is "education" is accepted, if psychological and social action steps are fostered, and if individuals and society begin to view it as an educational principle of practical significance. If this becomes a reality, then rural Americans will be the beneficiaries.

BENEFITS OF LIFELONG EDUCATION AND LIFELONG LEARNING

Rural America is experiencing a crisis of social, educational, political, and economic dimensions. At the heart of resolution, lifelong education must be present, for it is through our ability to change as well as draw upon our existing resources and mind power that a revitalization of rural America will be realized. Lifelong education and learning are the foundation on which change and progress must be constructed. It is through the benefits of lifelong education and learning that personal, societal, and economic developments are advanced.

Peterson (1979b) provides a framework for examining the benefits of lifelong education and learning. He has divided his typology as follows: (1) individual benefits as distinct from (2) social benefits, and (3) personal or noneconomic benefits as distinct from (4) economic benefits.

Perhaps the primary benefit of lifelong education and learning is to the individual. As a result of this process, individuals experience noneconomic benefits such as enhanced literacy; skills and knowledge for effective living as a consumer, parent, and participant in politics; a general and academic education; and the intellectual capacity of continuous learning throughout life. Individuals of all ages receive personality benefits such as a sense of self-reliance, personal autonomy, and empowerment. They gain an increased sense of self-esteem, self-worth, meaning, and fulfillment. An increased appreciation and tolerance for differing social attitudes, values, and ethics are fostered through lifelong education and learning. In addition, avocational and cultural benefits are realized such as increased interest and skill in recreational activities, artistic and esthetics skills and appreciations as well as consumption benefits that are experienced during participation in learning activities.

To society, the direct and indirect benefits of lifelong education and learning are multiple. Direct benefits include a literate population comprised of informed and skilled citizens that utilize their capabilities wisely in family, community, and political situations. Overall, then, society has a population that is generally more educated and knowledgeable. It contains many lifelong learners and citizens that are not dependent on institutions for all their educational, economic, social, and recreational needs. Communities of lifelong learners strive to exist in a harmonious and trustful existence and are interested in the pursuit of a humane culture that appreciates diverse and cultural interests. Indirect benefits also affect societal development through reduced welfare dependency and reduced crime and incarceration rates. Peterson suggests that improved general health, more equitable distribution of wealth, and the distribution of other life amenities are also indirect benefits.

A lifelong education and learning society also provides economic advancement to individuals. This benefit is directed toward adults and not young children or adolescents, although they will benefit as they move into adulthood and into the workforce. Individuals engaged in lifelong education benefit from the opportunities of entry level training, job upgrading, and vocational renewal as well as training for a new or different vocation. Subscribers to lifelong education enjoy the potential for occupational flexibility and continued growth and development.

The benefits of economic advancements to the individual also enhance the economic development of society. First, society has an increased availability of trained and skilled people. Job satisfaction, the general standard of living, and tax revenues are increased which affects the general economic conditions of society. As a result, the economy experiences higher employee productivity and lower unemployment rates. Finally, the economy benefits because the majority of employees are capable of readily moving among related jobs as a result of their capacity to critically evaluate the transferable skills they possess.

The economic and noneconomic benefits to individuals and to the society provide various implications for those engaged in community planning and program development in rural America. They imply new directions for financing education, the role of local communities and the involvement of volunteers, the role of schools and institutions of higher education, and the expanded role of community-based organizations. This suggests that we reevaluate our information bases and mass media outlets, as well as our planning and decision-making approaches and the design of learning services. Lastly, the implication is that rural America must reconceptualize the concept of education, the meaning of educator, and the educational resources at its doorstep.

CONCLUSION

Nothing will promote the idea and concept of lifelong education in the rural American community if the perpetual dependency on the establishment continues to exist. A bold new conceptual leap and the desire to change are necessary. The critical question must be whether or not lifelong education has the potential of freeing the rural society from the crisis that some say exists. Can it provide for self-fulfillment and an improved quality of life? The foundation of lifelong education is the individuals who seek out independence and autonomy that result in meaningful cultural experiences and personal development. To reach these people educators must develop new concepts of school, lifelong curriculum, and educator. Communications is the key. It is imperative to translate the philosophy of lifelong education into clear statements about what it means to the school curriculum, the professional and life educator, the teaching and learning encounter, the workplace, the community organization, and the individual.

Rural America cannot afford to dismiss the idea of lifelong education. The concept holds great potential for rural communities to become vital communities of learners and educational providers. It provides an opportunity for rural America to socially and contextually construct a lifelong education process to meet their unique present needs as well as those confronting them in the future.

REFERENCES

American Association of Retired Persons. (1987). *A profile of older Americans, 1987.* Washington, DC: Author.

Apps, J. W. (1985). *Improving practice in continuing education.* San Francisco: Jossey-Bass.

Biggs, J. (1973). Content to process. *Australian Journal of Education,* 17, 225–238.

Brockett, R., & Hiemstra, R. (1991). *Self-direction in adult learning.* London and New York: Routledge.

Brookfield, S. D. (Ed.). (1985). *Self-directed learning: From theory to practice.* New Directions for Continuing Education, no. 25. San Francisco: Jossey-Bass.

Brookfield, S. D. (1986). *Understanding and facilitating adult learning.* San Francisco: Jossey-Bass.

Brookfield, S. D. (1987). *Developing critical thinkers.* San Francisco: Jossey-Bass.

Candy, P. (1991). *Self-direction for lifelong learning.* San Francisco: Jossey-Bass.

Carnevale, A. (1986). The learning enterprise. *Training and Development Journal,* 40(1), 18–26.

Center for Educational Statistics. (1984). *Trends in adult education, 1969–1984.* Washington, DC: U. S. Government Printing Office.

Cervero, R. M. (1988). *Effective continuing education for professionals.* San Francisco: Jossey-Bass.

Cetrone, M., Soriano, B., & Gayle, M. (1985). *Schools of the future.* New York: McGraw-Hill.

Claxton, C., & Murrell, P. (1987). *Learning styles: Implications for improving educational practice.* (ASHE-ERIC Higher Education Report 4). Washington, DC: ASHE-ERIC Clearinghouse on Higher Education.

Cornett, C. (1983). *What you should know about teaching and learning styles.* Bloomington: Phi Delta Kappa.

Cremin, L. A. (1976). *Public education.* New York: Basic Books.

Cropley, A. J. (1977). *Lifelong education: A psychological analysis.* Toronto: Pergamon.

Cross, K. P. (1979). Adult learners: Characteristics, needs, and interests. In R. E. Peterson & Associates, *Lifelong learning in America* (pp. 75–141). San Francisco: Jossey-Bass.

Cross, K. P. (1981). *Adults as learners.* San Francisco: Jossey-Bass.

Daloz, L. (1986). *Effective teaching and mentoring.* San Francisco: Jossey-Bass.

Dave. R. H. (Ed.). (1976). *Foundations of lifelong education.* Oxford: Pergamon.

DeYoung, A. J. (1987). The status of American rural education research: An integrated review and commentary. *Review of Educational Research,* 57(2), 123–148.

Dillman, D., & Hobbs. D. (Eds.). (1982). *Rural society in the U.S.: Issues in the 1980s.* Boulder: Westview.

Dubin, S. S. (1974). The psychology of lifelong learning: New developments in the professions. *International Review of Applied Psychology,* 23, 17–31.

Egan, G. (1986). *The skilled helper: A systematic approach to effective helping* (3rd. ed.). Monterey: Brooks/Cole.

Elias, J., & Merriam, S. (1980). *Philosophical foundations of adult education.* Malabar, FL: Krieger.

Florini, B. (1990). Communications technology in adult education and learning. In M. W. Galbraith (Ed.), *Adult learning methods: A guide for effective instruction* (pp. 367–390). Malabar, FL: Krieger.

Galbraith, M. W. (1987). Assessing perceptual learning styles. In C. Klevins (Ed.), *Materials and methods in adult and continuing education* (pp. 263–269). Los Angeles: Klevens.

Galbraith, M. W. (Ed.). (1990a). *Education through community organizations*. New Directions for Adult and Continuing Education, no. 47. San Francisco: Jossey-Bass.

Galbraith, M. W. (1990b). Attributes and skills of an adult educator. In M. W. Galbraith (Ed.), *Adult learning methods: A guide for effective instruction* (pp. 3–22). Malabar, FL: Krieger.

Galbraith, M. W. (Ed.). (1991a). *Facilitating adult learning: A transactional process*. Malabar, FL: Krieger.

Galbraith, M. W. (1991b). The adult learning transactional process. In M. W. Galbraith (Ed.), *Facilitating adult learning: A transactional process* (pp. 1–32). Malabar, FL: Krieger.

Galbraith, M. W., & Gilley, J. W. (1986). *Professional certification: Implications for adult education and HRD*. Columbus: ERIC Clearinghouse on Adult, Career, and Vocational Education.

Galbraith, M. W., & Sundet, P. A. (1988). Educational perspectives of rural adult learners: A key informant analysis. *Journal of Adult Education, 17*(1), 11–18.

Galbraith, M. W., & Sundet, P. A. (1990). Comparative analysis of barriers to participation in rural adult education programs. *Proceedings of the 31st Annual Adult Education Research Conference* (pp. 89–94). Athens: University of Georgia.

Galbraith, M. W., & Zelenak, B. S. (1989). The education of adult and continuing education practitioners. In S. Merriam & P. Cunningham (Eds.), *Handbook of adult and continuing education* (pp. 124–133). San Francisco: Jossey-Bass.

Gilley, J., & Eggland, S. (1989). *Principles of human resource development*. Reading: Addison-Wesley.

Griffin, C. (1983). *Curriculum theory in adult and lifelong education*. London: Croom Helm.

Gross, R. (1977). *The lifelong learner*. New York: Simon and Schuster.

Heermann, B. (1988). *Teaching and learning with computers*. San Francisco: Jossey-Bass.

Hiemstra, R. (1985). The older adult's learning projects. In D. B. Lumsden (Ed.), *The older adult as learner* (pp. 165–196). Washington, DC: Hemisphere.

Hiemstra, R., & Sisco, B. (1990). *Individualizing instruction: Making learning personal, empowering, and successful.* San Francisco: Jossey-Bass.

Jarvis, P. (1986). *Sociological perspectives on lifelong education and lifelong learning.* Athens: The University of Georgia.

Jarvis, P. (1987). Sociological perspectives on lifelong education. *Educational Considerations,* 14(2 & 3), 5–8.

Jeffs, T., & Smith, M. (Eds.). (1990a). *Using informal education: An alternative to casework, teaching and control.* Philadelphia: Open University Press.

Jeffs, T., & Smith, M. (1990b). Educating informal educators. In T. Jeffs & M. Smith (Eds.), *Using informal education: An alternative to casework, teaching and control* (pp. 125–143). Philadelphia: Open University Press.

Jeffs, T., & Smith, M. (1990c). Using informal education. In T. Jeffs & M. Smith (Eds.), *Using informal education: An alternative to casework, teaching and control* (pp. 1–23). Philadelphia: Open University Press.

Knowles, M. S. (1975). *Self-directed learning: A guide for learners and teachers.* Chicago: Follett.

Kolb, D. (1984). *Experiential learning: Experience as the source of learning and development.* Englewood Cliffs: Prentice-Hall.

Lewis, L. H. (1989). New technologies for the future. In S. Merriam & P. Cunningham (Eds.), *Handbook of adult and continuing education* (pp. 613–627). San Francisco: Jossey-Bass.

Lindeman, E. C. (1926). *The meaning of adult education.* New York: New Republic.

Long, H. B. (1974). Lifelong learning: Pressures for acceptance. *Journal of Research and Development in Education,* 7(4), 2–12.

Long, H., Apps, J., & Hiemstra, R. (1985). *Philosophical and other views on lifelong learning.* Athens: The University of Georgia.

Marsick, V. J. (Ed.). (1987). *Learning in the workplace.* London: Croom Helm.

Nadler, L., & Nadler, Z. (1989). *Developing human resources* (3rd. ed.). San Francisco: Jossey-Bass.

Naisbitt, J. (1982). *Megatrends: Ten New Directions Transforming Our Lives.* New York: Warner Books.

Peterson, R. E. (1979a). Introduction: On the meaning of lifelong learning. In R. E. Peterson & Associates, *Lifelong learning in America* (pp. 1–12). San Francisco: Jossey-Bass.

Peterson, R. E. (1979b). Implications and consequences for the future. In R. E. Peterson & Associates, *Lifelong learning in America* (pp. 422–453). San Francisco: Jossey-Bass.

Peterson, R. E. & Associates (1979). *Lifelong learning in America*. San Francisco: Jossey-Bass.

Phillips, L. E. (1987). Is mandatory continuing education working? *Mobius*, 7(1), 57–63.

Pitman, W. (1984). Education for a maturing population in Canada: Reactions and speculations. *Educational Gerontology*, 10, 207–217.

Rice, J., & Meyer, S. (1989). Continuing education for women. In S. Merriam & P. Cunningham (Eds.), *Handbook of adult and continuing education* (pp. 550–568). San Francisco: Jossey-Bass.

Rosenwaike, I., & Logue, B. (1985). *The extreme aged in America: A portrait of an expanding population*. Westport: Greenwood.

Schön, D. A. (1983). *The reflective practitioner*. New York: Basic Books.

Schön, D. A. (1987). *Educating the reflective practitioner*. San Francisco: Jossey-Bass.

Sher, J. (Ed.). (1977). *Education in rural America*. Boulder: Westview.

Sher, J. (1981). Education in the countryside: Establishing the context. In J. Sher (Ed.), *Rural education in urbanized nations: Issues and innovations* (pp. 3–20). Boulder: Westview.

Skager, R., & Dave, R. H. (1977). *Developing criteria and procedures for the evaluation of school curriculum in the perspective of lifelong education*. Oxford: Pergamon.

Smith, R. M. (1982). *Learning how to learn*. New York: Cambridge.

Sundet, P. A., & Galbraith, M. W. (1990, April). *Adult education as a response to the rural crisis: Factors governing utility and participation*. Paper presented at the annual meeting of the American Educational Research Association. Boston, MA

Toffler, A. (1980). *The third wave*. New York: William Morrow.

Tough, A. (1979). *The adult's learning projects*. Toronto: The Ontario Institute for Studies in Education.

Van Tilburg, E., & Moore, A. B. (1989). Education for rural adults. In S. Merriam & P. Cunningham (Eds.), *Handbook of adult and continuing education* (pp. 537–549). San Francisco: Jossey-Bass.

U. S. Bureau of the Census. (1987). *Statistical abstract of the United States, 1987*. Washington, DC: U.S. Government Printing Office.

World Future Society. (1988). *Outlook '88*. Bethesda: Author.

APPENDIX

Rural School, Higher Education, and Nonformal Education Resources for Rural Lifelong Education

JACQUELINE D. SPEARS
GWEN BAILEY
SUE C. MAES

I. RURAL SCHOOL RESOURCES

Clearinghouses/Centers

ERIC Clearinghouse on Rural Education and Small Schools (ERIC/
CRESS)
Appalachia Educational Laboratory
1031 Quarrier Street
P.O. Box 1348
Charleston, WV 25325–1348
1-800-344-6646 (Inside WV)
1-800-624-9120 (Outside WV)

Provides information on educational programs and practices relevant to: (1) rural residents, (2) small schools, (3) American Indians/Alaskan Natives, (4) Mexican Americans, and (5) migrants. The clearinghouse conducts free ERIC searches and provides free and for sale publications. It was formerly located in Las Cruces, New Mexico.

Appalachia Educational Laboratory (AEL)
1031 Quarrier Street
P.O. Box 1348
Charleston, WV 25325–1348
(304) 347-0400
States Served: KY, TN, VA, and WV

AEL has tested a model of rural school-community partnerships, built a regional information base on rural schools, and tested a process to enable schools and communities to make data-driven decisions. It publishes a quarterly newsletter, *The Link*.

Far West Laboratory for Educational Research and
Development
1855 Folsom Street
San Francisco, CA 94103
(415) 565-3020
States Served: AZ, CA, NV, and UT

The Far West Laboratory has established the Rural Schools Assistance Center. Projects have included: (1) replicating innovative uses of instructional technology, (2) establishing a four-county collaborative to provide tele-learning services, (3) assisting small schools' response to Nevada's new graduation requirements in the arts/humanities, (4) serving at-risk students in rural areas of California, (5) helping rural schools in California and Nevada deal with science curricula, (6) providing funds to support school-based improvement plans in rural Nevada, and (7) coordinating cooperative curriculum planning across district lines in Arizona. The laboratory disseminates *Policy Briefs* and *Resources and Practices*, quarterly newsletters.

Mid-continent Regional Education Laboratory (McREL)
12500 E. Iliff Avenue
Aurora, CO 80014
(303) 337-0990
States Served: CO, KS, MO, NE, ND, SD, and WY

McREL is engaged in a number of rural projects, including: (1) Project Access designed to increase student access to information about postsecondary education, (2) Decisions about Technology designed to help schools organize themselves to use expanded course offerings made possible through collaboration and technology, and (3) Community Development Project designed to involve schools more directly in the community development process. McREL has also had substantial experience in clustering, working with groups of rural schools around common issues. McREL publishes the *McREL Update* three times annually, *Policy Notes* quarterly, and *Noteworthy*.

North Central Regional Educational Laboratory (NCREL)
295 Emroy Avenue
Elmhurst, IL 60126
(312) 941-7677
States Served: IL, IN, IA, MI, MN, OH, and WI

The NCREL effort has examined rural education in terms of the broader educational reform movement. Efforts have focused on reading and thinking skills, with individual projects underway in Illinois, Michigan, Ohio, and Wisconsin. Minnesota is pursuing a related project, using communication skills as the focus of school activities. In Indiana, rural projects are focused on school improvement; and in Iowa, efforts to introduce plans for performance-based pay and identify statewide issues in rural education are underway. NCREL distributes a *Rural Education Information Packet* quarterly.

Northwest Regional Educational Laboratory (NWREL)
101 S.W. Main Street, Suite 500
Portland, OR 97204
(503) 275-9547 or
1-800-547-6339 Ext. 547
States Served: AK, HI, ID, MT, OR, and WA

NWREL has been working with five clusters of schools spread across four states in implementing distance education technologies to expand learning opportunities in rural areas. In addition, the laboratory is exploring a strategy for installing and diffusing rural school improvement efforts. The *Northwest Report* is published monthly.

Regional Laboratory for Educational Improvement of the
Northeast and Islands (NE/IS)
290 South Main Street
Andover, MA 01810
(508) 470-1080
States Served: CT, MA, ME, NH, NY, RI, VT, Puerto Rico, and Virgin Islands

The laboratory maintains a rural and small schools network across the region. Projects include: (1) assessing regional data, (2) identifying exemplary programs and practitioners, (3) conducting forums for network members, and (4) building local capacity to direct school improvement efforts focused on enhancing basic skills and critical thinking. A bimonthly newsletter, *Alert*, and exchange packets of school practice materials are disseminated within the network.

Research for Better Schools (RBS)
444 N. Third Street
Philadelphia, PA 19123-4107
(215) 574-9300 Ext. 204
States Served: DE, DC, MA, NJ, and PA

The Rural and Small Schools Project has: (1) provided technical assistance to three rural sites where a computer-managed instruction program is being implemented and (2) assisted three states in developing statewide plans for improving rural education. In addition, it maintains a network of rural educators.

Southeastern Educational Improvement Laboratory (SEIL)
P.O. Box 12748
200 Park, Suite 200
Research Triangle Park, NC 27709-2748
(919) 549-8216
States Served: AL, FL, GA, MS, NC, and SC

SEIL is engaged in a number of rural projects, including: (1) the identification of promising practices in rural education, (2) the delivery of technical assistance to two rural schools per state in attacking persistent problems, and (3) support of the development of school-based enterprises. A newsletter, *The Key*, is disseminated six times annually.

Southwest Educational Development Laboratory (SEDL)
211 East Seventh Street
Austin, TX 78701
(512) 476-6861
States Served: AR, LA, NM, OK, and TX

SEDL is supporting staff development efforts focused on: (1) improving student thinking skills and (2) supporting school improvement. The laboratory is exploring a model that links staff development more tightly to school improvement efforts.

Programs

State Departments of Education

Contact your local State Department for information on state initiatives or collaborative work with the university centers or regional laboratories.

University Based Programs

A complete listing of university based programs and centers for rural education is available in: Rios, B.R. (1986). *Directory of Organizations and Programs in Rural Education.* Las Cruces, NM: ERIC Clearinghouse on Rural Education and Small Schools.

National Center for Smaller Schools
Texas Tech University
P.O. Box 4560
Lubbock, TX 79409
(806) 742-2391

Illustrative of university programs designed to research and assist rural and small schools, the National Center supports workshops, conferences, and seminars.

Rural Schools Program
408 Roberts Hall
Cornell University
Ithaca, NY 14853
(607) 256-7756

Illustrative of university programs designed to research and assist rural schools, the Rural Schools Program was established in 1978. In addition to research and technical assistance, the program sponsors conferences and disseminates rural school profiles.

University of Alaska
College for Human and Rural Development
University of Alaska—Fairbanks
Fairbanks, AK 99701
(907) 474-6431

The College for Human and Rural Development maintains a substantial field-based program for training rural professionals, including rural teachers and administrators. Eight regional centers are linked electronically and collectively offer complete degree programs to local residents.

REAL Enterprises Federation
658-B Old Lystra Road
Chapel Hill, NC 27514
(919) 929-3939

REAL Enterprises Federation unites organizations in three states (North Carolina, South Carolina, and Georgia) working to support the development of school-based economic enterprises as a part of rural school curricula. The enterprises offer: (1) schools a strategy to involve students more directly in the learning process and (2) communities a manner by which to support local economic development. The North Carolina Center publishes a newsletter, *The Real Story.*

Big Sky Telegraph
Western Montana College
Box 11
Dillon, MT 59725
(406) 683-7011

Big Sky Telegraph is an electronic bulletin board linking rural educators in the Northwest, with special services offered to teachers in one-room schools throughout Montana.

Organizations/Associations

National Rural Education Association (NREA)
300 Education Building
Colorado State University
Fort Collins, CO 80523
(303) 491-7022

NREA is the oldest national association devoted to rural schools. It sponsors an annual conference and newsletter, *REA Newsletter,* released quarterly. In addition, NREA publishes a professional journal, *The Rural Educator,* and acts as a distributor for an informal journal of ideas for teachers, *The Country Teacher.* NREA works at the national level to encourage financial support and policies appropriate to rural schools.

Special Interest Group: Rural Education
American Educational Research Association (AERA)
1230 17th Street, NW
Washington, DC 20036
(304) 347-0400

As a special interest group within the association, Rural Education sponsors a number of sessions at the annual AERA meeting and distributes a newsletter, *The Rural Education Newsletter.* Recent newsletters have summarized presentations, making it especially useful to those who are unable to attend the conference.

Rural and Small District Forum
National School Boards Association (NSBA)
1680 Duke Street
Alexandria, VA 22314
(703) 838-NSBA

The Rural and Small District Forum was formed to represent the issues and concerns of school boards in rural and small schools districts. Within NSBA's annual conference, the forum sponsors a Rural and Small District Education path, which focuses on major issues and concerns affecting rural and small school systems. One of the highlights is the "Rural and Small Education Excellence Fair" where school districts have the opportunity to showcase exemplary programs. Additionally, the Rural and Small District Forum hosts an annual conference.

Small Schools Committee
American Association of School Administrators (AASA)
1801 North Moore Street
Arlington, VA 22209
(202) 528-0700

The Small Schools Committee was formed to represent the issues and concerns of small district superintendents and administrators. It sponsors an annual conference, offers workshops, and inservice programs. *Leadership News,* AASA's newsletter, includes columns on rural issues. AASA Foundation is currently integrating small schools into work on Laborforce 2000.

American Association of Educational Service Agencies (AAESA)
1801 North Moore Street
Arlington, VA 22209
(202) 528-0700

AAESA is a contract organization affiliated with AASA. Recent projects have included a survey of rural school use of distance education and efforts to form Board of Cooperative Educational Services (BOCES)-type cooperatives for small schools.

Communicating for Agriculture
Southwest State University
Marshall, MN 56258
(507) 537-7021

This nonprofit organization engages in a number of activities related to sustaining rural lifestyles as an option for the American population. It supports an annual competition among schools, the Rural Knowledge Bowl, designed to increase knowledge about rural communities. Schools participating in the competition receive a teacher's guide and practice tests developed around themes selected each year. A newsletter, the *CA Communicator* is available to members.

National Rural Development Institute
Western Washington University
Bellingham, WA 98225
(206) 676-3576

An umbrella organization for a number of efforts, the National Rural Development Institute was established in 1984. It houses the National Rural Teacher Education Consortium, the National Rural Education Research Consortium, National Jobs Services, and the National Rural and Small Schools Consortium. Annual conferences, a monthly newsletter (*Rural School Classroom Clips*), and journal (*Journal of Rural and Small Schools*) support networking efforts.

American Council on Rural Special Education (ACRES)
National Rural Development Institute
Western Washington University
Bellingham, WA 98225
(206) 676-3576

This part of the National Rural Development Institute bears special mention. ACRES is the only national effort devoted to rural special education. Established in 1981, it sponsors an annual conference, a newsletter (*RuraLink*), and a journal, *Rural Special Education Quarterly.*

National Association of State Directors of Special
Education (NASDSE)
2021 K Street, N.W. Suite 315
Washington, DC 20006
(202) 296-1800

This umbrella organization supports a number of projects helpful to rural special educators. *Counterpoint,* a newsletter published quarterly, routinely includes articles relevant to rural practitioners. The Clearinghouse on Careers and Employment in Special Education maintains manpower supply/demand analyses specific to rural areas.

New Jersey Rural Special Education Coalition
Moore School
Highway #77
Seabrook, NJ 08302
(609) 451-4589

The coalition offers a forum for special education administrators in rural schools to discuss mutual concerns and development strategies for resolving problems.

Publications

Newsletters:

Newsletters are available from most of the state and national associations, as well as from some of the university centers. Contact the appropriate agency directly to be added to their mailing list. Some are distributed on a subscription basis or to association members, but others are free.

Journals:

Country Teacher. Available from NREA, 230 Education Building, Colorado State University, Fort Collins, CO 80523. Published three times annually. An informal journal designed to provide an exchange of ideas and resources for rural teachers.

Journal of Rural and Small Schools. Available from National Institute for Rural Development, Miller Hall 359, Western Washington University, Bellingham, WA 98225. Published three times annually. Subscription included with NRSSC membership. Professional journal with field-based orientation.

Research in Rural Education. Available from College of Education, University of Maine, Orono, ME 04469. Published three times annually. Formal research journal.

Rural Educator. Available from NREA, 230 Education Building, Colorado State University, Fort Collins, CO 80523. Published three times annually. Subscription included with membership in NREA. Professional journal designed to further communication between rural practitioners and university research faculty.

Rural Special Education Quarterly. Available from ACRES, MH 359, Western Washington University, Bellingham, WA 98225. Published quarterly. Subscription price included with ACRES membership. Professional journal devoted to rural special education issues.

Books:

Barker, R.G., & Gump, P.V. (1964). *Big school, small school.* Stanford: Stanford University Press. Presents evidence that small schools have strengths, for example the ability to involve more students in extracurricular activities or expose all students to a much broader array of general courses.

Cubberly, E.P. (1914). *Rural life and education: A study of the rural school problem as a phase of the rural-life problem.* Boston: Houghton-Mifflin. Historically interesting because of the perspective it offers and the extent to which that perspective continues to drive rural school consolidation efforts.

Cyr, F. (1959). *Catskill area project in small school design.* Oneonta, NY: State University Teachers College. One of several works written during the 1950s and 1960s from the perspective that small schools have special strengths.

Nachtigal, P.M. (Ed.). (1982). *Rural education: In search of a better way.* Boulder: Westview Press. Presents case studies of thirteen projects designed to support rural school improvement. Introductory and closing chapters set the stage for understanding why schools are different in rural settings and identify common threads in successful rural school improvement projects.

National Association of Secondary School Principals. (1987). *The best of the NASSP Bulletin: Leadership in the small school.* Reston, VA: Author. Selection of articles on small schools that appeared in the NASSP Bulletin since 1980. Chapters explore leadership, management, instruction, supporting teachers, and promoting student achievement.

Peshkin, A. (1978). *Growing up American: Schooling and the survival of community.* Chicago: University of Chicago Press. Powerful case study that documents the extent to which the survival of rural communities is tied to the survival of their schools.

Sher, J.P. (Ed.). (1978). *Education in rural America: A reassessment of conventional wisdom.* Boulder: Westview Press. Analyzes beliefs, assumptions, policies, and practices that shape rural schooling. The book challenges conventional wisdom and offers suggestions for needed change in rural schools.

Sher, J.P. (Ed.). (1981). *Rural education in urbanized nations: Issues and innovations.* Boulder: Westview Press. The worldwide context from which education in sparsely populated regions is examined makes this report especially interesting. An introduction that examines the reemergence of rural education in urbanized nations is followed by case studies that document delivery/support systems as well as in-school innovations in Europe, Australia, New Zealand, and the United States.

Tyack, D. (1974). *The one best system: A history of American urban education.* Cambridge: Harvard University Press. Equally valuable to those concerned with urban education, this book examines the extent to which a single model of schooling has proven inappropriate in the variety of community contexts, especially urban inner city and rural environments.

Monographs:

Armstrong, G. (1983). *The sourcebook: A directory of resources for small and rural school districts.* Arlington, VA: American Association of School Administrators. Lists organizations and projects by region (Midwest, Northeast, South and West) as well as national organizations and projects in rural education. While the contacts are a little dated, the directory itself is still extremely useful.

Augenblick J., & Nachtigal, P. (1985). *Equity in rural school finance.* (Paper presented at the National Rural Education Forum.) Las Cruces, NM: ERIC Clearinghouse for Rural Education and Small Schools. This paper reviews equity issues from the perspective of rural schools, examines strategies used by states to equalize funding, and recommends the development of a comprehensive database on rural school finance.

Barker, B.O. (1986). *The advantages of small schools.* Las Cruces, NM: ERIC Clearinghouse on Rural Education and Small Schools. A summary of the research literature on strengths/advantages of small schools, paying particular attention to research on optimum school and/or class size. Excellent set of references for those interested in exploring the topic further.

Campbell, A. (1985). *Components of rural school excellence.* (Paper presented at the National Rural Education Forum.) Las Cruces, NM: ERIC Clearinghouse for Rural Education and Small Schools. This paper reviews both the progress and challenges facing rural schools in response to legislative mandates and agency rules and regulations.

Conklin, N.F., & Olson, T. (1988). *Toward more effective education for poor, minority students in rural areas: What the research suggests.* Portland, OR: Northwest Regional Educational Laboratory. A rare effort to explore schools from the context of rural poverty, this monograph synthesizes research related to education of poor, rural, minority students.

Council for Educational Development and Research. (1988). *End of the road: Rural America's poor students and poor schools.* (National Rural, Small Schools Taskforce Report to the Regional Educational Laboratories). Washington, DC: Author. A curious mix of two reports: (1) work by NWREL in using common core data and state data to identify rural schools beset by limited resources and students from poor families and (2) review of regional laboratory work during the first year of the rural initiatives.

Elliott, J. (1988). *Rural students at risk.* Elmhurst, IL: North Central Regional Educational Laboratory. This study presents an analysis of extensive taped interviews with rural school administrators, teachers, and students in selected communities in Iowa.

Forbes, R.H. (1985). *State policy trends and impacts on rural school districts.* (Paper presented at the National Rural Education Forum.) Las Cruces, NM: ERIC Clearinghouse for Rural Education and Small Schools. This paper reviews educational reform activities and their impact on rural schools, recommending actions for policy makers and educational researchers.

Gardener, C., & Edington, E. (1982). *The preparation and certification of teachers for rural and small schools.* Las Cruces, NM: ERIC/ Clearinghouse for Rural Education and Small Schools. One of several studies that explores the appropriateness of current teacher preparation and certification requirements for rural practitioners.

Gjelten, T. (1978). *Schooling in isolated communities.* North Haven, ME: North Haven Project for Career Development. Using a remote community off the coast of Maine as the setting, this teacher explores one approach to helping rural youth use the entire range of opportunities available to them, from staying within the community to striking out on their own.

Hobbs, D. (1985). *Bridging, linking, networking the gap: Uses of instructional technology in small rural schools.* (Paper presented at the National Rural Education Forum.) Las Cruces, NM: ERIC Clearinghouse for Rural Education and Small Schools. This paper explores rural school experiences with technology and recommends the use of multiple technologies, collaboration among schools, and coordination in distance technology offerings.

Hofmeister, A.M. (1984). *Technological tools for rural education.* Las Cruces, NM: ERIC Clearinghouse on Rural Education and Small Schools. Reviews technology available to support computer managed instruction (CMI), computer assisted instruction (CAI), and videotext systems from the perspective of rural schools.

Horn, J.G. (1985). *Recruitment and preparation of quality teachers for rural schools.* (Paper presented at the National Rural Education Forum.) Las Cruces, NM: ERIC Clearinghouse for Rural Education and Small Schools. This paper reviews current practices in the recruitment and preparation of quality teachers for rural schools and closes with recommendations to program and policy decision makers.

Jaquart, M., & Newlin, J. (1988). *Rural school source book: Exemplary programs, practices and resources for rural educators.* Aurora, CO: Mid-continent Regional Educational Laboratory. A collection of 104 exemplary programs or practices drawn from rural schools in the McREL service area (CO, KS, MO, NE, ND, SD, and WY) available as a monograph or computer disk package for Apple IIe computers.

Killian, J.E., & Byrd, D.M. (1988). *Teachers' perspective on what promotes instructional improvement.* Paper presented at the Annual Meeting of the American Educational Research Association. New Orleans, LA.

Lewis, A.C. (1981). *Creative ideas for small schools.* Arlington, VA: American Association of School Administrators. Well written summary of ideas submitted by AASA members. Ideas reflect adaptations appropriate to rural or small school settings and include topics such as curriculum, teacher enhancement, class scheduling, cooperation, management, cutting costs, community relations, and working with students.

Lick, D.W. (1985). *Rural school partnerships with higher education and the private sector.* (Paper presented at the National Rural Education Forum.) Las Cruces, NM: ERIC Clearinghouse for Rural Education and Small Schools. This paper explores the conditions under which rural schools can form partnerships, illustrates current partnerships, and explores avenues by which partnerships can be built between rural education and higher education.

Mid-continent Regional Educational Laboratory. (1988). *Redesigning rural education: Ideas for action.* Aurora, CO: Author. Reviews activities undertaken under the Rural/Small Schools Initiative and briefly describes other exemplary programs.

Mid-continent Regional Educational Laboratory. (1989). *What's noteworthy: Rural schools and community development.* Aurora, CO: Author. Articles on rural schools of the future flank a series of blueprints based on current practices. Articles discuss: (1) schools and community development, (2) community input and investment, (3) studying the community, (4) entrepreneurship, (5) redesigning classes, and (6) learning by example.

Miller, B. (1988). *Teacher preparation for rural schools.* Portland, OR: Northwest Regional Educational Laboratory. Describes the need for preservice and inservice training appropriate to rural settings and presents examples of nine approaches to delivering such training.

Muse, I., Smith, R.B., & Barker, B.O. (1987). *The one-teacher school in the 1980s.* Las Cruces, NM: ERIC Clearinghouse on Rural Education and Small Schools. Contrasts more recent (1984) studies of one room schools and the performance of their students with an earlier (1960) study released by NEA. Includes a listing of 402 one-room schools that participated in the study, about half of those thought to still be operating.

Rios, B.R. (1986). *Directory of organizations and programs in rural education.* Las Cruces, NM: ERIC Clearinghouse for Rural Education and Small Schools.

Rios, B.R. (1988). *Rural: A concept beyond definition?* Las Cruces, NM: ERIC/Clearinghouse for Rural Education and Small Schools. Explores the many definitions of rural, rural education, rural school districts, and rural schools.

Rosenfeld, S. (1981). *A portrait of rural education: Conditions affecting vocational education policy.* U.S. Vocational Education Study Publication #6. Columbus, OH: Ohio State University. An outcome of research conducted into vocational education, this monograph describes the trends and issues in rural regions which will require changes in vocational education.

Sher, J.P. (1978). *Revitalizing rural education: A legislator's handbook.* Washington, DC: National Conference of State Legislatures. Although somewhat dated in the statistics cited, this monograph still presents valuable perspectives to legislators concerned with framing educational policy less harmful to rural schools.

Sher, J. (1988). *Class dismissed: Examining Nebraska's rural education debate.* Kansas City, MO: Mid-continent Regional Educational Laboratory. Result of an analysis of Nebraska's rural schools commissioned by the Nebraska Rural Community School Association. A similar study by the author, *Heavy Meddle,* explores rural education in North Carolina.

Spears, J. D., Combs, L. R., & Bailey, G. (1990). *Accommodating change and diversity: Linking rural schools to communities.* Manhattan, KS: Rural Clearinghouse for Lifelong Education and Development. This monograph explores strategies that involve rural schools in community development, social services, and lifelong learning. Two case studies examine rural school change in detail.

Spears, J. D., Oliver, J. P., & Maes, S. C. (1990). *Accommodating change and diversity: Multicultural practices in rural schools.* Manhattan, KS: Rural Clearinghouse for Lifelong Education and Development. Five case studies examine multicultural reform in a variety of rural community environments, ranging from all minority to all Anglo settings. Multicultural practices identified by more than 60 rural schools offer strategies for schools interested in initiating change.

Stephens, E.R. (1988). *The changing context of education in a rural setting* (Occasional Paper 26). Charleston, WV: Appalachia Educational Laboratory. An excellent report which examines: (1) diversity found among rural communities and rural schools; (2) economic, social, and political changes affecting rural areas; and (3) educational reform measures. A concluding section examines the implications of these trends/realities on rural school improvement efforts.

Stern, J.D. (Ed.). (1989). *Rural education: A changing landscape.* Washington, DC: U.S. Department of Education. Selected papers based on presentations at a national symposium on rural education held in 1987. Includes a closing section that explores school improvement strategies for rural education.

Stoddard, S., Wall, M., Luther, V., & Baker, K. (1988). *Schools as entrepreneurs: Helping small towns survive.* Lincoln, NE: Heartland Center for Leadership Development. The past, present, and future of a fictitious rural community sets the stage for profiles of seven rural school projects that illustrate school-business partnerships. The publication includes a list of ten strategies for making the connection between rural schools and economic development.

Journal Articles:

Bass, G.R. (1988). Financing for small schools: A study. *Rural Educator, 9*(2), 9–14.

DeYoung, A.J. (1987). The status of American rural education research: An integrated review and commentary. *Review of Educational Research, 57,* 123–148.

Dunne, F. (1983). Good government vs. self-government: Educational control in rural America. *Phi Delta Kappan, 65*(4), 252–256.

Helge, D. (1981). Problems in implementing comprehensive special education programming in rural areas. *Exceptional Children, 50*(4), 294–305.

Helge, D. (1984). The state of the art of rural special education. *Exceptional Children, 50,* 294–305.

Jacobsen, S. (1988). Effective superintendents of small, rural districts. *Journal of Rural and Small Schools, 2*(2), 17–21.

MacBrayne, P. (1987). Educational and occupational aspirations of rural youth: A review of the literature. *Research in Rural Education, 4*(3), 135–141.

Monk, D.H. (1987). Secondary school size and curriculum comprehensiveness. *Economics of Education Review, 6*(2), 137–150.

White, F., & Tweeten, L. (1973). Optimal school district size emphasizing rural areas. *American Journal of Agricultural Economics, 55*(1), 45–53.

II. HIGHER EDUCATION RESOURCES

Clearinghouses/Centers

Rural Clearinghouse for Lifelong Education and
Development
Division of Continuing Education
College Court Building
Kansas State University
Manhattan, KS 66506-6001
(913) 532-5560

The only national center devoted to rural adult education, the Rural Clearinghouse maintains an information base and network of formal and nonformal educational providers active in rural regions. Past research has included surveys of rural adult learners, barriers to rural adult access, effective delivery strategies, education's response to the farm crisis, effective literacy practice, and the link between education and rural economic development. Some of this work is published under the Action Agenda Project. The Clearinghouse publishes a newsletter, the *Rural Adult Education FORUM*, six times annually.

ERIC Clearinghouse on Adult, Career and Vocational
Education
Ohio State University
Center on Education and Training for Employment
1960 Kenney Road
Columbus, OH 43210-1090
(614) 292-4353

At one point the National Center for Research in Vocational Education was also housed here. This clearinghouse collects materials relevant to all levels and settings of adult and continuing, career and vocational/technical education. It includes some materials specific to rural practice.

ERIC Clearinghouse for Junior Colleges
University of California at Los Angeles
Mathematical Sciences Building, Room 8118
405 Hilgard Avenue
Los Angeles, CA 90024-1564
(213) 825-3931

Collects documents relevant to public and private community colleges, technical institutes, and two-year branch university campuses. Their holdings include some materials specific to rural practice.

Programs

Instructional Television for Students
Instructional Media Center
California State University—Chico
Chico, CA 95929
(916) 895-6112

The university uses an Instructional Television Fixed Services (ITFS) system to reach remote parts of its service area. Sixteen learning centers have been placed in community and corporate sites. Classes selected for ITFS delivery are then advertized throughout the region. Students enroll on the first day of class. Instruction is live, with one-way video and two-way audio, allowing students to interact with and respond to the instruction.

CGF-Telecom
College of Great Falls
1301 20th Street South
Great Falls, MT 59405
(406) 452-8651

The College of Great Falls combines the flexibility of videotapes with the interaction of audio conferences to deliver courses to remote sites in Montana. Students receive assignments and videotapes at one of fourteen remote sites. Students and their instructor meet by audio conference once each week, with the conference repeated at a different time and day to accommodate schedules. The system is relatively inexpensive to maintain and allows students flexibility in scheduling their work.

Rural Education
University of Alaska
3605 Arctic Boulevard
Anchorage, AK 99503
(907) 564-3350

A network of thirteen Rural Education centers extends university programs to rural communities throughout rural Alaska. Centers provide a student-centered curriculum that emphasizes professional education, professional development, job related skills, and academic preparation leading to associate and baccalaureate degrees. Statewide projects include Community Health Aides, Health Careers, Gerontology, and Vocational/Technical Education.

Washington/Alaska/Montana/Idaho (WAMI) Program
University of Washington Medical School
Puget Sound Plaza, 20th Floor
4th and Union
Seattle, WA 98101
(206) 543-5560

Initiated in 1971, WAMI is a multistate program designed to increase the availability of primary care physicians in rural areas. Medical students complete their first year's studies in their home state, the second at the University of Washington, and the third back in their home state. The program has increased both the number of students electing to train in primary care and the number establishing practices in rural areas. Success is attributed to the program's structure, which enables students to maintain strong ties with their home state, as well as the value placed on rural practice by the University of Washington School of Medicine.

Center for Rural Pennsylvania
607 North 2nd Street
Harrisburg, PA 17101
(717) 787-9555

Formed in 1988, the Center for Rural Pennsylvania is a unique partnership between state decision makers and higher education. Governed by an 11-member board, the center conducts research and offers grants in the areas of: rural people and communities; economic development; local government finance and administration; community services; natural resources and environment; educational outcomes; rural values; and social change. As a response to the broader needs of present day rural communities, the center illustrates one strategy for focusing a broader array of university resources on rural needs and linking information more closely to the policy process.

Dental Hygiene Mobile Program
University of Kentucky Community College System
Room 213, Breckenridge Hall
Lexington, KY 40506
(606) 257-5900

A creative solution to small enrollments, high costs, and demonstrated need for dental hygienists in rural areas, this program rotates a portable dental hygiene clinic and laboratory among rural community colleges. The clinic remains on sites for three years or until there is no longer a need for additional dental hygienists in the region, training approximately twenty-four students in each cycle.

Organizations/Associations

Division of Rural Continuing Education
National University Continuing Education Association (NUCEA)
One Dupont Circle
Washington, DC 20036
(202) 659-3130

Founded in 1987, the Division of Rural Continuing Education hosts four issue sessions at NUCEA's national conference, recognizes excellence in creative rural programming through an annual award, and publishes a newsletter. Regional affiliates of the association, especially those in predominantly rural regions, also offer excellent opportunities for interaction with rural colleagues. NUCEA publishes a journal, *Continuing Higher Education Review.*

Committee on Agriculture and Rural Development
American Association of State Colleges and Universities (AASCU)
One Dupont Circle, Suite 700
Washington, DC 20036-1192
(202) 293-7070

With over 60 percent of its membership rural, AASCU's work related to rural higher education is ongoing. The committee recently adopted a policy statement, "The Revitalization of Rural America," outlining guidelines for college involvement in service to rural communities. AASCU also works closely with the American Association of State Colleges of Agriculture and Renewable Resources (AASCARR), a forum for strengthening undergraduate programs in agriculture and renewable resources. "Rural Affairs" is included as an insert to AASCU's newsletter, *Memo: To the President.*

Commission on Small and/or Rural Community Colleges
American Association of Community and Junior Colleges (AACJC)
One Dupont Circle, Suite 410
Washington, DC 20036
(202) 293-7050

Formed in 1976, the commission sponsors rural forums at AACJC's annual conference, identifies issues of common concern, initiates research, and produces monographs. Recent projects have examined fiscal equity; business partnerships; and surveyed practices in areas such as literacy, economic development, and access. AACJC publishes a journal, *Community, Technical and Junior College Journal,* and a newsletter.

American Association for Adult and Continuing Education (AAACE)
1112 Sixteenth Street, N.W. Suite 420
Washington, DC 20036
(202) 463-6333

Formed in 1982, AAACE is a membership organization designed to provide leadership in advancing the education of adults in the lifelong learning process. While it has no rural division, rural educators form a substantial part of its membership and are involved in divisions and units across the association. Two units, the Cooperative Extension Service Unit and Continuing Education for the Professions Unit, are especially active in dealing with rural issues. AAACE publishes a research journal (*Adult Education Quarterly*), a practitioner's journal (*Adult Learning*), and a newsletter (*Online with Adult and Continuing Educators*).

Council of Independent Colleges (CIC)
One Dupont Circle, Suite 320
Washington, DC 20036
(202) 466-7230

CIC serves a membership of about 270 privately controlled colleges and universities, more than half of which operate in rural settings. Members have recently become involved in: (1) exploring the role of the private liberal arts college in community economic development and (2) understanding the linkage between rural schools and teacher education programs in rural private colleges.

Western Interstate Commission for Higher Education (WICHE)
P.O. Drawer P
Boulder, CO 80302
(303) 497-0205

An interstate compact, WICHE serves higher education in thirteen western states, North Dakota, and South Dakota. Given that its region is predominantly rural, WICHE has been active in projects on telecommunications, rural development, and minority populations. Recent projects include the creation of a telecommunications cooperative and sponsorship of a legislative workshop that explored the link between higher education and rural development.

Council for Adult and Experiential Learning (CAEL)
223 West Jackson Boulevard
Suite 510
Chicago, IL 60606
(312) 922-5909

Established in 1974, CAEL works to improve service to adult learners. Projects have included efforts to clarify and standardize procedures for assessing experiential learning, as well as assist businesses in assessing employee needs. A recent project, Pathways to the Future, offers long-term employees (members of Communication Workers of America and the International Brotherhood of Electrical Workers) the opportunity to assess their career. If a change is desired, counseling and tuition support is provided for the additional education. Employees at a distance have been identified as a target population. CAEL publishes a newsletter, *CAEL News.*

Association for Continuing Higher Education (ACHE)
College of Graduate and Continuing Studies
University of Evansville
1800 Lincoln Avenue
Evansville, IN 47722
(812) 479-2472

Formed in 1938, ACHE serves 2,000 continuing educators in higher education. Acknowledging the different context in which its rural members work, ACHE established a Rural Education committee in 1986. The committee surveyed its members on rural problems, compiled a directory of model programs, and organized rural sessions for ACHE's annual conferences. ACHE publishes a newsletter, *Five Minutes with ACHE.*

Western Governors' Association (WGA)
600 17th Street
Suite 1705 South Tower
Denver, CO 80202
(303) 623-9378

Increased concern with rural economic development led the Western Governors' Association to commission a study on the impact of university public service in rural areas and strategies for strengthening that linkage. The report led to a resolution, Higher Education Involvement in Supporting Rural Communities (89-021), identifying higher education as a critical link in rural revitalization and calling for expanded public service and applied research directed to rural needs. The report, *A Time of Challenge . . . A Time for Change: The Role of Higher Education in the Rural West,* is available from the association.

Publications

Newsletters:

Newsletters are available from most of the associations and organizations. But since these groups serve urban as well as rural institutions, it is more difficult to predict the extent to which rural issues will be included.

Rural Adult Education FORUM. Designed for formal and nonformal educational providers serving rural adults, this newsletter is published six times annually. Individual installments alternate between issues common to all providers (leadership, use of technology, or economic development) and a focus on a single provider (community colleges, libraries, universities). Available from the Rural Clearinghouse for Lifelong Education and Development, College Court Building, Kansas State University, Manhattan, KS 66506-6001.

Journals:

There is no single journal devoted to rural adult education within the higher education community. The following journals occasionally include articles on rural practice.

Adult Education Quarterly. Available from AAACE, 1112 16th Street, N.W., Suite 420, Washington, DC 20036.

Adult Learning. Available from AAACE, 1112 16th Street, N.W., Suite 420, Washington, DC 20036. Published eight times annually. Subscriptions available. Formerly published under the title *Lifelong Learning.*

Community, Technical, and Junior College Journal. Available from AACJC Publications, 80 South Early Street, Alexandria, VA 22304. Published bimonthly. Free to members. Annual subscriptions available to non-AACJC members.

Continuing Higher Education Review. Journal of the National University Continuing Education Association (NUCEA). Available from One Dupont Circle, Washington, DC 20036. Published three times a year. Free to NUCEA members. Subscriptions available to nonmembers. Formerly published under the title *Continuum.*

Journal of Continuing Higher Education. Available from ACHE, University of Evansville, College of Graduate and Continuing Studies, 1800 Lincoln Avenue, Evansville, IN 47722. Published three times yearly. Subscriptions available to nonmembers.

Books:

Darkenwald, G.G., & Larson, G.A. (Eds.). (1980). *Reaching hard to reach adults.* New Directions for Continuing Education, no. 8. San Francisco: Jossey-Bass. This book provides an excellent overview on hard-to-reach adult populations, including those located in rural settings, in efforts to deliver continuing education.

Feasley, C.E. (1982). *Serving learners at a distance: A guide to program practice.* Washington, DC: ASHE-ERIC. This study reviews more than 140 publications related to distance learning, exploring effective strategies and structures for using technology to reach students at a distance.

Treadway, D. (1984). *Higher education in rural America.* New York: College Entrance Examination Board. Excellent review of rural postsecondary education. After establishing the character of rural communities and adult needs for education, the author reviews types of programs available, program development strategies for reaching isolated populations, institution policies supportive of rural service, and national/state policies.

Willingham, W.W. (1970). *Free access higher education.* New York: College Entrance Examination Board. While the information is a little dated, this study examines the issue of access to higher education, concluding that rural and urban inner city populations are the least effectively served.

Monographs:

American Association of Community and Junior Colleges (AACJC). (1988). *Small-rural community colleges.* Washington, DC: Author. Synthesis of data collected in a survey of 600 small and/or rural community colleges during the 1986–87 academic year. Individual chapters are devoted to economic development, cultural and civic responsibility, high school connections and partnerships, literacy practices, uses of technology, resource development, and commitment to access.

American Association of State Colleges and Universities (AASCU). (1987). *1987 AASCARR Directory.* Washington, DC: Author. Listing of faculty and programs in institutions offering baccalaureate degrees in agriculture or renewable natural resources.

American Association of State Colleges and Universities (AASCU). (n.d.). *Rural funding guide: Resources and funds for rural and agricultural programs at colleges and universities.* Washington, DC: Author.

American Association of State Colleges and Universities (AASCU). (1988). *Allies for enterprise: Highlights of the 1987–88 national conferences in higher education and economic development.* Washington, DC: Author. Summaries of four regional conferences held to bridge the gap between higher education and the economic development community. Rural issues and models are included.

Atwell, C.A., & Sullins, W.R. (1984). *Curricular comprehensiveness in small, rural community colleges*. Alexandria, VA: ERIC Clearinghouse for Junior Colleges. Synthesizes data gathered from 250 small or rural community colleges in an effort to test commonly held beliefs about rural community colleges.

Bruce, R.L. (1983). *Adult education for rural Americans: An introduction*. Information Series #173. Columbus, OH: National Center for Research in Vocational Education. Includes an overview of the field and excerpts from the literature.

Continuing Higher Education Leadership Project (CHEL). (1987). *Challenges for continuing higher education leadership: The transformation of rural America*. Washington, DC: National University Continuing Education Association. Synthesizes presentations and panel discussions at a university forum that explored the role of continuing higher education leadership in assisting rural economic adaptations.

Cossaro, K. (1981). *Rural education programs that work: Sharing ideas*. Washington, DC: Office of Vocational and Adult Education. Descriptions of successful programs in adult, community, and vocational education.

Easton, S.M. (1989). *Barriers to education for rural adults in 13 Western states*. Paper presented at Rural Education Research Forum. Reno, NV. Explores barriers identified in a survey of educators and policy makers in 13 Western states.

Easton, S.M. (1988). *Overcoming barriers to education for rural adults. A consideration of public policy proposals*. Paper presented at 29th Annual Adult Education Research Conference. Syracuse, NY. Results of a modified Delphi survey that examined public policies considered important and feasible for ensuring adequate access to education for rural adults. Some 89 policies were compiled.

Emery, M. (1987). *Some potentials and limitations of technology in serving rural postsecondary learners*. Manhattan, KS: Action Agenda Project. Commissioned for the National Invitational Conference on Rural Adult Postsecondary Education. This paper reviews the use of technology from the perspective of equity, access, and quality. Other sections review the types of technology available and policy issues related to the effective use of technology in reaching rural populations.

Emery, M. (Ed.). (1987). *Education and the rural economy*. Manhattan, KS: Action Agenda Project. Brief descriptions of postsecondary programs illustrative of the link between education and rural economic development. The editor presents a taxonomy with which to organize education's contribution to economic development and reviews data collected on sources of funding, types of collaboration, clientele, and other features of the programs.

Hobbs, D. (1987). *Knowledge based rural development: Adult education and the future rural economy.* Manhattan, KS: Action Agenda Project. Commissioned for the National Invitational Conference on Rural Adult Postsecondary Education. This paper explores the link between education and economic development from the perspective of human capital, concluding that educational programs must be more responsive to local needs in order to support rural development.

Hone, K. (1984). *Serving the rural adult: Inventory of model programs in rural adult postsecondary education.* Manhattan, KS: Action Agenda Project. A survey conducted by the Western Interstate Commission for Higher Education led to profiles of 54 programs that illustrate innovative organizational structures, curricular adaptations, or delivery systems.

Lewis, R. (1983). *Meeting learners' needs through telecommunications.* Washington, DC: AAHE. Directory and guide to the use of telecommunications in higher education. This collection includes several rural-based programs.

Margolis, D. (1981). *The Kansas City initiative. Proceedings of the national invitational meeting on rural postsecondary education.* Manhattan, KS: Action Agenda Project. Synthesis of papers presented at the conference. Includes a rural "Bill of Rights" and an agenda for future work adopted by conference participants.

McCannon, R. (1983). Serving rural adult learners. In C.E. Kasworm (Ed.), *Educational outreach to select adult populations* (15–30). New Directions for Continuing Education, no. 20. San Francisco: Jossey-Bass. One of the earlier works that explores characteristics of rural adult learners and principles of practice for rural continuing education.

McCannon, R. (1985). *Serving the rural adult: A demographic portrait of rural adult learners.* Manhattan, KS: Action Agenda Project. An analysis of the rural (non-SMSA) cohort of data collected in the 1980 NCES Survey of Participation in Adult Education augmented by additional data collected at five midwestern colleges.

McDaniel, R. (Ed.). (1986). *Barriers to rural adult education: A report of the Northwest Action Agenda Project*. Pullman: Washington State University. Results of a survey of educational providers and rural adult learners in the Northwest. The report explores barriers identified in the survey and policy implications for states, institutions, and rural communities.

McLaurin, S., & Coker, R. (1987). *Notes toward the establishment of educational partnerships in rural communities*. Manhattan, KS: Action Agenda Project. Commissioned for the National Invitational Conference on Rural Adult Postsecondary Education. This paper suggests the need for an educational coordinator in rural communities, primarily to articulate needs and facilitate the provision of services. Much of the article focuses on the appropriateness of community colleges in such a role.

Rosenfeld, S. (1988). Rural vocational education for a technological future. In J.C. Hackett & L.A. McLemore (Eds.), *States' agenda for rural economic development*. Proceedings of the First National Conference on States' Rural Economic Development, Lexington, KY. Lexington, KY: Council of State Governments.

Spears, J.D. (1985). *Serving the rural adult: Private funding resources for rural adult postsecondary education*. Manhattan, KS: Action Agenda Project. Profiles of 91 foundations who fund programs related to rural adult education.

Spears, J.D., & Maes, S.C. (1985). *Postsecondary and adult education in rural communities*. (Paper presented at the National Rural Education Forum.) Charleston, WV: ERIC Clearinghouse for Rural Education and Small Schools (ED 258-790). This paper explores the different perspectives of education held by rural adult education providers, reviews research conducted in the field, and makes recommendations to educators and policy makers.

Spears, J.D. (1986). *Proceedings 1985: Four regional conferences*. Manhattan, KS: Action Agenda Project. Synthesizes the four regional "Serving the Rural Adult" conferences held in the spring of 1985. The proceedings explore the different images of rural adult education presented by the different providers, successes, concerns the providers share, and the next steps to be taken on behalf of rural adult postsecondary education.

Spears, J.D. (1987). *Proceedings 1986: Second national invitational conference*. Manhattan, KS: Action Agenda Project. This conference explored the role of postsecondary education in rural life, the educational developments seen as being most helpful to increasing rural access, and the realities of current finance and policy issues. An agenda for continued work on behalf of rural adult access was adopted.

Spears, J.D. (Ed.). (1987). *Education's response to the rural crisis: Model programs in the midwest.* Manhattan, KS: Action Agenda Project. A review of the many educational programs developed in response to the farm crisis. Programs were drawn from a variety of agencies in eight states (IA, KS, MN, MO, NE, ND, OK, and SD). An introduction provides a structure with which to organize the programs and explores implications for adult education.

Spears, J.D. (1988). *State policy and rural adult access to education.* Unpublished Ph.D. dissertation. Case study that explores state statutes, state agency rules and regulations, and governing board rules and regulations affecting the provision of education in rural areas. The study proposes a structure with which to organize these policies and identifies ways in which state policy acts as a barrier to improved rural access to postsecondary education.

Sullins, W.R., Vogler, D.E., & Mays, S.B. (1986). *Report from the Appalachian regional steering committee on rural postsecondary education.* Blacksburg, VA: Appalachian Action Agenda Project. This report explores barriers to rural access identified by the Appalachian Regional Steering Committee and suggests strategies for eliminating or reducing the barriers.

Sullins, W.R., Hoerner, J.L., & Whisnant, W.T. (1988). *Increasing rural adults' participation in collegial programs: Exemplary programs.* Blacksburg, VA: Appalachian Action Agenda Project. Conference proceedings, including a description of 20 Appalachian models.

Thomas, M. (Ed.). (1989). *A portfolio of community college initiatives in rural economic development.* Kansas City, MO: Midwest Research Institute. Profiles of 20 community college initiatives in rural economic development illustrate the range of activities that link these institutions with their regions. In addition, the monograph examines state programs that are community college based in terms of their appropriateness to rural settings.

Treadway, D. (1988). *Higher education and rural development: The next frontier.* St. Paul, MN: Northwest Area Foundation. Explores the extent to which colleges and universities are being asked to be more active in economic development and establishes a framework from which appropriate roles can be established.

Western Governors' Association (WGA). (1989). *A time of challenge . . . A time for change: The role of higher education in the rural west.* Denver: Author. Examines the character of educational institutions in the rural west from the perspective of rural economic changes currently underway. Identifies obstacles to increasing higher education involvement in rural development and profiles exemplary programs at Eastern Oregon State University and the University of Colorado.

Western Interstate Commission for Higher Education (WICHE). (1989). *Higher education's response to rural needs: Selected model programs.* Boulder, CO: Author. In collaboration with the staff at the Rural Clearinghouse for Lifelong Education and Development, WICHE staff have identified and profiled 22 programs which illustrate the expanded role higher education can play in rural development.

Western Interstate Commission for Higher Education (WICHE). (1989). *Evolving partnerships: Higher education and the rural west.* Boulder, CO: Author. Synthesizes comments and concerns of 75 key legislators, state directors, and economic development and higher education leaders in five states (MT, NE, ND, SD, and WY). Explores the major problems facing their state's rural communities and the role higher education can play in responding to those needs.

Journal Articles:

Allen, L.D., & KeKerif, M.V. (1986). College credit for rural high school seniors. *Continuum, 50*(1), 29–33.

Atwell, C.A. (1981). Doing more with less. *Community and Junior College Journal, 52*(2), 30–32.

Bailey, G., & Hesser, J.E. (1988). Rural professionals: An untapped audience for continuing education. *Continuing Higher Education Review, 52*(1), 40–49.

Ballantyne, J. (1989). Health education for rural adults: Challenges for nurses and adult educators. *Lifelong Learning, 12*(5), 6–7.

Barker, B.O. (1985). Understanding rural adult learners: Characteristics and challenges. *Lifelong Learning, 9*, 4–7.

Cosby, A.G. (1980). The urban context of rural policy. *Interstate Compact for Education, 14*(3), 38–39.

Currin, E.C., & Sullins, W.R. (1988). The community college's role in rural economic development. *Community Junior College Review, 12* (1), 37–46.

Dewees, P. (1988). Information technologies: Shaping state policies to serve rural learners. *Continuing Higher Education Review, 52*(3), 155–164.

Eaton, J.M. (1981). A vital component of the delivery system. *Community and Junior College Journal, 52*(2), 15–16.

Emery, M. (1988). Three models for improving access for rural adults with community connections. *Continuing Higher Education Review, 52*(1), 21–28.

Galbraith, M., & Sundet, P. (1988). Educational perspectives of rural adult learners: A key informant analysis. *Journal of Adult Education, 17*(1), 11–18.

Gray, W.H., & Sullins, W.R. (1988). Comparative analysis of the barriers to rural postsecondary education in two regions of the United States. *Continuing Higher Education Review, 52*(1), 29–39.

Hesser, J.E., Spears, J.D., & Maes, S.C. (1988). Action priorities for rural adult education. *Continuing Higher Education Review, 52*(1), 11–20.

Maes, S. (1988). Ensuring rural people access to education: Opportunities for continuing higher education. *Continuing Higher Education Review, 52*(1), 1–2.

McCannon, R.S., & Crom, R.L. (1988). Whose role is it to serve rural learners? Can/should continuing higher education assume the leadership? *Continuing Higher Education Review, 52*(1), 3–10.

Sullins, W.R. (1981). Leadership in the 1980s. *Community and Junior College Journal, 52*(2), 27–29.

Sullins, W.R., & Atwell, C.A. (1986). The role of small rural community colleges in providing access. *Community College Review, 13*(4), 45–51.

Sullins, W.R., Hoerner, J.L., & Whisnant, W.T. (1989). Programs that enhance rural adults' opportunities to participate in higher education. *Journal of Continuing Higher Education, 37*(2), 11–14.

Sundet, P., & Galbraith, M. (1991). Adult education as a response to the rural crisis: Factors governing utility and participation. *Journal of Research in Rural Education, 7*(2), 41–49.

TenHoeve, T. Jr. (1981). To serve 'even the last man in line.' *Community and Junior College Journal, 52*(2), 17–20.

Treadway, D. (1988). Rural adult education: A limited annotated bibliography. *Continuing Higher Education Review, 52*(1), 49–56.

Vineyard, E.E. (1978). The rural community college. *Community College Review, 6*(3), 29–45.

Wall, M. (1988). Clues to rural community survival: How education fits in. *Continuing Higher Education Review, 52*(2), 97–103.

III. NONFORMAL EDUCATION RESOURCES

Clearinghouses/Centers

Center for the Study of Rural Librarianship
College of Library Science
Clarion University of Pennsylvania
Clarion, PA 16214
(814) 226-2383

Established in 1978, the center supports rural library service in Pennsylvania and throughout the United States. It conducts research, disseminates information, and hosts conferences/continuing education activities on issues related to rural libraries. A recent conference, for example, explored the role of the rural public library in the informational infrastructure of rural America. Publishes a newsletter and a semiannual journal, *Rural Libraries.*

North Central Regional Center for Rural Development
216 East Hall
Iowa State University
Ames, IA 50011
(515) 294-8320
States Served: IL, IN, IA, KS, MI, MN, MO, NE, ND, OH, SD, WI

Established in 1971, the North Central Regional Center supports research and educational programs to improve rural communities throughout the region. Responses to the farm crisis led to several multistate rural development activities. The "Rural Revitalization Initiative" has explored educational programs that offer support to rural families in transition, community leadership and economic development, and innovative delivery of community services. Publishes a newsletter, *Rural Development News,* five times annually.

Northeast Regional Center for Rural Development (NERCRD)
104 Weaver Building
The Pennsylvania State University
University Park, PA 16802
(814) 863-4656
States Served: CT, DC, DE, MA, MD, ME, NH, NJ, NY, PA, RI, VT, WV

Like its rural development center counterparts, NERCRD supports community development activities through the region's land-grant universities and extension activities. Seed funds are awarded to multistate efforts that explore rural economic and social development, local government needs, national resource and environmental changes, and community leadership training and development. Publishes a quarterly newsletter, *Northeast Rural Development Network*.

Southern Rural Development Center
Mississippi State University
Box 5406
Starkville, MS 39762
(601) 325-3207
States Served: AL, AR, FL, GA, KY, LA, MS, NC, OK, SC, TN, TX, VA,

Established in 1974, the Southern Rural Development Center works with land-grant universities in strengthening community and rural development within the region. Publishes two newsletters, *Capsules* and *Bits and Bytes*.

Western Rural Development Center
Oregon State University
Corvallis, OR 97331
(503) 754-3621
States Served: AK, AZ, CA, CO, HI, ID, MT, NV, NM, OR, UT, WA, WY

Supports the activities of rural development specialists and researchers within the region. Typically supports one or two major projects and five to eight seed projects annually. Recent efforts have supported the development of an evaluation packet for community economic development, a workshop on community venture capital, a study on the potential for high technology industries in non-metropolitan areas, and trade area analysis. Publishes *Western Wire* three times annually.

Rural Information Center (RIC)
Room 314
National Agricultural Library
Beltsville, MD 20705
(301) 344-2547

A joint project of the Extension Service and National Agricultural Library, the Rural Information Center is designed to provide information, referral, and briefs to elected and appointed community leaders, community development professionals, and volunteer community leaders.

Programs

Federation of Southern Cooperatives
Rural Training and Research Center
P.O. Box 95
Epes, AL 35460
(205) 652-9676

The federation provides service, information, technical assistance, research, and advocacy to cooperatives and credit unions created during the civil rights movement. Made up of black and white family farmers in the rural South, these cooperatives offer strategies for helping families maintain their land and way of life. The federation assists new cooperative ventures, supports and offers training programs supportive of both activities.

Highlander Research and Education Center
Route 3, Box 370
New Market, TN 37820
(615) 933-3443

Founded in 1932, Highlander Research and Education Center is an adult education center devoted to helping low-income and minority people in Appalachia and the South gain the knowledge and skills with which to work toward social change. Recent projects include residential educational programs, workshops for community leaders, participatory research in land ownership patterns, and the development of an economic literacy curriculum for use with community groups.

Land Stewardship Project
512 W. Elm
Stillwater, MN 55082
(612) 430-2166

A private, nonprofit organization, the Land Stewardship Project is devoted to increasing public awareness of farm problems and promoting a sustainable land ethic. Publishes a newsletter, *The Land Stewardship Letter.*

Minnesota Food Association
2395 University Avenue, Room 309
St. Paul, MN 55114
(612) 644-2038

In response to problems created by the farm crisis, the Minnesota Food Association sponsored a program entitled "The Urban Legislator and Rural Policy Program." The program conducted research and sponsored workshops to better inform urban legislators on issues related to land tenure, biotechnology, and sustainable agriculture.

Rural America: The Search for Solutions
Pioneer Hi-Bred International, Inc.
700 Capital Square
400 Locust Street
Des Moines, IA 50309
(515) 245-3500

The corporation sponsors a series of seminars designed to inform their employees about current problems and promising solutions in rural America. The seminars are intended to enable the employees to return to their communities as informed leaders. Seminar topics have focused on health care, education, and the economy.

Rural Development Leadership Network
P.O. Box 98
Prince Street Station
New York, NY 10012
(212) 477-0367

This program offers educational programs to men and women from low-income rural communities. A study program and field project are designed to help these individuals develop the skills and knowledge needed to provide leadership in their home communities.

Prairiefire Rural Action, Inc.
550 Eleventh Street
Des Moines, IA 50309
(515) 244-5671

Prairiefire is an independent, nonprofit organization that supports education, research, and community action in rural areas. Dedicated to supporting family farm agriculture, Prairiefire works directly with farm and rural families, as well as with rural and religious organizations. The organization believes that education must be linked to social action and explores projects that will accomplish this linkage. Supports a Rural Women's Leadership Development Project and the Iowa Farm Crisis Hotline.

Heartland Center for Leadership Development
941 "O" Street, Suite 920
Lincoln, NE 68508
(402) 474-7667

The Heartland Center is an independent, nonprofit corporation created to support the development of effective leadership. The center has been involved in several projects concerned with rural communities. "20 Clues to Rural community Survival" explored characteristics common to communities that were surviving the farm crisis. A community leadership program was created from the information gathered. The Center publishes a newsletter, *Visions from the Heartland,* quarterly.

Center for Rural Affairs
P.O. Box 405
Walthill, NE 68067
(402) 846-5428

Created in 1973 by rural Nebraskans concerned about the role of public policy in the decline of the family farm and rural communities. Its purpose is to provide the public with information about the social, economic, and environmental issues affecting rural Americans. Supports research and education in sustainable agriculture, conservation techniques, leadership development, and rural community development. Publishes a monthly newsletter, *Center for Rural Affairs Newsletter.*

Intermountain Community Learning and Informational
Services (ICLIS)
Utah State University
Logan, UT 84322-0700
(801) 750-1134

A four state collaboration involving libraries, extension services, and universities, this project is exploring the use of rural libraries as information centers for their communities. The libraries are equipped to receive telecommunication courses that will, in turn, be developed collaboratively with land-grant universities and extension personnel. The centers will also offer access to state, federal, and private databases. The program is currently supported by the Kellogg Foundation.

Organizations/Associations

Association for Community-Based Education (ACBE)
1806 Vernon Street, N.W.,
Washington, DC 20009
(202) 462-6333

While it serves both urban and rural members, ACBE is involved in a number of activities of relevance to rural education. Minigrants, training, and technical assistance are offered to member organizations. In addition, the association opened the Rural Development Center in the heart of the Salinas Valley. This one hundred acre farm project acts as a training center for farmworker families, helping them gain the farming skills necessary to become economically self-sufficient farmers. Another recent project identified community-based literacy efforts, many of which were located in rural communities. Publishes a semimonthly newsletter, *CBE Report.*

National Association of Development Organizations (NADO)
400 N. Capitol Street, N.W. Suite 372
Washington, DC 20001
(202) 624-7806

Created in 1967, NADO promotes economic development in America's small towns and rural areas. Members include development districts, multicounty planning and development organizations, state, county, and city agencies. A weekly newsletter, *NADO's News,* addresses legislative, administrative, and local issues related to economic development in nonmetropolitan areas. The association sponsors an annual conference, workshops, technical assistance, and publications in response to member needs.

National Association of Towns and Townships (NATaT)
1522 K Street, N.W. Suite 730
Washington, DC 20005
(202) 737-5200

NATaT is a nonprofit membership organization whose mission is to strengthen local governments in small towns through America. Activities include educational programs and workshops on both effective management and rural development policies. Recent examples have explored the appropriateness of enterprise zones in rural areas, strategies for financing public services and facilities, and approaches for keeping and creating local businesses. Publishes a news journal, *The National Community Reporter* and sponsors an annual conference, often called America's biggest town meeting.

National Governors' Association (NGA)
444 North Capitol Street
Washington, DC 20001-1572
(202) 624-5300

NGA is the organization through which governors share information on effective programs and collectively influence the development and implementation of national policy. A Task Force on Rural Development adopted a twelve point agenda to be addressed collaboratively with federal and local initiatives in restructuring rural America. This agenda includes items relevant to education, including calls for increased rural school involvement in community development and programs that upgrade the skills of workers in rural areas.

Rural Coalition
2001 South Street, N.W. Suite 500
Washington, DC 20009
(202) 483-1500

A national alliance of groups concerned with the problems that confront disadvantaged rural people, this organization acts as a vehicle for rural policy advocacy. Work is accomplished through five task forces: Agriculture, American Indian, Natural Resources, Rural Economy and Development, and Military Issues. Task forces engage in research and publication activities designed to inform policy makers and grassroots organizations. Publishes a newsletter.

Community Transportation Association of America (CTAA)
725 15th Street, N.W. Suite 900
Washington, DC 20005
(202) 628-1480

Formerly known as Rural America, CTAA is a professional association dedicated to improving the mobility of all people. Emphasis is placed on transportation needs in rural areas and in response to the needs of the elderly, disabled, or poor nationwide. The association offers technical assistance, training seminars, and an annual exposition which includes some 40 educational workshops. Publishes a monthly magazine, *Community Transportation Reporter.*

Rural Sociological Association
Department of Sociology—Wilson Hall
Montana State University
Bozeman, MT 59715
(406) 994-5251

Professional association for researchers interested in rural individuals, families, and communities. It sponsors an annual conference and publishes a newsletter, *The Rural Sociologist,* and a journal, *Rural Sociology.*

National Rural Health Association (NRHA)
301 E. Armour Boulevard, Suite 420
Kansas City, MO 64111
(816) 756-3140

Membership organization created to provide leadership on rural health care issues. NRHA advocates rural health care needs to relevant publics, offers a forum for the exchange of information on effective rural health care, and builds coalitions that work toward solutions to rural health care problems. It sponsors an annual conference and regional seminars. Publishes a newsletter, *Rural Health Care,* six times annually.

Edwin Vincent O'Hara Institute for Rural Ministry Education
3700 Oakview Terrace, NE
Washington, DC 20017-2591
(202) 635-2365

Created in 1977, the Rural Ministry Institute's mission is to identify and voice the needs of communities of faith in small towns and rural areas. The institute sponsors an annual conference, assists in rural ministry preparation and placement, consults in the development of appropriate curricula, and has developed computer services appropriate to rural ministry efforts. Publishes *Rural Roots,* a bimonthly publication, and *Listening Post,* a monthly bulletin of rural resources.

Small Towns Institute
P.O. Box 517
Third Avenue and Poplar Street
Ellensburg, WA 98926

Founded in 1969 in response to the need for increased local citizen participation in solving community problems, the Small Towns Institute is a membership organization. It maintains the Small Town Resources Center, a comprehensive library on the issues and problems that face small communities. *Small Town,* a bimonthly magazine, shares ideas and programs currently working in small communities. Ideas are submitted by citizens, professional planners, elected officials, educators, business and religious organizations, and governmental agencies.

Publications

Newsletters:

Newsletters are available from most of the centers, organizations, and associations. Contact the appropriate agency directly to be added to their mailing list. Some are distributed on a subscription basis or to association members, but others are free.

Journals:

Community Education Journal. Available from the National Community Education Association, 119 N. Payne Street, Alexandria, VA 22314. Published quarterly. Free to members of the association. Available to others on a subscription basis.

Human Services in the Rural Environment. Available from Inland Empire School of Social Work and Human Sciences, Eastern Washington University, Cheney, WA 99004. Professional journal designed to serve mental health, health care, and social work professionals working in rural areas. Subscriptions available.

Journal of Extension. Available from Journal Extension, 432 North Lake Street, Madison, WI 53706. Written for extension professionals and other adult education practitioners, the journal blends research and practitioner-based articles. Published four times a year. Available on a subscription basis. This is the official, refereed journal of the Cooperative Extension Service.

Journal of Rural Health. Available from the Center for Health Policy Research, Box J-177, J. Hillis Miller Health Center, University of Florida, Gainesville, FL 32610-0177.

National Resources and Rural Development. Available from USDA-ES-NRRD. 3805 S. Building, Washington, DC 20250. Quarterly publication of new ideas in rural development.

Rural Development Perspectives. Available from the U.S. Department of Agriculture, 1301 New York Avenue, N.W., Washington, DC 20005-4788. Published 3 times a year. Available on a subscription basis.

Rural Libraries is a semiannual journal which combines research articles with notes from the field. Available from the College of Library Science, Clarion University of Pennsylvania, Clarion, PA 16214.

Rural Library Service Newsletter. Available from the Northwest Iowa Regional Library, 6th and Jackson Streets, Sioux City, IA 51105. Published quarterly.

Rural Sociology. Available from the Rural Sociological Society, Department of Sociology, Montana State University, Bozeman, MT 59717. Published 4 times a year. Available to members of the society. Available to others on a subscription basis annually.

Small Towns. Available from Small Town Institute, P.O. Box 517, Ellensburg, WA 98926. News journal useful to local officials, planners, business people, and citizens concerned about community. Reports on community development, economic development, and social science delivery. Available free to members of the institute. Subscriptions for others available.

Books:

Draves, W., & MacRunnels, C. (Eds.). (1978). *The free university manual.* Manhattan, KS: University for Man. Many of the free universities of the 1960s have become community education organizations of the 1980s. This manual explores the free university movement and its transition into a new form of community education.

Galbraith, M. W. (Ed.). (1990). *Education through community organizations.* New Directions for Adult and Continuing Education, no. 47. San Francisco: Jossey-Bass. This book suggests that the community provides a rich environment for lifelong education opportunities. It examines how community-based organizations use education as an allied function to reach their missions.

John, D., Batie, S.S., & Norris, K. (1988). *A brighter future for rural America? Strategies for communities and states.* Washington, DC: National Governors' Association. This study examined rural communities who were experiencing higher rates of growth than would be predicted by conventional wisdom. Case studies of the communities led to the identification of successful strategies and recommendation for state involvement.

Monographs:

Brown, H. (1985). *Keys to successful funding: A small town guide to community development block grants and other federal programs.* Washington, DC: National Association of Towns and Townships. Written for the first time applicant, this booklet presents useful guidelines for submitting proposals to the Community Development Block Grants and other federal programs.

Christenson, J. (1988). *Catalogue of catalogs.* Mankato, MN: Traverse des Sioux Library System. A 14 page catalog that identifies community development publications, main street business manuals, agricultural books, farming manuals, how-to books, seed catalogues, and rural education publications available through interlibrary loan.

Draves, W., & Bryant, C. (Eds.). (1980). *The rural and small town community education manual.* Manhattan, KS: University for Man. A workbook for community groups and leaders interested in starting a community-based education program. Sections explore how to get started, organize a class schedule, and recruit teachers as well as learners.

Emery, M., Horton, D., & McDaniel, R. (1988). *Community education and economic development: Activities in the field and potential new models.* Pullman, WA: Washington State University. Survey of community education activities in local economic development. Includes some models taken from rural communities.

Heartland Center for Leadership Development. (1989). *7 Secrets to coping with change in small towns.* Lincoln, NE: Author. Suggests a positive approach to responding to the economic changes currently underway.

Heartland Center for Leadership Development. (1989). *The entrepreneurial community; A strategic planning approach to community survival.* Lincoln, NE: Author. Practical guide to strategic planning for small to medium-sized communities.

Heasley, D.K. (1987). *Directory of statewide rural and agricultural leadership programs.* University Park, PA: Pennsylvania State University. Compilation of programs developed both with and without Kellogg Foundation support.

Hustedde, R., Shaffer, R., & Pulver, G. (1984). *Community economic analysis: A how to manual.* Ames, IA: North Central Regional Center for Rural Development. Takes the reader or community groups through the process of measuring the economic health of their community.

Jackson, G., & Chaudhuri, K. (1989). *National directory of community based adult literacy programs.* Washington, DC: Association for Community Based Education. Presents the results of a national survey of community-based literacy programs, many of which operate in rural areas.

Kellogg Foundation. (1984). *Rural development and higher education: The linking of community and method.* Battle Creek, MI: Author. This monograph explores eight projects funded by the Kellogg Foundation in response to their need for rural development assistance.

Kellogg Foundation. (1988). *The land grant university and local government: Examining a growing relationship.* Battle Creek, MI: Author. Proceedings of a conference designed to involve local governments, land-grant universities, and cooperative extension services in developing a cooperative relationship to solve community problems.

Kabak, S.E., & McCormack, N. (1987). *Workshop on developing feasibility studies for community based business ventures.* New Market, TN: Highlander Center. Describes in a step by step fashion how a community group can conduct a feasibility study for a new business idea.

Killacky, J. (1984). *Furthering nonformal education in rural America: The rural free university and three traditional providers.* Las Cruces, NM: ERIC Clearinghouse for Rural Education and Small Schools. Explores the free university model and its usefulness in helping Cooperative Extension, libraries, and community colleges reach out more effectively to rural adults.

Lewis, H., & Gaventa, J. (1987). *The Jellico handbook: A teacher's guide to community-based learning.* New Market, TN: Highlander Center. Part of the economic literacy project, this publication describes how teachers can use the community as the resource and guide for education.

Luttrell, W. (1987). *Claiming what is ours: An economics experience workbook.* New Market, TN: Highlander Center. Describes a series of activities that community groups can complete as part of a process of better understanding the economic condition of their community.

National Governors' Association (NGA). (1988). *New alliances for rural America: Report of the Task Force on Rural Development.* Washington, DC: Author. Suggests a four point agenda for supporting rural revitalization: (1) helping communities prepare for the future, (2) making wise investments in rural America, (3) making the most of opportunities for economic growth, and (4) focusing federal agenda on rural needs.

Office of Rural Development Policy. (1984). *Rural resources guide: A directory of public and private assistance for small communities.* Washington, DC: Author. Lists 440 sources of public and private assistance available on a national or regional basis. Organized into four areas— community facilities, services, general community improvement, and natural resources. While the guide was sorely needed, it is now somewhat dated.

Rural Coalition. (1988). *Saturn: Tomorrow's jobs, yesterday's wages and myths.* Washington, DC: Author. A case study of the effect "successful" industrial recruitment had on a rural community.

Rural Coalition. (1988). *National rural agenda.* Washington, DC: Author. States what members believe is needed to ensure the health and vitality of rural communities for the future.

Stark, N. (1988). *Growing our own jobs: A small town guide to creating jobs through agricultural diversification*. Knoxville, TN: National Association of Towns and Townships. This guide explores a community's capacity to create jobs. Separate chapters discuss diversifying agricultural production, adding value through local processing, marketing produce locally, tourism, and crafts industries. Excellent resources provided in the Appendix.

Wall, M., & Luther, V. (1987). *20 clues to rural community survival*. Lincoln, NE: Heartland Center for Leadership Development. Case studies of five rural Nebraska communities that are surviving the economic crisis. Led to the identification of 20 clues and a leadership training program that is now available to rural communities.

Video Materials:

Harvesting Hometown Jobs. Shows practical, affordable, locally initiated approaches to keeping existing jobs and creating new ones. Available from the National Association of Towns and Townships. Format in 1/2 inch VHS or 16mm film.

Changing Rural America. Explores how and why rural America is changing. Presents examples of what can be done to positively affect change. Available from U.S.D.A. Economic Research Service.

Search for Solutions. A two part video series that explores the problems of rural health care. Available from Pioneer Hi-Bred, International.

Index

Cooperative societies, role of, 197–
199 (*see also* Special interest
organizations)
Cultural diversity (*see also* Rural
America)
rural education for, 263–267
Curriculum (*see also* Elementary
education; Higher education;
Lifelong education; Rural lifelong education; School curriculum; Secondary education)
school and lifelong education differences in, 305–309

Demographic communities, 9 (*see
also* Adult education; Community)
Dispositional change, need for,
303–305 (*see also* Rural lifelong education)

Economic vulnerability (*see also*
Cities; Rural America; Urban-
rural)
centrifugal effects of, 30–31
independence or dependence,
29–30
of rural residents, 28–31
Education (*see also* Community
adult education; Elementary
education; Higher education;
Lifelong education; Secondary
education; Special education;
University extension; Vocational education)
definition of, 4
rural context for, 21–40
rural development relationship
with, 35–37
Elementary education, 45–71 (*see
also* Curriculum; Principals;
Students; Teachers)
achievement of rural students in,
53

characteristics of rural principals
in, 60–61
external challenges, 51–52
future of the, 68–71
inservice/staff development of
teachers in, 59–60
internal challenges, 49–51
preparation of teachers in, 58
problems of rural students in,
53–54
recruitment of principals for,
61–62
recruitment of teachers for, 58–
59
responsibilities and challenges of,
47–52
rural student in, 52–54
rural teacher in, 54–60
school curriculum of, 63–68

Farmer's organizations (*see also*
Adult education; Special interest organizations)
farm bureau, 196–197
farmer's union, 197
the grange, 196

Gemeinschaft, 8 (*see also* Adult
education; Community; Rural
community adult education)
communities described as, 10–
11
Geographic communities, 9 (*see
also* Adult education; Community; Rural community adult
education)
Gesellschaft (*see also* Adult education; Community; Rural community adult education)
communities described as, 8–9
Good community, 10 (*see also*
Community)
Government publications (*see also*
Public library)
learning with, 215–217

DATE DUE

DEC 1 5 '92	
AUG 2 5 '93	
AUG 1 4 1995	
JAN 0 4 1999	
FEB 1 5 1999	
AUG 0 9 1999	
OCT 0 7 2001	

BRODART, INC.   Cat. No. 23-221